History

of

Cuba

THE CHALLENGE OF THE YOKE AND THE STAR
BY PROFESSOR JOSÉ CANTÓN NAVARRO

> *The present second edition and fifth printing has been updated by the author, adding the main historic events occurring between the years 1995 and 2000.*

José Martí

History of Cuba

THE CHALLENGE OF THE YOKE AND THE STAR
BY PROFESSOR JOSE CANTON NAVARRO

Biography of a People

Editorial SI-MAR S.A.
La Habana, Cuba/2001

Edition Manager
Sara Molejón

Design and reproduction:
Milagros de León

Corrected and translation:
Juan Jacomino

Cover and illustrations:
Amílkar Feria Flores

Coordination:
Carlos Molejón

© 2001 by José Cantón Navarro.
© On the present edition by
SI-MAR S.A. Publishing House

ISBN 959-7054-75-2

Editorial **SI-MAR S.A.**
Calle 47 No. 1210 e/36 y Lindero, Nuevo Vedado
Plaza de la Revolución, Ciudad de La Habana, Cuba.
Telephones: 81-8168 and 81-80-33

4

This is a comprehensive history of Cuba. Despite its relative brevity, and perhaps for that very reason, Professor José Cantón has managed to catch, in flight, that which is transient and also imperishable in it, in these pages bound to become classic. Here is everything that is inescapable, all that which is indispensable for a smooth, uninterrupted journey along the Cuban historic process. There will be facts and events missing here and there, passages that some might consider important but which are not fundamental in the course of the story that is so passionately told that history seems to unfold. For not all that is important demands recording, as it would turn the story into an encyclopedia, and one of the purposes of this book is to make Cuban history more easily available to millions of people, both abroad and in this country.

In writing about history there are several approaches. There is the study of periods and epochs, of developments that are unique in their political, social, or military content, and also the review of that which encompasses the global events, like the roots and movements of whole populations in their shaping of nations and countries.

The biographies of outstanding individuals generally carry descriptions of the prevailing situation during their life and times. Regardless of whether they were illustrious and benevolent, or sinister and backwards, they are all approached from the point of view of their own personalities.

It is no easy task writing about the intricate domain of society. But it becomes all the more difficult when the objective of the chronicler or historian is to compile a biography of a people, from their first steps until they become the nation they are today.

In the present correlation of contemporary society, in which today is but the date when before the hand was raised to reach the printing press, The Challenge of the Yoke and the Star has as its background an exalted culture, a philosophy of everyday life, and a legitimate, proven veracity; a pedagogical and ecumenical impulse. This is the history of a small modern nation, which has been marked by great events and has become a banner for millions of men and women, youth, and even children. It deals with a fundamentally Spartan people who have refused to sell their freedom to the imperial bidder, and who have been ready to simply succeed or die in the effort.

This is a biography of paramount events and episodes, all of them as true as a sunrise. A synthesis of science, arts, and courage. The Cuban epic, that struggle between "the yoke and the star", that labyrinth full of heroic deeds and heroes, outstanding among them José Martí, and more recently Fidel Castro, deserves a legitimate and truthful narration capable of impregnating the minds, eyes, and skin of millions, allowing them to find resistance to evil, love for human and social freedom, and that acting in solidarity and firmness in the face of declining social strata whose existence was necessary at one time, but whose social death is inevitable.

Professor Cantón has seen the global nature of ages and epochs, from the naturalism and credulity of Cuba's indigenous roots to the complex texture of a country where for the first time in 1898 the imperial greed of "the American Rome" surfaced in the form of a US military intervention in the war Cubans were waging against a monarchic, reactionary, recalcitrant Spain, to the detriment of the Spanish people and their culture, already pervasive in the Cuban scenario in the blood, the language, the virtues, and the shortcomings of its people.

The United States took hold of Cuba, a country devastated by a war that had brutally brought its population down to a third of its original size but whose people had bravely fought and defeated a powerful Spanish army of more than 200 thousand men.

Like in a movie, Indians are slaughtered, black slaves are brought from Africa, savagely exploited and subdued, and despotic, corrupt Spanish colonial rulers take turns in power, while Cubans wage successive independence wars.

We then witness the formation of a neo-colonial republic, in which the worst of the Cuban nation pledges servitude to the US aggressor.

Also the development of the Republic, and the first social explosion: the 1933 Revolution. Until we arrive at the last bourgeoisie-large landowners' dictatorship at the service of the United States: the March 10th, 1952 military coup.

And then... the advent of an honest, liberating, socialist, true revolution, of whose echo or reality the world has taken careful note.

The images of Fidel and Che, the two together, in brotherly association, are found today in posters, books, newspapers, and electronic screens. But above all they are also found in the hearts of many good, kind people in the world, people whose beliefs may differ but whose projection is humanistic.

I am sure the reader will appreciate having available such a truthful and effective text. If anything is missing in it, the readers will certainly tell Professor José Cantón, who will no doubt attend to their concerns.

This frugal book is bound to become indispensable in all contemporary libraries. Read it; you will certainly not regret having done so.

Lionel Soto

6

The Yoke and The Star

"Oh, blossom of my chest, oh, generous homagno,
Summary and reflection of myself and of Creation,
Fish turning into bird, into horse, into man,
Look at these two things I in sorrow offer you,
These two emblems of life, then make a choice.
This one's a yoke: whoever chooses it, rejoices,
Works as an obedient ox,
And since he pays a service to his masters,
Sleeps on warm straw, and feeds from plenty
Of the nicest of oats.
This other one, oh, mystery born of myself,
Like the summit was born of the tall mountain,
This shining, killing thing, is a bright star,
And since it sheds light,
Sinners avoid whoever carries it,
And so, through life, whoever carries this light
Goes alone, like a criminal monster.
But he who easily accepts to play the ox,
An ox becomes, and so, a vacuous brute,
He once again begins the universal scale.
Yet he who bravely holds on to the star,
  Since he creates, he grows!.
                                And when all the sap
Of the world has been drained from him,
When his own heart is all he has been left with
To gladly, sadly offer mankind's blood-thirsty feast,
And when his sacred voice
He's cast to North and South,
The star enshrouds him in its light,
Lights up the air, as in a feast,
And so he who faced life with pride and courage,
Steps forward from the shadows!"

Give me the yoke, oh, Mother, so that standing
On the yoke, the star that shines and kills
  shines on my forehead all the more brightly.

José Martí

I
Geographic, political, and administrative aspects

Cuba is not just an island; it is an archipelago comprising more than 1600 keys and smaller islands. Of the islands, the most important are Cuba itself and the Isle of Youth, which up to 1978 was known as the Isle of Pines.

The Cuban archipelago is located in the torrid or tropical area of the planet, very close to the Tropic of Cancer. It is in the Caribbean Sea, or Sea of the Antilles, at the entry of the Gulf of Mexico, which is why Cuba has also been called "the key to the Gulf". The nearest countries are Haiti and the Dominican Republic in the east, 77 kilometers away; Jamaica in the south, 140 kilometers away; the United States (Florida Peninsula) in the north, 180 kilometers away; and Mexico in the west, 210 kilometers away.

The archipelago extends over an area of some 111,000 square kilometers. The main island of Cuba has the shape of a crocodile; it is some 1 200 kilometers long, and its width ranges from 32 kilometers at the narrowest point to 190 kilometers at its widest.

The country's territory is administratively divided into 14 provinces and 169 municipalities, one of which, that of the Isle of Youth, has a special category, as it is directly subordinated to the central government. The provinces are Pinar del Río, the westernmost, Havana, Havana City, Matanzas, Cienfuegos, Villa Clara, Sancti Spiritus, Ciego de Avila, Camagüey, Las Tunas, Holguín, Granma, Santiago de Cuba, and Guantánamo, the easternmost.

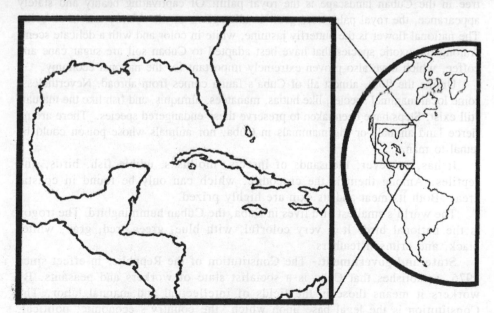

Cuba's geographic position

9

Cuba has a population of 11 million people (January 1996), 59 per cent of which lives in urban areas. Its demographic density is 99 inhabitants per square kilometer. Approximately 66 per cent of Cubans are white; 12 per cent are black; 21.9 per cent are mixed; and 0.1 per cent are of Asian background. Cuba has ten cities whose population exceeds 100,000 people. First comes Havana, the capital, with 2 172 400 people. The rest are Santiago de Cuba, Camagüey, Holguín, Santa Clara, Guantánamo, Pinar del Río, Matanzas, Cienfuegos, and Bayamo. Indeed Havana is the capital of two provinces: Havana and Havana City. It is the political, administrative, and scientific center of the country.

The climate.- One of the geographic characteristics of Cuba that is more highly appreciated by visitors, especially those from cold regions, is its semi-tropical climate. Although climatic conditions slightly vary in some areas of the country, with micro-climates in the mountains and along the coast, the differences are barely noticeable. It could be said that there is a permanent summer, with stable, high temperatures in mid-year months (in July and August it can exceed the 35 degrees Centigrade) and lower, more variable temperatures toward the end and beginning of the year, although almost never lower than 6 degrees Centigrade even in the coldest months of January and February. The average annual temperature is 25.4 degrees Centigrade (in summer it is 27 degrees and in winter 23 degrees). In the eastern part of the country, the temperature is usually 1 or 2 degrees higher than in the west.

Flora and fauna.- Cuba is one of the few countries in the world whose flora is essentially of native origin. It has more than 8000 species of plants, from cactuses in the dry areas to orchids in the humid ones. There is a rich variety of hard woods. The vegetation covers valleys, plains, mountains, and shores. The most representative tree in the Cuban landscape is the royal palm. Of captivating beauty and stately appearance, the royal palm trees grow in all regions of the country and in all soils. The national flower is the butterfly jasmine, white in color and with a delicate scent. Among the exotic species that have best adapted to Cuban soil are sugar cane and coffee, which have also proven extremely important for the national economy.

Unlike the flora, almost all of Cuba's fauna comes from abroad. Nevertheless, some local mammal species, like hutias, manatees, almiquis, and fish like the majuarí still exist. Steps have been taken to preserve these endangered species. There are no fierce land animals or big mammals in Cuba, nor animals whose poison could be lethal to man.

It has, however, thousands of insects, mollusks, edible fish, birds, and reptiles. Among them is the crocodile, which can only be found in coastal areas. Both its meat and its skin are highly prized.

The world's smallest bird lives in Cuba, the Cuban hummingbird. The trogon is the national bird. It is very colorful, with blue, green, red, gray, white, black, and crimson feathers.

State and government.- The Constitution of the Republic, in effect since 1976, establishes that Cuba is a socialist state of workers and peasants. By workers it means those in the fields of intellectual and manual labor. The Constitution is the legal base upon which the country's economic, political, social, and cultural organization is built, including the preservation of the

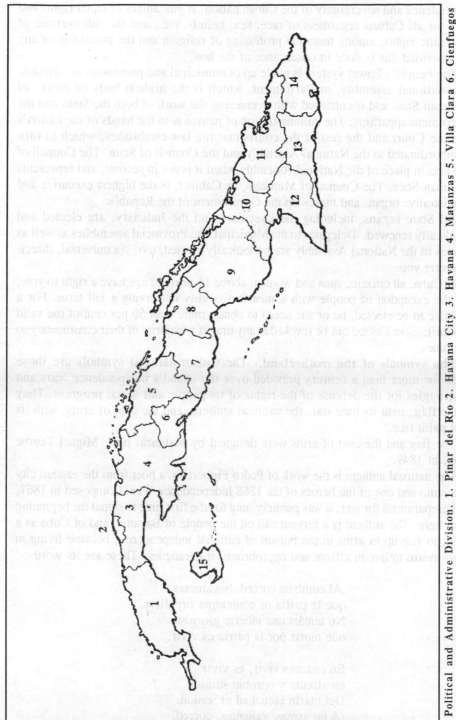

Political and Administrative Division. 1. Pinar del Río 2. Havana City 3. Havana 4. Matanzas 5. Villa Clara 6. Cienfuegos 7. Sancti Spíritus 8 Ciego de Ávila 9. Camagüey 10. Las Tunas 11. Holguín 12. Granma 13. Santiago de Cuba 14. Guantánamo 15. Isle of Youth.

independence and sovereignty of the Cuban nation. It guarantees of equal rights and duties for all Cubans regardless of race, sex, beliefs, etc., and the full exercise of democratic rights, among them the professing of religion and the practicing of any cult, provided this is done in observance of the law.

The People's Power system is made up of municipal and provincial assemblies, and a national assembly, or Parliament, which is the highest body of power of the Cuban State and is entrusted with overseeing the work of both the State and the Government apparatus. The administration of justice is in the hands of the nation's Supreme Court and the rest of the courts that the law establishes, which in turn are subordinated to the National Assembly and the Council of State. The Council of State acts in place of the National Assembly when it is not in session, and represents the Cuban State. The Council of Ministers, or Cabinet, is the highest executive and administrative organ, and makes up the Government of the Republic.

All State organs, including the Executive and the Judiciary, are elected and periodically renewed. Delegates to the Municipal and Provincial assemblies as well as deputies to the National Assembly are periodically elected, too, via universal, direct, and secret vote.

In Cuba, all citizens, men and women, above 16 years of age have a right to vote, with the exception of people with a mental disability or serving a jail term. For a candidate to be elected, he or she needs to obtain more than 50 per cent of the valid votes cast; those elected can be revoked at any time if a majority of their constituency so determines.

The symbols of the motherland.- The Cuban national symbols are those which for more than a century presided over the island's independence wars and the struggles for the defense of the rights of its people and social progress. They are the flag, with its lone star, the national anthem, and the coat of arms, with its royal palm tree.

The flag and the coat of arms were designed by Matanzas poet Miguel Teurbe Tolón, in 1849.

The national anthem is the work of Pedro Figueredo, a poet from the eastern city of Bayamo and one of the heroes of the 1868 Independence War. Composed in 1867, amid preparations for war, it was publicly sung for the first time to signal the beginning of the fight. The anthem is a fervent call on the people of Bayamo, and of Cuba as a whole, to rise up in arms in the pursuit of national independence, because living in chains means to live in affront and opprobrium, it harangues. These are its words:

> Al combate corred, bayameses,
> que la patria os contempla orgullosa.
> No temáis una muerte gloriosa,
> que morir por la patria es vivir.
>
> En cadenas vivir, es vivir
> en afrenta y oprobio sumido.
> Del clarín escuchad el sonido.
> ¡A las armas, valientes, corred!

SOME IMPORTANT DATES:

January 1st: National Liberation Day. Anniversary of the victory of the Cuban Revolution, in 1959.

January 28th: Birthday of José Martí, Cuba's National Hero, in 1853.

February 24th: The Cry of Baire, or Cry of Calicito. Re-initiation of the independence war, in 1895.

March 13th: Attack on the Presidential Palace in Havana, in 1957.

April 16th: Militia Day. Burial of victims of air attacks that preceded the Bay of Pigs mercenary invasion in 1961. Declaration of the socialist character of the Cuban Revolution.

April 19th: Cuban Victory at Bay of Pigs, in 1961.

May 17th: Peasants Day. Passage of First Agrarian Reform Law, in 1959.

July 26th: National Rebellion Day. Anniversary of the attacks on Moncada Garrison, in Santiago de Cuba, and Carlos Manuel de Céspedes Garrison, in Bayamo, in 1953.

July 30th: Day of the Martyrs of the Revolution. Assassination of revolutionary leader Frank País, in 1957.

August 12th: Ousting of the Gerardo Machado dictatorship, in 1933.

October 8th: Day of the Guerrilla Fighter. Capture of Ernesto "Che" Guevara, in 1967.

October 10th: The Cry of Yara, or Cry of La Demajagua. Beginning of independence war, in 1868.

October 20th: National Culture Day. Cuban National Anthem publicly sung for the first time, in 1868.

October 28th: Disappearance of Commander Camilo Cienfuegos, in 1959.

November 27th: Brutal, unjustified execution of 8 medical students in Havana at the hands of Spanish authorities, in 1871.

December 2nd: Day of the Revolutionary Armed Forces. Landing on Cuban soil in 1956 of the "Granma" boat expedition, organized by Fidel Castro in Mexico.

December 7th: Day of the Heroes of the Independence Wars. Death in combat in 1896 of Lieutenant General Antonio Maceo, called the Bronze Titan of the Cuban Independence Wars.

Christopher Columbus' arrival

II
A new world and an unknown civilization

Christopher Columbus and the "new world".- The existence of Cuba, and of the American continent, remained practically unknown to Europeans until the end of the 15th century. It is true that stories were being told of Norman incursions into territories west of Europe, beyond the cold Northern Sea, and that names like Eric the Red and his son Leif were being mentioned as the protagonists of those adventures. But in practice nothing was known about those lands, and much less about their inhabitants.

So when Christopher Columbus, an experienced sailor from Genoa, set about organizing a voyage across the Atlantic, his purpose was not to discover a new world but to find a shorter, less dangerous route to India, an important market of spices and other items in great demand in countries of Western Europe.

In his journey Columbus could of course come across territories not yet occupied by any European power, so in accepting the project, the Catholic King and Queen of Spain, Fernando and Isabel, not only agreed to share with Columbus the commercial benefits resulting from the undertaking but also appointed him Admiral, Viceroy, and Governor General of the lands he might discover.

This is how, authorized by the Capitulations of Santa Fe, and with supplies provided by the Spanish Crown, Columbus began his voyage. His three ships—the *Santa María*, the *Niña*, and the *Pinta*—set sail from Palos de Moguer harbor, in the southern Spanish province of Huelva, on August 3rd, 1492.

Columbus sailed for 72 days. Longer than expected, the voyage created panic among the ever more restless sailors, who feared Columbus might have gone insane, and pressed him to return to Spain. But before the agreed 3 day term expired, in the early morning of October 12th, 1492, Andalucian sailor Rodrigo de Triana sighted land. Columbus' intrepidity, willpower, and skills had paid off. They had arrived at an island the indigenous inhabitants called Guanahaní—presently Watling—in the Lucayas or Bahamas, and which the Admiral called San Salvador, since it had saved his efforts from disaster. Columbus did not know it then, but he had discovered a new continent for Spain.

Advised by the native inhabitants through signs and gestures that there was more land nearby, he continued his voyage southeast. Fifteen days later, on October 27th, Columbus arrived at the coasts of Cuba, which he called Juana in honor of Prince Juan, the first born of the Spanish royal couple. Later, in 1515, the island would be renamed Fernandina by a decision of King Fernando, although all along it would retain its primitive name of Cuba.

This is how Europeans arrived in Cuba, a land whose pristine natural scenery prompted Columbus to call it "the most beautiful land the human eye has beheld".

Columbus found in Cuba a hospitable, industrious, and peaceful civilization whose members he called *Indians*, in the belief he had arrived in India, the legendary Asian peninsula he had originally set off to find.

15

This civilization had a very low level of development. They had not moved beyond the Stone Age yet, and were the oldest inhabitants on the island.

With the beginning of the conquest and colonization in 1510, and with Columbus already dead, the representatives of the Spanish Crown also started a brutal subjugation of the local Cuban population. In their thirst for wealth, the Spanish conquistadors outdid their peers in other regions, not only replacing the existing relations of production with new, more advanced ones, but also physically eliminating in the process those whose traditions and customs they were transforming. That stopped the natural process of evolution, which could have probably resulted in a Cuban nationality with characteristics different from those of today.

Indeed, the influence of the indigenous culture on the development of Cuban society was very little compared, for example, to the role played by the indigenous communities of Mexico, and other regions of Central and South America in the formation of the present nationalities of those countries.

This violent elimination of the Cuban primitive community in the 16th century, which cut it off from socio-economic formations that followed, poses in addition a serious obstacle for the study of that society. And since the original inhabitants of Cuba had not advanced beyond the Stone Age, they left no written record of their life. Yet, we will learn more about them one day when the writings found in caves in eastern Cuba, the Isle of Youth, and other places in the archipelago are deciphered. The archeological findings recorded prior to the victory of the Cuban Revolution, although useful in providing knowledge about the time immediately before the discovery by Columbus, shed little light on the origin and social evolution of the Cuban Indians.

At the same time, the important contribution of the testimonies of Spanish discoverers and colonizers has been rendered limited for a number of reasons. Most of the documents belonging to Christopher Columbus have been lost, and the written works of Father Bartholomew de las Casas and of other Spanish chroniclers and historians on the Conquest contradict each other in part, as de las Casas favored the Indians while Oviedo and others had negative things to say about them.

Yet, despite these limitations, important aspects having to do with the life of Cuban Indians have surfaced, allowing us to have a general view of what their society was like. Gaps remain, of course, but a basic picture can be drawn of the socio-economic developments that marked the Cuban pre-historic scenario.

Origin of the first inhabitants.- When the Spaniards arrived, no less than three Indian groups, with varying levels of development, inhabited the Cuban territory. Historians have defined them as *Tainos, Siboneyes* (also spelled *Ciboneyes),* and *Guanajatabeyes*. The origin of the last two groups is still uncertain, although the theory that they might have originated in Cuba is generally discarded. Archeological research has not come up with a single clue supportive of the idea that Cuba could be their place of origin; there are no signs of the existence of other men on the island before our Indians, nor is there evidence of the presence of any other mammals who could have been their ancestors.

16

On the other hand, Cuba emerged from the bottom of the sea, and may have stayed under water for thousands, perhaps millions of years. Petrified or fossilized remains of sea animals dating back to those remote times have not been found, the conclusion being that signs of the ancestors of the Cuban Indian could have been equally discovered had they had their origin here.

As it stands, there is no certainty as to the ethnic trunk from which they descended nor the exact place from where they migrated to Cuba, although it is believed that they could have only come from Florida, Yucatan, in Mexico or South America. Most researchers point to South America as their likely point of departure.

The origin of the Tainos, however, seems to be clearer. Historians agree that they are descendants of the Aruacos, of South America, and that they came from the northwest coast of Venezuela, specifically from the basin of the Orinoco river, where the character, way of life, and customs of the indigenous inhabitants are very close to those of the Tainos. The Aruacos have a culture similar to that of other Indian groups of the Dominican Republic and the Lesser Antilles, which seems to indicate that they may have come in waves, moving from island to island along the arch of the Antilles, pursued perhaps by the belligerent Carib tribes.

When Columbus arrived in Cuba, many of the Tainos had been living there for decades, even centuries. It was probably the Tainos who pushed the Guanajatabeyes toward the Guanahacabibes peninsula, where they were found by the Spaniards.

Unequal development of the Cuban primitive groups.- Contrasting opinions regarding the number of indigenous cultures that existed in Cuba and the rest of the Antilles, and lack of coordination concerning the archeological terminology led to the need for a unifying efforts. It eventually made the National Archeology Board of Cuba to convene a round table of Caribbean archeologists, which took place in 1950.

The meeting agreed to place Cuban Indians under three groups it called cultural complexes I, II, and III. They respectively correspond to the Guanajatabeyes, the Siboneyes, and the Tainos.

The most backward of all, the Guanajatabeyes did not build houses. They were practically nomadic, lived in caves, and engaged in fishing. They did not cultivate the land nor carve or polish stones, their culture thus belonging to the Paleolithic period.

The staple foods of the Guanajatabeyes were fish and mollusks, and their main tool the shell. The huge shell sites they left along the coast and at their burial places has resulted in Guanajatabeyes being called a "shell culture".

According to Father de las Casas, the Siboneyes, or Cultural Complex II, lived together with the Tainos, acting as servants, though not as slaves. More than a culture of their own, they could be considered to have had a pre-Taino culture. They carved the stone in a very rudimentary way, and did not master symmetry as skillfully as Tainos did. They made axes of soft, polished stones, and rough, undecorated clay vessels.

Rough, imperfect objects have been found in Taino cemeteries next to items belonging to an advanced culture. They are undoubtedly from an inferior culture, though one that was superior to that of the Guanajatabeyes. Those objects belong to the Siboney culture.

17

According to historian Fernando Portuondo, unlike the burial sites of the Guanajatabeyes, sites believed to be from the pre-Taino culture of the Siboneyes are located in fertile areas. This leads to the conclusion that the makers of those anthill-like sites might have practiced some kind of agriculture. Shells are not abundant in these sites, while food waste is plentiful, from turtles to fish, birds and mollusks, which indicates that their diet was richer than that of the Guanajatabeyes.

From the point of view of their level of development, the Tainos, or Cultural Complex III, are the most representative of pre-historic Cuba. Theirs is the most advanced of the cultures. They carved and polished stones, cultivated the land and had a higher social organization than the rest of the groups. The Tainos left a more complete source of information than the previous two groups.

Level of development.- It certainly seems that when the first indigenous groups settled in Cuba, they knew long before how to make their instruments of labor; they were no longer animals but men. They had left their life in hordes or herds, and even the most backward of them practiced not only the first activities of man in history—gathering and hunting—but also fishing. They already used fire, and had come down from the trees to find shelter in caves.

When the Spaniards arrived, they found the Tainos engaged basically in fishing, hunting, cultivating the land, and domestic labors. The instruments used in all these occupations were manual and very rudimentary. Except for some mute dogs they were said to have had, which they used for hunting, they knew of no other tamable mammals. In that respect, they differed from other primitive peoples of Europe, Asia, and Africa: while they went from hunting to herding and then to agriculture, in the fertile American continent indigenous groups jumped from hunting to agriculture without going through herding.

This was especially true of Cuba, where not even the llama was known. So, the barbarian age, which for the peoples of the East began with the practice of herding and cattle-raising, began in Cuba with the growing of vegetables and other plants. The presence of the mute dogs does not have an impact on agriculture since those animals—if they ever existed—were used in a gathering activity, in this case hunting, and not in a producing activity.

One other characteristic of the development of productive forces then has to do with the knowledge and use of metals. The Cuban Indians knew gold, but they did not use it. And they did not know how to obtain tin, iron, or bronze, for that matter. This might have been so because there was no coal in our soil, and because the Tainos did not know of another natural resource that could produce enough heat to work with metals.

The chief instrument of the Cuban Indians was the "*coa*"—a stick one of whose ends was hardened in fire and which they used to break the ground for cultivation. In his diary, Columbus describes how Tainos worked hard to cultivate the land; he talks about the beauty of their fields of cassava, corn, pepper, pumpkin, potato and sweet potato, peanut, tobacco, etc. It was thanks to the Tainos that the Spaniards were introduced to corn and tobacco.

To fish the Indians used hooks they made of fish bones, nets made of cotton, and canoes made from hollowed-out tree trunks, which they moved by oar. Ingeniously,

18

they used the "*guaicán*", a type of remora fish, to catch bigger fish. Their hooks could not have been made of iron or copper since, as we said, they did not know how to use or work with metals. The Cuban Indians caught sea animals as diverse as turtles, manatees, shad, mullets, mollusks, etc. When animals were big, they hit them on their heads with their "*macanas*" —hard, short shafts they used as weapons.

Hunting was another of their favorite activities, although they also practiced it in a very rudimentary way. They hunted the hutias, big rodents still existing in Cuba, with their mute dogs, finishing them off with the "*macanas*". And they used a number of tricks to catch water birds.

No references from direct sources exist as to the use of bows and arrows for hunting, although we do know that under the leadership of a cacique called Hatuey, they used them as weapons in an effort to stop Diego Velázquez from landing. "They went about setting up their defenses"—wrote Father de las Casas—"with their bare bellies and their few, poor weapons: bows and arrows, which looked more like children's bows."

The Cuban Indians are known for their wooden tools and objects. They used wood to build their houses, which were spacious, clean, and simple. From wood they also made seats, tools for cultivation, canoes, oars, shafts, and decorative items. Most of the articles of home use were made by women.

They used cotton skillfully. With it they made hammocks, which they used for sleeping, as well as a type of skirt for women, which they called "*naguas*", that covered from the waist to the knee. With plaited leaves of a type of palm tree they called *yarey*" they made bags and baskets for carrying and storing food; and with the plaited leaves of yet another palm-tree, the "*corojo*", they made ropes, which they used for several purposes.

The walls of their houses were made of planks obtained from the trunk of royal palm-trees and tied with vines.

One other major activity in which Cuban Indians engaged and in which they attained higher levels of development than other groups in the Caribbean was the carving and polishing of stone, typical of the Neolithic character of their culture. The symmetry of their sculptures is admirable. A good example of their skills in carving the stone are their petaloid axes, which they used as weapons and work instruments and also in their liturgy and ceremonies. Axes used for ceremonial purposes usually had faces, human bodies, or animal figures carved on them. Idols and other figures carved on the stalagmites of some caves have also been found.

Aside from axes, they carved and polished stone idols, beads for necklaces and pendants, scrapers, mortars, and other objects. Strikingly enough, some of these items were carved on very hard rocks like porphyry, granite, diorite and serpentine.

In pottery they also achieved development, although not as much as some of their Caribbean peers and much less than the Aztecs and the Incas. The Tainos knew how to amass, shape, and burn clay to make vessels. Many of those vessels, like pots and trays, with grotesque figures on them have been found in their settlements and cemeteries.

As can be seen, the level of development of the working tools used by the Cuban Indians was very low. But as low as it might have been, it was enough to help them solve their basic needs. Cuba was an immense forest; one could go from one end of the island to the other practically without missing the shade of the trees.

But as if this prodigality were not enough, Cuba was free from wild animals or poisonous snakes, and its peaceful inhabitants went unbothered about their work activities, without fear of the constant raids of the Caribs, who caused havoc among the population in the Dominican Republic and other territories of the Antilles. That is why Spaniards found Cuban Indians in possession of no effective weapons with which to put up resistance.

It might be a logical conclusion, too, that surrounded by such an abundant flora and fauna, and sitting on such a fertile soil, Cuban Indians may not have suffered from the shortages of food supplies that led other primitive peoples of the world to the conquest of other lands and the practice of anthropophagy. In addition, Cuban Indians had already learnt to store reserves for the future, as demonstrated by the mullet fishponds they had in the today Cienfuegos and Santiago de Cuba bays, which for a long time Spanish conquistadors used for their own food supplies. "They had food in abundance", wrote Father de las Casas, "and they had every thing they needed for living; they had crops, many of them, and very orderly arranged, of which—their abundance of everything and the quenching of our hunger with it—we are witness."

Another consequence of that relative abundance of supplies, the mildness of our climate, and the fertility of our land was, in our view, the fact that Tainos were not men of great physical strength and resistance. They never had to do strong physical work, and they proved generally unable of withstanding it when Spaniards submitted them to it.

Work was done collectively by the Indians. It required many people to break large plots of land with the "*coas*", and to kill large animals like turtles and so on. Indians did these jobs on the basis of simple cooperation. Collective property and work also presupposed an equal distribution of products. "I seem to have seen", recalled Columbus, "that what one had he shared with all, especially eatable things".

In conditions of such a low development of productive forces, the social character of production was confined to the boundaries of each separate Indian community. Tainos necessarily depended on a natural economy, i.e. they produced just for the internal consumption of their little community and not for exchange. Only occasionally did groups traded what they produced.

They ignored completely the value of what they produced. That economic category—value—did not exist for them. For instance, they would give Spaniards very useful items in large amounts, like tens of pounds of spun cotton threat and baskets of fruits, in return for just any worthless thing. Columbus told of how he had to defend Indians against the bad faith of many Spaniards who would take products from them in exchange for broken pieces of bowls, pieces of glass, broken barrel rings, etc.

All this points to the fact that, like all other primitive peoples of the world, the fundamental economic law of that Indian society was producing the main means of

20

subsistence, with rudimentary instruments and through collective work. Joint ownership over land and working instruments, and the use of collective work were not the conscious result of knowledge of the laws of social development.

Man was still blindly ruled by the then unknown forces of nature. An although man was already a conscious being, his consciousness only vaguely reflected his condition. Religious beliefs of the Tainos show perhaps more clearly than anything else how deformed that reflection of reality was.

Guanajatabeyes did not leave religious elements through which to judge them in this regard; most likely they did not have such beliefs. If it were so, it would confirm for Cuba too the thesis advocated by Mortillet in 1903 and shared by many other scientific materialists that "the first stages of the Paleolithic lacked religiousness".

This is not the case of Tainos. Creators of a Neolithic culture, they had advanced enough in the field of material production as to think, feel, and somehow reflect on their consciousness and the independent place they occupied in nature. The roots of religion were still purely Gnostic; conditions had not developed yet for it to acquire a class character.

The hurricanes that swept across the Caribbean, the plagues that destroyed crops, the floods, the dry spells, lightning, the sunshine, the darkness of the night, and the many other natural phenomena that affected the life and economic activities of Tainos must have reflected in their consciousness, in a fantastic, distorted way, man's helplessness before nature. This is how natural forces became almighty, associated with the unknown, and supernatural for them.

In trying to explain those forces, Cuban Indians also created their myths. According to chronicler Roman Pane, Tainos of the island of Hispanola believed that the sun, the moon, and man came from a cave; they talked about men becoming other creatures due to the power of the sun; they narrated the adventures of the founders of their race; and they tried to explain the origin of certain rites, of the female sex, of social castes, and of their main crops.

As in the case of other primitive peoples, the religion of Tainos was complex. They believed in the magical powers of their "*behiques*", or priests, and in their ability to speak with the dead, foretell the future, and understand the wishes of the "*cemi*", a supernatural, mysterious power.

It seems that by the time of the Spanish arrival, the Taino society was already showing signs of decomposition. The move from the patriarchy to the matriarchy seems to confirm it, as well as the emergence of hierarchics in society, the possible servant role of Siboneyes, the existence of a mythology, and other factors. But that state of decomposition did not lead to a gradual and natural replacement of the primitive community by a slave regime or some form of transition. As Engels asserted, "the Spanish conquest prevented altogether any further independent development".

Ordeal of Chief Hatuey

III
From Indian servitude to African slavery

Conquest and colonization.- After the discovery, the first American territory to be colonized was Hispanola, the name given by Columbus to the island that today is known as Haiti and the Dominican Republic. Cuba remained virtually neglected until 1510 despite the Spanish Crown's interest in it being explored to see whether it had gold.

Except for some occasional visits, the only important Spanish trip to the island during these years was that of Sebastián de Ocampo, who left Hispanola with the official mission of exploring the Cuban coastline. De Ocampo was indeed the first to sail all along the Cuban island, confirming in so doing that Cuba was not mainland like Columbus had thought. De Ocampo also discovered two of the island's most important bays: Havana on the northern coast, which he called "*Carenas*", and Cienfuegos, in the South, which he called "*Jagua*".

Information compiled by de Ocampo about the island's fertile soil, peaceful inhabitants, and magnificent coastline made Spanish ruling classes want to conquer it and colonize it.

This mission was entrusted to influential military man Diego Velázquez, who was Hispanola's richest person and had experience in the "pacification" of Indians and the founding of villages. With him came men who would later be well-known in the Americas: Pánfilo de Narvaez, Hernán Cortés, Juan de Grijalba, Pedro de Alvarado, Diego de Ordaz, and others. Velázquez was to take control of the whole island; force the Indians into submission and convert them to Catholicism, "without causing them harm"; find out whether there really was gold in Cuba; and found settlements, to give a lasting sense to Spanish domination. The expedition arrived at the southern coast of Cuba's easternmost region in mid 1510, and unleashed the occupation.

Despite the peaceful character of the indigenous population, the conquest started with violence. Indians in eastern Cuba were aware of the cruelty with which their brothers and sisters were treated at Hispanola because many of them had come to Cuba fleeing the conquistadors there, and because there had been Spanish raids into eastern Cuba to hunt for Indians and take them to the nearby island.

One of those who fled Hispanola was Hatuey, an old cacique from the Guahaba region, in what is Haiti today. Upon his arrival in Cuba he organized a group of Indians with the aim of putting up armed resistance to the Spaniards. Hatuey and his men fought for several months in a mountainous region, but their weapons and level of organization could not match those of the conquistadors. Their resistance was eventually crushed, Hatuey was captured, and sentenced to be burnt alive.

Father Bartholomew de las Casas wrote that as flames engulfed Hatuey, who had been tied up to a pole in the center of the fire, a priest tried to convert him to Christianity. The Indian chief asked why he should become a Christian, and the priest answered that so that he could go to heaven. Then Hatuey asked whether

23

Spaniards went to heaven too, and when the priest said yes he then said: "I do not wish to go to heaven to find them there again".

The initial resistance crushed, the conquest continued, first across the eastern region. The first Spanish village in Cuba, *Nuestra Señora de la Asunción de Baracoa*, was founded in 1512, later becoming the first Cuban capital. The conquistadors then split into three groups and started their advance west: one group through the south, another through the center, and the third through the north.

The conquest of Cuba was marked by the cruelty and abuses of Spaniards against the local population. The so-called "Caonao Onslaught" was a good example of it. When Spaniards arrived at this Indian village, near what is today the city of Camagüey, many of the inhabitants gathered in bewilderment to watch the newcomers.

As the Indians peacefully observed them, a Spanish soldier drew his sword. As if in agreement, the rest also brandished their weapons, beginning a cold-blooded murdering of innocent men, women, and children. The begging, threatening, and shouting of Father de las Casas went unheeded. Narváez, the head of the expedition, stood by undisturbed as the massacre took place. The priest would later describe the event as an uncalled for, barbaric, and cruel act and a consequence of the habit by colonizers at Hispanola to viciously shed human blood.

But if the conquest was marked by such outrageous actions, the colonization process was even more nefarious for the Indian population. This process began parallel to the conquest. Upon arriving at each location, the conquistadors would read a so-called "*requerimiento*"—a document informing Indians that the Sovereign Pontiff, vicar of Christ, had donated the Indies to the Catholic King and Queen of Spain and their successors, and that they were to show obedience to the Crown and to their representatives.

Indians did not understand, of course, what they were being told. But Spaniards would later make sure they understood if only through violence and force.

During the process of conquest and colonization, the first villages and towns were established, as Spaniards began taking control of the land and the Indians around them. Seven were the villages founded then, which today are major cities: Baracoa, which we already mentioned; Trinidad; Santi Spiritus, Puerto Principe, Santiago de Cuba, Bayamo, and Havana. Almost all of them were located along the coast, to facilitate relations with the outside world, especially Spain. Spaniards also took into consideration the existence of Indian settlements near the villages, since at the beginning Indians were the chief source of labor. Some of the villages were later moved to other locations. The system followed for the establishment of all these villages was that of building an open square—the *Plaza de Armas*—next to which the church, the garrison, and the town hall were built. The narrow streets all led to the square, and along them were the private houses, whose sizes varied according to the wealth of their owners.

Each village had its town hall, consisting of two mayors, and three regents or councilors. The mayors were in charge of the administrative and judicial work. Supreme authority was in the hands of the Governor of the island, who also held the positions of Vice-Patron of the Church and Distributor of Indians. Above the Governor was only the Spanish Audience at Hispanola, and ultimately the King of Spain.

Land distribution was done along feudal cannons, with the first plots generally going to the *Plaza de Armas*, the church, the townhall, and the garrison. Other plots were then provided for the town dwellers, who were supposed to quickly build their houses; for neighbors to cultivate in tribute to the Council; and for common use, mainly in the form of forests, pastures, and watering places. The rest was distributed among the conquistadors-turned-settlers, with plot sizes varying according to the beneficiary's hierarchy and influence.

Plots were usually distributed in three sizes: *hatos*, a piece of land with a two league radius used for cattle raising; *corrales*, with a one league radius and meant for pig raising; and *estancias*, for general farming and varying in size. The conquistadors were only given land in usufruct; the owner of their land was considered to be the King. Yet, under certain conditions the conquistadors were also allowed to own land. The townhalls were for some time empowered to also distribute plots that had not been given out.

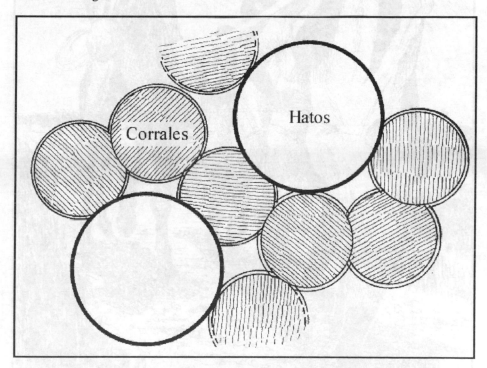

Way in which *hatos y corrales* were marked out

Forced to work in servitude, Indians were also distributed—"*encomendados*", or entrusted, was the Spanish word used. Each conquistador was "entrusted" a number of Indians according to his rank and influence. Formally, the idea was to convert Indians to the Christian faith, to teach them how to work, and to make them acquainted with civilized life. The King had instructed that they be treated well, be properly fed and provided with clothes, and that their rights be fully recognized as subjects of Spain.

A type of abuse against slaves

But such good intentions were never carried through. Driven as they were by greed and the desire to become rich as fast as they could, the colonizers did not hesitate to exploit Indians, abusing them and victimizing them in every way. And since Indians were supposed to be only temporarily "entrusted" to them, the colonizers tried to exploit them as much as they could, aware that it was free labor that could be replaced as soon as exhausted.

Initially, work consisted mostly of searching for gold, making cassava, and looking after the animals. Agriculture was generally disregarded, as practically every thing needed was brought from Spain. Most Indians were therefore employed in searching for gold. And since gold was scarce in Cuba, Indians were forced to work for long hours. Hard work made many of them sick; others would ran away or killed themselves, sometimes resorting to collective suicides, all of which made punishment and precautionary measures against the remaining much more severe.

Ilustrative of Spanish cruelty were the confessions of a wealthy colonizer called Vasco Porcallo de Figueroa. De Figueroa, who had numerous children with Indian and African women, confessed before he died that he had killed many Indians, by burning their mouths so they would not eat mud—an Indian form of mass suicide—or by forcing those caught trying to run away to swallow boiling oil.

But despite their helplessness before the Spaniards, not all Cuban Indians passively accepted the abuses or sought to commit suicide. Many ran away to the mountains, where they settled, frequently raiding villages and burning houses. Others resorted to an even more active fighting, like the cacique Guamá, who attacked and harassed Spaniards for 11 years (1522-1533) at Baracoa mountains.

Whatever the case, 40 years after the conquest the Cuban indigenous population had been practically wiped out. When the *encomienda*, or "entrustment", system was abolished in 1542, only a few thousand Indians were left.

Black slavery.- The fast pace at which the Indian population decreased made Spaniards have to look for new labor. They resorted then to black Africans, whose low level of social development and weak resistance to slave hunters made them an ideal substitute for Indians. In addition, blacks were known to be four times more productive than Indians and much more resisting.

Black slavery was already known in the Iberian peninsula, probably since the time of Arab domination. But it was the Portuguese who made slave trade thrive and who established a direct link with the African countries for this purpose. The first black slaves were brought to Hispanola in the early 16th century (1503), and some of them presumably traveled from there to Cuba with the conquistadors. A document dating back to 1513 authorized the entry into Cuba of black slaves.

Slave labor increased gradually thereafter, acquiring large proportions by the end of the century, when the first sugar mills were established in Cuba.

Blacks were hunted for in Africa, and then loaded like animals on board slave ships, so many of them thrown together that quite a few died during the journey across the Atlantic. They ended up being sold in the American continent to the big landowners and other wealthy people.

Black slaves were brutally forced to work, usually under the most inhuman of conditions. Only those who went to work as house slaves received a less savage treatment, but the ones assigned to the mines, the sugar cane plantations, or the farms had to work 14, 16, or more hours a day. They were poorly fed, dressed in rags, and slept in unhealthy barracks. They were of course denied any education, except for that of the Church, seeking to convert them to the Christian faith. When slaves did not work as hard as they were expected to, or when they committed a fault, they were punished: cruelly beaten with sticks or whips, chained and shackled, placed in a pillory, or even killed.

But like Indians before them, black slaves also ran away, to safe hideouts far from the reach of the Spaniards. There they built their own settlements, or *palenques*. Slave owners hired *rancheadores*, or slave hunters, to track them down with weapons and dogs. A run-away slave captured was usually killed: hanged from a tree for others to see.

As time went by, slaves became aware of their collective capacity to fight, and organized rebellions in demand for freedom. Slave work prevailed in Cuba for three and a half centuries.

IV
Foreign hostility and social conflicts

Corsairs and pirates.- Europe's colonialist powers (England, France, Spain, Holland and Portugal) were constantly involved in the struggle for the domination of the rest of the world's lands and markets. After the conquest of America, Spain exerted an absolute commercial monopoly over the conquered lands, which could only export and import to the empire and only through one port: Seville.

This iron-clad monopoly fueled conflicts between other European nations and Spain and made it possible for piracy to extend to the New World too, with the object of not only contending commerce with America to Spain, but also important possessions on the continent. As of the third decade of the 16th century, Cuba began to experience the siege of the English, the French and the Dutch.

Another factor that encouraged piracy was the monopoly by Spain itself. This monopoly upset many of the island's producers, especially the cattle ranchers, as it forced them to sell to only one buyer and also imposed very low prices on their products. As a result, smuggling became a flourishing business, carried out between these sectors and the corsairs that visited Cuban shores. Spanish authorities and other top officials in many Cuban regions became involved in this activity.

But Cuba was not always at peace with these sea bandits. The island also suffered numerous pirate attacks on its main cities (Havana, Santiago de Cuba, Puerto Principe, Baracoa, Cárdenas, Mariel, etc.), some of which were pillaged with impunity. Among the main attackers of the island and its adjoining seas were: Francisco Nau, Henry Morgan, Jacques de Sores, Francis Drake, and Gilberto Girón. There were also Spanish pirates a Cuban one, Diego Grillo.

Gilberto Girón's attack on Manzanillo in 1604 has a special meaning for Cuban culture. During the battle, a black slave, Salvador Golomón, killed the pirate and rescued Bishop Juan de las Cabezas Altamirano, who had been kidnapped. To honor the event, Canary Islands poet Silvestre de Balboa, who lived in Puerto Principe, composed the first poem to be recorded in Cuba: "*Espejo de Paciencia*".

> "An Ethiopian worthy of praise
> called Salvador, a brave Black man
> from those Yara has on its farmland,
> son of Golomón, a prudent old man…

In view of the constant attacks, the Spanish government took numerous measures: severe sanctions against the island's inhabitants who took part in the smuggling, a more intense surveillance of the coasts, the organization of the fleet system in a way that ships loaded with merchandise didn't travel alone and defenseless, and above all, the building of fortresses to protect cities. Thus, the following castles were built: La Fuerza, La Punta and El Morro; the Fortified Towers of Cojimar and La Chorrera (all of them in Havana), and El Morro in Santiago de Cuba.

Havana fortress: La Fuerza

No wonder historian once said that "El Morro and La Punta castles were monuments to Sir Francis Drake".

Internal contradictions.- Differences between the various classes and social sectors sharpened throughout the 17th century. The indigenous were being exterminated and the Black slaves were increasing; both were the most exploited and mistreated classes among the island's inhabitants, and we have already referred to their discontent and their struggles. But class contradictions also deepened among the Spaniards and their descendants born in Cuba (known as Creoles).

Rich slave-owners who owned sugar plantations, large amounts of land, farm animals and large industries—such as slave traders and import merchants—formed a powerful oligarchy. The Spanish authorities, headed by the Governor of the Colony, were generally concerned about how to get rich quick and, although they frequently got into conflicts with the oligarchy, they always came to an agreement.

Another very different situation was that of the small and medium producers (rural landowners, artisans, retailers, modest professionals, etc.), on whom the main burden of fiscal and religious contributions fell. Aside from this burden, they had to sell their products or services at low prices and had great difficulties in obtaining the necessary resources for their work.

The struggles of tobacco farmers, for example, were long and grievous. They had to fight the eager, expansionist desires of large landowners who tried to forcibly remove them from their lands. These struggles began with the increase of sugar and cattle production and continued throughout the entire colonial period. It even continued into the period of the pseudo-Republic, which was dominated by the bourgeoisie and large landowners.

30

Small and medium producers had to wage battles against the pillage of the rulers and against the commercial monopoly of the Metropolis, Spain. Since they were forced to sell their products to only one buyer -the colonial government- they were subjected to imposed conditions, which were generally abusive.

One of the ways in which they improved their situation was smuggling, an activity we referred to before. They ran the risk of suffering severe sanctions if they were discovered.

In some cases, they also decided to carry out protest actions, occasionally violent. This was the case, for example, of the tobacco farmer on the outskirts of Havana (Santiago de las Vegas, San Miguel del Padrón and Jesús del Monte), during the end of the second decade and the beginning of the third of the 18th century.

In 1717, taking into account the great popularity of Cuban tobacco in Europe, the government resolved to decree the *estanco* or state monopoly of this product, effectively monopolizing its sale.

Tobacco farmers could only sell their crops to a factory established in Havana, with branches in the island's provinces, at a price set by the government. This measure notably worsened the situation of tobacco farmers: buyers would discard the part of the tobacco leaves they did not want, they set very low prices, they delayed payments and committed other types of abuses.

Tobacco farmers were extremely annoyed with the *estanco* and repeatedly complained to Havana authorities, but they paid no attention to them. Then, in 1717, some 500 tobacco farmers from Jesús del Monte armed themselves with machetes, picks, and other agricultural instruments. They marched to the capital and surrounded the La Fuerza castle, where the governor had his office, demanding an end to the monopoly. To calm them down, they were promised that the estanco conditions would be modified. The Governor and the factory's officials fled to Spain. But the promises were not kept and there was a second rebellion in 1720, when protesters burned the houses and crops of some of the *estanco*'s supporters. New promises calmed the protest, but the new tricks upset the farmers. In 1723, they agreed not to sell tobacco unless they were paid in cash, and nearly 900 armed tobacco farmers prepared to burn the houses and crops of some of those who didn't respect the agreement. The authorities found out about their plans and ambushed them, killing a number of the farmers and wounding others. Eleven tobacco farmers were captured and lynched, their bodies left hanging from the trees along the road to Jesús del Monte as a warning.

The rebellion, however, was not in vain. It had repercussions in Spain, and the King decreed that the tobacco farmers could sell their produce freely. This was the first big uprising of farmers that took place in Cuba.

Although these struggles were not yet an expression of Cuban nationalism, they began to mark important differences between the colonial government and the island's producers.

On the other hand, the slaves' resistance also grew. Besides the escapes and the increase in the number of maroons and *palenques* (maroon settlements), other more resolute actions began to take place. In 1727, over 300 slaves revolted at the Quiebra Hacha sugar mill, located west of Havana. Also of great importance was the uprising of the El Cobre mine workers, in Santiago de Cuba in 1731. The miners stayed in the mountains for a month with the help of 50 black slaves in their settlement. They only ended their action when they were assured there would be no reprisals and received promises of better treatment. Several slave revolts also occurred at the end of the 18th century, at farms located in Mariel, Havana, Güines, Trinidad and Puerto Principe.

However, the most important and best organized of these initial rebellions broke out in 1812. It was led by a free Black man, José Antonio Aponte, a carpenter by trade, who had some education and was aware of the political problems of his time. His aim was to unite Black slaves and to make a revolution that would abolish slavery. Actions were carried out in several places in Oriente and Camagüey, as well as in Jaruco and Guanabacoa (in Havana province); but the revolution was defeated. Prisons were filled with Black slaves, who were subjected to severe torture; Aponte and his main collaborators died on the gallows.

The taking of Havana by the British.- The British always wanted to possess some of the most important Spanish enclaves in the Americas, Havana among them. In 1740, Admiral Vernon, heading a powerful squadron, came up to the entrance to the city but, after noticing it was well protected, decided not to attack. He then headed to Oriente's southern coast, and went ashore in Guantánamo, where he founded a colony named Cumberland. Vernon's purpose was to advance on Santiago de Cuba. But after five months, besieged by Creole guerrillas and diseases, the British were forced to give up the attempt.

A few years later, in 1761, while France was at war against England, Spain became involved in the conflict. King Charles III signed, along with his relatives and the King of France, the so-called "Family Pact". In response to this pact, England declared war on Spain and decided to attack Havana. A powerful British squadron arrived at Havana Bay in June 1762; attacking the city, Britain took control after battles that lasted over a month.

The British did not occupy the entire island—only the portion that extends from the port of Mariel, 55 kilometers west of the capital, to the city of Matanzas, located 105 kilometers to the east. The rest of the territory continued to be under Spanish administration, which once again selected Santiago de Cuba as the island's capital, as it did in the 16th century.

The taking of Havana by the British proved that Cuba's natives still identified with the Spaniards, that they didn't distinguish between Creoles and natives of Spain. It was actually the natives who showed a greater determination to struggle against the British, despite the fact that England's ideas of free trading coincided with those of Creole producers. It was a Creole, José Antonio Gómez—known as Pepe Antonio—who organized the guerrilla struggle against the British.

Another characteristic of those events, was the large number of US colonists that supported the British troops in their siege on Havana. This was a demonstration of the 13 colonies' interest in developing economic relations with the island.

But perhaps the most relevant factor of British domination was the impulse it gave to commerce between Cuba and other countries, especially with England itself and with its American colonies. The monopoly of the Royal Company of Commerce—which was Spanish—ceased immediately.Havana Bay was full of merchant

32

ships: during the eleven months of British domination, some one thousand ships unloaded cargo in the capital's port. At the same time, the export of sugar, tobacco and some other of the country's products, multiplied.

Economic and cultural progress. Love for the native land.- Once Spanish domination over Havana was re-established in early July 1763 as a result of the Treaty of Versailles, restrictions for commerce on the island were reinforced, however the basis for a necessary opening had already been set up. With the so-called "Wise Despotism" that Charles III represented for Spain, a time of certain progress began for Cuba. Governors that arrived in Cuba during those years did away with commercial monopolies, reduced taxes and took a series of measures for the development of agriculture, commerce and education. A plan to rebuild El Morro and to build other fortresses in order to strengthen the country's defenses was initiated. Commercial relations with US contractors began. The first newspaper, **"La Gaceta"**, was published in Cuba in 1764. In 1773, the San Carlos Seminary was founded. This religious and aristocratic college—along with the University of Havana, founded in 1728—constituted the country's highest seats of learning.

Since 1776, when the independence war of the 13 American colonies began, Cuba offered support to the insurgents. Cuba sent them weapons and ammunition, it offered protection to their ships and carried out smuggling operations in favor of the independence fighters. In 1778, when France began its new war against England, Cuba became the point from where expeditions regularly sailed to Florida, Jamaica and other territories, giving the island a privileged situation.

This prosperity notably increased after 1790, under the administration of Don Luis de Las Casas. To carry out his government work, he surrounded himself by eminent personalities, many of them Creoles: **Francisco de Arango y Parreno,** a statesman who promoted freedom of commerce and made important contributions to the development of agriculture; **José Pablo Valiente,** a specialist in fiscal matters who organized and strengthened the country's finances; **Dr. Tomás Romay,** a doctor and a politician who introduced and applied anti-viral vaccines for the first time in Cuba; and Presbyterian **José Agustín Caballero**, professor, orator and man of liberal ideas who helped reform out-dated methods of teaching. All of them contributed their knowledge and directed their efforts to the progress of their native land.

This period saw the creation of institutions that largely promoted agriculture, industry, commerce and education in general. Among them: the *Amigos del País* Economic Society; the Royal Consulate of Agriculture, Industry and Commerce; the Poorhouse, and the *Papel Periódico de La Habana*. Teaching methods at the San Carlos Seminary were updated.

The rebellion of Black slaves in Haiti in 1791 contributed greatly to the island's economic boom. The destruction of sugar mills and coffee plantations by the rebels and the abandonment of others by the French colonists—many of whom took refuge in Cuba—forced sugar and coffee production in that country to decline drastically. For that reason, Cuba began to assume the sugar and coffee demand that previously corresponded to its sister island and also benefited from the considerable rise in the prices of these products.

The Cuban governor warmly received the Haitian colonists; he gave them land in the eastern region of the island and money to start their farms. These colonists, in turn, contributed their vast experience in coffee and sugar production, in the creation of small industries and even in the propagation of artistic and literary culture (language academies, theaters and other activities). These colonists changed the appearance of some of the regions. The number of sugar mills and coffee plantations notably increased, which brought on a significant increase in the introduction of Black slaves during the last years of the 17th century. Between 1770 and 1800, the number of Blacks taken to Cuba was greater than during the previous three centuries.

As in science and technology, the subject of nationalism also appeared in the field of literature as the main theme of this generation. Although the concept of homeland did not have a political connotation for these men and they frequently praised the glories of Spain, they began to express a love and pride for their native land, and often considered it superior in riches and natural beauty. For example, Manuel de Zequeira y Arango from Havana and Manuel Justo de Rubalcava from Santiago de Cuba—both in the military—wrote verses that became symbolic of a nation in birth.

V
The nation in birth. Currents and ways

In late 18th century, contradictions within Cuban society stood out. The Spanish government prohibited free trade by Cuban producers again; but opposition to this measure was so strong, that the island's governors could not implement it. The Black population's growth, mainly due to the massive importation of slaves and their growing struggles for emancipation, caused apprehension among the white population. They feared a Black revolt, as had taken place in Haiti, which undoubtedly inspired slaves and freed slaves in Cuba.

There were also contradictions between Creole plantation owners born of Spaniards in Cuba and Spanish merchants, who charged high interest rates for the money they lent to producers. The merchants raked up big profits from the purchase and sale of sugar, tobacco, coffee, etc., at the expense of plantation owners and foreign merchants. They were cut out as intermediaries.

The seed of freedom was also watered by important international events, such as the declaration of independence by the 13 British colonies of North America, the victory of the Great French Revolution of 1779 and the triumphant revolt of Haiti's Black slaves. And during the first decades of the 19th century, the ideas of independence and freedom were helped by the liberation wars carried out by many of Spain's American colonies.

Early revolts. Control of reformist ideas.- A joint conspiracy of Blacks and whites was forged in 1795, headed by a free Black, Nicolás Morales.

It was centered in Bayamo, with insurrectionary plans in several other places in the eastern region. It was not a separatist movement; its main demands were "equality between mulattos and whites" and the abolition of sales taxes and other burdens "that oppress the poor". Discovered before breaking out, the conspirators were jailed.

The first separatist rebellion—organized in 1809 and 1810—emerged from the richest layer of Creole aristocracy. Among its leaders were: Roman de la Luz Silveira and Joaquín Infante. Infante drafted the nation's Magna Carta—the first Cuban Constitution based on independence—which considered Cuba a sovereign state, presumed the rule of the country's wealthy, maintained slavery as long as it was necessary for agriculture, established a social classification based on the color of one's skin and declared Catholicism the official religion.

The government aborted the conspiracy and its main leaders were condemned to prison and deported to Spain.

The main reason for the failure of these attempts was that the vast majority of Creoles, especially plantation owners, did no t consider independence to be a solution to Cuba's problems and, therefore, they rejected any separatist action. They thought that Spain's power was essential to maintain the pro-slavery system and to prevent a Black revolt. Nationalism had not developed among the rich Creole sector nor Black slaves. At that time, Black slaves only aspired to their emancipation and Creoles relied on in Spain to grant the political, economic and social reforms necessary to guarantee the country's progress: the maintenance of slavery and slave trade, the end to a commercial monopoly imposed by Madrid, granting Cuba the rights other Spanish colonies enjoyed or the establishment of an autonomous government on the island.

It was precisely in the early 19th century when the three currents that characterized political struggles of the 1800's took shape: reformism, annexation and independence.

Moreover, it was during these years when spontaneous and isolated actions—which slaves had been carrying out for some time—grew in organization and formed a well-defined current of social character: abolitionism.

All these currents existed simultaneously throughout the century; but their substance and importance varied during different stages.

The independence movement was extremely weak until 1820 and pro-annexation ideas (which supported Cuba's annexation to the United States) took their first steps during those years, encouraged by the words and actions of several US presidents. At this stage, Reformist ideas had an almost absolute predominance.

The confidence of Creole producers in the policy of reforms consolidated in the first lustra of the century, when the colonial government administered the island intelligently, protected the interests of Creoles, efficiently handled public finance, promoted culture and placed some representatives of native landowners in prominent positions. Francisco de Arango y Parreno, the most outstanding of them, was appointed Counselor of Indies; the abolition of the tobacco monopoly was achieved and free commerce between Cuba and the rest of the nations was authorized. In an also favorable international situation, Cuban sugar and tobacco reached a high demand, their prices went up, public income notably increased, and Cuba entered a new stage of prosperity.

Under these conditions, the struggles of other colonies of The Americas for their independence influenced very little in the spirit of Creoles.

Two decades of separatism. Varela and Heredia.- The influence of South American wars strengthened after 1820. After the re-establishment of the Spanish Constitution on the island in 1812, the political struggle between the two parties began. one of them responded to the most reactionary Spaniards, the so-called *integristas* (advocates for preserving national traditions and ways of life), especially big importers, enemies not only of Cuba's independence, but also of any reform that could benefit native producers.

The other party represented the interests of Creole society, defended liberal reforms and had many young people among its followers, who were already influenced by the ideas of the French Revolution and by the example of the Spanish colonies that successfully won their independence.

The struggle between *integristas* and Creoles became so belligerent that cries of "Long Live Independence!" began to be heard and separatist posters appeared everywhere. Due to their conservative appearance, Masonic lodges served as centers where independence fighters planned their next moves.

Numerous secret societies also emerged: the most important of them was the so-called "*Soles y Rayos de Bolívar*", founded in 1821 to free Cuba and to establish the Republic of Cubanacán. The movement was led by José Francisco Lemus, a member of the Creole Party who, years before, had been appointed Colonel of the Colombian Army. An Argentinean was also well-known—José Antonio Miralla. His connection with the South American patriots was evident. The organization had branches in five provinces and its forces were known to exceed 600 fighters. In 1823, two years after its creation and when the insurrection was drawing near, the leadership was arrested and condemned to exile.

The destruction of this conspiracy coincided with the re-establishment of absolutism in Spain, after almost three years of constitutional rule. In Cuba, the governor was granted broad powers. He dissolved the national militia, created the Permanent Executive Military Commission which was under his power, closed newspapers, removed provincial representatives and suppressed other liberties; as a result, the island returned to the worst days of tyrannical and despotic rule.

A number of independence conspiracies took place during the 1820's and 1830's: one led by Second Lieutenant Gaspar Antonio Rodríguez, which joined separatist Cubans and pro-constitution Spaniards (1824); another led by young Cubans from eastern Camagüey province—Francisco Agüero and Andrés Manuel Sánchez—who established connections with Colombian revolutionaries abroad and disembarked in Cuba in 1826; the Expedition of the Thirteen (*Expedición de los Trece*) (1826), which returned to Jamaica after docking in several ports without being able to go ashore; the Great Legion of the Black Eagle (*Gran Legión del Aguila Negra*), linked to Mexican revolutionaries and formed by members of different social classes, including workers and artisans (1829); and the Triangular Chain (*Cadena Triangular*) and *Soles de la Libertad* (Liberty Suns) (1837). All of these conspiracies failed and many of the leaders paid for their efforts to free Cuba with their lives.

Two figures that played a leading role when Cuban nationalism was conceived rose to prominence during this first stage of independence struggles: Presbyterian Félix Varela and poet José María Heredia.

Varela revolutionized teaching methods, delivering a devastating blow to educational techniques in his capacity as a professor at San Carlos Seminary; he adopted Reformist positions, but soon understood the impossibility of achieving any progress under the colonial regime and fought for independence. As a congressional representative in 1823, he introduced legislation for a "Project of Autonomous Government of Overseas Provinces". According to this bill, territories would not be under military rule and slavery would be eradicated in Cuba. By supporting the independence of Spanish colonies, he defended the right of all people to freedom. Due to his positions, Félix Varela was condemned to death. He was forced to leave Spain and went to the United States.

José María Heredia was Cuba's first revolutionary poet and, according to critics, the greatest Spanish-American poet of his time. At 18 years of age, he fought for the independence of his homeland in the "Soles y Rayos de Bolívar Society". When authorities discovered the society, he had to flee Cuba and sought refuge in Mexico. The poem *Al Niágara* (To Niagara) and his *Himno al Desterrado*

(Hymn to the Exiled) stand out among his finest works .From the latter are the following verses:

It's better to confront the enemy's sword
without fear
than to lie in bed
while suffering a thousand deaths.

....

Cuba! At last you'll be free and pure
like the radiant air you breathe,
like the seething waves of your beaches
kissing the sand.
Although served by despicable traitors
the tyrant's rage is useless,
'cause not in vain between Cuba and Spain
the immense sea stretches out its waves.

Second reformist stage. Saco, Luz and Del Monte.- Beginning in 1830, a new growth of reformism took place, but its demands were different compared to the first period. With free trade achieved in 1818, the main economic demand was the reduction of customs tariffs on imports not coming from Spain. Spanish products were imported with very low tariffs, but those from other countries were excessively high, which limited the advantages that free trade could offer.

In the political arena, reform advocates continued to demand that Cuba be "assimilated" as a Spanish province or that it be granted full autonomy. However, facing the despotic regime that was in power, their main efforts were aimed at end the all-encompassing powers held by the governors.

In the social field, reform advocates continued to support the institution of slavery, but now they demanded that no more slaves be brought over from Africa. Slave trade had been taking place secretly since 1820—when England and Spain had agreed to stop it. The steam engine was introduced in Cuban sugar mills in 1819, and many sugar plantation owners realized that the new techniques required qualified, skilled workers and they increasingly replaced the slaves. On the other hand, fearful of a race revolt, they tried to stop the Black population from increasing on the island.

However, coffee and some sugar plantation owners who continued to use old procedures in their factories wanted more slaves from Africa, since they needed the labor force.

These disagreements between Creole producers divided the reform advocates and contributed to the height of pro-annexation ideas.

Slave traders also disagreed with the reform advocates, since they made substantial profits from this illegal commerce. Colonial government officials also disagreed, given that they were paid for every slave clandestinely brought to Cuba.

The main leader of the Reformist movement was José Antonio Saco, from the eastern city of Bayamo. A brilliant writer, historian and politician, Saco defended the interests of the powerful Cuban plantation owners, along with two prominent intellectuals: José de la Luz y Caballero and Domingo del Monte. The three of them stood out for their criticism of Spanish despotism and for their positions against slave trade.

Saco strongly denounced the illegal trade that was taking place under the protection of Spanish governors, he engaged in debates with advocates of *Integrismo*, opposed to annexation, and did not try to conceal the fact that when he spoke about his homeland, he was talking about Cuba.

One of the most despotic governors of colonial Cuba, General Miguel Tacón, deported him from the central town of Trinidad and then to Spain. In 1836, when a mutiny forced the Spanish Queen to re-establish the constitutional regime in Madrid, the island was given the possibility of choosing four members of the Spanish Parliament. Four of them were Cuban and three of them were well-known reform advocates. Saco was one of the delegates, but in face of the defeat suffered by colonialists, the Spanish Parliament refused to accept the Cuban congressional representatives.

José de la Luz y Caballero reached his greatest prominence as an educator of several generations of wealthy Creoles. Several of his students would stand out, years later, as independence combatants. He was a friend of abolitionists and was implicated, without any evidence of such activity, in anti-slavery conspiracies.

Domingo del Monte belonged to a family of rich plantation owners, but he mainly excelled as a writer and teacher of Cuban intellectuals. He contributed to the emancipation and literary development of Black poet Juan Francisco Manzano and to the height of Cuban culture. An enemy of despotic regimes, he was persecuted and was forced to leave Cuba.

The Reformist offensive of the 1830's ended in complete failure. Spain did not concede to any of the demands, and instead deprived Cubans of the right all Spaniards had to send their representatives to the Spanish Parliament. Furthermore, Madrid stepped up repression against all those that called for reforms. Contradictions between the colony and the Metropolis noticeably intensified.

Height of Abolitionism. La Escalera Conspiracy.- While hopes of Reformist ideas were frustrated at this stage, a considerable number of struggles for the abolition of slavery took place. Two main factors contributed to this: first, the development of an awareness for struggle among slaves and many Blacks who were emancipated with the support of a small sector of white Creoles; and second, the encouraging significance of English government pressures on Spain to end the slave trade.

In 1817, Spain had to sign a treaty that forced it to definitely suspend the admission of slaves to its colonies. But since Spain did not meet that commitment, England forced Spain to sign another agreement in 1835, which extended the right of English vessels to capture Spanish slave ships on the open sea. England had abolished slavery in its colonies in 1838 and was concerned that Spain's commercial competition would ruin producers in those colonies. Sugar produced in Cuba by slave labor was cheaper than that produced by salaried workers.

England and Spain established a court in Havana in 1837 to judge traders who were caught with cargoes of Black slaves. Moreover, England appointed an abolitionist as a consul in the island's capital, to guarantee the fulfillment of commitments made by Spain.

In 1843, the situation became very dangerous for Spanish domination, so revolts were put down with massive killings and executions of Blacks. But abolitionist actions occurred over and over again, and the situation reached its climax in 1844, when a vast conspiracy that included both free Blacks and slaves was discovered. White intellectuals and professionals from several social classes were also implicated.

Known as "La Escalera Conspiracy", it took its name from the Spanish word *escalera,* or ladder. Blacks were tied to a ladder and whipped until they confessed or died. According to an investigation made by outstanding Cuban professor Sergio Aguirre, over 300 Blacks and mulattos died from torture; 78 were condemned to death and executed; over 600 were imprisoned in Cuba and over 400 were expelled from the island. Among the executed, there were renowned mulatto intellectuals and professionals, such as famous poet Gabriel de la Concepción Valdés (Plácido), musician José Miguel Roman, dentist Andrés Dodge, and plantation owner Santiago Pimienta—all from central Matanzas. Also implicated—but without their participation ever proved—were José de la Luz y Caballero and Domingo del Monte.

This brutal repression placed obstacles in the way of abolitionist struggles in the following years; but Spain was forced to take measures to reduce the introduction of Black slaves. Slave traders began to look for other sources of cheap labor—Chinese colonists and Indians from Yucatan—also in conditions of utter slavery.

The road to annexation. "The Ripe Fruit" Theory.- A series of abolitionist revolts at a time when Blacks were 58% of the population, along with Spain's apparent incapacity to resist England's pressures to abolish slavery, motivated many wealthy Creoles —die-hard defenders of slavery—to advocate for Cuba's annexation to the United States. Slavery existed in the southern US states, so the Creoles believed that if they could successfully annex Cuba to that region, slavery on the island would continue.

Moreover, Cuban pro-annexation thought that the power of the US was sufficient to protect the pro-slavery regime against England's anti-slavery drive, something they could not expect from Spain.

This was the basis of pro-annexation ideas in the 1840's. However, there were other types of annexation advocates: those who longed for development similar to that of the industrial North in the US, with democratic freedoms, and thought that annexation would carry the island along the path of political democracy and economic and social progress.

They could not expect this from the exploitative, backwards and despotic Spain and did not believe that Cuba alone could conquer its independence.

US rulers always encouraged Cuban pro-annexation. Since 1805, Jefferson expressed his intentions of taking possession of Cuba due to strategic reasons and in 1809 he sent secret agents to the island to negotiate with Governor Someruelos. The same happened with presidents that followed. In April, 1823, US Secretary of State, John Quinsy Adams, formulated his "ripe fruit theory": "there are laws of political gravitation, like there are laws of physical gravitation, and Cuba, separated from Spain, will necessarily fall in the grasp of the United States, the same way a ripe fruit detached from a tree has to necessarily fall to the ground".

In December of the same year, the Monroe Doctrine was proclaimed: "America for the Americans", which is directly related to Cuba, Puerto Rico, and other European colonies. But in 1826, on the occasion of Panama's Congress, the US government prevented Spanish-American nations from joining to support Cuba's independence. Washington preferred that the island continue as a Spanish colony before it fell in the hands of the English, or conquered its independence. That's why Washington

40

officially expressed its opposition to possible agreements between Spain and England—even threatening with the use of force to prevent them— and disapproved, also in an official way, the preparation of military expeditions to Cuba from US territory.

Several secret organizations with pro-annexation purposes were created between 1845 and 1855, the most outstanding of which was the La Habana Club; several newspapers of the same character were published in Cuba and in the United States, and there were unsuccessful conspiracies and uprisings in several provinces. But the most resounding actions of pro-annexation character were those carried out by Spanish Army General Narciso López—born in Caracas, where he had fought against Venezuelan patriots—who conspired on the island since 1847 and who prepared four expeditions to Cuba in the United States. His annexation defense was based on a pro-slavery position.

López joined forces with the US military and settlers, among them Colonel John Anthony Quitman, governor of the state of Mississippi, who had great experience in these matters. He had participated in the invasion of Mexico in 1847 and had been a military governor there.

The first two expeditions organized by López failed before their departure (in 1848 and 1849), due to opposition by the US government. The third one, made up of over 600 men, of whom only five were Cubans, went ashore in the central city of Cárdenas, which was taken. But, lacking popular support, the expeditionary force went home.

In his fourth and last attempt, López gathered 400 men, most of them foreigners, who disembarked in western Pinar del Río province, in August, 1851. After several victorious encounters, they were defeated by Spanish troops. After being captured, López was executed.

Failure of reformist ideas. The Board of Information.- Pro-annexation ideas could not recover from its overwhelming setbacks. Very few followers were left, and the number decreased even more beginning in 1865, when slavery was abolished in the US southern states, as a result of the victory of the North in the Civil War. Future annexation advocates would not carry the pro-slavery banner.

The defeats suffered by reform advocates, abolitionists and annexation supporters reinforced the idea that neither white Creoles nor Blacks (slaves or free) could achieve their aspirations under Spanish domination. However, there was one last hope among Creole plantation owners with respect to reforms approved by Spain. Between 1859 and 1866, Cuba had two governors of liberal ideas, who won the sympathy of the Creole population: Generals Francisco Serrano (married to a Cuban) and Domingo Dulce. They began to attract the attention of Cubans, who had been absent from the colonial administration since the Tacón government in the 1830's; they consulted them about important problems on the island, they showed respect for their opinions and allowed them to have certain liberties which had been previously forbidden. The tradition of reading literary works at tobacco factories began during that stage (1865). Serrano prepared a bill— though unsuccessfully—that established Cuba's representation before the Courts of Spain, and created several insular organizations in which Creoles could participate, aimed at elaborating budgets and studying the tax system. And even more surprising, the two governors encouraged the creation of a Reformist Party, despite the fact that in Cuba the existence of political parties was forbidden.

The main leaders of that party were renowned economist and politician Francisco de Frías, Count of Pozos Dulces, prominent lawyer José Morales Lemus, and Miguel Aldama, one of Cuba's richest plantation owners. All three had pro-annexation histories, and colonial authorities had persecuted the first two on charges of conspiracy. They were also allowed to publish a newspaper, **El Siglo**, directed by the Count of Pozos Dulces, who played a prominent role in political struggles of the time.

The main aspirations of the new party were more ambitious than those of the Reformist movement of previous epochs. In the economic field, they called for free trade by eliminating customs taxes on all imports from all countries, and by eliminating indirect taxes that affected the population, replacing them with a single 6% indirect tax on profits from all capital invested in Cuba.

In the public sphere, they supported the separation of the civilian and military powers; the creation of national corporations to deal with the major issues of interest for the island, and respect for civil liberties, constitutional rights and guarantees, including the election of Cuban parliamentarians to Spain's legislature. Some reform advocates, like José Antonio Saco, opposed these congressional posts at the Spanish Parliament and demanded an autonomous regime for Cuba, similar to that of Canada.

Socially, the reform advocates took a significant step ahead: they not only demanded the total elimination of the slave trade, including its clandestine nature, but also supported the gradual abolition of slavery through economic compensation for slave owners.

Madrid responded by organizing an assembly that was called the "Board of Information", made up of people knowledgeable about overseas problems, to discuss ways to solve them. Cuba was granted the right to choose 16 delegates to represent the island at the Board. The election of those delegates took place in May, 1866, and was an overwhelming victory for the Reformist Party over Spanish reactionaries: 14 of the 16 chosen were reform advocates.

The performance of those delegates at the Board of Information was brilliant: they maintained their demands with an arsenal of irrefutable arguments. But the response of the Metropolis constituted a scandalous mockery. The Spanish government, instead of establishing free trade and eliminating indirect taxes, dictated a new 10% tax on capital investment. Instead of guaranteeing constitutional rights and giving Cubans participation in their country's affairs, it maintained the governors' all-embracing powers, ignored the demands of assimilation and autonomy, and sent a new despotic and reactionary governor to Cuba, general Francisco Lersundi. This governor suppressed liberties granted by Serrano and Dulce, prohibited gatherings of a political character, as well as the reading of books and newspapers at cigar factories, and unleashed a campaign of repression against people of liberal ideas. At the same time, the colonial government maintained the pro-slavery regime with all of its rigor. This failure of Reformist ideas was definitive. Most Cubans finally understood that there was only one alternative: armed struggle for independence.

42

VI
The Ten Year War

Madrid's stepped-up abuses against Cubans after the demise of the Information Board, alongside with other factors like the economic crisis that swept the island during 1866-67, made the life of the Creole population unbearable. Coffee production continued in crisis and sugar prices plummeted. Plantation owners became more indebted and workers, artisans and entrepreneurs were forced to migrate—many of them settling in southern United States, in Tampa and key West.

Nevertheless, the colonial administration was making huge profits in Cuba, and did not bother to invest in the island's development. In 1862, for instance, only 3 per cent of revenues were earmarked for economic development. Yet, 44 per cent of revenues were used in military spending, and 41 per cent to cover the expenses of the country's colonial government, all of which exclusively benefited Spaniards. In addition, 12 per cent of the revenues collected was sent to Spain and Fernando Poo Island. With slight variations, this panorama would be repeated year after year. At this rate, the Spaniards, who amounted to only 8 per cent of the island's population, appropriated over 90 per cent of the its wealth.

In the meantime, the overwhelming majority of the native population had no political rights, while an insignificant peninsular minority ruled the destiny of the island at its will. The failure of the latest Reformist efforts gave way to a new scenario.

Carlos Manuel de Céspedes. La Demajagua. After the failure of the Board of Information, conspiracies ensued, mostly in the eastern part of the country, where the crisis was more acute. In July, 1867, the Revolutionary Committee of the City of Bayamo was established under the leadership of Francisco Vicente Aguilera, one of the country's wealthiest plantation owners.

Aguilera was a cultivated man, well known for his generosity and spirit of sacrifice. He would later become Military Commander of Oriente and vice-president of the Republic in Arms. He was assigned to go to the United States to foster the unity of Cuban immigrants who were feuding among each other. With no money, and thread-bare, he accomplished his mission on the streets of New York. He died in absolute poverty in 1877, admired and loved by all Cuban patriots.

The conspiracy rapidly expanded to Oriente's most important towns, principally in Manzanillo. There, Carlos Manuel de Céspedes, a lawyer and landowner, would become the main protagonist of the uprising.

Céspedes was born in Bayamo to a well-to-do family. He acquired his lawyers' degree in Barcelona, traveled through Europe and was very cultivated. He loved music and poetry, and was also a great horseman and fencer. In 1851, he denounced colonial rule, and expressed his sympathy with Cubans who had revolted against Spain. He wrote satiric poems against the Spanish government. As a result of his political positions, he served prison terms and was deported twice.

His situation in Bayamo became very tenuous, forcing him to move to Manzanillo, where he opened his lawyers' office and bought an estate known as "*La Demajagua*".

He would soon be acknowledged as the leader of the independence conspiracy in that territory.

His anti-colonial intransigence endured many tests. On one occasion, his son Oscar was imprisoned by the Spaniards. They immediately contacted Céspedes with an offer: if he would strike up a deal, the life of his son would be spared. Céspedes replied: "Oscar is not my only child. I am the father of all Cubans who have died for the Revolution". The young man was executed and ever since, Céspedes has been known as the Father of the Nation.

In early October, 1868, Spanish authorities discovered plans for an uprising and immediately ordered the arrest of its main leaders. Once Céspedes heard the news, he moved up the date of the uprising and in the early morning of October 10 he issued the independence cry in his sugar mill "*La Demajagua*". So started the war against Spanish rule in Cuba. As the first act of sovereignty, Céspedes freed his slaves, and called on them to join in the liberation struggle. He then issued a proclamation explaining the reasons for the insurrection.

The 10th of October Manifesto.- The document denounced the intolerable situation in which Spain kept Cuba, charging that oppression was rampant. "Spain governs the island with bloody swords, civic freedoms are non-existent. Cubans lack the most elementary rights, they are banished form their own land or are either executed without due judicial processes. They are left with no choice but to remain silent and obey".

In the economic order—continued the document—there is an ominous exploitation. "The Customs House does not allow Cuban producers to cover their expenses; the single taxation ruins their properties, and the endless flow of starving Spaniards that flood the island takes from Cubans available goods and jobs; the Spanish government deprives Cuba's best children of public employment and finances, and pays with Cuban money for an army and navy that depletes private and public sources of wealth".

The situation is one of total stagnation. The immigration of whites is forbidden and slavery is maintained. "We believe that all men are equal", said the document, and "we call for the emancipation of slaves".

Once the document was read, the patriots headed to the nearby town of Yara with the purpose of seizing it. In route, they were surprised by a strong Spanish Army column, suffering numerous casualties and dispersed. This clash is considered the first action of war and is historically known as the Cry of Yara.

It identifies the beginning of the first emancipation war in Cuba. When the few patriots that remained regrouped, Céspedes stated: "there are still 12 of us left, we are enough to achieve the independence of Cuba".

The Seizing of Bayamo.- The uprising was supported in various regions in Oriente. On October 13, the rebels took 8 towns in the province. These victories favored the enrollment of more personnel and the acquisition of more weapons, and boosted the prestige of the liberation forces . With the assistance of Dominican Luis Marcano, Céspedes provided the Liberation Army with a rudimentary organization and continued the struggle. He was recognized as General in Chief of the Army.

The group led by Céspedes headed to the important city of Bayamo, which they seized after three days of fierce combat. It was there, amid popular enthusiasm, where Bayamo's poet, musician and patriot, Pedro Figueredo, while riding on his horse wrote the lyrics of what would later become Cuba's national anthem.

The first government of the Republic in Arms was established in Bayamo. It was headed by Céspedes. It immediately took to the task of reorganizing public administration according to the needs of the free territory. Military and civilian powers were separated, and the first town council was elected which, alongside white Creoles, included two Spanish and two Black aldermen. The government decreed the liberty of slaves who joined the independence war and of those whose masters were willing to set them free with compensation.

The first independent newspaper ever to be published in Cuba, "*El Cubano Libre*", saw the light.

The city of Bayamo remained under the control of independence forces for three months. On January 12, 1869, faced with the impossibility of controlling it any longer, a huge popular assembly agreed that before relinquishing it to Spanish troops, the city would be torched so that the colonial troops would only find burning ruins. Tents were their only shelter in the destroyed city.

Bayamo in flames

Camagüey and Las Villas. Ignacio Agramonte.- While the war began to extend in Oriente, patriots in other provinces were preparing to join the independence forces. On November 4, 1868, Camagüey rose up in arms, and in early February, 1869, Las Villas followed.

If we were to illustrate the revolutionaries of Camagüey in two of its men, we would choose Ignacio Agramonte y Loináz and Salvador Cisneros Betancourt, the Marquis of Santa Lucía.The latter enjoyed one of the highest economic and social

45

positions. He also freed his slaves and took to the bushes. He would fight in all of Cuba's independence wars.

Ignacio Agramonte was a young man born to a wealthy family. He was one of the pupils of José de la Luz y Caballero, lawyer and patriot heavily influenced by the French Revolution. Agramonte was the soul of the revolution in the province. His boldness was proverbial. On one occasion, one of the fighters, brigadier Julio Sanguily, was captured by the Spaniards. Without thinking twice he picked 34 members of his cavalry and ordered a machete charge against an enemy column of 120 men, rescuing the *mambí* officer. Due to his courage, gentlemanship, and gallantry, he is known as the Daredevil of the Cuban Revolution.

The West. José Martí.- The three westerly provinces (Pinar del Río, Havana and Matanzas) did not support the uprising, because their big plantation owners—as opposed to their counterparts in the Eastern provinces—were of conservative traditions and enjoyed a favorable economic situation. They remained by the side of the Spanish government.

They did not want to risk their wealth and they feared the attitude their slaves would assume once the war reached them.

However, many western patriots organized clandestinely and supported the insurrection movement. Some of them took to the bushes, others were involved in unsuccessful uprisings, above all in Pinar del Río, in places like Vuelta Abajo. José Morales Lemus headed the revolutionary forces in Havana. He had already participated in numerous conspiracies.

Since the early stages of the conflict, a 15 year old young man named José Martí Pérez stood out in Havana. Born to Spanish parents in 1853, since childhood he had manifested his rebelliousness against injustice, oppression and despotism. While a student, he published revolutionary journals and contributed in others; he wrote and published fiery patriotic poems and expressed solidarity with those who were fighting in the countryside. At the age of 16 he was detained and condemned to 16 years of hard labor. He was later deported to Spain. From there he restlessly expressed his support for the independence of Cuba, engaged in debate with reactionaries and monarchists, and wrote in 1873 his essay "Political Imprisonment in Cuba", a harsh denunciation against the crimes committed by the Spanish government. For his unyielding commitment to the liberation of Cuba, to which he gave his life, he is known as the island's National Hero and the Apostle of the Independence of Cuba.

Internationalism. Máximo Gómez.- As can be observed, the first national liberation war was headed by the most radical sector of Cuban plantation owners and wealthy intellectuals and professionals.

It also enjoyed the decisive support of freed black salves and mulattos, *campesinos*, artisans and other exploited sectors of the population. Abroad, the Cuban revolutionary emigration, made up of Cubans of all classes and social origins, organized in various independent revolutionary clubs, playing a decisive role in the support of the war.

Since its beginning, the revolution counted on the disinterested support and the military expertise of men born in other countries who made theirs the Cuban independence cause. Examples of this are Modesto Díaz, Luis Marcano and Máximo Gómez Báez, former officers of the Spanish Army in Santo Domingo.

Máximo Gómez arrived in Cuba in 1865, and contacted conspirators in Bayamo. He joined independence forces as soon as the war broke out and soon achieved fame during military operations due to his courage, intelligence and capacity to organize and command. He introduced the famous machete charges that became the terror of the Spanish columns. Under his leadership, many Cuban combatants were trained. During the 1895 war, he would rise to the rank of General in Chief of the Cuban Liberation Army. Alongside José Martí and Antonio Maceo, he was one of the war's most important leaders.

The Assembly of Guáimaro.- In April, 1869, with the purpose of providing the revolution with greater organizational and juridical unity, an important assembly was held with representatives of the various territories that had joined the uprising. The gathering took place in the town of Guáimaro, in the province of Camagüey.

Several opinions on how to conduct the Revolution collided in the meeting. Céspedes was supportive of a centralized leadership that would be in charge of both

Machete charge

military and civilian affairs. Agramonte was the major spokesperson for another trend, which called for the establishment of a civilian government, separated from a military leadership that was to be subordinated to the civilian authorities.

The overwhelming majority of delegates supported Agramonte's thesis, and the consensus was registered in a charter known as Guáimaro's Constitution. This constitution established that the House of Representatives was the state's supreme power: it would be in charge of appointing the President of the Republic and the Chief of the Army, and it could freely remove them form their posts. It would also make decisions on how to organize the army and had the power to amend the constitution. In fact, the House would be in charge of resolving even the most trivial administrative problems. Among other provisions, this law established civil liberties and abolished slavery, stipulating that "All of the Republic's inhabitants are completely free".

Once the Constitution was passed, the Assembly became the House of Representatives and appointed Carlos Manuel de Céspedes as the President of the Republic. Manuel de Quesada y Loynaz, who had earned the rank of General in Mexico fighting the French invasion forces, was appointed Army Chief.

Spain's Policy: Extermination. The Execution of the Eight Medicine Students.- In the early months of 1869, the colonial government tried to reach an agreement with the insurrection forces, but it soon abandoned the idea. Recalcitrant Spaniards in the colonial government vehemently opposed any agreement. A war of extermination was unleashed against the *mambises* and all sympathizers of the independence cause.

Besides its own Army, Spain relied upon the so-called Voluntary Corps, which had been created a few years before to face the announced invasion by Narciso López. The corps was disbanded after López's defeat, but the so-called *integristas* brought it back to life. In a few months it had a force of 30,000 troops in the capital and thousands of others in all towns of the country.

Fortune seekers made up the bulk of the Voluntary Corps. They were generally illiterate and lead by wealthy Spaniards, who counted on the support and financing of the Spanish government for the training of this paramilitary institution that would soon be notorious for its barbaric and bloody acts. The power enjoyed by the Voluntary Corps was so huge, that at times not even the Island's Captain General dared to defy its designs.

As absolute masters of the streets, one night the volunteers opened fire on the centric Louvre Café, a point of gathering for youths supporting the independence cause, assaulted the Villanueva Theater while a comic play was underway, and attacked the palace of Miguel Aldana, one of the richest plantation owners of the country known for his separatist ideals. These actions left several people dead and wounded.

But one of the most despicable crimes was the execution of eight students of the first year of Medicine at the University of Havana in 1871. One day a professor did not attend classes. A group of students spent the idle time playing with a cart used for taking corpses to an adjacent cemetery. One of them took one flower from a wreath.

Colonial forces falsely accused the students of desecrating the tomb stone of Spanish journalist Gonzalo Castañón, enemy of the independence cause, who had died in a duel with a Cuban. A war council sentenced some of the students to prison terms to appease the volunteers. But they were incensed by the sentence and demanded another trial, which didn't satisfy them either. The war council met for the third time, and acquiescing to the volunteers' thirst of Cuban blood, eight of the accused young men were sentenced to death, while others received prison terms of 30 years. A raffle

48

to pick the eight was conducted among 45 students, and for greater mockery, among the eight chosen to be executed, one of them had not even been in Havana on the day of the events. The pleas pointing to a lack of evidence were futile, as was the impeccable defense by Spanish Captain Federico Capdevilla, attorney for the students. The eight students were executed on November 27, 1871. Years later, Castañón's son admitted that his father's tomb had been intact, that it was never desecrated, and officially recognized the innocence of the medicine students. The crime demonstrated to the entire world the barbaric character of Spanish rule and deepened the gap that existed between the colony and the Metropolis.

Faced with the momentum of the insurrection, the colonial government enacted several laws seeking to sow terror island wide: all arrested insurgency leaders and all individuals caught collaborating with them would be executed on the spot, without any type of judicial proceeding. Ships sailing through Spanish waters or in free waters near Cuba carrying en, weapons and ammunition would be seized and all individuals on board would be immediately executed. Males of 15 years of age or older caught outside of their plantations or places of residence, and unable to justify this "abnormality", would be summarily executed. All towns were ordered to raise a white flag. Those that did not comply with the order, would be burnt to the ground. Any woman caught away from her farm or place of residence would be concentrated in cities. These laws were obeyed to the letter, and they led to innumerable crimes. Even rebel Cubans who surrendered to the Spanish troops, believing in the promise that the life of those who abandoned the war would be spared, were also executed. Terror forced many families out of the country. It is estimated that during the first year of the war, 100,000 people left Cuba.

Glory and Doom. The Defeat.- The war of extermination declared by the colonial government had a severe impact on the liberation forces. Notwithstanding the situation, the war spanned for a decade, during which years of great revolutionary spirit alternated with critical situations. Nevertheless, it was demonstrated that achieving Cuba's independence through armed struggle was viable. Under permanent conditions of inferiority in terms of weapons and people, the Cuban troops accomplished great heroic deeds. They conducted numerous successful campaigns, they frightened the enemy with their famous machete charges, they fooled the enemy and bypassed well-defended and fortified military roads and took the invasion to the West, reaching the province of Las Villas, in the central part of the country. They also waged important strategic combats, among them the battles of La Sacra, Palo Seco, El Naranjo and Las Guásimas, in which the ratio between the contending forces was of one Cuban per five Spaniards. Even so, the Cubans overwhelmed the colonial troops.

But in the long run, Spain would win the war. The failure, however, was not due to the overwhelming superiority of Spanish troops and resources, which found compensation in the fighting spirit and revolutionary moral of the Cuban troops, as well as in their knowledge of the theater of operations and other advantages attained by fighting in their own terrain. The fundamental factors that led to the defeat of the war were mistaken conceptions, regionalism, racial prejudices and other contradictions and evils that could not be overcome during the war. All of them affected Cubans both on the island and abroad. As Martí very accurately asserted in following years, "by taking advantage of the internal conflicts, Spain was able to win a war that it couldn't win with its weapons".

From the very onset of the war there were deep divisions with respect to the organization of the liberation struggle. They became even more pronounced after the Assembly of Guáimaro, and they reached a climax when the House of Representatives dismissed President Céspedes and Army Chief, Manuel de Quesada. Céspedes retired to his farm in San Lorenzo, in the Sierra Maestra mountains, and devoted his time to teaching campesino children. There he was surprised by the Spaniards and died fighting in February, 1874. Some months before, in May, 1873, Major General Ignacio Agramonte had died in combat, so the revolution lost two of its most prominent figures during the early years of the war.

Regionalist sentiments, together with fears that the slaves in Matanzas would join the Liberation Army and break the weak existing balance between whites and blacks to the benefit of the latter, prevented Cuban independence troops from going further in the invasion of the three westernmost provinces. This amounted to a significant setback for the Revolution's strategic plans.

Likewise, regionalism led to irreparable differences between Liberation Army leaders, to military insubordination, the collapse of the struggle in Las Villas, a general leadership crisis and the progressive weakening of the insurrection forces.

The crisis was coupled by another very important factor. The government of Spain, aware of the crisis, acted wisely and changed its policy towards the *mambises*. Instead of the extermination war, it launched a campaign aimed at demoralizing Cubans, offering to forget the past, to forgive political crimes, to release prisoners, pardon Spanish defectors, and facilitate exile from Cuba for anyone who so wished. Cuba would be ruled by the same special laws that ruled Puerto Rico and slaves that fought in the Cuban independence army would be recognized as free individuals, among other attractive promises.

In the meantime, in an effort to force the acceptance of those conditions, the Spanish Army was reinforced with fresh troops until it surpassed 250,000 men, and the budget for military spending was considerably increased.

The person in charge of applying this new policy was General Arsenio Martínez Campos, who had previously fought in Cuba. He was considered a skillful politician and enjoyed the trust of the Spanish government.

It took Martínez Campos almost two years to bring an end to the war. The Government of the Republic in Arms finally disbanded and a Negotiating Committee signed peace with the Spaniards on February 10, 1878, by means of the so-called Pact of Zanjón. The document covered most of the promises made by the Metropolis.

A few weeks later, only a few troops in Oriente led by Generals Vicente García and Antonio Maceo did not acknowledge the capitulation. General Ramón Leocadio Bonachea, in Las Villas, was the last known military chief to surrender.

During the last three years of the Ten Year War a change in course was noticeable. While the influence of the great plantation owners subsided, the role of some leaders of humble sectors of the population strengthened, as was the case of General Antonio Maceo y Grajales. On the same days that the Pact of Zanjón was being signed, Maceo

was achieving in Oriente one of his most brilliant military victories: the destruction of the famous San Quintín Battalion, in the San Ulpiano Hills.

The Protest of Baraguá. Antonio Maceo .- Maceo was a mulatto farmer from Santiago de Cuba. He had joined the Liberation Army as a soldier on October 12, 1868, two days after the beginning of the war. Due to his heroism, courage and natural talent, he quickly attained ranks and merits. When the Ten Year War was over, he had achieved the rank of Major General. Because of his size, skin color, and courage he was known and the Bronze Titan. The Maceo brothers and sisters were nineteen. All of them fought in the war, and 15 of them died in it. Antonio's father also died in combat; his mother, Mariana Grajales, took to the bushes and died in exile after the war: she is today considered the prototype of the Cuban revolutionary woman.

On March 15, 1878, in his campsite of Mangos de Baraguá, in Oriente province, Maceo held talks with General Martínez Campos to become acquainted with the offer. Maceo flatly rejected peace without independence and without the abolition of slavery, which is why he decided to carry forward the struggle.

This historic event is known as the Protest of Baraguá, and during more than a hundred years of struggles of the Cuban people it has been a symbol of revolutionary intransigence.

Those gathered in Baraguá agreed to approve a brief Constitution, which established a provisional government made up of a President, a Vice President and one General-in-Chief. Major General Antonio Maceo was entrusted with the command of the Army in Oriente. However, the disillusion prevalent among the troops was irreversible at the time. Cuban troops were inactive and the Spaniards avoided possible encounters. To go on with the fight would have amounted to a useless holocaust.

Under those circumstances, the provisional government convinced Maceo of the futility of carrying on the struggle and of the suitability of sending him out of the country to prepare conditions for the continuation of the war. In this way the 10 Year War concluded. It was May, 1878.

Meaning of the war.- Despite the setback suffered by Cubans, this war had a vital importance for the independence movement. Firstly, it was the melting pot that forged a Cuban nationality. The slavery regime—huge obstacle to the success of the war—could not survive after the armed conflict. The abolishment of slavery within the ranks of the insurrectionaries who had joined the liberation war resulted in the fusion of two of the main elements of Cuban nationality: black and white Creoles.

The war also helped to definitively integrate within the Cuban nation an increasing number of Spaniards who had established roots on the island and whose interests coincided with those of the native population. In making theirs the independence cause, these Spaniards by birth showed they were Cubans due to their interests, aspirations and sentiments. Something similar occurred with the mass of Chinese that were forcibly brought to the island, as well as other minorities opposed to a system that enslaved them. They were already building Cuban families whose offspring would fully integrate into the new nationality.

Hence, when the Spanish colonial government sat at the bargaining table in El Zanjón or Baraguá, it was forced to admit that it was not dealing with a group of "social outcasts", as they hatefully called them, but with the representatives of the Cuban nation.

VII
The rewarding truce

The defeat suffered by the Cubans with the signing of peace without independence in 1878 led to an upsurge of Reformist ideas and an ebb of the revolutionary movement. But ever since, Spain was obliged to grant Cubans certain liberties and political rights and to gradually abolish slavery. In the meantime the experiences drawn from the conflict would be of utmost important for the creation of the indispensable conditions for the resumption of the armed struggle with more hope of success. This stage, leading up to the resumption of a war that lasted 17 years, is known in Cuban history as "The Rewarding Truce".

As a rule, the defeats of revolutionary movements lead to the demoralization of its forces and a retreat of the movement itself. This is what happened in Cuba in 1868. The Pact of Zanjón was a severe blow to independence forces, and it took them several years to recover.

Naturally, however, the war left behind innumerable experiences for struggles to come. It is also true that many patriots maintained their revolutionary spirit and attempted to resume the armed struggle, devising new plans and organizing more uprisings. But all these efforts were unsuccessful, though they did provide for the continuity of the revolution, and the prelude of victorious actions that were yet to come.

Meanwhile, Cubans opposed to independence reaffirmed their stance after the war's failure. Others, who had even fought against Spain, lost faith in getting rid of the colonial yoke and devoted themselves to improve Cuba's situation and to demand from Spain the fulfillment of the accords provided by the Zanjón Pact. Some of them worked for the Spanish government.

Pro-Autonomy ideas and Integrationism.- In that same year, 1878, and taking advantage of the few liberties granted by the Zanjón Pact, the former reform advocates, now working in cooperation with some important personalities of the recently concluded war, founded the Liberal Party, which was later called Liberal Autonomist Party. Well known intellectuals of the Cuban bourgeoisie (lawyers, journalists, historians, economists, orators) like José María Gálvez, Eliseo Giberga, José Antonio Cortina and Rafael Montoro made up its leadership.

Some of the main items of their platform were: make Spain grant Cuba the same rights enjoyed by Spaniards at home, that the Island be ruled by the same laws and codes used there, the separation of the civilian power from the military, the abolition of slavery through compensation for slave owners, the encouragement of white immigration exclusively, and the achievement of reforms on tariffs and taxes to benefit Cuban producers. Four years later, in 1882, the Liberal Party would demand "the immediate and absolute freedom" of slaves.

Also in 1878 the Constitutional Union Party was organized by reactionary and conservative Spaniards, rabid enemies not only of Cuba's independence but also of any autonomous status or any reform that would weaken colonial rule. Its stated

53

goal was to defend Spain's integrity and its colonies, hence their name "*integristas*", or integration advocates.

In the struggles unleashed between the two organizations, for a while the Autonomist Party unconsciously played a positive role by fighting the most recalcitrant enemies of independence. Its forums and journals were used by some patriots to denounce the unfair and arbitrary economic and political regime imposed on Cuba by the Metropolis. Later, when the independence forces were involved in the preparatory details of the new war, and during the war itself, autonomy advocates in fact became instruments of the colonial government, as they flatly rejected independence.

The Small War and other insurrection efforts.- The failure of the 1868 War and Maceo's efforts to continue the fight after the Zanjón Pact did not discourage the most consequential and committed leaders of the independence war. Before the end of 1878, inside the country and abroad preparations were undertaken for a new uprising. Its main leaders were Calixto García, who had the supreme command, and Antonio Maceo, who would be in charge of Oriente province. Other important figures included Flor Crombet, Pedro Martínez Freyre, José María Rodríguez (Mayía), Belisario Grave de Peralta, Guillermo Moncada, José Maceo, Quintín Banderas, Serafín Sánchez, Francisco Carrillo, and Emilio Núñez.

During these preparations, 25 year old José Martí began to excel as a leader and organizer. He was appointed deputy-delegate of Havana's Revolutionary Committee. Arrested, he was deported to Spain. From there he traveled to New York, where he presided over the Revolutionary Committee created there by Cuban patriots.

In August of 1879, the first uprisings took place in Gibara, Holguín, and Santiago de Cuba, with the rebels taking to the mountains in Eastern Cuba and operating from there. There were also uprisings in Sancti Spiritus, Remedios, Sagua la Grande, and other places in central Cuba.

The rebels relied on the weapons and other supplies that were to be shipped from abroad, principally from two large expeditions arranged by Calixto García and Antonio Maceo. But after 9 months of struggle only one small expedition was able to reach the island. It was impossible for Maceo to arrive due to information provided by a traitor, which led to the seizing of weapons and money collected, and because of the relentless persecution of the Spanish Navy against the Cuban independence leader. Calixto García did manage to disembark in Cuban territory, but by then it was too late.

The absence of the most important leaders, the shortage of weapons and ammunition, coupled with the skillful propaganda spread by the Spanish government with the support of the reform advocates, weakened the Cuban independence forces. Taking advantage of the prevailing racial prejudices and of the fact that the main independence leaders were black and from the eastern part of the country, the Spaniards spread the rumor that the patriots were interested in founding a Black Republic in Oriente. On the other hand, the autonomy advocates sent messengers to the patriots seeking to convince them that the movement was untimely. When Calixto García arrived, many of the rebels were already considering capitulation.

General Calixto García wandered through the countryside for over three months without finding any armed groups, finally giving up. The last chief to lay down his weapons was General Emilio Núñez, in the province of Las Villas, in December, 1880.

54

Although known as "The Small War", the movement was not as small as one would think. To illustrate its magnitude, more than 2,000 armed and 4,000 unarmed men surrendered to the Spanish.

Other insurrection efforts ensued in the following years, all of which failed. The expeditions of Ramón Leocadio Bonachea (December 1884), Carlos Agüero (April 1885) and Limbano Sánchez (May 1885) failed, and the expeditionary force were executed.

Beginning in 1884 a new effort gained in momentum: the so called Gómez-Maceo Plan. At the beginning it had the support of José Martí. But he withdrew his backing the same year arguing that it was organized authoritatively, without paying attention to democratic principles. The plan failed in 1886, without having led to an insurrection. In April of 1893, the unsuccessful uprising of the brothers Manuel and Ricardo Sartorious took place, in Purnio, Velasco and Holguín, in eastern Cuba.

Social changes. The abolition of slavery.- The principal achievement of Cuban independence forces during the Ten Year War was the abolition of slavery. As early as 1870, with the intention of weakening the abolitionist movement, Spain passed the so called "Free Womb Act", that granted liberty to every child born to slave parents in Cuba as of September, 1868, to those slaves who had aided the Spanish troops, and to those who were 60 years old or near that age. In 1878, as a result of the Zanjón Pact, Spain agreed to acknowledge the freedom of all black slaves and of Asian contracted workers who had fought with the Cuban *mambí* troops. With the current state of affairs, it would have been a contradiction to keep from freedom slaves who had served Spain. So, in February 1880, the "Patronage Law" was enacted, putting an end to slavery in Cuba. However, emancipation remained formal, for free slaves stayed under their masters patronage for 8 more years after passage of the law.

Finally, in October, 1886, the Spanish Government scrapped the patronage law, introducing full abolition of slavery in Cuba. This is how the three and a half century slave system on the island came to its end.

The national liberation war, the abolition of slavery and the expansion of sugar production in other regions of the world brought about important changes in the structure of Cuban society. Former slaves joined the ranks of wage earners, artisans, farmers, and other free laborers. Most wealthy Cubans lost their properties, and many of them joined the urban middle class; while in the countryside, those who lost their sugar mills or land devoted themselves to harvesting sugar cane for mills they no longer owned.

Formerly, sugar plantation owners owned both the plantations and the mills. But the ruin brought by the war, Spain's confiscations, and the growing need to invest immense resources in the modernization of the mills to competitively face the challenge of other sugar-producing countries led to the concentration of capital and of sugar production. The number of sugar mills drastically dropped and efficiency increased, with ownership being transferred to companies and the most powerful plantation owners. The agricultural area and the amount of sugar growers at each sugar mill expanded. The number of *campesinos* swelled, as did that of the *colonos,* or tenant farmers, people who engaged in growing sugar cane to sell sugar mill owners.

This is a period when US capital began flowing to Cuba, mostly in the sugar, mining, and tobacco sectors. In 1895, US investments on the island reached 50 million dollars, a huge amount for the time. Politically, Cuba remained a Spanish colony, but economically , it began to be dependent on the United States.

The Labor Movement.- With the end of the 10 Year War, the labor movement reached a new stage of development, gaining in quantity and quality. Numerous associations, cooperatives and mutual assistance societies were organized in different parts of the island.

The sectors of cigar makers, typographers, tailors, masons, carpenters, bakers, coachmen, cartdrivers, and salesmen were among the most outstanding. At the time, and for many years after, the workers of the island's main industry, the sugar industry, were unable to organize themselves.

The first labor organization created then was the Cigar Makers Guild, founded in September, 1878, and led by Saturnino Martínez. The following year, the Central Board of Artisans was established, also in Havana, and other workers organizations began appearing, both in Havana and other regions (Santiago de Cuba, Puerto Príncipe, Santa Clara, Cienfuegos, Cárdenas, San Antonio de los Baños, Santiago de las Vegas, and so on).

In 1885, the Havana Workers Club was created. Its purpose was to bring together the capital's workers guilds, and to find sites and resources for the opening of schools and the holding of social, cultural and political activities.

Many of these labor organizations began to publish their periodicals, so that in a few years hundreds of them were circulating across the island. Some of the most outstanding, in chronological order, were: *Boletín Tipográfico* (Havana, 1878), *El Obrero* (Cienfuegos, 1884*), El Artesano* (Havana, 1885) *El Productor* (Havana, 1887*), La Unión* (Havana, 1888); *La Tribuna del Trabajo* (Key West, 1889); *El Acicate* (Santiago de Cuba, 1891).

Conditions in which the labor movement developed were extremely difficult, due to three main factors: a) the class-in-the making character of the proletariat, without a clear-cut consciousness of its interests and living in sub-human conditions; b) the anti-labor and anti-national character of the colonial authorities at the service of the exploiting class, c) the divisions and clashes that occurred among workers themselves.

Many of them, just released from the shackles of slavery, had not freed themselves from their slave mentalities, and others maintained a semi-artisan mentality. Labor rules were still tainted with strong semi-feudal elements, and included corporal punishment and full submission to employers. An example of this was an event that sent shock waves through public opinion: on February 7, 1881 a blaze destroyed a cigar factory in Havana, and alongside the material damages, it caused the death of two apprentices who had been tied to a rack as punishment. Unable to move, they burned to death.

On the other hand, in all labor conflicts colonial authorities always took side with the employers. Workers who revolted were persecuted, beaten, incarcerated or murdered. Nevertheless, hundreds of strikes were organized during the 80's, several of them successful.

One of the most resounding labor actions of the time was the 1888 workers strike at the "Henry Clay" Cigar Factory in Havana, first demanding better salaries, and then the reinstatement of fired colleagues, and a halt to employer's lock-outs. This

56

strike garnered the solidarity of almost all the other factories and workshops of the trade, with other sectors also supporting them. Despite repression, the drastic measures adopted by management, and the capitulating position adopted by reform advocates, the strikers' demands were met.

During the strike, the seriousness of differences among workers became evident. The Reformist leaders adopted positions that favored management while the anarchist leaders firmly stood by the workers until their victory.

Divergence of opinions during the strike resulted in the founding of two parallel labor organizations: the Workers' Alliance and the Workers' Union. The former was led by radical individuals, mainly anarchists, among them the "three Enriques", Enrique Roig San Martín, the most brilliant labor leader of the time, Enrique Crecci, and Enrique Messonier. They had a periodical called "*El Productor*", led by San Martín and considered to be the most important and combative publication defending workers interests during the last two decades of the 19th century.

The Workers Union grouped in its leadership Reformist leaders like Saturnino Martínez, members of the Autonomist Party, and even integration supporters—enemies of Cuba's independence, like Domingo Menéndez Areces. Their journal, "*La Unión*", played a dividing, anti-labor role.

The preponderance of reform advocates in the Cuban labor movement began to lose ground by 1880, with its leadership going to the hands of the anarchists. The periodical "*El Productor*" carried out a remarkable job of spreading the ideas, achievements, and positions of the international labor movement, and made an outstanding contribution to the ideological and organizational advancement recorded by the Cuban working class.

Cuba's labor movement expressed solidarity with the US workers who later were known as the Martyrs of Chicago. Thanks to the work of local unions, Cuba became the only Latin American country—with the sole exception of Argentina—that in 1880 observed May 1st as International Workers Day. It was the first time that such a celebration was being held in the world.

Workers made a decisive contribution to the independence struggle in Cuba. José Martí relied mainly on working class Cuban émigrés for the organization of the Cuban Revolutionary Party and the war itself.

In Cuba, meanwhile, anarchist leaders—opposed to any political activism—tried to convince workers that the independence struggle was only a matter of interest for the bourgeoisie, and did their very best to keep them away from the struggle. But the activism of Martí and labor leaders in exile helped unveil this false idea. Finally, in an important congress held in January, 1892, the first National Workers Congress, the conclusion was reached that there was no contradiction between the struggle for individual liberties and the struggle for the independence of the country from a foreign colonial rule. From that moment on, the island's working class movement joined ranks with the émigrés in the struggle for independence.

José Martí and "The Necessary War". The Cuban Revolutionary Party.- Ever since José Martí separated himself from the Gómez-Maceo insurrection project in 1884, he abstained from actively participating in the mobilization of Cuban patriots in exile so as not to interfere with Gómez and Maceo's plans. But once those efforts failed and Gómez announced the end of preparations for an insurrection movement in late 1886, Martí wholeheartedly threw himself into the organization of the war.

On October 10, 1887, Martí delivered a militant and enlightening speech at a gathering of Cuban émigrés at New York's Masonic Temple. This event represents the beginning of Martí's commitment to bring émigrés together, organized them, and prepare the indispensable conditions for the final struggle to attain Cuba's independence. He visited veterans from the 1868 war and wrote to others outline his ideas regarding the war.

The following month, the Executive Commission in charge of initial preparations for the war was set up, with Martí as chairman. The foundations for the future revolutionary organization were laid.

A major task was convincing Cuban patriots of the urgent need of unity among all sectors, unity in organizing and unity in action. This was extremely difficult due to the intrigue and divisionist campaigns launched by the Spanish government, and the misleading actions of autonomy advocates, which together sparked numerous prejudices, confusion, contradictions and other internal ills that affected the patriotic forces. Many patriots lost their faith after the defeat of 1878, and others were desperate to start the war again even without any foreseeable possibility of success. It was also necessary to prevent new outbreaks of regionalism and indiscipline, evils that led to the failure of the previous war. Prejudice against blacks was still strong, even among some *mambí* leaders, while many former slaves still bore natural resentments against their old masters. Jealousy grew among veterans of the 1868 war and the new cadres getting involved in the struggle. There were remnants of old feuds between exiled patriotic groups, and differences between them and patriotic groups on the island.

Contradictions between workers and their employers heightened, and there was an upsurge in strikes and other forms of class struggle. Some sectors were afraid that, like in other countries, the end of the colonial period would give way to an authoritarian state, ruled by anti-democratic forces or undermined by anarchy.

Faced with these problems, Martí conducted a patient and relentless political activism aimed at recovering trust in the Revolution, at demonstrating the inevitability of the war and the need for its efficient preparation. He worked on the elimination of racial prejudices against blacks, defending the most advanced concepts with regard to equality among human beings. He explained that the war was not against good, honest and hard-working Spaniards but against colonialist Spaniards. He tried to mediate in differences between émigré patriots; demonstrated the common interests between émigrés and Cubans on the island; convinced everyone of the need for strong unity between old and new independence fighters; and called upon seasoned chiefs of the 1868 war to occupy decisive military responsibilities.

Speaking as a representative of an entire nation, and not of a portion of it, Martí managed to subordinate class feuds to the supreme goal of attaining independence. He warned about the danger stemming from the creation of class or race-centered movements and managed to gather behind the cause of national emancipation the masses of city and rural workers, the patriotic intellectuals, a significant sector of the small and medium bourgeoisie, and former wealthy Cubans, ruined by the previous war. It was at this time that he launched his slogan: "With all and for the good of all".

This unifying drive did not keep Martí from expressing his identification with the poor, with the oppressed, particularly workers, and from expressing his total confidence in them. One of Martí's essential contributions was his advanced social thinking. According to him, the two roots that were to feed the republic were: the labor of men and women and homegrown ideas. No one, he stressed, should exploit someone else's work. He aspired to founding a workers republic. Martí saw in the working classes, both manual and intellectual workers, the guarantee that the emancipating revolution would take roots.

The anti-imperialist, Latin America-oriented and internationalist activities carried out by Martí were of tremendous importance for his time and for posterity. He called US Imperialism by its name; denounced the role of monopolies and US finance capital; put Latin American peoples on alert regarding the US's voracious expansionism. He firmly rejected the possibility of a US intervention in the Cuban war, and stressed that the importance of the independence of Cuba and Puerto Rico consisted in not only building two free and prosperous republics but also in the decisive role that they were to play in saving all of Latin America from the US threat and striking world balance.

In essence, Martí expressed with clarity the Latin American and universal character of the revolution that was in the making.

He called attention to the existence of two Americas, very different in origin, history, interests and purposes: on one hand, Anglo-Saxon America, and on the other, the America stretching from the Río Grande to the Tierra del Fuego, the one he called "Our America". Our America, he said, is made up of peoples with the same origin, same language, who suffered from the same kind of foreign domination for centuries, which has fought common enemies and faced common threats; an America made up of peoples who are to survive together or perish together, because spiritually, they constitute one single nation.

This unifying and democratic will, spirit of freedom, love for work and social justice, the revolutionary, patriotic, anti-imperialist, Latin Americanist and universal sentiments present in José Martí's ideals and works, were conveyed by this remarkable leader to all Cuban émigré clubs and also transmitted to Cubans on the island.

In December of 1891, Martí addressed the large community of Cuban émigrés based in Tampa and Key West, many of whom were cigar workers. It was here that Martí drafted the Secret Platform and Regulations of a new independence organization, the Cuban Revolutionary Party. These documents were acclaimed by the patriotic clubs created in other US cities, and in other nations of the Antilles, in Mexico and in Central and South America. Together with the Party, the periodical *Patria*, or Motherland, was created in March, 1892. It would play a remarkable role in the task of uniting, organizing and guiding the patriotic forces.

On April 8, assemblies were held to elect the leaders of the organization, and two days later, on April 10, the party of all revolutionary Cubans was officially proclaimed. Martí would be elected Delegate, the Party's highest position, along with a Treasurer.

The Cuban Revolutionary Party was based on two essential principles: strict democracy and tight discipline. Since its founding, it proclaimed its primary goals: to achieve Cuba's full independence and lay the foundations for a democratic republic, as well as to promote and assist in the independence of Puerto Rico. In the Cuban Revolutionary Party there were no national barriers, it was open to "all good men from all countries" who shared similar independence ideals. This is why in various branches of the Cuban Revolutionary Party, as well as in the staff of *Patria*, and in all independence efforts, side by side with Cuban patriots, Puerto Rican and Dominican patriots would occupy leadership roles. Cuban revolutionary clubs would count among their members the sons and daughters of many countries, among them Jamaica, Haiti, Italy, and even Spaniards and North Americans. The revolutionary clubs became a creative solution for the organizing of a political party that was very similar in structure to the one that would appear later on in Russia, guided by the principles Lenin outlined for that nation's Social Democratic Party.

With such a party, the successful preparation of "the necessary war" was guaranteed. To attain this goal Martí devoted all his energies beginning in 1892. Under his instructions and his constant visits, the clubs elected those who became the war's military leaders; raised funds; purchased weapons and ammunitions; and rented ships. The Party would also send envoys to Cuba to prepare conditions, and frequent meetings would be held among revolutionary leaders, both in the US and in the Dominican Republic, as well as in other countries. Latin American governments with clear anti-colonialist positions were contacted for help, and the requests were heeded.

By late 1894, the basic conditions for the launching of the war were ready. On December 8, the Uprising Plan was outlined, and on the 25th Martí ordered the departure for Cuba of three ships loaded with fighters and weapons: the "Lagonda", the "Almadis" and the "Baracoa". They left from Fernandina port, near Florida. But US authorities, despite their expressions of solidarity with the Cuban cause, were in fact assisting the Spanish government. They seized two of the ships and a good deal of the weapons in early January 1895, an action that dealt a severe blow to patriotic efforts.

Despite the setback, plans went full steam ahead and Cuban patriots on the island were authorized to launch the war without waiting for the supporting expeditions. On January 29th, the order for the uprising was signed. The outbreak of the independence war was inevitable.

VIII
The 1895 War

February 24th.- Just as it was agreed, the cry of independence was heard in several places of Cuba on February 24th, 1895. In Oriente province the most important uprisings occurred in Santiago de Cuba, Guantánamo, Jiguaní, San Luis, El Cobre, El Caney, Alto Songo, Bayate and Baire. The latter, a part of the municipality of Jiguaní, symbolized the beginning of the new war, since the rebellion is better known in history, not without criticisms, as the **Cry of Baire.**

In the western and central part of the island there were several uprisings: in Ibarra and Jagüey Grande (Matanzas province) and in Aguada de Pasajeros (Las Villas province). But none were successful, due mainly to the lack of coordination. The main leaders were captured, some were deported and others were executed. In the province of Havana, the movement's leaders were detained before the rebellion. Fellow countrymen in Pinar del Río were ordered to wait until the war started in the rest of the country. A week after the cry was given, some 2500 men had taken up arms.

The three political parties legally organized in the country (the Autonomist, the Unionist and the Reformist) condemned the rebel movement. The Autonomist Party leadership tried to persuade the *mambí* leaders to lay down their weapons. Both the Autonomy advocates and the Spaniards began a vigorous campaign, using promises and intrigue as during the previous war. But they failed.

On March 25th, a very important document was made public, the **Montecristi Manifesto,** signed in Santo Domingo by José Martí as Delegate of the Cuban Revolutionary Party and Máximo Gómez, as General in Chief of the Liberation Army. Besides laying out the objectives of the insurrection, the Manifesto was aimed at destroying the cunning campaigns of the Spanish government and its followers, strengthening the unity of all Cubans and encouraging confidence in the Revolution, ensuring Spaniards who resided in Cuba that they should not fear for their lives or be concerned about their properties as long as they respected the liberation cause.

But the strongest boost to the rebellion occurred with the arrival in Cuba of the main *mambí* leaders in two expeditions: Major General Antonio Maceo and 22 expedition members landed near Baracoa on the northern coast on April 1st; and on April 11th, José Martí, Máximo Gómez and four other expeditionary members arrived in Playitas, also in the eastern part of the island but on the southern coast. The news that the war's three main leaders were already in the Cuban countryside sparked a general uprising in Oriente, led by Antonio Maceo, which had very favorable repercussions in the rest of the country.

The meeting of La Mejorana. José Martí's death in combat.- The independence fighters needed to design the strategy of the Revolution. With that aim, the three main *mambí* leaders (Martí, Maceo and Gómez) met on May 5th at La Mejorana sugar mill, in San Luis municipality. At the meeting, they dealt with several issues related to the missions each of them had to fulfill and to the idea of

The invasion to the west

launching an invasion in the west; but, as during the provisos war, the most controversial issue was the organization of the civilian government and the military command and the relationship between them.

Maceo remembered the destructive consequences of the military command's absolute obedience from the House of Representatives in 1868 and rejected the need for a civilian government during the war. Martí, supported this time by Gómez, understood that a civilian government was necessary; but at the same time, and to avoid the problems of the previous war, he came out for greater autonomy for the military command concerning war operations. In order to give legal form to these issues, Martí stated the need to call for an assembly of representatives of the Cuban people in arms. Even though he maintained his views, Maceo obeyed Martí's and Gómez's decision and prepared to continue his military operations in Oriente. The Delegate and the General prepared to head towards Camagüey to organize the uprising there and to put together a constituent assembly.

But the cause of independence received an unexpected blow, which, in the long run, would have an unfortunate influence in the course of the Revolution. On May 19th, Spanish troops found the camp of Gómez and Martí at Dos Rios, in Oriente province, where the Cuban Hero lost his life in combat. His death deeply shook the independence fighters and particularly the revolutionary immigrants whom he had united and organized. That loss would dramatically weaken the Cuban Revolutionary Party from a political, ideological and organizational point of view and would help thwart the patriotic, democratic and socially advanced objectives of the Revolution.

Insurrection boom.- After the meeting at La Mejorana, Maceo took the war to all parts of Oriente. He threatened the main cities, used the railways, taxed the big landowners and waged strategically important and successful battles like those of Jobito, Peralejo and Sao del Indio. In addition, this military offensive helped train the *mambí* troops, most of whom were self-trained in military operations, and carried the rebellion to other provinces.

Camagüey, which was waiting for Gómez's arrival, took up arms during the first days of June. Gómez carried out a series of tactical, military operations which were known as "the circular campaign", consisting of surprise attacks around Puerto Principe, the provincial capital, harassing the enemy, seizing weapons and ammunition and training the young troops. Before the end of June, all of Camagüey was at war. Then Gómez ordered Maceo to prepare a contingent of troops from Oriente and they headed to Camagüey together in order to jointly carry out the invasion to the west. By late July, the rebellion gained momentum in Las Villas, where small and limited uprisings had taken place in several areas since April. It was precisely in that province, south of Sancti Spiritus, that 1868 war veterans—Polish internationalist, General Carlos Roloff and Serafín Sánchez, landed with other high-ranking military officers. it was an important support in weapons, men and military experience. The expeditions were an essential contribution of the revolutionary émigrés during the war.

A newspaper of the patriotic forces, named after the one edited by Céspedes in 1868, **El Cubano Libre** (The Free Cuban), was published in early August.

The Jimaguayú Assembly.- In the middle of September 1895, the representatives of the five Liberation Army corps met in Jimaguayú, Camagüey province. The Assembly approved the Jimaguayú Constitution, which established a centralized government that grouped the executive and legislative powers in one entity called Government Council.

This Council was made up of a President and a Vice President. Two 1868 war veterans—Salvador Cisneros and Bartolomé Masó, respectively—were elected to the two posts. The Liberation Army's Supreme Authority would be exerted by a General in Chief, while the second in command would be a Lieutenant General. Máximo Gómez and Antonio Maceo, respectively, were named for those posts. Tomás Estrada Palma, who had replaced Martí as Delegate of the Cuban Revolutionary Party, was named representative abroad.

In an attempt to avoid the mistakes committed during the previous war regarding the relationship between the government and the military command, the Constitution limited the functions of both: the Government Council would deal with issuing the regulations on civilian and political life, passing the military law which would be proposed by the General in Chief and granting military ranks from Colonel up. The General in Chief would assume the leadership of military operations, and the Government Council could only get involved in this area when it was "absolutely necessary for important political purposes". But this involvement depended on the President and the Vice President. Civilian interference into purely military affairs occurred later, causing serious conflicts between the civilian government and the army's high command.

Following the Jimaguayú Assembly, the establishment of an orderly civilian life in free territory and the organization of the Liberation Army, the greatest commitment of the *mambí* leaders was to take the war to the western provinces.

The invasion to the west.- The invasion to the west, a dream that the Ten Year War combatants were unable to turn into reality, was of utmost important for the independence cause—militarily, economically and politically. For this reason, as soon as the struggle was consolidated in the three eastern provinces, Maceo set up a contingent with part of his troops to go to Camagüey, join Gómez in Las Villas and head west.

After gathering a little more than 1400 troops in Baraguá where the historic Protest had taken place in 1878, Maceo began the march on October 22nd, 1895. After tricking the Spanish command in Holguín, which launched all its forces to prevent Maceo's advance, the invasion contingent entered the province of Camagüey, crossed the well-defended military road from Júcaro to Moron without a single casualty and joined Máximo Gómez's troops, just as planned, in Las Villas. The "Generalisimo" designated Maceo as head of the invasion contingent. Taking an inventory of weapons and ammunition on December 15th, Maceo realized that they only had an average of two bullets per soldier: they had to take weapons and ammunition away from the enemy.

64

They had the chance in Las Villas, where 3600 men were already facing 8000 Spanish troops. There they fought several battles, including one on December 15th, 1895 in the pasture grounds of El Naranjo. That battle was to be the most successful for the Cuban troops during the entire invasion. As few as 400 troops inflicted more than 200 casualties upon the enemy. They captured a large cache of weapons and ammunition, at the cost of 4 Cubans dead and another 40 wounded.

Marching for 16 hours, the liberation forces arrived in Matanzas province, well-defended by 30 000 Spanish soldiers led by an experienced general, Arsenio Martínez Campos. In the central part of the province, Gómez and Maceo utilized a tactical maneuver, turning back toward the province of Las Villas, as if they were going east. When Campos thought they were far away, they turned back westward and approached the province of La Habana. This operation is popularly known as "the knot of the invasion" and was an excellent maneuver that enabled them to deceive the powerful Spanish forces and continue moving west.

Already in Havana with reinforcement, the *mambí* troops advanced, took eight important towns and threatened the capital. Maceo and Gómez split their forces at this point; Gómez stayed in Havana with 2500 men, while the Titan moved toward Pinar del Río with 1500.

In order to facilitate Maceo's actions in Pinar del Río, Gómez distracted the attention of the Spanish troops in Havana through the tactics of "*la lanzadera*", or the shuttle tactics, characterized by a constant going and coming which confused the enemy troops deployed against him.

Maceo went through the province of Pinar del Río, took over numerous towns, went around others and victoriously arrived on the island's western tip, in the city of Mantua, where he raised the flag of the Cuban flag on January 22nd, 1896, exactly three months after the invasion began in Baraguá. The Liberation Army and its two main leaders had carried out an extraordinary feat which, according to a foreign expert, was "the most audacious military event of the century".

In fact, in 92 days the independence fighters walked more than 1800 kilometers, crossed a long and narrow island cut by numerous rivers, challenged an enemy which had some 100 000 men at the beginning and more than 180 000 soldiers and 42 generals at the end; which controlled the main cities and well-fortified towns, magnificent camps and military roads; which had the most modern weapons of the time and a good communications system. Under those conditions, the invasion troops completely fulfilled their military objectives: taking the war to all corners of the country, urging thousands of their fellow countrymen to take up arms and strengthening the insurrection materially and morally.

Important economic objectives were also met: they destroyed a large amount of Spain's economic resources in such a way that production and the Spanish colonial government's income decreased.

As for the political point of view, the independence movement's international prestige increased; Cuba demonstrated that there was a popular army on the island and not a "gang of villains", as the Spaniards reported. They encouraged the interest of international media outlets in learning about and spreading the news of Cuba's struggle.

After the invasion, the people's faith in victory strengthened and many world figures understood that Spain could not win the war in Cuba.

Weyler and the Relocation.- The invasion's success also sealed the fate of General Arsenio Martínez Campos, who months earlier had noticed the independence movement's strength and had asked to be replaced as the head of the Spanish Army. In February of 1896, general Valeriano Weyler—an experienced military officer who had already served in Cuba during the previous war under the command of bloody Blas Villate, Count of Balmaseda—took over as head of the government and army.

Since that date, Weyler proved he liked cruel methods such as periodic executions, mass exile, destruction of farms and crops, in short, subjecting people to hunger and fear. The terror, which began following Martínez Campos' replacement, reached its height on October 21st, 1896, when Weyler issued an order: "All residents in the countryside and outside fortified towns will gather **within eight days** in the towns occupied by the troops. Any individual who remains in rural areas when that term expires will be considered a rebel and will be treated as such".

Hundreds of thousands of people had to leave their homes, farms and other properties, and gather in the cities. They stayed on front porches, in the parks and on the streets, sleeping in the open air, living of public charity. Those who suffered most were the elderly, women and children, since young men and the adults generally joined the Liberation Army instead of complying with the order.

Spanish politician and lawyer, Alvaro Figueroa, Count of Romanones, referred to "more than 300 000 agonizing and starving people, dying of hunger and disease in the towns". And renowned Spanish political and intellectual leader, José Canalejas stated before the war was over that the hostilities and the forced relocation had caused the death of at least one third of Cuba's rural population.*

But Weyler's monstrous measure didn't bring about the results Spain expected. If it's true that it wiped out a large portion of the civilian population and wreaked havoc among the rebel ranks, it also forced thousands of men to take up arms against Spain and sparked a wave of indignation against Spanish colonialism throughout the world. The course of the war continued favoring the Cubans. The forced relocation, however, was maintained until March 1898.

The military campaign in the west. Antonio Maceo's Death.- Following the invasion and fighting constant battles, Maceo returned to Havana, where he met Máximo Gómez. They carried out operations in this province and in Matanzas and split up again: Gómez went to the island's central region while Maceo went back to Pinar del Río.

_____

* It's been said that the relocation was the first modern expression of what later were the Nazi concentration camps during World War Two and the "strategic villages" created by the United States in Vietnam during the war it waged against the heroic people of Indochina.

66

The Titan's military operations in Pinar del Río were characterized by bloody battles which were not always successful and which inflicted a large number of casualties on both sides, although having a favorable balance for the Cuban rebels. In a bid to stop the *mambí* offensive, Weyler took over the direction of operations in Pinar del Río with the aim of surrounding and destroying General Antonio Maceo. With the construction of a formidable military line (the military road from Mariel to Majana), it was thought that the *mambí* troops wouldn't be able to cross it.

Called from the center of the island to mediate in a crisis between the Government and the General in Chief, Maceo left Pinar del Río, tricked the Spaniards at the road from Mariel to Majana and instead he crossed by sea, entering the province of Havana again. Camped in San Pedro, some 20 kilometers southwest of the capital, the camp was surrounded by Spanish troops. In the battle which ensued, Maceo was shot and killed. His aide-de-camp, Francisco Gómez Toro, Máximo Gómez's son, died with him.

The body of the "Bronze Titan" had 26 wounds. He had fought in more than 900 battles and was a legend of invulnerability. For that reason, it was difficult for the *mambí* troops to accept his death. Cuba not only lost a military chief and extraordinary warrior, but also a leader of radical revolutionary thinking and extremely loyal to the cause of independence, to the unity of the island's patriotic forces and the people in general. Antonio Maceo's anti-imperialist, Latin American and internationalist ideas guided his life.

The La Yaya Assembly. Cuban supremacy in the countryside.- On october 10, 1897, another Constituent Assembly met in La Yaya in Camagüey province as agreed upon by the Jimaguayú Assembly two years before. There, a new constitution was adopted which subordinated the military command to civilian rule and passed all the powers of the General in Chief over to that civilian authority. The Assembly reconfirmed the government, named Bartolomé Masó President and Dr. Domingo Méndez Capote Vice President. The Assembly also agreed that the War Secretary, General José B. Alemán, should be the supreme head of the Liberation Army. In fact, no one questioned, however, Máximo Gómez's position as General in Chief.

In 1897, the war continued on the island and the Cuban troops maintained a privileged position in Camagüey and Oriente, the country's two largest provinces. In those territories, the Spaniards only controlled a few big cities, while Cubans were the absolute owners of the countryside and towns. During this year, Gómez carried out his famous operation of La Reforma between Las Villas and Camagüey with so much success that a biographer of the great Dominican wrote: "Butcher Weyler was unable to take over that little piece of territory defended by a handful of Cubans, despite the fact that he had 260 000 soldiers".

General Calixto García achieved a big success in Oriente, with the occupation of Victoria de Las Tunas and Guisa, important supply and operation centers of the Spanish Army. In Las Tunas, the Cubans captured hundreds of prisoners, who were later released, and seized, among other things, 1200 rifles, 1 500 000 bullets

The Explosion of the "Maine"

and ten wagons loaded with medicine. Liberal leader Praxedes M Sagasta, who weeks later was named the President of Spain's Council of Ministers, was forced to admit in May 1897 that: "After having sent 200 000 men and shed so much blood, we don't own any more land on the island than that which our soldiers are stepping on".

The Autonomous government: A delayed decision.- In view of the situation, the Spanish government decided to change its policy towards Cuba in a last attempt to preserve it. Weyler was replaced and a "colonial Constitution" which established an autonomous system for Cuba and Puerto Rico was drawn up. In Cuba, a government was set up with five leaders of the Autonomist Party, one of whom was named President of the Council of Secretaries. But the advocates of an autonomous government had already lost their meager credibility: most of their followers had joined the independence movement or gave up the political struggle.

With half of the island completely in the hands of Cuban forces and the other half affected by the war, the relocation, epidemics and other diseases, the autonomous government was nothing other than pure fiction. Welcomed by angry protests carried out by pro-integration advocates, the autonomous government was firmly rejected by the rebels.

The delayed autonomous regime was so obviously useless that, according to what had been said, when Sagasta put the decree which established it on the desk of the Queen of Spain María Cristina to be signed, she said: "I've been told, however, that with autonomy Cuba is lost". And the Minister replied: "Well, my lady! It can't be more lost than it already is!"

Explosion of the "Maine": US Intervention.- On February 15th, 1898 only weeks after the autonomous regime was installed and just before the island's parliamentary elections were held, an event occurred that clearly announced the future: the explosion of the US battleship Maine in Havana Bay, with a toll of 266 crew members and two officers dead. The US government had sent the ship three weeks before with the pretext of serious unrest promoted in Havana by integration supporters against the autonomous regime. The "Maine" was an obvious sign that the United States was willing to directly intervene in the Spanish-Cuban war.

According to a US commission, the explosion had come from outside the ship; but a Spanish commission found that the blast had occurred inside. Actually Spain was doing everything possible to prevent a war with the United States and was careful not to commit any act of provocation. Hence, the Spaniards were not responsible for the blast. On the contrary, the US authorities were seeking a pretext to wage war against Spain. Besides meeting its old ambitions over Cuba, Puerto Rico, the Philippines and other militarily and economically important possessions could fall into US hands as a result of a war with the European country. And fearing that Cuba would obtain its independence and slip through its fingers, the US needed an incident like that of the "Maine". Consequently, everything points to a self-provocation. The theory concerning US responsibility was reinforced by the fact that almost all white officials escaped the catastrophe because they were not on deck at the time of the blast.

Máximo Gómez

In a desperate attempt to prevent the US from getting involved in the conflict, the colonial government took two steps that had been demanded by that country's President, William McKinley, and which until that moment it had refused to accept: an end to the forced relocation and an end to hostilities with the island's independence fighters in order to reach a peaceful settlement. But both the Republic's Government Council and the Liberation Army's General in Chief immediately rejected the late truce offered by the Spaniards, claiming that they would only accept Cuba's absolute independence.

In the United States, the explosion of the "Maine" was blamed on Spain, sparking a wave of indignation. President McKinley sought authorization in Congress to put an end to the Spanish-Cuban war. On April 11th, 1898, congress granted the permission through a so called Joint Resolution, which also stipulated that "the island of Cuba is, and by right should be, free and independent". The road had been cleared for US intervention in Cuba.

On April 21st, the Joint Resolution was presented to the Spanish government as an ultimatum and Spain and the United States broke off diplomatic relations. Hours later, a US contingent led by Admiral William T. Sampson blockaded several Cuban ports, and President McKinley called on 150 000 volunteers to take arms, a figure which rapidly rose to 200 000. Artillery fire began falling on Cuban ports, paving the way for the arrival of the invasion army. Cannon shots were also heard over San Juan de Puerto Rico. At the same time, another US contingent entered Manila Bay in the Philippines, sinking the Spanish boats anchored there.

For its war in Cuba, the United States decided to begin the invasion in Oriente, the province where the Cubans had almost absolute control. With that objective, the US asked for and obtained the Liberation Army's cooperation. Cuban troops played a decisive role in establishing a "beach-head" and protecting the US landing in Daiquiri on June 20th, as well as the successful battles over El Caney and San Juan. Santiago de Cuba surrendered on July 16th. The Cubans completed the siege of the city and prevented the arrival of Spanish reinforcements. The Battle of Las Guásimas in which the Cuban troops did not participate was a disaster for the US Army. The Spanish contingent, led by Admiral Pascual Cervera, was destroyed in Santiago de Cuba's Bay on July 3rd. Cervera was captured by the Cubans, who supported the attack from the coast.

With Oriente under control and sure of its victory, the United States began to show its real intentions regarding Cuba. After the city of Santiago de Cuba was taken over by Cuban and US troops, General Nelson A. Miles would not allow the Cuban troops to enter in the city, claiming that they wanted to prevent clashes between Cubans and Spaniards. General Calixto García, head of the *mambí* forces in the Eastern department, ordered his troops to defend their respective areas, presented his resignation to the Government Council and wrote a memorable and dignified protest letter to general William R. Shafter, head of the US troops.

After having lost the Philippines and Puerto Rico and without hope of holding on to Cuba, Spain asked the United States to begin peace talks. On August 11th, the first agreements were reached and, hostilities came to an end. On December 10th, the Paris Treaty was signed, putting an end to the war and leaving Spanish colonies in US hands.

With total disregard for the Cuban people, who had fought heroically for their independence for more than 30 years, the United States prevented Cuban representatives from taking part in the peace talks and in the signing of the Paris Treaty.

On January 1st, 1899 the government of Cuba was transferred to the United States.

IX
The first US occupation

When the first US governor, General John R. Brooke officially took over the administration of Cuba, the United States realized one of its oldest and dearest ambitions. It considered Cuba a vital enclave in its economic, political and military strategy, as well as a testing ground where it could try out all forms of domination that it would then implement in other countries of the Americas. At that moment, however, the US hadn't yet decided on the form in which it would exert that control. Though it intended to annex the island, its plans found serious obstacles both in Cuba and in the United States.

There were those who advocated annexation, but the steps taken by the US in that direction clashed with the fierce resistance of the patriotic forces. The Cuban people had fought fierce battles for their independence for 30 years, they had been the main protagonist of Spain's defeat; they had an experienced and well organized army with a deep-rooted independence ideal, and though their most enlightened leaders had been killed, their ideas were still firmly rooted in a group of *mambí* officers, in outstanding revolutionary professionals and intellectuals, as well as in the people, who wouldn't passively accept the nation's collapse. On September 29th, 1898, the Liberation Army's General in Chief, Máximo Gómez, who had camped with his troops in Yaguajay, Las Villas province, issued a document in which he warned that the island was "neither free nor independent yet", and stated his decision not to lay down his arms until the conclusion of the work to which he had devoted his life: the independence of Cuba.

On the other hand, there was harsh opposition to pro-annexation projects inside the United States. The Cuban people's heroic struggle had garnered the sympathy of large sectors of US society, which demanded compliance with the Joint Resolution's statement that Cuba must be free and independent. In addition, an influential portion of the US ruling classes, including the beat sugar growers from the south and the tobacco producers, saw a serious danger in Cuba's annexation. Their interests might be affected by the competition which Cuba could offer with its cane sugar and tobacco potential, products which, in case of annexation, would enter freely into the United States.

The struggle between those issues caused hesitation in the interventionist government, which couldn't determine Cuba's future status beforehand or how long the occupation would last. But, besides the form of domination that it would adopt (annexation or protectorate), the United States had big obstacles to overcome, and immediately started to clear the way.

The United States against the Cuban nation. Elimination of Cuba's representative bodies.- Governor Brooke quickly strengthened his ties with both Cuban and Spanish classes as well as sectors who could be his allies: the big sugar bourgeoisie, import traders, land owners, the clergy, intellectuals with ties to those classes and sectors, as well as with a group of Cubans coming from the pro-annexation, Reformist and even pro-independence, right-wing ranks, who favored US rule.

Without consulting the Cuban people or their institutions, Brooke set up a civilian government; divided the island into seven departments ruled by US governors; named civilian governors in the provinces as well as mayors and representatives in the municipalities, and kept many Spanish colonial government officials in their posts. In addition, he ordered people to turn in their weapons and, completely ignoring the *Mambí* Army, he created a repressive force, the Rural Guard, and a municipal police corps, both at the service of the occupation forces. The Rural Guard was, from that moment on, the most loyal defender of the interests of large landowners and the big sugar bourgeoisie. The US administration created the judicial power with its courts legally based on the same civil and criminal codes of the Spanish government.

On the other hand, even before taking over the country's government, the occupation forces began maneuvering to get rid of the Cuban nation's three representative bodies: the Cuban Revolutionary Party, the Liberation Army and the Assembly of Representatives of the Cuban People in Arms (usually called Santa Cruz or Cerro Assembly, depending on where it gathered). The interventionist government ignored them completely; but they existed and were faithful forces. That's why the US used all possible means to get rid of them, something which was achieved in the first six months of 1899.

The first one to be eliminated was the Cuban Revolutionary Party. The United States relied on Tomás Estrada Palma for that. Estrada Palma had taken over as Delegate of the Cuban Revolutionary Party following Martí's death and had reduced the organization's activities to raising funds and preparing expeditions, depriving it of all political functions. After the war was over, Estrada Palma thought that those activities were no longer necessary and dissolved the party in December 1898, just a few days after the signing of the Paris Treaty. There was neither an independent country nor a democratic republic yet, the party's two main objectives, but Estrada Palma, who admired the American way of life and refused to believe that the Cuban people were able to govern themselves, explained the dissolution claiming that the objectives for which the party had been set up had already been met. Thus, one of the Cuban people's main tools to confront US role disappeared.

By means of maneuvers and skillfully taking advantage of the lack of future vision and contradictions among the Cuban patriots, the occupation government managed to destroy the Liberation Army and the Cerro Assembly. Previously it had managed to bring Máximo Gómez at odds with the Assembly, which dismissed "the Great Dominican" as General in Chief.

Consequences of the war and US interference.- The elimination of the national liberation movement's three representative institutions allowed the United States to reach its objectives of economic and political domination. The disastrous situation of Cuba after the war also helped.

A census conducted in 1899 revealed the great human loses and destruction of the island's wealth, as well as the backwardness to which education, health and other important sectors of the country's life had been subjected by the colonial regime.

Cuba's population amounted to 1,572,000 inhabitants, a considerable reduction from four years before. It is estimated that 400 thousand people, including 100 thousand children, died from 1895 to 1898. The western part of the island was the most affected, since the war was harshest there and forced relocation more rigorous.

Seventy-five per cent of cattle were lost during those three years; 81 percent of the sugar mills were completely or partially destroyed, causing the sugar harvest to be cut by one third; tobacco production didn't even reach 20 percent of that which was achieved in 1895.

The neglect of public health and education was worse than during the years of the war. Yellow fever and other epidemics decimated the population, and there were only 904 public schools across the island.

Thousands of people who had lost their homes and other properties due to the forced relocation wandered about on the streets without shelter or employment. Most Liberation Army members were also without a job or a salary.

With this situation, many thought the help of a powerful and prosperous nation like the United States was needed to rebuild the country. And the occupation government also took advantage of that. Using the island's economic reconstruction as a pretext, the US laid the groundwork for US capital's absolute control over the Cuban economy by direct investments in that area, the restructuring of a local oligarchy which would historically be its ally, and the annulment of an incipient and weak national bourgeoisie which was never able to play an important role in the country's destiny.

Since the 1860's, the economic ties between Cuba and the United States had been strengthened in such a way that the United States was already replacing Spain as Cuba's trade metropolis. First, it granted credits for sugar production, and starting in 1880, direct US investments were made mainly in the sugar industry and in mining. It is estimated that in 1895, the United States had invested some 50 million dollars in Cuba—a remarkable figure for those times.

In 1898, before it officially took over the government, the US administration cut tariffs on US goods which were brought to Cuba, without granting the same privileges for Cuban products which the United States purchased. Washington also ordered the free circulation of US currency and ruled that all government payments must be made in US dollars, devaluating the moneys which had historically been used in the country: Spanish and French currencies. And as soon as general John R. Brooke took power, a wave of US citizens (business executives, settlers, traders, speculators, etc.) invaded the island to settle in a land which they already considered their own.

Cuban independence fighters raised their voices against the threat posed by those developments and demanded protection for the island's wealth. Inside the United States and for different reasons, powerful interests came out against the Americanization of the island, mainly beet sugar and tobacco growers. Mobilizing their forces, they pressured the US congress to pass the so-called Foraker Amendment, which prohibited the US occupation government from granting privileges and concessions to US investors in Cuba during the occupation.

The US authorities, however, repeatedly violated that ban by making up excuses. Their principal interest was sugar production, given the Cuban soil's conditions for the development of that crop, the island's experience in the field, its trade perspectives and the possibilities it provided to control the world market of sugar. For that reason and despite the Foraker Amendment, the properties of US companies like the United Fruit Co. dramatically increased and new ones like the Cuba company, the McCann Sugar Refinery and the Gramerey Sugar Refinery also appeared. Very closely linked with sugar production was the railway system; that is why, they also took over part of the railroads, clashing with the English companies which had taken possession of the rails in the island's western region at the end of the 19th century.

Sugar development required large extensions of land, and Military Order N. 62 was issued to mark the limits of common farms, cattle ranches and fenced—in areas to benefit US companies. They were purchased at very low prices and to the detriment of Cuban *campesinos*. The growth of large US estates was so quick that in 1905, according to their own confession, nearly 10 percent of Cuba's total land area belonged to US citizens.

Another example illustrating violations of the Foraker Amendment could be found in mining and tobacco. Important mining licenses were granted and by 1902, US companies controlled 80 percent of Cuban ore exports.

US capital also impetuously entered tobacco production, replacing the English investors who controlled that area. At the end of the military occupation in 1902, US citizens owned most of the cigar and cigarette factories.

Completing the easy terms given to US investors on the island, the US government ignored the demand for credits to prevent agricultural and small and medium sized industries from going bankrupt, which allowed US companies to evict many of them for their lands and facilities.

That was how the occupation period laid the groundwork for Cuba's economic growth in the following decades, characterized by a total dependence on the United States: the destruction of an economy practically based on the production of only one product, the exportation of only one crops and the extensive importation of raw material and manufactured goods at high prices.

The US aspirations of annexing Cuba, and even its aspirations of turning it into a protectorate, forced the occupation forces to take measures regarding public health, education and other areas. However, those measures did not respond to a coherent and systematic plan aimed at solving the country's problems but at meeting its objectives of domination and at providing a favorable image of the military occupation.

In that way, and because it was obviously convenient for the occupation troops, the Health Department was established up to the municipal level, carrying out a sanitation campaign to fight endemic diseases which caused high mortality rates, mainly yellow fever. Since the 1880's, a Cuban doctor, Carlos J. Finlay, upheld the thesis that the disease was transmitted by the *Aedes Aegypti* mosquito. When the occupation government organized a scientific team to study and fight the causes of the disease, health authorities at first rejected that thesis, but in the end, several

Cuban and US scientists proved that Finlay was right. Although the arrogance of some US authorities wanted to take that glory away from the outstanding doctor and patriot, his merits have been recognized worldwide.

In the fields of public education, totally neglected by the Spanish colonialists, there were also important gains. The occupation government was interested in training the work force that the US companies and the local oligarchy needed for a more profitable exploitation of the country. To that end, the education system was organized at all levels, the number of primary schools increased four-fold, education was compulsory for children from 6 to 14 years of age and a training system was set up for teachers.

That educational policy also had the objective of politicizing teachers and the younger Cuban generations in favor of the "American way of life" and of US interests. The General School Superintendent, Alexis E. Frye, was an American as was the team of instructors that came with him. The first school texts were also produced in the US, and Cuban teachers had to take intensive courses in the United States. They even tried to bring US teachers for the Cuban schools, and idea that didn't materialize due to its rejection by Cuban teachers and outstanding figures.

Popular resistance, labor movement and socialist parties.-The measures and anti-national positions of the US occupation government faced the active rejection of the classes and sectors interested in achieving the island's absolute sovereignty in the shortest term. That resistance was headed by some representatives of the former *mambí* forces, including various generals and other members of the disbanded Liberation Army, as well as revolutionary immigrant leaders, the most radical sectors of the middle class, the labor movement and some isolated representatives of the island's weak bourgeoisie.

Harsh criticism was made of the terms under which the Paris Treaty was written, from which Cubans were left out, which excluded the Isle of Pines from Cuba and didn't limit the time of the US military occupation. They protested the pro-annexation campaign, the elimination of the Cuban nation's representative institutions, the licenses granted to US business executives, the hypocritical US "humanitarian" attitude, the autonomists' participation in the government and the absence of workers from public posts. Particularly important were the protests against replacing the military authorities by a US civilian government, which meant consolidating and extending the occupation.

Those national feelings were expressed in different ways including patriotic rallies organized against the US authorities' will; speeches at the so-called *asambleas de notables* (consultations made by the military government); denunciations in various nationalist newspapers, and above all, the establishment of patriotic clubs and other organizations in many parts of the country which brought together members of the dissolved *Mambí* Army and all independence fighters. A strong movement aimed at setting up a broad nationalist party began and the call for a Constituent Assembly was demanded.

In February of 1899, outstanding intellectual and revolutionary immigrant fighter, Diego Vicente Tejera, founded the Cuban Socialist Party, the first political organization of the working class in Cuba. Although utopian, it gathered a growing number of Cuban workers, including many immigrants who had returned to the country, it advocated the ideas of José Martí and became an organization struggling for the full equality of all Cubans, for the independence of Cuba and against all measures which affected the island's sovereignty.

But the party faced strong opposition. The middle class was reluctant to accept a workers party; most bourgeois press and various outstanding political figures claimed that the existence of such a party was an obstacle for the nation's unity and the need to face foreign occupation. Anarchists also fought against it, because they rejected political action. In that way, the party lasted only a few months. Another effort by Tejera—the Cuban People's Party—was also doomed to failure in the year 1900.

Guilds and other workers organizations were more successful. The end of Spanish rule and the return to Cuba of many workers and working class immigration leaders reactivated the labor movement. Workers clubs were set up as well as guilds, cooperatives, artisans centers, various trades associations and even a national organization: the Cuban Workers General League, considered a rudimentary workers confederation.

The League published a newspaper, ¡Alerta! (Alert), through which it not only upheld the specific interests of the working class, but also denounced the foreign occupation forces' anti-national policy, the domination of US monopolies, pro-annexation attempts, and the submission of many Cubans to the United States. At the same time, it demanded an end to discrimination against the island's workers and women, came out for respecting *mambí* traditions and for turning Martí's ideas into a reality, calling workers and *campesinos* to unite against the foreign trusts and local exploiters and to fight for a socialist government.

The League led many workers actions in several areas of the country during the US occupation, such as the important construction workers strike in August and September, 1899, which was brutally repressed by authorities.

Interference and Republic. Political hustling.- In December, 1899, in view of harsh opposition to pro-annexation plans both in Cuba and the United States, the US War Secretary was forced to assure that the occupation was temporary, and announced that municipal elections would be held, that a Constituent Assembly would be set up and that, following general elections, the island's government would be handed over to the Cubans.

At the same time, President McKinley spoke about the links that should exist between the two nations. The US administration had obviously decided to admit that Cubans could have a formal government of their own, but totally directed from Washington. Then Cuba's Military Governor, General Leonard Wood replaced John R. Brooke to oversee the transition.

Before that date—December, 1899—some political parties had been created to fill the vacuum left by the elimination of the official institutions that represented the Cuban nation. But the most influential were created in the year 1900. They included the Cuban National Party, which was very heterogeneous although bourgeois sectors with certain nationalist aspirations prevailed; the Federal Republican Party of Las Villas and the Federal Republican Party of Havana, which included some radical figures from the *mambí* ranks; and the Democratic Union Party, made up of the main advocates of Autonomous regime tied directly to the United States.

On June 16, 1900 the first elections were held to elect mayors, treasurers and attorneys of the country's 110 municipalities for a one-year term. Balloting was limited: only Cubans older than 21 who could read and write and had properties worth more than $250.00 were eligible to vote (members of the dissolved Liberation Army need not comply with these two requirements). Spanish subjects who had not reaffirmed their condition as Spaniards also had the right to vote. The balloting restrictions took their toll: out of **417,993** male citizens of age to vote, according to the 1899 census, only **150,648**—that is to say, 36 percent— were actually eligible to vote. In addition, women were excluded from the election and 359, 423 women over 21 years of age could not cast their ballots.

New municipal elections were held one year later, also with a limited vote, to elect mayors, treasurers and attorneys for a one-year term, as in the previous balloting.

The Constituent Assembly and the Platt Amendment.- New elections were held on September 15, 1900, to elect 31 delegates to the Constituent Assembly, but with the same balloting limitations. Both in the municipal elections and in those for the Constituent Assembly, the people overwhelmingly voted for the pro-independence candidates, although they included right-wing, progressive and even former Autonomist candidates.

From November of that year to February, 1901, the assembly drew up and passed the first Constitution of the Republic, which included a large part of the Cuban people's democratic aspirations, thanks to the participation of a large number of *mambí* delegates. The Constitution, however, contained a series of contradictions and limitations stemming from the Assembly's heterogeneous nature and from the inconsistent positions adopted by some pro-independence activists. It established the republican form of government and Cuba's sovereignty over all neighboring islands and keys. It granted Cuban citizenship to Spaniards residing in Cuba from April 11, 1899 who had registered as Spaniards, and to Africans who had been slaves or emancipated. It declared that all Cubans are equal before the Law, but women were not granted the right to vote. It proclaimed internationally recognized individual rights and liberties, the right to practice any religion, and the separation between Church and State. It established the composition, structure and functions of State powers, as well as the obligations and authority of its institutions and of people who held public positions.

After signing that Magna Carta, the Assembly fulfilled the objective for which it had been created. But, rather than dissolving itself, it was forced by Washington to fight a new and unequal battle, which led to the castration of the nation's sovereignty.

In February, 1901, President McKinley signed the Military Expenditures Law, which contained an amendment put forward by congressional representative Orville Platt and which was passed by the Senate. The amendment's eight articles went against the dignity and sovereignty of Cuba. Among other things, it prohibited the Cuban government from reaching agreements which "damaged" the nation's independence or granted part of its land to foreign governments (the US government was the first to violate this dictate); granted the United States the right to military occupy Cuba when the US authorities considered that the life, properties and rights of citizens were in danger; excluded the Isle of Pines and other islands and keys from Cuba; forced the country to grant large portions of its land to the United States to build naval bases or coal stations, and recognized all actions carried out by the military occupation government. That amendment had to be approved fully by the Constituent Assembly and attached as an appendix to the Constitution of the Republic of Cuba. There were strong protests against the Platt Amendment nationwide. Most delegates firmly opposed its content and even its discussion by the Assembly. They made a counter proposal, with a number of changes, and set up a commission to discuss the issue in Washington. But the United States announced an ultimatum: If the amendment was not passed in its entirety without any change, the United States would not withdraw the occupation troops from the country.

With this dilemma, the amendment was approved by a small margin of only four votes. Various delegates who rejected it and fought against it since the beginning, gave up to US pressure, publicly claiming that they did so in order to prevent the extension of the foreign occupation. Of particular note was Juan Gualberto Gómez's speech and Salvador Cisneros' vote against the amendment as a symbol of the Cuban people's integrity and opposition to US imposition. The 1901 Constitution formally gave Cuba a bourgeois-democratic republic, respectful of private property and of the main postulates of the 1789 French Revolution and a superior legal status than the one it had to date; but, as Governor Wood himself admitted, "little or no independence had been left to Cuba with the Plat Amendment and the only thing appropriate was to seek annexation". They would never reach that objective, but the truth was that the island ceased being a colony of Spain to become a semi-colony of the United States.

The first presidential elections. The United States imposes Estrada Palma as President.- Cuba already had a Constitution and the United States had guaranteed its control over the new republic. The next step was to call general elections to elect the republican government: the Republic's President and vice-president, senators, representatives, governors and provincial counselors. The date for the elections was December 31, 1901.

The national liberation movement was unable to close ranks in a common front which could defend its aspirations, and the electoral battle began with a confrontation between two presidential candidates: Tomás Estrada Palma and General Bartolomé Masó.

Estrada Palma had been President of the Republic in Arms for a short period of time during the Ten Year War and when Martí died, he replaced him as Delegate of the Cuban Revolutionary Party. He always questioned the Cuban people's capacity to govern themselves, came out for the US intervention in the Spanish-Cuban war and maintained pro-annexation positions behind Martí's back. When he realized that those positions were firmly rejected by the Cuban people and by influential US sectors, he proposed a status through which Cuba would remain under US control without annexing the island. That proposal materialized later in the Platt Amendment. He was therefore the favorite candidate of the United States.

Bartolomé Masó had been one of the first Cubans to take up arms in October, 1868, he was among the twelve men who remained with Céspedes at the defeat in Yara and served as second chief of the Liberation Army during the First Independence War. He was one of those who first launched the Cry of Independence in February, 1895. He always opposed any US interference in Cuban affairs, publicly condemned the Platt Amendment and drew up a government plan based on Cuba's absolute independence. He was seen as a serious danger by the US occupation forces.

From the beginning, the electoral race showed Masó's popular roots and, as a result, the occupation government used all its power to support Estrada Palma's candidacy. In a unilateral and anti-democratic move, the United States did not admit the participation of a representative of Masó's coalition on the Central Electoral Board, pressured government officials to support and help Estrada Palma and became an accomplice of the fraudulent actions committed during the electoral race.

As a protest against US favoritism and the manipulation of the political machine by Estrada Palma's followers, Masó withdrew his candidacy, and Estrada Palma was left as the only candidate. With no adversary, his victory was guaranteed.

Estrada Palma was a US citizen still living in the United States and returned to Cuba four months after the elections to occupy the presidential seat on May 20, 1902. Thus, the country's military occupation ended and the pseudo-republic made its debut on the island's political scenario.

Matanzas poet Bonifacio Byrne expressed the Cuban people's frustration for the US occupation with the following poem:

My Flag

Upon returning from distant land,
in mourning and with a gloomy soul
anxiously, my flag I looked for
and another one I've seen besides mine!
Where is my Cuban flag,
the most beautiful flag that ever was?
From the boat I saw it this morning,
and I've never seen anything so sad..!

With the faith of austere souls
today I energetically maintain
that two flags should not wave
where one is enough: Mine!
In the fields that today are an ossarium
it saw the valiant soldiers fighting together,
and its been the honorable sudarium
of the poor dead warriors

Proud it looked in battle
without childish or romantic vanity:
A Cuban who doesn't cherish it
should be whipped for being such a coward!

....

Although weakly and sadly it waves,
my goal is that the sun
shines on it alone. Alone!,
on the plains, on the sea and on the summit.

If torn to pieces
one day my flag turns out to be,
our martyrs raising their arms,
will know how to defend it still!

X
First Republican government and second US military occupation

Tomás Estrada Palma.- Tomás Estrada Palma, the president chosen and imposed on Cuba by the United States government, confirmed his renunciation of independence ideals when he formed his Cabinet.

All of his selected cabinet members ged held Autonomist ideas: there wasn't a single revolutionary emigrant, or anyone who had suffered imprisonment or deportation for defending his homeland's independence. That Council of Secretaries could not do much good for the Cuban people's interests.

In 1904, Estrada Palma's government contributed to the indebtedness of the Republic, by arranging a 35 million peso loan from US banks, in order to pay pensions to members of the dissolved Liberation Army.

In 1903, an ill-named Treaty of Commercial Reciprocity was concluded, stipulating that a small list of Cuban products entering the United States would benefit from a tariff 20% lower than the products of other countries. In exchange, a long list of US products would enter Cuba with tariffs reduced by between discount that ranged 25 to 40%. As it can be seen, the advantage for US products was notable. Moreover, taking into account the penetration of US capital in the Cuban economy, the tariff reduction for the island's products would mainly benefit US investors. This Treaty's mechanism made it possible for the United States to place a good part of its surplus production in Cuba, thus obstructing the development of a strong national bourgeoisie on the island.

In accordance with the Platt Amendment, a Permanent Treaty of Relations between Cuba and the United States was signed. This Treaty reproduced the eight articles of that constitutional amendment, with its limitations on Cuban sovereignty. Also under the Platt Amendment, portions of Cuban territory were rented to the United States. This land was located in Bahía Honda (on the north coast of western Pinar del Río province), and in Guantánamo bay (southern coast of the former eastern province of Oriente), where Washington constructed a naval base still maintained by the United States against the will of the Cuban people.

Years later, the United States abandoned the territory it occupied at Bahía Honda, in exchange for an important expansion of the Guantánamo Base area. Guantánamo bay is Cuba's third largest bay. As a deep-sea bay that was well protected it was of strategic importance for the United States: its location guaranteed military control over the Caribbean and Central and South America, including the Panama Canal. The base covers 117 square kilometers of Cuban territory, 78 of which correspond to its terrestrial part and 39 to its maritime area. This foreign enclave in Cuba has represented a constant threat to the Cuban people.

Under Estrada Palma's government, the penetration of US capital into the sugar and tobacco industries, real estate, railroads, mines and other branches of the economy continued, in competition with British, French, German and Spanish capital, among others. British investments still surpassed those of the United States. In 1905, there were 29 US-owned sugar mills, which produced 21% of Cuba's sugar and owned large tracts of land; 13,000 Americans worked on the island, with land holdings to the tune of 50 million dollars; the US tobacco trust had already surpassed that of Great Britain: it possessed the majority of brand names and controlled close to 90% of cigar exports.

Estrada Palma's financial policy was based on fiscal saving. The budget surplus reached 27 million dollars in 1905, although the acquisition of weapons and other military expenditures reduced it to less than 14 million at the end of his mandate, despite having increased his treasury with an 11 million peso loan.

In his eagerness to fill the state's coffers, Estrada Palma did not use these substantial resources to repair the devastation caused by war or to foster the development of the national economy. Agriculture remained abandoned; the soldiers of the liberation war were not granted the land or the resources they were demanding. Their living conditions remained precarious. Doors were opened to imports from the United States, in an unequal competition with national products. National products were slapped with high taxes to pay for government loans. Public works limited themselves to 256 kilometers of roads, very few bridges and aqueducts, less than 150 public schools and some other investments of minor importance.

Popular discontent and workers agitation.- Discontent with Estrada Palma's administration and against the country's increasing dependence soon became generalized. A year after Estrada Palma took possession of office, his government faced two armed uprisings, which were brutally put down. That same year, 1903, there were huge popular protests against the unfavorable terms in which the Treaty of Commercial Reciprocity and the Permanent Treaty of Relations had been agreed upon. Prestigious representatives of the *mambí* movement, even inside the Republic's Congress, energetically condemned the government's submission to the United States. Senator Manuel Sanguily presented a bill—which did not prosper—against large land holdings and the sale of land to foreigners.

The workers movement played a major role in the defense of the *mambí* legacy, of the country's national wealth and sovereignty. In November, 1902, shortly after Estrada Palma was sworn in as president, the first general strike of the Cuban republic took place, the so-called "strike of the apprentices". This strike was led by tobacco workers and was later supported by other proletarian sectors, including those in Tampa and Key West. Renowned *mambí* fighters like Juan Gualberto Gómez, Manuel Sanguily, Fermín Valdés Domínguez and Diego Vicente Tejera also expressed their active solidarity with the labor mobilization. The protest was in response to the discrimination of Cuban workers, especially blacks. Though adhesion was massive, the strike was brutally put, with several workers killed and wounded. The first important mobilizations of sugar workers took place in these years, which were also violently repressed. Through their actions and their media outlets, workers came out against the penetration of US capital and the submissive attitude of the government, while at the same time specifically establishing their demands.

The first political organizations of a Marxist character were created in 1903—in Havana, Manzanillo, and other regions—headed by labor leader and independence

84

fighter Carlos Baliño and other leaders of the revolutionary emigration who returned to Cuba. Among them: the Club for Socialist Propaganda (1903) (*Club de Propaganda Socialista*), the Labor Party (1904) (*Partido Obrero*), the "Karl Marx" Center" (*Círculo Carlos Marx*), the Socialist Party of Manzanillo (1905) (*Partido Socialista de Manzanillo*), Havana's Socialist Group (1905)(*Agrupación Socialista de La Habana*), and the Socialist Party of the Isle of Cuba (1906) (*Partido Socialista de la Isla de Cuba*).

Electoral fraud and the "August Small War". The end of Estrada Palma's mandate was close, and elections were called for September 23rd, 1905. Popular discontent grew further with the president's re-election aspirations were revealed. Those aspirations were encouraged by Washington and Estrada Palma's local supporters.

Several political organizations joined the Moderate Party (*Partido Moderado*), which nominated Estrada Palma, and others joined the Liberal Party (*Partido Liberal*), which had General José Miguel Gómez as presidential candidate. Neither candidate presented a program of popular benefit; but the Liberal Party included a group of men who were more popular, many of them veterans of independence wars.

The pro-government group that promoted Estrada Palma's re-election aspirations formed a so-called "Combat Cabinet" and resorted to every means to guarantee his victory. Mayors, officials and authorities who opposed fraud and corruption were dismissed; members of the Moderate Party took control of all the voting stations and elaborated voters' lists as they pleased; and the Rural Guard was prepared to intervene in the process in favor of Estrada Palma. Independence Army Colonel Enrique Villuendas, liberal leader in central Las Villas province, was murdered the day before the elections. This assassination sparked widespread indignation, and the Liberal Party withdrew from the dispute. Estrada Palma was left as the only candidate, as occurred in 1901, automatically becoming the winner of the elections.

However, liberal leaders did not passively accept the fraud and took up arms in several regions of the country beginning in August, 1906. The insurrection became strong in the provinces of Pinar del Río, Havana, and Las Villas. Independence veterans attempted to mediate in the confrontation but Estrada Palma demanded the total and immediate surrender of the rebels. There were arrest orders against liberal leaders, incarcerations and assassinations. The Rural Guard, using machetes, assassinated General Quintín Banderas in Havana, one of the most courageous leaders of Cuba's independence wars. But the insurrection, historically known as the "small war of August", became increasingly strong, even threatening the Cuban capital. In view of the serious situation, Estrada Palma again demonstrated his pro-annexation vocation, and instead of seeking a peaceful agreement among Cubans, he again requested US military intervention. The US government accepted the petition and on September 29th, 1906, US Secretary of War, William H. Taft, took up the post of Provisional Governor in Cuba.

The second US occupation.- Taft dissolved Congress functions and assumed legislative faculties; he disbanded insurrection forces and the militias created by Estrada Palma, and named US supervisor and several US advisors for the Rural Guard. But the true purpose of his mandate was to pave the way for the person who would take control of the Cuban government during the intervention: Charles E. Magoon.

Washington justified the intervention with moral arguments, but this period was characterized by the waste of public funds, political and administrative corruption and the Republic's indebtedness. Magoon established the unrestricted use of bribes and the *botella* (a post for which a person was paid without working). Public works were a rich source of speculation: each kilometer of road, for example, cost seven times more under Estrada Palma's government.

From the Republic's Treasury, Magoon paid for the material damages caused by "the small war of August", increased the salaries of the Rural Guard, reimbursed Washington for the cost of the US intervention and gave the Catholic Church a large sum as compensation for the properties the Spanish government had taken possession of in the 19th century, despite the fact that Spain had compensated the Church with interest and Leonard Wood had given it another large sum. At the same time, Magoon left Cuba with a 16 million 500 thousand debt on a public works loan for Havana's sewage system. That is, from the funds he had received from the previous government, 13 million 625 thousand and 539 dollars, Magoon only left 2 million 800 thousand to his successor, from which one million were in foreign debt bonds. It can be said that the second US intervention definitively established the foundation for unrestrained corruption, which since then would be one of the neocolonial republic's greatest social ills.

Another negative characteristic of this period was the violent repression against workers who clamored for reasonable demands, such as an 8 hour working day, fair salaries, job safety, and adequate treatment. The only proletarian action that developed normally was the so-called "coin strike", to demand that salaries be paid in US currency since Spanish currency was devaluated. This was a legitimate demand, but it wasn't for this reason that the government was receptive: what interested Magoon was generalizing the use of American currency to contribute to the strengthening of Washington's control over the Cuban economy. The strike was won by the workers. The strikes of railroad, tobacco, and sugar workers and those of other sectors, however, were not successful. Repression of those labor actions left workers killed, wounded, detained and fired, and even strikebreakers were brought in from New York. The anti-labor essence of the US intervention was clearly manifested in all of its cruelty.

There were, nevertheless, armed uprisings against the intervention. One of them, headed by a group of Independence Army officers, was discovered the day before the uprising, in September, 1907, and its main leaders were condemned to prison. Another attempt took place the following month, in the eastern region, at Manzanillo, which was put down by the Rural Guard.

Perhaps the only acceptable aspect of this US administration was the elaboration of a series of complementary laws to the 1901 Constitution, such as the municipal law, the organic law of the Judicial Power, the civil service law, an electoral law, and other resolutions needed for the return of a government led by Cubans. With the purpose of elaborating these laws, a Advisory Commission was created, formed by three Americans —one of whom was the head of the commission—and by nine Cubans of diverse political tendencies. Old independence combatant Juan Gualberto Gómez played a decisive role in that commission. He achieved important democratic victories in issues such as universal suffrage and the autonomy of municipalities, as opposed to the thesis of limited suffrage and of centralized government defended by the three US delegates and some reactionary Cubans.

Once the island was pacified and the continuity of US domination guaranteed, the work of the Advisory Commission concluded, provincial and municipal elections were called for August 1st, 1908, and presidential elections for November 14th of the same year. Following the first elections won by liberals—who were divided internally during the process—attention was focused on general elections. The Conservative Party (formerly the Moderate Party) had a typical representative of the native oligarchy as presidential candidate, General Mario García Menocal. The Liberal Party (its two factions united) nominated a skillful politician, General José Miguel Gómez. When elections concluded, the liberal candidacy triumphed by a wide margin, and on January 28th, 1909, General Gómez took possession of the presidency of the Republic. Thus ended the second US intervention, which had lasted two years and four months.

Julio Antonio Mella

XI
Absolute domination of the United States
(1909-1925)

The stage following the second occupation is characterized by the consolidation of US domination over Cuba's economy and politics, and by the development of serious evils that damaged the bourgeois republic and latifundia owners until its disappearance. The three governors from that period (José Miguel Gómez, Mario García Menocal and Alfredo Zayas), who were liberals and conservatives, shared the responsibility for the permanent political and moral crisis in which the country was submerged, and the misery and abandonment of the masses.

US investments.- A rapid growth of US investments takes place during this stage, which towards 1915 reaches and surpasses that of English capital and begins a significant rise, especially in the sugar industry. This situation reached its climax between 1925 and 1926. With US investments in 1906 calculated at some 160 million pesos, in 1914 they reached 215 million (1.3 times more) and, in 1925, they totaled 1 billion 360 million (6.3 more than in 1914).

During the 1915-1925 boom of the sugar industry, US capital took control of several strategic sectors of the Cuban economy: besides sugar, it took control of mining, public services, banking, foreign debt and land. They were almost entirely owned the electricity and telephone companies, numerous energy industries (charcoal, oil, alcohol); as well as of most of the railroad; cement, tobacco, and canned food factories.

But the bulk of investments in this period were dedicated to the sugar sector. In 1914, US companies owned 38 sugar mills producing 38 percent of Cuba's sugar. In 1927, they had at least 75 sugar mills, with 68 percent of production. Only one of its enterprises, the Cuban Cane Company, obtained 580 million dollars between 1916 and 1925 for the selling of sugar and molasses, with a 105 million dollar net profit.

The US sugar latifundia also had a disproportionate growth, and in 1927-1928 comprised it 40 percent of the country's best lands. As few as 18 US companies owned 103,992 *caballerías* (1,395,572 hectares).

During the first decade of the 1990's financial penetration was carried out mainly through loans, with very few US banks. These proliferated with the "sugar fever" after 1915, the National City Bank of New York being the most important of them. Banks from Canada and other countries were established and even the Cuban bourgeoisie founded some 30 small banks, which went bankrupt with the 1920 financial crisis.

Between 1914 and 1927, Cuba received six loans from US banks worth 118 million pesos, and had to pay them 170.8 million. US banks obtained 59.8 million pesos in profits from these operations, at the expense of Cuba's national treasure.

With the expansion of the sugar industry, US monopolies and the island's bourgeoisie linked to that industry needed a cheap and abundant labor force, especially to cut and collect sugar—cane during the harvest season. In 1913, the government

89

signed the first official authorization to import laborers from the Antilles, mainly from Jamaica and Haiti, which were contracted and placed on sugarcane plantations under semi-slavery conditions; they were housed in unhealthy living quarters, with salaries that were not enough to buy food. This immigration increased notably after 1915, with the sugar boom prompted by World War I. It is estimated that over 250,000 Haitian and Jamaican laborers entered the country that way between 1913 and 1915.

Moral decomposition.- Political and administrative corruption was also present during the period 1900-1925. Political corruption had already appeared during the first general elections under the US occupation, with the purpose of imposing Estrada Palma as president; Estrada Palma used corruption in order to be re-elected after 1905.

Corruption manifested itself especially in two ways: trying to win the favor of voters before elections by bribery or pressure—or by totally ignoring the results of an election. Large landowners, enterprises or employers, used to get votes by threatening workers and their families with layoffs and evictions or promising future jobs to the unemployed.

Many political bosses bought votes from the poor, either by giving them money or by offering them some indispensable services: the entrance to a hospital or school, a visit to a doctor's office or the acquisition of medicines, an invoice of food stuffs at a given establishment and even the means to bury a dead relative.

Falsifying voter registration lists was also a common practice, or the use of the rural police and army to prevent supporters of the opposition from voting. When these practices were not enough, they used the *cambiazo*: the outright stealing of voting booths or a similar action to alter the election results.

Some of these fraudulent measures, or all of them together, were took place in each of the elections that occurred in the Republic.

Something similar happened with administrative corruption, inseparably linked to the ruling politicians. It developed during the government of Leonard Wood, and particularly during the government of Magoon; and Creole governors learned their lesson very well. They were often involved in turbulent businesses and embezzlements of the public funds. But, moreover, all public works were planned in such a way that they left large material and monetary benefits to those who supported the projects. Construction works, loans, commercial transactions, concessions to private enterprises, budgets, credits to assist victims of natural disasters, in short, any government project was a source of illegal income for the corrupt politicians. Almost all republican governments left a number of useful construction works unfinished; but these projects, even if they had a social function, remained as monuments to irresponsibility and speculation. There were, of course, exceptions during republican history; but honest politicians were invariably few, and some of them committed suicide.

Demagogic measures alternate with the most violent repression during this period, and at the end of it the first symptoms of crisis in the neocolonial system appeared.

Government of José Miguel Gómez.- The first president during this period, José Miguel Gómez, who ruled from 1909 to 1913, had become a general in the 1895 war, but he soon sold out his commitment to the national liberation cause.

Gómez was known for his demagogy and for the deals in which he and his followers were involved. This earned him the nickname of "Shark"—and the fact that he occasionally shared the spoils with those around him resulted in a very popular phrase: "The shark bathes himself, but only splashes those standing next to him".

His government authorized cockfights and re-established the "National Lottery", a game of chance that turned in million of pesos every year, most of which went to the private coffers of politicians.

Concessions made to Cuban and US enterprises to dredge Cuba's ports and to drain the Zapata Swam were among the most well-known frauds of that government. Despite popular indignation, highly lucrative taxes were created, tremendous amounts of money were given to concessionaires and they were granted the right to exploit the area's forestry resources. The United States intervened diplomatically and the dispute lasted several years. But, in the end, the ports were not dredged and the swamp was not drained and millions of pesos disappeared into the accounts of politicians and concessionaires.

Another important and juicy deal was the exchange of the Villanueva plot—where the central railroad station was located and where they wanted to build the Capitol—for that of the Arsenal. They paid a much higher price for the Villanueva land; while the Arsenal plot was worth four million more than the Villanueva land.

Substantial profits were also obtained from the vast construction plan that was carried out: six agriculture schools, one in each province; and agricultural station in Santiago de las Vegas, on the outskirts of Havana; a 51 kilometer-long canal in central Matanzas province (initial steps); over 500 kilometers of roads, various slaughterhouses, aqueducts and cemeteries; projects for some one thousand houses for the workers, senior citizens' homes in Havana and other places; a hospital in eastern Manzanillo; and the repair of highways, roads and bridges. Moreover, the State subsidized three large railroad enterprises (from the US and England) so they expanded railways they owned on the western side of the island, and in Las Villas and Camagüey provinces.

Some laws that benefited the people were approved, such as the granting of a *caballeria* (33 acres) of land to each rural family without land, prohibiting payment of salaries to workers in money vouchers or tokens rather than legal currency, and the Closing Law, which established hours for stores. But these measures were never carried out during those years.

Gómez' regime, known for its demagogy, also repressed popular and trade union demonstrations. With that purpose, he created the Permanent Army, he re-organized the Rural Guard, he strengthened the structure of the armed forces and advanced his own military and ideological preparation. The Government Secretary, General Gerardo Machado, became known from that time on for his repressive actions.

The military apparatus was used, in the first place, to silence popular protests. In 1912, a powerful sugar workers' strike on several sugar plantations in eastern Cuba—led by the Socialist Party in Manzanillo— was savagely repressed by the Rural Guard. Similarly, another important strike of Havana's sewage system workers was repressed in 1911, which ended with the imprisonment or expulsion from the country of its leaders.

But the most brutal repressive action of that period was the crushing of the so-called "Small War of the Blacks" in 1912. Racial discrimination, inherited from the colony, increased notably during the US military interventions and corroded the republic. Blacks were not allowed into the police force; they could not attend official ceremonies or occupy a number of public posts, nor could they work as employees in numerous public services, banks, etc., or enter the main hotels or restaurants. Wealthy whites had large schools and recreational, sports and social institutions, as well as other facilities, in which blacks were not allowed; blacks were forced to get jobs for inferior salaries, as compared to those of whites.

There were many protests by the workers movement, independence war veterans, personalities and progressive organizations. In order to struggle against that state of exploitation, Evaristo Estenoz, former leader of the labor movement and small contractor at the time and Liberation Army Colonel Pedro Ivonet founded the Independent Colored Group in 1908. This organization's program was aimed not only at doing away with racial discrimination, but also at abolishing the death penalty. It supported compulsory and free education, as well as other demands of social benefit. In 1910, the Group became a political party and tried to participate in the elections; but a law prohibiting the existence of single race parties was approved.

With legal avenues closed, the Independent Colored Party appealed to arms. On May 20th, 1912, the uprising began. Its main focus was in Oriente, on the eastern side of the island, but it also took in areas of Pinar del Río, Havana, and Las Villas provinces. The government mobilized all its forces against the rebels and destroyed the movement. Most of the rebels fell in combat and many of them, such as Colonel Ivonet, were assassinated. As many as 3000 Blacks were killed in the massacre.

This crime has no justification at all, although the idea of forming a party only for blacks was a mistake. The scourge of discrimination against blacks continued to spread throughout the entire republican period.

Government of Mario García Menocal.- Mario García Menocal y Deop followed José Miguel Gómez as the first magistrate of the Republic on May 20th, 1913. A civil engineer graduated at Cornell University in the United States, Menocal had been one of the youngest generals of the 1895 war, but was not involved in any major military action. He had conservative and pro-US ideas, he collaborated with Leonard Wood as chief of police in Havana and was a typical representative of US monopolies, excelling as administrator of properties of the Cuban American Sugar Company and other enterprises. The US press affirmed that Menocal was more American than Cuban. Due to his aggressive anti-labor and anti-popular policies, Menocal was called "The Foreman" and "Cuba's Keiser".

Menocal ruled for two consecutive terms, until 1921. When he was re-elected through a scandalous fraud in 1916, an uprising headed by José Miguel Gómez and other leaders took place, which had the support of a large number of Rural Guard and Army officers. This uprising went down in history as "*La Chambelona*", referring to a popular tune sung at activities and used in Liberal Party propaganda.

The insurrection involved five provinces, from Havana to Oriente, but it was defeated by the government's military superiority and the intervention of the United States, which managed to land infantry at various points on the island. Rebels were accused of being "Germanophiles" and some of their leaders were assassinated. Others were imprisoned and were later granted amnesty.

Shortly after Menocal became president, World War I broke out, which had great economic and political repercussions in the country. In October 1914, two months after the beginning of the war, an Economic Defense Law was approved. This law included, among other measures, the introduction of economies in the State's Administration, issuing treasury bonds, raising taxes, increasing rates of interest over mortgage loans, re-organizing the Army and the Rural Guard, the setting of export premiums for tobacco, creating a maritime insurance for exporters, and minting of a national currency.

"Fat Cows" and "Meager Cows".- Due to the war, all beat crops in Europe were practically devastated, so demands for Cuban sugar increased considerably and prices rose in an unprecedented manner. The year before the war—1913—Cuba produced 2,428,000 tons of sugar and had contributed 14.3 percent of world production. In 1916, production increased to 3,000,000 tons—18.48 percent of world production and, in 1919, it reached 4,000,000 tons, to cover 26.6 percent of the world's sugar. And the price of the sweet product, which had been 1.15 cents a pound in 1913, increased to 18.5 cents in May 1920. The country's mining works also increased notably, especially those of iron and manganese. The balance of trade was favorable for Cuba during those years, since exports substantially surpassed imports. National budget revenues of 43,077,394 pesos in 1913, increased to 114,675,438 in 1920.

This economic bonanza was known as "The Dance of the Millions" or "The Fat Cows".

But that prosperity mainly benefited monopolies and sugar magnates, big dealers and the banks, especially US banking, and not popular sectors. The war also provoked a drastic scarcity of commodity items and dealers shamefully speculated with the scarce supplies. The cost of living increased 100 percent, while salaries only rose 30 percent.

The important English market for Cuban tobacco closed due to the war, and other items of the island's economy were frozen for the same reason. There were production restrictions, factory closings and massive unemployment. Similarly, the "sugar fever" caused a lack of attention to other agricultural development (except sugar cane) and was a great disadvantage to farmers, who were deprived of large areas of land to increase sugar latifundia.

But that was not the worst thing that happened. The fact that the "fat cows" were followed by "meager cows" with unexpected speed led to a real catastrophe in the mid-1920's. The recovery of sugarcane areas affected by the war (which had ended two years before), caused an avalanche of sugar to flow onto the US and world markets, which produced an accelerated price fall. From 22.5 cents a pound in May, it went down to 17.5 in June, 15.5 in July, 11 in August, 9 in September, 7 in October, 5.25 in November and 3.75 in mid-December.

In early October of that year, in view of the evident disaster, depositors panicked and converged on the banks to withdraw their deposits. But the banks did not have funds to pay: they had make considerable loans and conducted other business on the basis of large sugar harvests—counting on prices of up to 30 and 40 cents a pound. When prices dropped dramatically, they found themselves deeply in debt and without any possibility of having an answer for the anguishing demands of their creditors.

As a consequence, bankruptcy occurred due to a shortfall of resources. Hardest hit were Cuban banks, sending landowners, tenant farmers and other agriculture workers, traders and small property owners into ruin.

The two large banks that were not from the United States—the so-called *Banco Cubano* and the *Banco Español*—disappeared in the economic storm. The only two banks that survived were two powerful enterprises that answered to strong ventures with limited reserves. So US banks took possession of the credit sector and of many sugar businesses, land, numerous enterprises and real estate properties.

This disaster could have been avoided, but Menocal was essentially a representative of US monopoly interests and gave them the key to Cuba's economy.

Despite the impressive economic boom that Cuba experienced until 1920 and the considerable loans it received, the performance of Menocal's administration was mediocre. A number of works initiated by José Miguel Gómez were suspended and the construction of several highways, roads, hospitals and schools continued. Among the most significant results: the completion of the Presidential Palace and the creation of six Teachers' Training Schools (to train primary teachers), the National Archives and the National Museum. The founding in Cuba of so-called "regional centers" — Spanish societies for health care and recreation—corresponded to this period.

Menocal substantially contributed to the Republic's going into debt. He arranged four loans for a total of 52 million pesos; he created a bond issue worth five million and increased the island's internal debt to seven million pesos in order to cover payments to the enterprise in charge of the fraudulent port-dredging scandal.

One of the most important steps in the area of finances was the minting, for the first time in Cuba, of a national currency in 1915. US currency—stronger than Cuba's—continued to circulate and the control of US banking over Cuba's finances greatly limited the significance of the new coins.

Menocal made huge investments in the military. He equipped the Army, the Navy, and the Rural Guard, reorganizing them after the "*La Chambelona*" liberal uprising. He also established a naval academy and an aviation school.

The October Revolution and the rise of social struggles.- During Menocal's government, the workers' organizational level increased and popular struggles intensified. Two ideological currents were predominant in the labor movement: anarcho-syndicalism and reformism. The socialist current, which developed certain strength during the first years of the century, weakened after 1908, and even the Socialist Party Carlos Baliño was a member of, not the leader, was dominated by the ideas of the Second International. Cuba also suffered, in a way, the setback the world revolutionary movement received with the defeat of the 1905-1907 Russian Revolution.

The Reformist influence came mainly from Spain, through Pablo Iglesias' followers, and from the United States, by means of relations some Cuban leaders already had with the American Federation of Labor. Among the latter was renowned novelist and railroad leader Carlos Loveira, who participated with Mexican revolutionary forces in Yucatan.

Several social reformers created the so-called Cuban Association for the Legal Protection of Labor; they were able to influence Menocal at the beginning of his mandate, and convinced him to sponsor a national labor congress, with the purpose of winning the workers' favor. The event, financed by the government, took place in August 1914 and was attended by 1400 delegates from around the country. But the fact that the workers' guild could choose their delegates freely gave the congress a different character from the one the sponsors wanted it to have. Participants at the event advocated for a series of demands that were deeply felt by workers themselves, but also by farmers, sugarcane tenant farmers, women and the people in general, as well as by the rest of the sectors interested in total independence and the nation's progress. Among the many demands were: 8-hour work shifts and the right to strike; laws providing protection for victims of occupational accidents, social security, protection for children and women; measures against the transfer of workers, against unemployment and the high cost of living, and in favor of cultural education for the workers. Participants demanded policies that would defend a national economy, laws prohibiting the sale to foreigners of land and real estate, the annulment -or a beneficial modification- of the Treaty of Reciprocity. Militarism and war were condemned, and several delegates defended the ideas of Karl Marx.

But these demands were not taken into account by the government. Very few laws benefiting the people were approved during these years, such as the Law on Occupational Accidents—which was never enacted—and those of School Retirement and Railroad Retirement.

On the other hand, there was a strong anarcho-syndicalism current in Cuba, whose main promoters were Spanish immigrants. They also organized an important congress in Cruces, in central Las Villas province, in 1912. Among Cuban workers who embraced these ideas were typographers' leader, Alfredo López, who played a key role in the workers' organization and struggles of those years.

During this stage, hundreds of guilds, trade unions, provincial and branch federations were established or grew in membership in Cuba. The most outstanding of them included the maritime and port sectors, railroad, tobacco, construction, sugar and graphic and manufacturing industries. In all these sectors—particularly sugar, maritime and railroad—the workers carried out important actions. The workers carried out partial or general strikes which were violently repressed by Menocal, although occasionally the workers obtained some of their demands.

Large protest demonstrations against the high cost of living were also organized, which were violently put down. As a result, several people were killed and more were wounded, arrested and deported.

Under the pretext of the world war, the government charged the workers with being "Germanophiles". The Cuban people, who did not lose their sense of humor even during the most difficult times, used to sing tunes like this:

> Cut the cane
> and move fast
> the foreman is coming
> whipping the lash.

> I won't cut the cane
> leave it for the wind
> let Lola cut it
> swinging her hips

Another sector that suffered the consequences US rule during those years was that of the farmers. The sugar industry expansion was carried out at the cost of the eviction of thousands of families from their land in all provinces, especially in Oriente. Generally, the evictions were accompanied by the destruction of crops, houses and other properties that belonged to the farmers. These evictions, along with the entire system of exploitation they were submitted to, brought on the creation of the first organizations within this sector, such as the Association of Farmers of the Island of Cuba, as well as struggles that often were joined by workers.

The triumph of the Great Revolution of Russia in 1917 gave a considerable impulse to workers' organizations and struggles as well as to other sectors. Guilds and workers' actions multiplied, the Socialist Group of Havana and the Socialist Party of Manzanillo gained new life. At the same time, Reformist parties that called themselves socialist, labor, radical, etc., proliferated. In these parties, honest leaders, full of hope to find legal ways, mixed with opportunistic elements at the service of employers and the government.

Two positions also manifested themselves among the followers of anarcho-syndicalism: those who supported unity of all workers and those who rejected any alliance with socialists and reformists and attacked the Soviet regime.

Most of labor organizations had united leaderships, formed by socialists, reformists, and anarcho-syndicalism followers, in which the latter predominated. In all of their activities, especially every May 1st, they expressed their support to the incipient Soviet state. They also formed the Pro-Russia Committees and carried out solidarity campaigns. An important workers congress held in April 1920 agreed to send fraternal greetings and show their solidarity to "the brothers that had established the Soviet Socialist Republic in Russia", which they considered to be a "guiding light and an inspiration for those ill-treated, eager for justice".

Also in 1920, a group of followers of anarcho-syndicalism proclaimed themselves "a section of the Third International" and organized a workers congress, whose main document was called the "Program and Basis of the Communist Republic of the Soviets of Cuba".

Government of Alfredo Zayas (1921-1923).- The presidential candidacy of lawyer Alfredo Zayas y Alfonso (1861-1934)—who took office on May 20, 1921, won the general elections of 1920.

Zayas, known for always changing his mind, had been an Autonomist, but later on became an independence fighter; he was Secretary of Justice under US domination, but was one of the eleven Cubans that voted against the Platt Amendment in 1901; he assumed nationalist and anti-intervention positions, but US intervention reached spectacular forms under his mandate. He had served as Havana's mayor and vice president of the Republic. Under his government, the nation was subjected to more and more political and administrative corruption.

Taking pride in pacification and reconciliation, he solved serious conflicts of his mandate without bloodshed, by means of gifts, jobs and bribes. He put up with criticisms and attacks, while becoming wealthy. He had to face the impetuous re-emergence of the patriotic, anti-imperialist and revolutionary movement, mainly impelled by workers, students and intellectuals.

Zayas came to power amid serious economic, financial and political crisis that had begun the previous year, and the process of an almost absolute domination of the Cuban economy by US capital was completed under his mandate. However, between 1923 and 1925, there was a distinct—although ephemeral—revitalization of the sugar industry which, along with the tolerance that characterized those years, gave some a positive image of the government.

But the facts contradicted that image. Zayas was a corrupt man. Since 1913, after he ended his term as vice president of the Republic, he appointed himself the island's official historian, with a 500 peso monthly salary. During his mandate, he "accidentally" won the national lottery's first prize twice, and was the only president who built a statue of himself while still alive. He gave the green light to gambling and other vices; he distributed "*botellas*" (people who appeared on payrolls and collected their money but never went to work), and promoted an amnesty law that benefited people convicted of committing fraud. At the end of his mandate, his personal fortune totaled several million pesos.

An example of the juicy businesses that Zayas promoted was the purchasing of Santa Clara's convent from a private enterprise. At the time of the "*vacas gordas*" (or fat cows), the Church had sold it for one million pesos to that enterprise, and then, amid the crisis of the moment, the State paid two million three thousand pesos for the convent.

The scandal fueled popular discontent and led to a movement that had great public resonance: the so-called "Protest of the 13". On the occasion of a tribute paid to Uruguayan writer Paulina Luissi at the Cuban Academy of Sciences, Erasmo Regueiferos was preparing to deliver a speech. Regueiferos was a member of Zayas' Cabinet and one of the people responsible of that shameful operation. Before the speaker began, several young intellectuals stood up, and one of them, lawyer and poet Ruben Martínez Villena, denounced the fraudulent purchase and accused Regueiferos before the auditorium. The group published a manifesto signed by the thirteen intellectuals after which the protest was named. Later, almost all of them would be known in the field of letters and politics, and would originate the so-called Grupo Minorista, which had great repercussion in the history of that time. Two of the protagonists, Martínez Villena and Juan Marinello, would occupy top positions in the workers and communist movement.

Even more shameful and irritating than administrative corruption was US intervention. During almost all of Zayas' mandate, the person who actually ruled was the representative of the United States, Enoch H. Crowder. This machiavellian character had served in Cuba during the two occupation governments; he returned to Havana in 1919 and drew up the Electoral Code, which was used to elect Zayas. He returned again in 1921, shortly before Zayas' took office.

Crowder arrived this time as a special envoy of US President Woodrow Wilson and was quite arrogant. It was announced that he was coming to study, on the ground, denunciations made by the liberals regarding recent fraudulent elections and to clean up public administration, sunk in corruption. In fact, the US government could not criticize Cuba, since it had introduced not only fraud in the first elections of the Republic, but also embezzlement, the "*botellas*" or salaries paid to people that were on pay rolls but never showed up for work), theft and speculation in the administration. US interference took place for other reasons: the mismanagement of Menocal's government and the 1920 crisis left public finances in such deplorable conditions that the Cuban government had not fulfilled its commitments regarding loans arranged with the United States, and the latter decided to safeguard the endangered interests of US banking, without having to resort to military intervention.

That's precisely why this procedure was called "preventive interference". That's how the US newspaper **The World** described it when it warned: "We hope that General Crowder's visit will awaken the Cuban people and make them realize that intervention is possible".

Crowder brought a team of US experts in finances and public administration, to whom Zayas' government opened the doors of the archives and other sources of information, no matter how secret they were. And the US proconsul instructed Zayas in all the measures he should take from then on. The most famous were the 13 secret memoranda—that everyone knew about—in which Crowder dictated his orders. If they were not carried out, Zayas' government would not receive the 50 million peso loan it had requested and would open itself to a military intervention.

Crowder ordered a 5 percent reduction of the national budget, and that the Cabinet be restructured, which was done. Crowder himself selected the new secretaries, men he relied on, constituting what was called the "Cabinet of Honesty". The memoranda dictated the way in which the loan could be used, it ordered the suspension of certain laws and the approval of others. In short, Zayas signed only what Crowder ordered. No other Cuban president had confronted such a degree of humiliation.

Once his mission ended, Crowder returned to the US. The loan was arranged, but under the most onerous conditions for Cuba. Then Zayas assumed some nationalist and anti-interventionist positions, and made statements against Crowder's conduct; but Crowder returned again, officially appointed by President Warren G. Harding as the US ambassador to Havana. And Zayas continued to bow down to the United States, so much so that he developed a whole campaign of "gratitude" to his government because at last that country's Congress recognized, in 1925—almost three decades after the end of the war against Spain—that the Isle of Pines and other adjoining lands were part of the national territory.

First National Students' Congress. Rise of the popular movement.- The third decade of this century began with a vigorous eruption of popular masses in the country's political and social life. The assault by US monopolies on the nation's riches, the insulting interference of the US government in the political life, the wearing down of the oligarchic governments and the financial and economic decline, provoked a feeling of frustration in important sectors of Cuban society, which looked for new ways to solve the country's problems. And it wasn't only the workers and the farmers who rebelled against the prevailing order. Student activists entered the arena with great strength, as well as groups of intellectuals and professionals, and even sectors of the small and medium bourgeoisie who were affected by the situation. They were favorably influenced by the victory of the Russian Revolution and by rising nationalist feelings in Mexico and other countries.

98

Students from the University of Havana—the country's only center for higher studies—and from high schools carried out a strong university reform struggle, led by the Reformist movement initiated in the Argentinean University of Cordoba in 1918 and inspired by the changes in the field of education made by the Russian and Mexican revolutions. Students demanded the autonomy of the university, the participation of the university in the government, the expulsion of corrupt professors, the up-dating of study programs and other important changes. They created the Federation of University Students in 1922 and in convened the National Students' Congress in 1923.

The Congress took place in October 1923. It gathered representatives from the University, secondary teaching institutes, private schools (including religious schools) and different youth associations and magazines. It met for 12 days, characterizing itself for its militancy, and adopted many and important agreements connected with teaching, the Cuban and Latin American students' movement, the struggle against colonialism and imperialism, the defense of Cuba's sovereignty and that of all the peoples, and the unity of students and workers.

The Congress assumed all the already mentioned demands regarding university reform; it elaborated an advanced Code of Students' Rights and Duties; it condemned corruption prevailing in schools and other public places, and agreed on creating the "José Martí" Popular University, in order to contribute to the cultural development of workers.

The Congress came out against imperialism in general, and particularly against US imperialism. It demanded the annulment of the Platt Amendment and of the Permanent Treaty, the ending of all US interference in Cuba's internal affairs and recognized Cuban sovereignty over the Isle of Pines. Likewise, Congress proclaimed itself against "universal capitalism", against the Monroe Doctrine, against the outrage suffered by colonial and dependent countries, against the existence of "tutors" in inter American relations, and advocated for the annulment of all treaties that were detrimental to the peoples' sovereignty. It condemned the isolation of Soviet Russia and called on the Cuban government to recognize it diplomatically.

The event dedicated several agreements to the establishment of fraternal ties between Latin American students, including the call for a student congress and the creation of a Latin American Federation of Students. It demanded the official celebration of all of the national holidays of Latin American countries in Cuban schools and the study of the history of the Americas.

In another example of its advanced positions, the Congress addressed fraternal greetings to the workers' organizations and agreed on carrying out joint actions with them in favor of student, class, and national demands.

A unique characteristic of this event, which showed the general discontent due to the situation prevailing in Cuba at the time, was the fact that despite the ideological heterogeneity of delegates and of the acute polemics that arose, all the agreements were decided upon unanimously or by a solid majority.

The soul of this Congress, and of all the students and the anti-imperialist movements of these years, was José Antonio Mella (1903-1929), a 20 year old athletic young man, with a vigorous and charismatic personality The son of a Dominican father and a North American mother, Mella rapidly became the most outstanding leader of Cuban youth. He founded, among other organizations, the José Martí Popular University, the Anti-Clerical League, the Anti-imperialist League, and the Cuban Communist Party, as well as the magazine **Juventud**. His brief life was entirely devoted to the cause of the Cuban and Latin American revolutions.

Zayas' government, pressured by the huge demonstrations, agreed to several demands in connection with university reform: he granted it autonomy, he recognized the participation of students in the ruling of the University and fired a group of corrupt professors. These measures only lasted until the end of Zayas' presidential term.

During this period, students carried out numerous protest actions, most of them in alliance with the workers. They prevented the attempt by some professors and politicians to appoint Enoch H. Crowder and Leonard Wood as Honoris Causa Rectors of the University; they rejected—through huge demonstrations—the visit to Cuba of the "Italia" boat, sent by Mussolini's dictatorship; and repudiated Zayas' flattery towards the US government when it recognized Cuba's sovereignty over the Isle of Pines.

The feminist movement was also formed at the beginning of this decade. In 1923, the first National Women's Congress was held, in which 31 women's organizations of the country were represented. They demanded the right to vote, equal rights with regard to men, material and moral protection of women at work, laws in defense of children, and other demands that were not as radical as those of the workers and students but constituted a step ahead on the road to Cuban women's struggles.

The Movement of Veterans and Patriots was among actions of a wider social basis during these years. Initiated by Independence War veterans in defense of their pensions, the movement expanded their demands and emphasized the ending of administrative corruption and in making public life more decent. Bourgeois politicians who only wanted to obtain personal profit joined the organization, which had clashes with honest young people with patriotic feelings, such as Ruben Martínez Villena and Juan Marinello. A little over a year after it began, following a failed insurrection attempt, the movement ended. Its strongest protagonists understood that no serious result could be expected under the leadership of bourgeois politicians.

Growth of the labor movement. Havana's Labor Federation (FOC) and the National Workers' Confederation of Cuba (CNOC).- This period had great importance in the ideological and organizational growth of the working class. Other organizations joined the ones created during the previous decade, most notable among them: Havana's Labor Federation (1921) and Cuba's Railroad Brotherhood (1924).

The first of them, led by anarcho-syndicalists and socialists, gave a considerable boost to the unity of the proletariat and their struggle for vindication as well as the eventual creation of an umbrella organization for trade unionists. The Federation, of a provincial character, promoted and supported numerous actions in sectors such as port, tobacco and cigarette making, typography, masonry, bakery, shoe repair, telegraph, taxi drivers, paper, cracker and candy industries. The most notable of these actions, led by the Trade Union of Manufacturing Industry, was the strike of the Polar brewery workers, which lasted for three years. During this strike, there were many clashes with the police, incarcerations and even death sentences which, in the end, were not carried out.

100

Founding of the Cuban Communist Party (1925). Mella and Baliño.

The Railroad Brotherhood, led by Reformist elements, came into being with strong militant actions. It opened with a 21—day strike against the English railroad monopoly, which relied on the solidarity of sugar workers in different areas of the country. The sugar workers were not nationally organized, but carried out vigorous strike actions that included dozens of sugar mills, refineries and sugar plantation railroads, with the mobilization of over 20,000 industrial and agricultural workers.

These actions were aimed at the recognition of trade unions by the enterprises and the government, the right to strike, improvements in salary and working conditions, the drawing-up of rotation lists at ports and even condemned the 50 million peso loan President Zayas was negotiating. Long-time working class leader Carlos Baliño said in the labor newspaper **Justicia**: "The Republic `with all and for the good of all' that Martí dreamt about it was nothing but a beautiful phrase. Today, following the fashion prevailing among the small and defenseless Spanish-American republics, it has become the Morgan and Company Republic".

The labor movement during this period crowned itself with two important events: the Cienfuegos Congress, in February 1925, and the most important of the ones held until that moment, that of Camagüey, in August of the same year. The latter, held after Zayas ended his presidential term, led to the first Cuban trade union confederation. 128 labor organizations from the country attended this congress, which was characterized by its eminently unified spirit and by the fact that all its agreements were based on the principles of working class struggles and on international solidarity among workers. The fraternal cooperation of the participating ideological currents was a practice of the event: anarcho-syndicalists, which were predominant; reformists and communists. One of its main weaknesses was the almost absolute absence of sugar workers, since they were not organized at a national level at the time; only a trade union from Puerto Padre, in Oriente province, represented this sector at the event.

The Congress made the working masses' main economic, political and social demands their own and expressed itself against all discrimination for reasons of race, nationality or any other type that could divide them; against wars and in solidarity with those that faced imperialism. It also advocated for the creation of a confederation of all workers of the Americas.

Nevertheless, the most important agreement was the creation of the first trade union confederation that comprised the entire country: The National Confederation of Cuban Workers (CNOC). The creation of the CNOC, along with the constitution of the Cuban Communist Party eight days later, were two of this period's top events.

Founding of the Cuban Communist Party.- Since 1922, Havana's Socialist Group had adopted the program and the tactics of struggle of the Third International and the following year it changed its name to Havana's Communist Group. Other similar communist organizations began to be created in several of the country's localities (Manzanillo, Media Luna, Guanabacoa, San Antonio de los Baños), as well as among Jewish people living in Cuba. Havana's Group published a newspaper, *Lucha de Clases,* and developed an intense political and ideological work in the labor and students' organizations. Among their most outstanding members was Carlos Baliño, a veteran independence fighter who founded the Cuban Revolutionary Party along with Martí in 1892; Julio Antonio Mella, a representative of the young, revolutionary generation; and José Miguel Pérez, a Spanish teacher and writer who enjoyed the esteem of progressive circles in Cuba, as well as several prestigious labor leaders.

The first congress of these groups was carried out, under semi-legal conditions, on August 16-17, 1925, after Zayas' presidential term. Delegates at the meeting were not even 20, representing some one hundred communists from the entire country. The first Marxist-Leninist party of the island was founded there, under the name of Cuban Communist Party.

Delegates were not prepared to put forward a proper Party Program; they were Marxists at heart, but without enough political and ideological preparation. They limited themselves to adopting a program of vindication for workers and farmers.

The Congress approved the structure of the Party and its Statutes; it agreed upon participating in the electoral campaigns as a way of publicizing their cause. This agreement was followed by a hot debate; it established the tactics to be followed regarding trade unions, the farmers and the women's movements; it outlined the task of creating an organization for young communists and decided to affiliate the Party to the Communist International. It elected a Central Committee of nine members, headed by José Miguel Pérez as General Secretary. It was also formed by Carlos Baliño, Julio Antonio Mella, a public employee, a journalist and four well-known and loved trade union leaders.

The preparation of the Congress and the event itself counted on the cooperation of a member of the Mexican Communist Party, Enrique Flores Magón, a representative of the Communist International.

Despite the low theoretical level of the founders and the small number of communist militants it represented, the founding of this party, as well as the creation of the first trade union confederation, marked a decisive step in the new historic stage that was about to begin.

CIVIC AND LYRICAL MESSAGE

To José Torres Vidaurre, Peruvian poet.

....

José: we're needing one old-time machete charge of those
whose warlike wing would gain valiant momentum,

when as in mad rush overwhelming hoofbeats
would bravely appear, kicking stars apart!

We're needing that charge to kill impostors,
to meet the commitment of the revolutions;

to vindicate our dead, victims of outrage,
to clean out the colonizer's tenacious crust;

103

so that with our reasons and prestige, one day
we can extirpate the appendix of our Constitution,

to not leave hunger, effort, wound and death
to useless and humiliating fate,

So that the Republic can sustain itself,
making José Martí's marble dream come true,

to keep our glorious homeland from spoiling hands,
to save the temple raised to Love and Faith,

to keep our children from begging on their knees for
the homeland which their parents fought for on their feet.

I swear for the blood of that much hurting,
to honor the salvation of this beloved land,

and in defiance of any unfair persecution,
I'll continue to offer caustic and whip.

Our sacred duty grows amidst increasing danger.
(infamy deserves but choleric words)

I pull at my soul as if it were my own sword,
and I kneel to swear before Mother America.

Rubén Martínez Villena, 1923.

104

XII

The Machado tyranny and the 1933 Revolution

General elections were held in November of 1924 where the Liberal Party candidate, general Gerardo Machado y Morales (1871-1939) was elected President. He was sworn in on May 20th, 1925.

Machado obtained his military ranks in the 1895 Independence war, even though, according to some researchers, he was then involved in shady business deals related to cattle rustling. He collaborated with the US occupation forces, was mayor of Santa Clara, ran and later owned a sugar mill with the support of US financial interests.

He had already shown his hatred for the people when he violently cracked down on the Independent Colored People's Movement and workers strikes, masterminding the murder of their principal leaders from his post as Interior Minister in the José Miguel Gómez administration. He had close ties to the Electric Bond and Share company which provided half a million pesos for his presidential campaign. He had a solid fortune. Imperialism and the country's oligarchy realized that he was the strong man capable of crushing the growing popular movement that sprang up during the Zayas government. Martínez Villena nick-named him "the donkey with claws" for his repressive brutality.

Despite that background, he obtained a large number of votes, due principally to two reasons: first, his opponent was Mario García Menocal, who had earned a sad reputation as President; and in addition, Machado presented a highly demagogic platform of promises based on the slogan "water, roads and schools", proclaiming as his objective the country's recovery. He called himself "Cuba's first worker". To challenge the Conservative Party's slogan "On horseback!", Machado raised the slogan "On foot!"

Submission to the United States and terror against the people.- Shortly before his inauguration, the new President felt he had to travel to the United States. There he met with bank, trade and industry representatives, politicians and military officers. He offered them absolute guarantees for their investments in Cuba, identified his personal class interests and those of his government as similar to those of the US, promised that there wouldn't be unrest during his administration because he had enough material support to repress the people and expressed his unlimited loyalty to the United States under any circumstances.

Back in Cuba he started his term in office beheading the country's popular movement and cracking down on all opposition. In August he ordered the murder of Armando Andre, conservative politician and Editor of **El Día** news daily. He expelled Mella from the University and took radical action against the student movement. Two weeks after the Communist Party was set up, Machado filed a suit against its leaders on charges of rebellion, exiled its Secretary General José Miguel Pérez, and detained the rest. He declared the Industrial Workers General Union illegal and ordered the murder of Enrique Varona, prestigious railroad worker leader from Camagüey. Police, the Army and the Rural Guard used terror to repress any popular movement.

105

On charges of terrorism and sedition, the administration began a process against Mella, who began a hunger strike on December 5th, 1925. Nineteen days after he started the strike, a powerful popular movement forced the administration to release the student leader, whose hunger strike had left him on the brink of death. After his release his life was in danger, and he was sent to Mexico, where he continued his revolutionary struggle.

Repression took the lives of many working class leaders, including Alfredo López, founding member and leader of the Havana Workers Federation and of the recently set up National Confederation of Cuban Workers. In mid-1926 most of the union's leaders had been physically eliminated. One of the most scandalous crimes of the times was the hanging of more than 40 *campesinos* of Spanish origin residing in Ciego de Avila, in Camagüey province, in retaliation for the kidnapping of a rich landowner in the area.

Public works plan and tariff reform.- Beside establishing a reign of terror in the country, Machado also took some of the measures he had promised in his campaign platform. Two months after being sworn in, Machado began an ambitious public works plan which helped alleviate unemployment and gave him an image of a good president, though also allowing him to considerably increase his personal fortune and those of his relatives and friends. The most important of those public works was the Central Highway, which stretched from Pinar del Río to Santiago de Cuba along 1142 kilometers. It was a useful and necessary road, but it also helped increase the private fortunes of many people. To cite one example: almost 100 thousand pesos were paid for each kilometer of the road when at that time the normal cost for that type of work was 9400.

Another important public work was the Capitol or Palace of Congress, which included a large park named *Parque de la Fraternidad* or Fraternity Park. The luxurious building was an imitation of Washington's Capitol and cost 22 million pesos. The main criticism Machado received for building the capitol was that he had spent a very large amount of money at a time when the island was going through a severe economic crisis.

The plan also included dredging ports and docks, repairing many roads in very bad shape, paving streets, constructing water pipelines and sewage systems and other workers which included schools, hospitals, the University of Havana's Stairs and the University Stadium.

Seventy five percent of the plan was contracted with the US company Warren Brothers and Company and the rest with the *Compañía Cubana de Contratistas* (Cuban Contractors Company) controlled by the President and his Public Works Minister, Carlos Miguel de Céspedes. Financing was contracted with the Chase National Bank of New York, despite the fact that Machado promised to carry out his projects without foreign loans.

In order to pay the debt the government taxed land transportation, gas, oil and other fuels, sales and income, and the money that was taken out of the country among other tax-prone activities. Cuba underwent a relative economic recovery, but at a high cost in terms of fraud, demagogy and indebtedness.

Machado: public works and people's blood

Machado also promised to protect the island's industry and diversify the country's economy. With that end, in October, 1926 he implemented a tariff reform on an experimental basis which increased tariffs on imported food items by 15 percent and on industrial goods by up to 25 percent. With that measure the government reduced imports from Europe and Latin America and some from the United States. Several items were not included, however, because the United States could consider them a violation of the Trade Reciprocity Treaty.

The reform protected certain economic areas and boosted the production of eggs, meat, butter, cheese, condensed milk, rice, coffee, corn, soap, cement, paint, shoes and other goods. National capital was encouraged and even Machado did some business in those areas. Foreign business executives also invested in some of the above-mentioned sectors; but with the predominance of big national and foreign capital, many small producers were ruined.

The tariff reform was a positive but short-lived step, and most importantly it didn't change the country's status as producer and exporter of a single product or its economic dependence. The reform promoters themselves admitted that "the spirit of the new tariffs" was "extremely moderate". Large US interests were not affected.

Machado decides to extend his term in office.- In 1926 and 1927 Machado still had a certain social support based on the measures he had taken and the weakness of the popular movement, which hadn't been able to recover after the harsh blows it had received. But beginning in 1927, several factors helped weaken that meager social base: the sugar restriction policy, the decrease in the price of sugar, an exaggerated tax increase, a certain recovery of the workers and student movement and the dictator's decision to prolong his term in office.

The ruling political parties used bribery and intimidation to forge a compromise with the opposition to "cooperate" with Machado's presidential reelection plan. That compromise was called the "cooperative spirit". A small fraction of the Liberal Party refused to support the plan and organized a new opposition party named Nationalist Union, headed by Army General Manuel Piedra Martell, of the Independence War.

Machado's "*guatacas*" or lackeys began a campaign to praise his political performance. They called him "The Illustrious", "The Caesar of the Americas", "The New Messiah", "The Peerless Citizen", "the Redeemer of the Republic". Distinguished titles were also conferred upon him including the Honorary Doctors Degrees at the University of Havana. The country's municipalities declared him "adopted child" and even a high ranking Catholic church leader publicly said: "God in Heaven and Machado on Earth".

Between march and June of 1927, the country's congress, mostly controlled by the so-called "collaborationists", passed the law that extended Machado's term until 1931. Subsequently elections were called to set up a Constituent Assembly without the participation of the political parties that opposed Machado's reelection. Only ten percent of eligible voters went to the polls. This assembly, in open violation of the 1901 Constitution and placing itself above congress, agreed to prolong Machado's term until 1935, and to extend those of representatives, senators and others for another two years.

As was to be expected, popular protest against Machado's reelection was immediate. A widespread campaign of denunciation and condemnation got underway.

People were called to meetings, demonstrations and other popular actions, in which the Nationalist Union Party and other bourgeois groups played a prominent role. Leading political leaders also played a major role, including Carlos Mendieta, Juan Gualberto Gómez, Cosme de la Torriente and José Martí Jr., as well as prestigious intellectuals like Enrique José Varona, Ruben Martínez Villena, Juan Marinello, Alejo Carpentier, Emilio Roig de Leuschsenrig and others, the Communist Party, unions and university students, who were also very active.

The Student Directorate of 1927 was set up at the University, challenging a University Council that was submissive to the regime. It led the struggle against Machado's reelection. Its most outstanding leaders included Antonio Guiteras, Gabriel Barceló, José Elías Borges,

Eduardo R. Chibás and others who would later play an important role in our people's struggles. As a result, a first group of 21 students were temporarily and definitively expelled from the university as well as others who were ousted later.

Machado was determined to impose his reelection against all odds, and so he did. This imposition, however, was an important factor in the steadfast growth of the people's opposition.

The 6th Pan-American Conference, new crimes, Julio Antonio Mella.- In January, 1928, amid Machado's reelection campaign, Havana was the venue of the 6th Pan-American Conference with the attendance of the President of the United States, Calvin Coolidge. Preparations for this event led the regime to step up terror. Among the victims were Claudio Bouzon and Noske Yalob, two communists who were caught when distributing a manifesto against the conference and in solidarity with Nicaraguan rebel leader Augusto César Sandino. They were taken to La Cabana fortress, murdered and thrown to the sharks.

The murder of outstanding communist leader, Julio Antonio Mella a year later shook Cuba and the rest of Latin America. Exiled in Mexico since 1926, Mella was closely linked to that country's revolutionary movement. He held leading posts and was very active in numerous Mexican popular organizations: The Anti-imperialist League of the Americas, the United Workers Confederation, the National Campesino League, the Communist Party (he was a member of its Central Committee), the League for the Defense of Persecuted Fighters, the Hands Off Nicaragua Committee, the New Cuban Revolutionary Immigrant Association and others. He was the soul of several newspapers like **El Libertador**, **Tren Blindado**, **¡Cuba Libre!** and **El Machete.**

Mella remained in close contact with the Cuban Communist Party, and beginning in 1928 began negotiations with groups of the island's opposition to organize an armed insurrection against Machado's dictatorship. In order to stop Mella's efforts, as well as his powerful anti-imperialist campaign, Machado, through the Cuban embassy in that country, and with the complicity of US circles and US agents in the Mexican capital, decided to eliminate the 26 year old courageous fighter and murdered him on the streets of that city on January 10th, 1929. A gigantic wave of protests swept across Mexico and other Latin American countries, further igniting the struggle against dictatorships and imperialism. Mella's murderers wanted to eliminate him forever, but instead they made him immortal.

Two months later outstanding Venezuelan revolutionary leader, Francisco Laguado Jaime was detained and murdered in Cuba. He cooperated with **Venezuela Libre**, which was printed in Havana and was an active fighter against the Juan Vicente Gómez dictatorship. Both dictators, Machado and Gómez, joined to execute the crime.

The 1929 to 1933 Economic Crisis. The Labor Movement.- It was precisely in 1929 when the big depression began. Cuba was seriously affected by this event, aggravated by Machado's disastrous sugar policy of limiting sugar production while most sugar producing countries increased theirs. In 1929 the island had manufactured more than 5 300 000 tons of sugar, but later the number of tons began to decline remarkably to a little more than 2 340 000 in 1933. On the other hand, sugar prices, which had already gone down to 1.72 cents a pound in 1929, plunged to 0.97 cents in 1933. And to make things worse, in 1930 the US government raised tariffs on Cuban sugar to 2 cents a pound, inflicting a shattering blow on the Cuban economy's principal economic area. The economic crunch also affected tobacco and other products to such an extent that Cuban exports went down by 66 percent.

As a result of this crisis, many industries closed and others reduced production, sparking an alarming rise in unemployment, which in 1933 reached more than one million people (41 percent of the island's population above 13 years of age). Salaries plunged by fifty percent or more. The payment of teachers' and public employees' wages was delayed for months and the poverty of all working sectors worsened. Many shanty towns sprang up in Havana and other cities during those years.

In the face of this situation the Cuban labor movement stepped up its struggle. The National Confederation of Cuban Workers, the CNOC, led by the communists with the assistance of Rubén Martínez Villena, had gradually recovered from the blows received by the dictatorship, and began organizing small strikes that increased in number and effectiveness.

In 1928 the Young Communist League was set up, not only to group the country's most radical youth and lead them in the struggle against the dictatorship, but also to decisively help organize workers, particularly those of the sugar industry. The government tolerated certain labor actions that weren't considered dangerous. However, in 1929 the CNOC decided to support an agreement of the Latin American Workers Confederation—recently set up in a continental congress in Uruguay— which set march 20th, 1930 as the Day of the Struggle for the demands of the unemployed in Latin America. In addition, it designed a plan which included hunger strikes, protest marches and other labor actions. Then Machado decided to declare illegal the CNOC, the Havana Workers Federation and other workers organizations.

The labor movement's answer was to call for a 24 hour general strike on march 20th, 1930 based on a series of economic, social and political demands. That action was extremely successful since more than 200 thousand workers participated nationwide. Its main coordinator and leader, Ruben Martínez Villena was sentenced to death and forced to leave Cuba for the United States. From there he traveled to the Soviet Union, where he was hospitalized in a sanatorium to receive treatment for advanced TB.

110

The general strike reinforced the Cuban working class movement, and along with the militant May Day demonstrations of that same year, brutally repressed by the dictatorship, changed the panorama of the struggle against Machado.

Another labor organization—the International Workers Defense—was set up during those months. This new group was affiliated with the International Red Relief Organization. For years this new group played an active role in helping political prisoners, in denouncing repression, in showing its solidarity with fighters against fascism, imperialism and reactionary forces in Cuba and around the world.

The student movement and other sectors. The University Student Directorate (DEU) and the Student Left Wing Organization (AIE). - The struggle against the dictatorship grew considerably from 1930 on, with the participation of *campesinos*, the radical petite bourgeoisie and some sectors of the island's national bourgeoisie. Along with strikes, demonstrations and other actions this period also saw the beginning of armed rebellion. In the vanguard of this fighting spirit were the most advanced sectors of the island's students and intellectuals. Following several actions against Machado's reelection in 1927 and the fierce repression unleashed by the regime, the students of schools taken over by the army were forced into silence. But the workers actions of march and may, 1930 gave a boost to the student movement, which held its first big demonstration on September 30th, 1930. More than one hundred university students joined by a group of workers began a protest march to the Presidential Palace to demand the dictator's resignation, chanting slogans like Down with the Dictatorship!, Death to Machado!, Down with Imperialism! They were intercepted and clashed with police leaving student, Rafael Trejo killed, several people injured and many arrested.

Trejo was a member of the University Student Directorate (DEU) and the 27th of November Committee. He was a 19 year old Law student with no political affiliation but with noble feelings and a rebel spirit, who used to repeat the phrase by Juan Montalvo: "Miserable is the nation whose youth bow to tyranny, where students don't make the world tremble".

The DEU, which had already been organized months before, was set up a few days before September 30th. It was a heterogeneous organization with a majority center-right wing trend and another left anti-imperialist and socialist wing. DEU's positions mainly coincided with those of the Nationalist Union, but it upheld a more advanced political platform and its methods were more radical. It published its newspaper **Alma Mater**, and was one of the most active organizations in the struggle against Machado.

Other organizations were set up during those days, including the University Women Student Directorate and other Directorates in several high schools and in Havana's School for Teachers. The student movement grew fast in the rest of the island's provinces.

But left wing students didn't agree with the DEU's limited Reformist program or with its positions, and three months after its establishment leftist students split from the University Student Directorate and set up a new organization—the Left Wing Student Organization (AIE) with its own newspaper, **Línea**.

The most advanced women's struggle also became more radical during those days. There were splits from the Cuban Feminine Club created in 1918, and from the National Feminist Alliance (1928) whose demands were limited to achieving women's political and legal equality. The Women's Labor Union was established in May, 1930 with the objective of defending working women and openly joining the struggle against the Machado dictatorship.

At the same time, left wing lawyers denounced the Havana based pro-Machado Lawyers Association, established the Radical Lawyers Directorate and joined the popular movement. Other intellectuals and professionals also joined the struggle.

The bourgeois rebellion and terrorism. Popular actions.- Popular rebellion and government repression gained momentum in Havana, Santiago de Cuba, Matanzas, Pinar del Río and other cities. Manifestos, demonstrations, strikes, school occupations, terrorist attacks and other actions occurred daily. Machado declared a state of war throughout the island in November, 1930. As the regime's repressive forces weren't sufficient, he created the Patriotic League, which the people called "*porra*": a paramilitary gang made up mainly of criminals, pimps, professional killers and other elements of the underworld, led by government agents and paid by authorities. Their role consisted of putting down any popular demonstration. The University was closed on December 15th and didn't reopen its doors during the duration of the Machado regime. The same measure was taken in high schools and other education centers.

In the on-going wave of repression, hundreds of opponents from all organizations and political affiliations were attacked, tortured and murdered: students, workers, *campesinos*, journalists, political leaders and even representatives and senators of bourgeois political parties, as well as military and police officers suspected of opposing the regime. Massacres also occurred, including the hanging of 44 people in a single night by Santiago de Cuba's military chief, Commander Arsenio Ortíz, known as "the Jackal of Oriente".

Brutal repression also forced the bourgeois opposition, including its ultra right wing sectors, to adopt more radical strategies. They created a so called "Revolutionary Committee" in New York and began an armed uprising in many parts of the country on August 8th, 1931. The rebellion was joined by all bourgeois parties that opposed Machado ("the Nationalists", followers of Menocal and Miguel Mariano Gómez), the DEU, Independence Army veterans (general Francisco Peraza and Captain Arturo del Pino), and some men inspired by patriotic feelings of freedom and justice like Antonio Guiteras.

A group from the capital led by Captain Del Pino was betrayed and trapped, and despite heroic resistance down to the last bullet, was annihilated. One hundred men headed by General Peraza took up arms in Pinar del Río, but were defeated by a superior army, arrested and murdered. The same occurred with other uprisings in which the massive murder of prisoners was very common. Meanwhile, bourgeois leaders Menocal and Mendieta were detained in Río Verde, Pinar del Río, without shooting a single shot and receiving a different treatment. The same occurred with other bourgeois chiefs in several regions of the country.

A group led by Antonio Guiteras took up arms west of Santiago de Cuba on August 11th, but was finally captured. An expedition led by former army lieutenant

Emilio Laurent and journalist Sergio Carbo landed in Gibara (northern coast of Oriente) on the 17th. They took over the city but were captured three days later.

The rebellion was crushed in a mather of days. The only group that survived was headed by campesino Juan Blas Hernández, who fought for two years in a vast area of Camagüey province without being caught. The insurrection's failure took a toll of dozens of people killed, hundreds jailed and a further rise in the regime's repression. Prisoners were granted amnesty in late 1931.

As a result of this failure, terrorism gained momentum. Under the leadership of young lawyer and economist Joaquín Martínez Sáenz, a group of ultra conservative elements of the country's petite bourgeoisie, which supported indiscriminate terror, decided to create a new secret organization of a cellular nature, the ABC. Some of its leaders sympathized with Fascist ideology and methods (racism, anti-communism, "green shirts", march on Havana) and upheld the need to set up a corporate system like that of Mussolini.

The ABC, however, initially garnered the support of many honest people tired of the traditional political parties and excited by the new organization's demagogic language and allegedly radical methods. The ABC called itself "the Hope of Cuba" and its slogans were very luring: "New men, new ideas and procedures, re-conquest of land, political freedom and social justice". It had strong influence in the University Student Directorate.

Other secret organizations which opposed Machado were set up during those days, including other right wing groups like the Revolutionary Radical Cellular Organization (OCRR), the Opposition Women Organization, and left wing groups like the Pro-Law and Justice Organization and the Revolutionary Union (UR).

The latter was founded by Antonio Guiteras in late 1932 to defend anti-imperialist and national liberation ideals. Guiteras began preparing a rebel movement for which he created action groups in Santiago de Cuba, San Luis, El Caney, Holguín, Bayamo, Manzanillo, Victoria de las Tunas and other regions. One of its first actions was the attack on Santiago de Cuba's Court of Justice, where they seized a large number of weapons. In April of 1933 they took over the town of San Luis, but were forced to withdraw later. During these actions several people were killed. The Revolutionary Union remained active until Machado was overthrown.

Organization and struggle of sugar workers.- There was also a boom in the country's labor movement A Collective Workers Joint Committee was established to group unions of all tendencies, including those which were not associated with the CNOC, in order to guide the growing struggles of the island's workers. An important conference attended by delegates from all over the country managed to organize the island's sugar workers in December, 1932. Then the National Union of Sugar Industry Workers was created, unleashing important mobilizations joined by agricultural and industrial workers, tenant farmers and *campesinos* in general. Workers set up Support Committees to help strikers and their families. They also created armed self-defense groups to fight back the attacks of the regime's repressive corps and the sugar mill guards.

The Campesino League appeared on the scene joining workers in sugar mill strikes and protest marches to support unemployed workers. Tens of thousands of sugar workers went on strike between the 1932 to 1933 sugar harvest and for the first time took over a sugar mill—the **Nazabal**—in Las Villas province, obtaining partial results. Railroad, port, tobacco, textile and transportation workers, among others, also staged important labor mobilizations. The rise in the country's popular movement was already heralding the end of the Machado dictatorship.

A new US Pro-Consul: Benjamin Sumner Welles. The mediation.- A Cuban Opposition Junta, also known as the Revolutionary Junta, was created in Miami in late march, 1933. The Junta was made up of old politicians of the country's oligarchy which opposed Machado, as well as the University Student Directorate, the ABC and university professors. The organization threatened Machado with a rebellion, but in fact it wanted the US government's mediation to solve "Cuba's political, social and economic problems".

As soon as US authorities learned about this movement, Washington began its interventionist maneuvers. The US ambassador to Havana, Harry F. Guggenheim, was replaced by Benjamin Sumner Welles, who arrived in Cuba on May 7th, 1933. According to then-US Secretary of State, Cordell Hull, Welles' mission was to negotiate a well-defined, detailed and compulsory agreement between Machado and the opposition that would lead to a political truce until elections were held.

Welles' mission was not to overthrow Machado, but to achieve a "legal" and "peaceful" transition in order to prevent a popular rebellion. In fact, his plan perfectly dovetailed with the dictator's: elections on November 1st, 1934 so that the new president would be sworn in 1935. That was what Machado had intended to do back in 1928: to hold the presidential seat until 1935.

After he met that objective, Welles planned to discuss a series of economic and commercial measures that would alleviate the country's economic crisis in favor of the bourgeoisie, landowners and the US monopolies based in Cuba.

Welles' mediation, as Crowder's mission 12 years before, was a sort of "preventive intervention", in order to prevent a direct military occupation in case of a popular revolution. Roosevelt advocated the "Good Neighbor" policy based on pressures and maneuvers as opposed to the "Big Stick" policy based on an open use of force. In Latin America, and particularly in the Caribbean, rejection of US military deployment was very strong, as seen in the 1928 Pan-American Conference. Powerful nationalist currents sprang up on the continent like that headed by Lázaro Cárdenas in Mexico; social forces polarized and new revolutionary winds blew over Latin America. In the face of this reality Roosevelt tried to solve the situation in an intelligent way, improving the US imperialism's image. He would only force when extremely necessary.

The mediation took place between May and August. Welles held separate and joint talks with the leaders of the Nationalist Union, with university professors, supporters of former Havana Mayor Miguel Mariano Gómez, leaders of the ABC, the OCRR and the DEU. In the meantime, he met with Machado and informed his government constantly and in detail. He easily manipulated Cosme de la Torriente, a former Independence Army Colonel at the service of the bourgeoisie and imperialism, who acted as his informer and messenger, and to whom he dictated what he had to write in the press. He also previously revised the statements that the dictator would

114

make, though Machado played both sides of the coin. While appearing submissive, he maneuvered on Welles' back. In addition, though he had requested the mediation, Menocal became angry when Welles showed his preference for Mendieta.

The Communist Party, CNOC, AIE, Revolutionary Union, Radical ABC and other left wing organizations condemned the mediation. The DEU, which was closely linked to the ABC, hesitated during the first weeks, but later came out against it under pressure from exiled members, the Havana Institute's Directorate and students in general. All these organizations were behind the popular movement, and there would be no solution without taking them into account.

The opposition that favored the US government's mediation made a long list of demands before the government, including the renewal of constitutional guarantees, an end to press censorship, the release of all prisoners not sentenced by criminal courts, a law to reorganize political parties and create new ones, the President's resignation and his replacement by an "honorable" and "impartial" Secretary of State, dissolution of congress and a constitutional reform.

Machado formally adopted some of those measures. On July 26th he enacted an amnesty law which not only benefited political prisoners but also criminals, torturers and embezzlers. Constitutional guarantees were reestablished, but the "*porra*" and the regime's repressive forces continued terrorizing the people.

General Strike and Machado's Overthrow .- Nevertheless, these measures didn't deceive the people and the protest movement couldn't be stopped, though Welles and his collaborators were incapable of understanding this reality. One day after the amnesty law was signed, Havana's public transportation workers went on strike with economic and social demands that included the reinstatement of unemployed workers, recognition of the sector's unions and salary hikes. The Communist Party and CNOC were leading the stoppage. The CNOC called for solidarity and other sectors joined the strike, including public transportation employees in various provinces, and later workers from other economic areas. Hundreds of assemblies, demonstrations and other actions took place as demands increased: activists were now demanding the legalization of unions, the Communist Party, the CNOC and other revolutionary organizations; they were demanding full democratic liberties, condemned the US mediation and began shouting "Down with US imperialism", and "Long live the agrarian and anti-imperialist revolution!

On August 1st, public transportation was paralyzed across the island; all economic activities ground to a halt in Santa Clara; tobacco workers in Pinar del Río joined the strike; young communists Marcio Manduley and America Lavadi were murdered during demonstrations; rallies and marches of workers and *campesinos* were held; thousands of sugar farmers joined the labor actions and some sugar mills were taken over by workers. The Mediation Committee called on the people to suspend all public rallies, but the movement was unstoppable. Journalists, port workers, doctors and others joined the stoppage. On August 5th the country was completely paralyzed. ABC suggested that Machado be replaced by a Secretary of State chosen by the bourgeois opposition. Welles was alarmed and wanted to get rid of the President before the people found their own solution, but Machado refused to resign.

On August 7th the rumor spread that the dictator had resigned. Hundreds of thousands of people and vehicles took to the streets of the capital and marched toward the Presidential Palace and the Capitol. The army and police received the order to machine-gun the demonstrators, an act of cruelty which left dozens of people dead and hundreds wounded. But the massacre only fueled the fire of the people's anger instead of frightening them. Machado understood that he had lost the battle and, maneuvering to remain in power, he agreed to grant most of the CNOC's economic, social and political demands. The CNOC and the Communist Party called Machado's proposal a great victory and subjected it to grass roots and workers assemblies. But the people had already become more radical, rejecting the dictator's proposal: their principal demand now was Machado's resignation. The strike continued under the leadership of the Communist Party and the CNOC, which made the workers' decision their banner. After the dictator's plan was rejected and without hopes for reconciliation, Welles requested the deployment of US battle ships and urged the Cuban military to oust the dictator. On August 12th Machado presented his resignation and fled the country. The general strike's victory translated into the failure of the US mediation. From that point on, everything depended on the popular movement's ability to consolidate the triumph and establish a revolutionary government.

President Céspedes. The reaction of workers and students.-All efforts by Army chief, General Alberto Herrero to take the presidential seat were futile. During the evening of August 12, congress agreed to name an insignificant figure, Carlos Manuel de Céspedes as President, with US approval. Céspedes formed his cabinet with opposition members who favored the mediation and other figures at the service of the US government. This team wanted to maintain the status quo and gave protection of Machado's supporters as they fled the country.

But neither Céspedes, nor the political parties or Welles himself, understood the magnitude of the popular movement boosted primarily by workers and students.

The Communist Party and other Communist-leaning organizations like the National Confederation of Cuban Workers, the CNOC, tried to give the Revolution an agrarian and anti-imperialist nature. More than 200 thousand sugar workers went on strike in August and September. Workers took over many mills, occupied rail roads, extended their control over large agricultural areas and set up armed self-defense groups, generally with the support of *campesinos*. In several places *campesinos* took over large landed estates. The disorganized repressive apparatus was unable to exert any authority.

Taking into consideration the country's revolutionary situation, the Communist Party called on workers, *campesinos* and soldiers to establish "soviets", or popular councils, wherever possible to act as provisional governments elected by the people to deal with solutions to the main problems of rural and urban industrial and agricultural workers, as well as those of the general population.

Starting in August, 1933, workers responded to the Communist Party call with the occupation of some 36 sugar mills and the establishment of "soviets" in many of them, including Mabay, Tacajo and Santa Lucía in Oriente; Jaronu, Senado and Lugareño in Camagüey; Nazabal, Hormiguero and Portugalete in Las Villas. Some of those "soviets" stopped operating when workers reached satisfactory agreements with the companies; others were crushed by the army months after Céspedes was overthrown.

116

But the truth is that during the weeks that followed that August 12th, the government was incapable of facing the people. Thanks to the people's action, and without Céspedes being able to prevent it, jails were filled with supporters of Machado, the regime's henchmen were executed on the streets, the properties of the dictator's officials were attacked, mayors and aldermen dismissed. An amnesty law released opposition members behind bars, and exiles of all parties, groups and tendencies returned to Cuba, something which creased the people's action.

There was a deep crisis in the army, which was now incapable of repressing the impassioned masses. Following Welles' request, two US battle ships moored in Havana Bay in a threatening attitude.

The people demanded the replacement of the Céspedes administration by one sympathetic with the popular revolution's aspirations. The University Student Directorate (DEU) became more radical, broke its ties with the ABC and called for a popular rebellion to wipe out all vestiges of the Machado dictatorship and establish a provisional revolutionary government designated by the students. The DEU published a Program that included numerous political, economic, social and educational reforms with a democratic and national liberation nature which the provisional government should meet until clean and fair elections were held. The DEU then became the coordinator of the most radical middle-class organizations. Some young army officers, who had created the so called Renovation Group, also joined the DEU and accepted its Program.

The Sergeants Revolution. The Pentarchy .- The insubordination against the government had another very important manifestation: the discontent of soldiers, corporals and sergeants over the mismanagement of funds earmarked for food, clothes and other logistics needed by the troops; over rumors of a decrease in salaries and of dismissals, and the ill-treatment they received.

This discontent is led by Major Sergeants Pablo Rodríguez, who led the Non-Commissioned Officers Club. He was initially supported by some army members including Sergeant Stenographer Fulgencio Batista, who set up the Revolutionary Military Union, better known as the Board of Eight due to its original membership.

The military conspiracy gained momentum very quickly, and in the morning of September 4th, 1933 the sergeants' movement staged a coup: the Army chiefs and officers were removed from office and the sergeants took over in what has been called "The Sergeants' Revolution". Through very skillful maneuvers, Batista assumed the movement's leadership, leaving leader Pablo Rodríguez as head of Columbia's military headquarters. Shortly after, Batista was promoted to colonel and officially named head of the Army's Chief of Staff.

The DEU arrived in Columbia's military headquarters, along with other left wing organizations, to take control of the situation. The Communist Party (PC), the National Confederation of Cuban Workers, the CNOC, the Anti-imperialist League and the Student Left Wing Organization, which had played the most outstanding role in Machado's overthrow, supported the coup and also arrived in Columbia; but their participation was not welcomed. The DEU and the coup leaders established the so called Cuban Revolutionary Group, which assumed control. President Céspedes was dismissed and at DEU's request, the Group named a five member collegiate government that included university professors Ramón Grau San Martí and Guillermo Portela; Sergio Carbo, a journalist with left wing demagogic positions; José Miguel Irisarri, anti-imperialist lawyer and active opponent of the Machado dictatorship; and insignificant banker and business executive Porfirio Franca. Welles was alarmed by the sergeants' revolution and asked his government to send war ships. On September 7th Cuba was surrounded by 30 US battle ships, and the Guantánamo Naval Base was reinforced. Batista had already contacted Welles and taken steps to become Washington's strong man in Cuba. The island's oligarchic sectors had asked for the US intervention.

The Provisional Government. The work of Grau and Guiteras.- The Pentarchy lasted only one week. Due to its contradictions it was dissolved by the DEU and designated Ramón Grau San Martín as President, who took office on September 10th.

The Grau administration was very heterogeneous. Three defined tendencies made up his government since the beginning: a majority of nationalist and Reformist trend headed by Grau himself, another pro-imperialist and reactionary current led by Army Chief, Colonel Batista, and an extreme left wing, whose main representative was Antonio Guiteras. As a result, there were serious contradictions, which confused popular forces.

Thanks to the government's most radical wing, and with Grau's approval, the administration adopted a large number of resolutions of a popular, revolutionary and national liberation nature. In order to overcome the economic crisis, it made decisions concerning the 1934 sugar harvest which benefited Cuban owners and tenant farmers (sugar growers), it dismissed American Thomas L. Chadbourne as President of the National Sugar Exporting Corporation, temporarily called off payments of the debt that Machado had contracted with the Chase National Bank of New York and took certain measures to protect agricultural production. In response to repeated popular demands, the government ordered a significant reduction in electricity rates and took steps that favored that sector's workers. It even intervened the US company that controlled gas and electricity services on the island, and also limited usury, temporarily suspended evictions and canceled 50 percent of taxes that had not been paid in due time.

The measures taken in favor of the island's workers had a great impact, including the establishment of an eight hour working day and the prohibition to pay salaries with vouchers or chips, the establishment of a one pesos minimum wage for industrial workers and 0.80 cents for agricultural workers; a ban on hiring people under 18 years of age for evening activities and children under 14 as apprentices, the creation of the Labor Ministry and the establishment of the management's responsibility for on-the-job accidents. Two of those very important social measures sparked antagonistic positions: the compulsory unionization of workers in defiance of employers, and the so called "labor nationalization law", which established the obligation that not less than 50 percent of the workers and employees hired at any work center had to be native Cubans.

In order to meet the demands of students, the government recognized University autonomy, devoted 2 percent of the national budget to that center of higher education, granted one thousand scholarships for poor students and began a purge of university professors.

The government took radical and courageous decisions concerning political and legal problems: 517 army officers were expelled and a Marine corps grouping revolutionaries and poor people was created; the infamous Secret Police Corps was eliminated; the amnesty law that Céspedes granted to the supporters of Machado who had committed crimes was annulled and a Court of Sanctions was set up to try them. The government disbanded the island's traditional political parties, called for a Constituent Assembly and designated de facto mayors and governors throughout the country.

The government's anti-imperialist nature was shown in many of the measures approved, as well as in the position it assumed at the 7th American International Conference held in Montevideo, Uruguay in December, 1933. There the Cuban delegation, headed by revolutionary intellectual and Labor Minister, Dr. Angel Alberto Giraudy, came out against US interference in Latin American affairs, saying that "Cuba was born with a congenital vice of intervention". He also denounced the Platt Amendment and the Permanent Treaty as steps taken against the Cuban people's will when the country "was occupied by US bayonets". Grau didn't abide by the 1901 Constitution and he had been sworn in before the people. In addition, he ignored the Platt Amendment.

Counterrevolutionary subversion. Batista's terror.- The measures taken by the Grau government increased the wrath of the bourgeoisie, of the officers who supported Machado and had been displaced from their positions, and of reactionary organizations like the ABC, Radical ABC, and DEU's right wing. They also sparked serious criticism in US government circles. Following Welles' bellicose instructions, a large number of former Machado army officers and ABC members gathered at the National Hotel located near Havana's sea side wall. On October 2nd, Guiteras ordered an attack and forced them out of the area. Batista, who had hesitated before the attack, gave a demonstration of his repulsive sentiments. Once the counterrevolutionaries had surrendered, Batista ordered his troops to summarily execute a group of the rebel officers.

The following month, on November 8th, there was another uprising that included the occupation of police stations. Also this time Guiteras led the defense of the revolutionary movement and crushed the rebellion in a few hours.

Nevertheless, while on the one hand radical measures were taken and acts of heroic revolutionary resistance reported, on the other the government's right wing and its main representative Batista terrorized workers and the masses. Grau did not take a consistent stance: he generally supported Guiteras' radical positions, but on other occasions he passively accepted Batista's cruelty. In order to crush the country's powerful strike movement, in October and November the army was launched against workers in several actions, trampling on and murdering them as in Machado's worst times. The massacre of the Jaronu Sugar Mill alone left ten people dead and sixteen wounded.

But repression not only affected striking workers. One of the worst examples of repression was the massacre against the peaceful popular demonstration organized to bury Julio Antonio Mella's ashes, on September 29th, 1933. A few days before the event, a commission headed by Juan Marinello had transferred Mella's remains from Mexico to Havana. In the Anti-imperialist League's headquarters people served as guards of honor to pay tribute to the leader. On the 29th, when hundreds of thousands of people were to deposit the ashes in a provisional monument built in Fraternity Park, army troops and anti-Communist groups including Radical ABC, Pro-Law and Justice, the Caribbean Army and members of the DEU's right wing fired upon the demonstration, killing several workers as well as a child, Francisco González Cueto.

Immediately after, several trade union headquarters were attacked and looted. This action opened a new stage in the offensive of the government's reactionary forces and oligarchic groups against the popular and labor movement.

As Guiteras was the Interior, War and Navy Minister and consequently Batista's superior chief, the Communist Party and the CNOC also considered him responsible for the massacres perpetrated by the army. Hence, the two organizations accused him as well as the rest of the government. Thus, Guiteras was attacked both by the right and the left. It was not until early 1935 that the Communist Party began to understand Guiteras' positions, and to realize its lack of capacity to correctly understand the different forces that made up the government or the role that each of them played within the administration.

The Government's crisis. The January 15th reactionary coup.- The government's crisis worsened at the beginning of 1934. On January 6th, after the DEU had dissolved itself, a general student assembly denounced the counterrevolutionary conspiracy financed by foreign companies, opposed any foreign interference, and rejected Grau "for having frustrated university ideals and for being incapable (...) of accomplishing the university program".

Also during those days—from January 12th through 16th, 1934—a major meeting of workers strongly condemned the government. The workers gathering was the CNOC's 4th Congress which was legally held in Havana with the attendance of 2400 delegates representing nearly 400 thousand workers from across the country. Its main organizer and inspirer was Ruben Martínez Villena who waged his last battle there, since he died at the end of the congress. His funeral was an impressive homage of the island's workers to their beloved leader.

The Congress reviewed the CNOC's activities since its creation, examined the country's situation and set guidelines for its struggle. Though it highlighted the workers' heroic battles and progress, and was a step forward in their organization and struggle, it continued to misunderstand the Grau administration. It rejected the labor nationalization Law or Law of the 50 percent as a measure that promoted division, ran against workers internationalism and was unable to solve unemployment, as its supporters also claimed. The CNOC Congress also denounced the crimes committed by the army, not blaming its reactionary wing but the government as a whole, which it accused of using terror on some occasions and demagogy on others.

At that difficult moment, the country's only labor confederation, with powerful influence in the working class, insisted on condemning a government in which the national-Reformist forces dominated. Not a single political party, representative, social organization or sector with real political strength supported that administration. Its days were counted.

In a plot with the United States, that included its new ambassador Jefferson Caffery, who had replaced Welles in December, 1933 and with the ABC and the bourgeois parties, Batista staged a counterrevolutionary military coup which overthrew Grau on January 15th, 1934.

The reactionary forces in power.- Deceitfully, the coup leaders named Grau's collaborator, Engineer Carlos Hevia, President of the Republic; but a few hours later they replaced him by colonel Carlos Mendieta, ultra right wing politician and Washington's obedient instrument. The army remained in the hands of Fulgencio Batista, coup leader and the US embassy's strong man. This gave way to the National Concentration Government, which the people called the Mendieta-Caffery-Batista Government in reference to its three most influential figures.

Without yet going to the extremes of the Machado dictatorship, the new government began to annul the gains achieved under the provisional revolutionary government. Several laws and decrees were issued in that direction: creation of the Emergency Courts which limited the defendant's defense possibilities and whose sentences could not be appealed; establishment of the death penalty for convicts accused of killing in sabotage or other terrorist attacks; a ban on strikes and demonstrations; an end to free labor organization; and elimination of university autonomy.

The army was organized and equipped with the aid of the United States. The troops' accommodations, clothes and salaries were improved, with which Batista held on to his leadership in the Army. Once the military took control of the country another evil was added: reactionary militarism. Persecutions, barbaric actions and political murders increased to the extent that even a racist crime was committed: the lynching of a black barber and journalists in Trinidad, Las Villas by ruling ABC party members.

The Cuban Revolutionary (Authentic) Party and the Young Cuba Organization.- The revolutionary forces that had lost power had not been destroyed and began preparing for the struggle. Dr. Grau San Martín and a large number of his supporters founded the Cuban Revolutionary (Authentic) Party—the PRC(A)—with a heterogeneous membership mostly dominated by nationalists. The party designed an advanced national-Reformist program with a radical slogan "Nationalism, Socialism and Anti-imperialism". The PRC quickly became the country's largest opposition party.

Also in 1934 Antonio Guiteras set up a new organization—the Young Cuba— which gathered a group of intellectuals, students and other representatives of the most radical sectors of the island's middle class, which also included many workers. Its program was of an advanced national-revolutionary nature.

The PRC(A), and particularly the Young Cuba Organization, established their anti-imperialist positions and their plans to organize an insurrection to re-take power.

The work of the Communist Party and the National Confederation of Cuban Workers.- The Communist Party held its 2nd National Congress in April of 1934, in which delegates approved the party's first Program and set guidelines for the struggle to install "a worker and campesino government". Blas Roca was ratified s its Central Committee's Secretary General. The PC and the CNOC developed a powerful strike movement during that year to demand better conditions for workers but also for the abolition of the Platt Amendment, against a project to reform the Reciprocity Treaty with the United States and other national demands.

Under the leadership of the PC and CNOC a wave of strikes joined by dozens of thousands of sugar workers was reported in numerous mills from January on. The stoppages took place in open defiance of Batista's threat that "there will be a sugar harvest or there will be blood". Soldiers were launched against the strikers, they attacked barracks with their bayonets, evicted families from their homes and expelled them from the mills, with people killed and wounded.

Railroad workers from Morón, Camagüey, went on strike for more than one month; Communications Ministry employees walked off their jobs for 20 days; industrial, transport, textile, printing, oil, tobacco, agricultural and forestry workers also carried out important labor actions as well as street car and steel workers, teachers, barbers and hairstylists, tobacco growers and doctors, among other sectors. A successful 24 hour general strike also took place in October.

Campesino struggle. The *Realengo 18*.- The *campesinos* who had fought important battles during the Machado regime increased their actions in 1934 in several sites, mainly in eastern Oriente province. An important example of their struggle was the Realengo 18 in eastern Guantánamo's mountainous area, when an order of mass eviction against some 5 thousand families was issued in the area. Those families took up arms with the aid of the Communist Party and, voicing the slogan "Land or Blood!, they faced the company and Batista's troops over and over again. At the end they prevented the company from taking their lands away.

Abolition of the Platt Amendment. The new Reciprocity Treaty.- In a bid to improve its image in Cuba and Latin America, the United States agreed to meet one of the Cuban people's most repeated demands during the Republic: the abolition of the Platt Amendment. In march, 1934, the Roosevelt administration annulled the interventionist Law. Nevertheless, a US journalist noted at that time that while US capital continued controlling industries, the land, banks and other resources, and the island remained dependent on trade with the United States, that country's decisive influence over Cuba wouldn't cease. But the fact that the infamous Amendment stopped being an appendix of the Cuban Constitution was a victory for the Cuban people's struggles.

In August, 1934, Cuba and the United States signed a new Reciprocity Treaty to replace the one from 1903. The northern nation was even more favored with this treaty than before. The island's economic area that somewhat benefited was sugar; but those benefits were never felt on the island, because the United States applied the Costigan-Jones Law, which set very low quotas for purchasing Cuban sugar in the United States.

The March 1935 General Strike. Guiteras' death.- The Reciprocity Treaty, the law of sugar quotas as well as the government's anti-popular measures and repression increased popular unrest in early 1935. Protests saw the participation of workers from virtually all economic sectors.

At the end of February a University Strike Committee urged all sectors to stage a general strike to demand the re-establishment of democratic liberties, an end to militarism, the release of political prisoners, the elimination of the Emergency Courts, and the urgent need to meet the demands of public schools and junior high schools, among others.

The Young Cuba Organization, Guiteras, the Communist Party and the CNOC, whose positions were now closer, considered the strike premature. Taking into consideration its importance for the Revolution's future, the strike needed to be organized in close cooperation with all sectors, and with the establishment of armed detachments capable of facing the repressive forces. Those organizations thought that without such requisites the strike was doomed to failure.

However, the masses were restless and impatient, and went on strike anyway. In view of the events, the revolutionary organizations decided to support the stoppage. Several economic areas were paralyzed from march 6th on; and on the 9th and the 10th the strike reached its highest point. Mendieta and Batista declared war, launched the army against the strikers, annulled constitutional guarantees, took over the University and authorized their supporters to open fire upon those who promoted the strike. The fierce violence unleashed by authorities and the lack of a real possibility of an armed response weakened the movement, which was finally defeated, as Guiteras and the PC had predicted. With this failure, the 1933 popular revolution was practically destroyed.

Guiteras decided to go to Mexico to look for weapons and recruit men to begin another revolution in Cuba. But the words of a traitor put Batista on the alert. Guiteras was caught when he was going to leave the country from El Morrillo beach, in Matanzas, dying in an uneven battle with army troops on May 8th, 1935. Venezuelan Communist and former Sandinista guerrilla colonel, Carlos Aponte also died in combat with Guiteras. Antonio Guiteras' irreparable loss closed one of the most heroic pages in the history of Cuba.

Significance of the 1933 Revolution.- Despite its defeat, the 1933 Revolution was one of the most important and instructive stages in the Cuban people's long struggle against their foreign and local oppressors. The country's political panorama changed dramatically in six years—from 1929 to 1935. The people's anti-imperialist and anti-capitalist consciousness reached a high level; for the first time after the establishment of the Republic, the people massively challenged the oligarchy's power and threats of US military occupation.

Those years considerably diminished the traditional political parties' absolute control over the island's political scenario, giving way to new organizations and nationalist, anti-imperialist and revolutionary parties. The young and small marxist-leninist party garnered extraordinary influence among manual and intellectual workers, gained invaluable experiences and laid the groundwork to later become a party of the masses.

The 1933 Revolution confirmed the working class as the most firm and consistent class in the struggle for profound economic, political and social change. It also showed the vital need for an alliance between workers and *campesinos*, and between them and left wing students, intellectuals and professionals—sectors which played a decisive role in the revolutionary process.

At the same time, the Revolution revealed the domestic bourgeoisie's weak, submissive and hesitant nature, and once more showed the anti-popular, reactionary, pro-imperialist role played by the local oligarchy, the bourgeois political leadership and the petite bourgeoisie's right wing.

Finally, among other lessons, the 1933 Revolution demonstrated that a revolutionary movement's victory depends to a great extent on its capacity to employ all forms of struggle, of creating its own military apparatus and of combining armed struggle with a broad and powerful mass mobilization.

Hence, the experiences, victories and setbacks of the 1933 Revolution, its victories and mistakes, its strategic guidelines and fighting tactics had a priceless value for future struggles, and demonstrated the historic continuity of the Cuban revolutionary process.

124

XIII
From reactionary militarism to a constitutional regime

The crushing of the general strike of March of 1935 dealt a severe blow to the revolutionary movement. The repressive emergency legislation—promulgated by the Government of National Concentration once it realized its inability to curb the revolutionary drive—was brutality enforced and enhanced with new laws and resolutions of exception. The Military regime scrapped the Constitution it had approved, vested all powers itself, declared a state of war, established the death penalty and ordered summary executions of those committing "crimes against public order". Coronel José Eleuterio Pedraza, was appointed supreme military chief of the Province of Havana, and the National Police and municipal police forces were given extraordinary powers that placed them above the rule of judges and courts.

Amid this setting of extreme terror, other laws were passed. They ordered the suspension of all school activities and shut down teaching-training, business and secondary schools. The university was militarily occupied and university autonomy was suppressed. Laws establishing press and mail censorship prohibited the dissemination of printed propaganda.

Jails were filled with workers, students and professionals, the implacable persecution and covert or outright murders (suicide, "the law against escape attempts", death by torture and poisoning in prisons) were authorized as official methods to eliminate prisoners of the regime, notwithstanding their political affiliation or social status.

Many trade union offices were destroyed, the army and the police would steal their funds and property, other union centers were occupied by members of the "reserve". Military intervention in trade union organizations was fully established.

Railroad services were militarized; military inspectors terrorized the work force at companies, factories and public offices and with their approval, staff would be downsized under the allegation of "necessities of the economy". Thousands of workers, teachers and civil servants who actively participated in past struggles were dismissed from their jobs.

Reprisals concentrated mainly on the sugar industry sector, their organizations were destroyed and their leaders and members were fired. In many instances, their homes were sacked, or they were either murdered or incarcerated.

New tactics of struggle.- Faced with such a situation, most of the opposition leaders fled the country. Grau San Martín, Prío Socarrás and other leaders of the Cuban Revolutionary (Authentic) Party settled in Miami.

Grau's passivity was expressed in his phrase: "We have to learn how to wait". Leaders of ABC left for Mexico and the United States.

While defeatism reigned in some sectors of the petite bourgeoisie, tendencies towards individual actions gained momentum: bombings, assassination attempts, propaganda announcing the coming insurrection, the arrival of armed expeditions, etc. These trends underestimated the need for a united and organized movement of the masses as the most important step to change the prevailing situation.

In late 1934, the Communist Party (PC) and the CNOC overcame their sectarianism regarding other left organizations. This change was openly expressed following the defeat of the March strike and reached its peak after the 5th Congress of the Communist International in July-August 1935, and the VI plenary meeting of the Communist Party two months later. Slogans like "classes versus classes" and "for a Soviet government of workers and farm workers" were dropped, and the ideas of the formation of a single front of all opposition parties and organizations were raised.

The sentiment of unity was also reaffirmed in other smaller organizations like Jóven Cuba (Young Cuba) Partido Agrario Nacional, Partido Aprista Cubano, Izquierda Revolucionaria, Organización Revolucionaria Cubana Antimperialista, Organización Auténtica (a fraction of the Cuban Revolutionary Party under the leadership of Carlos Prío Socarrás and Carlos Hevia) and Unión Revolucionaria (legal party with ties to the underground Communist Party). Some of these organizations made up the Unitarian Front, the Peoples Revolutionary Bloc; but it never consolidated due to the divisive attitude of Dr. Ramón Grau San Martín, who led the opposition's largest party, the PRC. He refused to take part in any united action.

Meanwhile, after the first attack against it, the popular movement began to recover at the grassroots level with the help of left-wing forces. Committees for the amnesty of political prisoners, opposed to the high cost of living, for a united front and others began to be set up. Students founded the September 30th Mobilization Committee in memory of Rafael Trejo. Actions included the boycott of elections called for January 1936, protests against terrorism in society, the legalization of all political parties, the return of exiles, the re-establishment of democratic rights, etc.

Workers changed their tactics of struggle: they organized new trade unions whose leaders were not known as revolutionary activists, they took their main actions to work centers and organized factory committees and committees demanding that those who were dismissed from their jobs be re-hired. In Havana, the Comité Conjunto de Colectividades Obreras (the Joint Committee of Work Collectives) was founded to coordinate activities of the majority of workers organizations from all political tendencies. Mobilizations to mark May Day grew in momentum as well as activities to oppose fascism and war, specifically against Italy's invasion of Ethiopia, and against other fascist abuses.

In January 1936, when Doctor Miguel Mariano Gómez was sworn in as President of the Republic, contradictions between the civilian and military power arose, despite the fact that the new leader was a carbon copy of Batista. Popular forces took advantage of these contradictions to fight against militarism and worked to gain support in the civilian sectors.

Demagogy and democratic changes.- Batista realized the strength of the mass movement and how they had recovered their mobilizing power by late 1935. He decided to combine terror with a mixture of several demagogic measures to create the impression that there was a real commitment to resolve the most important national problems such as education, health care and the country's economic development. With this purpose in mind, a series of important institutions were created in February 1936: a vast network of civil-military schools for remote rural areas, with sergeants as teachers; the National Corporation for Public Assistance and the National Council on Tuberculosis, all under the umbrella of the Corporate Council on Education, Health and Welfare. In January 1937, a Teaching Law was passed, which amounted to a great victory for the students movement, because it met their most important demands. In June of that same year, the drafting of a Triennial Plan was announced. This was an ambitious program for economic and social development that was presented as a panacea that would solve all the island's problems. In September, the Law for Sugar Coordination was approved, offering a series of benefits to sugar workers and tenant farmers.

The Communist Party and the National Confederation of Cuban Workers called on the masses to demand that the government fulfill its promises to satisfy the population's real needs. This would either force Batista to keep his word or demonstrate that he was deceiving the people. The demands were raised during large demonstrations legally held island wide on May 1st 1937 and hinted at an important change in the political situation.

The progress of the popular movement was also noticeable in other important events that occurred in 1937, among them: the creation of several regional workers confederations, above all, the important *Comité de Unificación Obrera de la Provincia de la Habana*, (Havana's Workers Unification Committee), the approval of a far-reaching amnesty in December, releasing more than 4000 political prisoners and allowing exiles to return to the country; the self-destruction of the *Ala Izquierda Estudiantil* (the Students Left-wing) and of the *Comité de Superación Universitaria* permitting the re-emergence of the University Students Federation (FEU) and the holding of a very important provincial small farmers congress in Camaguey.

From then on, important democratic achievements were attained, which reversed the country's political situation between 1938 and 1939.

Some of the most important achievements were: the freedom to organize unions and the legal status of all opposition groups and parties, including the Cuban Communist party, which was allowed to conduct propaganda and organizing tasks (1938), the foundation of the Confederation of Cuban Workers, led by the outstanding Communist leader Lázaro Peña (1939), and the celebration of a free and sovereign constituent assembly that the people had demanded (1939-1940).

Decisive factors internationally and domestically contributed to the realization of these changes. First, the birth and consolidation of Nazi-fascism amounted to a serious threat to the economic, political and military might of the United States. The United States needed the continent's support in order to impede that threat. The Big Stick policy, long pursued by US administrations, had evoked the rejection of the peoples of Latin America. Roosevelt began to use—without intending to change the essence of US imperialism—new and more subtle forms of domination in the continent, which achieved its peak with the Good Neighbor policy. This policy allowed for, among other things, the limiting of military interventions, the encouragement of substituting dictatorial regimes in Latin America through the holding of elections and the pursuit of some institutional changes strongly demanded in Cuba and other countries by sectors of the national bourgeoisie that

127

aspired to a civil government with free political game. Batista, always attentive to Washington's wishes and displaying his characteristic sharpness, made himself the main protagonist of these changes.

Another important factor was the huge activism waged by the Cuban people in solidarity with the Spanish Republic, which had been heroically fighting since July 1936 against a fascist uprising and aggression. Democratically-minded Cubans from the most diverse political trends, social origins and religious beliefs participated in the mobilization. The material and moral support provided by Cubans to the Spanish people was impressive and its greatest expression was the participation of one thousand Cubans as combatants on the frontline of battle; hundreds heroically gave their lives in Republican trenches. A symbolic martyr of this time was young journalist and writer Pablo de la Torriente Brau, who had participated in the struggles against the Machado and Batista dictatorships. He is one of the highest examples of revolutionary intellectual and fighter.

But this solidarity not only helped the Spanish people. It created the conditions for a wide and powerful movement that brought together the struggle in defense of the Spanish Republic with demands against the Batista dictatorship. The large demostration which the government was unable to disrupt, played an important role in the achievement of democratic changes on the island.

Likewise, popular activism contributed to actions in solidarity with the Mexican government led by General Lázaro Cárdenas, who had nationalized the oil industry and the railway system of the sister nation, encouraged the Agrarian Reform, protected Mexican products from foreign competition and took measures that put him at odds with the US government and monopolies. Fund-raisers, requests to the Cuban government to help Mexico overcome the US blockade and large solidarity rallies, helped weaken the positions of the oligarchic sector of the Cuban government and made democratic changes in its policies.

Domestically, the decisive factor was the rapid growth of the popular movement, which quickly recovered after the defeat of the March 1935 strike. One proof of the determining role of popular actions was the fact that in other Latin American countries, despotic regimes remained in power without noticeable changes, despite the fact that the US also exerted pressure on them and notwithstanding the influence of other international factors.

Founding of the Confederation of Cuban Workers.- The founding congress of the *Confederación de Trabajadores de Cuba* (CTC)—Confederation of Cuban Workers—was preceded by the celebration in Mexico (September 1938) of a continental workers congress, which concluded with the launching of the *Confederación de Trabajadores de América Latina* (CTAL)—Latin American Workers Confederation—led by Vicente Lombardo Toledano. A Cuban delegation was present at the event, which was made of up representatives from all prevailing political and ideological currents existing within the Cuban trade union movement. The delegation made the commitment to create a broad trade union federation on the island.

In late January 1939, a workers conference was held in Havana with the participation of 1500 delegates representing 789 trade union organizations from all over the country. Delegates came from the most diverse currents; the only trend absent from the event

128

was the *Comisión Obrera Nacional* from the *Partido Revolucionario Cubano* (*Auténtico*). This commission was led by Eusebio Mujal, an individual of rabid anti-Communist ideology who had always wanted to take over the Cuban labor movement.

The importance of this congress was that it led to the birth of a new trade union federation, whose leadership had a Unitarian character. The Federation's General Secretary, Lázaro Peña, and other members of its leadership were Communists that had gained prestige in the struggles against the Machado and Batista dictatorships, in the defense of workers and the people's interests. The CTC then began an era of important economic, social and political achievements for the Cuban working class.

The Constitution of 1940.- Of all the political events of the time, the Constituent Assembly, which met in Havana between February and June 1940, was the most prominent. Elections of delegates for the assembly were held in November 1939; 11 political parties contested for 76 seats. The PRC (A) won the most votes and sent 18 delegates. The *Unión Revolucionaria Comunista* Party (merger of the Communist Party with *Unión Revolucionaria* Party) which participated for the first time in elections, ended up in 5th place with 6 delegates.

The heterogeneous character of the Assembly, in which all social classes, layers and sectors were represented, prompted heated debates. But the firm positions of the Communist fraction, aided by the support of numerous delegates from other political trends, the live radio broadcasts of the debates to the entire nation which allowed people to follow the issues debated, and the mass pressure, combined for the success in the shaping of a constitution with a democratic content considered progressive for that time. Some articles were devoted to express principles like national sovereignty, as well as many other social achievements, individual liberties and political rights.

The Charter not only acknowledged the equality of all Cubans before the law, but it also declared "illegal and punishable any discrimination based on sex, race, color or class, and any other discrimination that would hurt human dignity".

Article 90 of the Constitution was also very important. It prohibited large landholdings and provided "to effect its disappearance, law will set the maximum extension of the estate that each person or entity might possess for each type of use which the land is submitted, taking into account the circumstances". In addition, the Constitution suspended the eviction of *campesinos* for a period of two years and instructed the Congress to approve, during this term, a law on Renting and Sharecropping, providing that the state's idle lands be distributed among campesino workers.

Regarding social aspects, the Constitution met basic demands by the labor movement. It outlawed the fixing of a minimum wage for all workers, even in the case of piecework salaries, it acknowledged the principle "for equal work, equal salary;" it prohibited the payment of wages or salaries with tokens or promissory notes and discounts not established by law; it set up social welfare for disability, aging, unemployment and for accidents in the workplace. It fixed the work day to a maximum of 8 hours in general and of 6 hours for youth from 14 to 18 years of age, the 44-hour work week, equivalent to 48 hours of salary, the right to proportional remunerated rest, protection of maternity and mandatory rest for pregnant workers for six weeks prior to and six weeks after delivery.

The Constitution acknowledged unions and the worker's right to strike, the system of collective bargaining, the universal access of Cubans by birth or naturalization to employment, as well as the equal opportunity to fill job vacancies without any kind of discrimination; it prohibited the dismissal of workers without prior records; it provided for the compulsory fulfillment of social laws by the employer and the procedure of setting up conciliatory commissions to settle labor disputes between management and the workers, etc.

Despite being a bourgeois constitution that acknowledged private property, although "in its widest concept of social performance", it was considered one of the most advanced constitutions of the continent.

General elections. Batista is elected President.- Once the constitution was approved, general elections were called for July 14, 1940. Two blocs contested for the elections: the *Coalición Socialista Democrática (CSD)*, whose candidate was Fulgencio Batista and the so-called Pact of Four, with Dr. Ramón Grau San Martín as candidate.

Despite the efforts of progressive forces since 1935, they were unable to unite in an organization that would group all left-oriented forces, a block that would have allowed for common action during the sessioning of the Constituent Assembly. The main hurdle to such an alliance was Ramón Grau San Martín's anti-unity, sectarianism and overbearing attitude, he dismissed repeated efforts to unite, proposed by the rest of the left forces. As Grau led the PRC(A) Party, the largest opposition party, there was no way to forge unity. In addition to Grau's critical attitude was his negative stance regarding Cuban's solidarity with Republican forces in Spain and his relations with institutions and individuals linked to the pro-fascist organization "*Falange Española.*"

But Grau's greatest offense, after having frustrated the unity of left-wing organizations, was teaming up in the Constituent Assembly with the bourgeoisie's most reactionary parties like the ABC Party, *Acción Republicana* Party and the *Demócrata Republicano* party, headed by the old oligarchic caudillo and former President of the Republic, Mario García Menocal.

Meanwhile, Batista adopted positions that distanced him from those of reactionary and pro-fascist forces. And given the external and internal reasons mentioned before, he played a starring role in the democratic transformations that were taking place in the country. Moreover, by the time of the general elections in 1940, the Socialist Democratic Coalition, led by Batista himself, launched a platform that included numerous demands of a democratic and progressive character, which included the call for the passage of complementary laws to the recently approved Constitution. Faced with such attractive postulates, Grau, who had not presented any program, accused Batista of having stolen the platform from his PRC (A) Party.

Having witnessed this movement, the *Union Revolucionaria Comunista* Party decided to join the Batista-led *Coalición Socialista Democrática (CSD)* and supported his candidacy. This decision, heatedly debated by the party's grassroots organizations island-wide, was finally approved. On the one hand, the decision led to a noticeable development of the labor movement and to the respect of democratic rights and liberties. On the other hand, it infuriated numerous revolutionary forces and some sectors of the petite bourgeoisie, who criticized the party's support of the man responsible of the defeat of the 1933 Revolution and of the bloody dictatorship that Cuba suffered after the March 1935 strike. This resentment was to be found in one way or another in subsequent decades.

The CSD won the general elections and Colonel Fulgencio Batista was elected President. The electoral process, as customary during neo-colonial times, was marred by all kinds of fraud and in some parts of the country, the army disrupted the polling. But other factors were decisive in the election results. The most important was the procedure to elect the president, which was not based on direct vote but in the number of votes garnered by senators or representatives of each party. Taking into consideration the power exerted by political bosses in provinces and municipalities, the congressional majority of the bourgeois parties was guaranteed, and through it, the presidential election. Moreover, one of the parties that had supported Grau in 1939, the *Demócrata Republicano* Party, joined the CSD in 1940, supporting Batista.

The influence exerted by important sectors of Cuban society on the elections cannot be disregarded, above all that of the farmers. All the economic measures, the political liberties, education, the social achievements and public health care that Batista had so demagogically announced, when applied, meant some positive change with respect to their former situation.

Cuba and World War II.- The new government took office on October 10, 1940. A new era of constitutional normality began, an era whose main characteristics were the preponderance of civil institutions instead of reactionary militarism that reigned during previous years. The educational, social and health care institutions created during military rule, were directed and supervised by the corresponding ministries of the civilian government.

A year before, World War II had broken out. Batista's Constitutional Government (1940-1944) passed with the world's progressive and anti-fascist forces as a backdrop. This reality was also reflected in Cuba.

Although the Cuban Army was never deployed to the battle fields, the country did contribute to the struggle with some industrial products, mainly sugar; diverse material aid in accordance with the island's limited resources; the people's political and moral solidarity and the voluntary participation of a number of Cubans in the Allied Armies. Two young men Enrique Vilar and Aldo Vivó, died fighting with the Red Army. Furthermore, Cuba also suffered some direct consequences: German submarines marauding in the waters of the Atlantic Ocean and the Caribbean Sea, sank several Cuban merchant ships, causing dozens of casualties. A German spy related to those attacks, Heinz August Luning, was caught in Havana, imprisoned and executed in 1942. The small Cuban Navy sank one German submarine.

The Cuban people closed ranks and made enormous sacrifices to contribute to the anti-fascist war. A National Anti-Fascist Committee was established to lead anti-fascist campaigns. It was widely represented and had branches all over the country. It was time for the creation of a government of national unity, which could not be consummated by the attitude of Grau's PRC (A) Party, which did not agree to join a War Cabinet.

The labor movement temporarily agreed to suspend strikes and other actions that would obstruct production and services. More than 250,000 young men enrolled in the General Military Service and thousands of citizens volunteered to go to the battle fields. In the framework of the struggle against fascism, diplomatic relations between Cuba and the USSR were established for the first time.

The mass movement gains momentum.- Between 1940 and 1946 a broad, solid and fighting mass movement developed. The CTC—which was made up of 790 organizations and 220,000 members at the time of its foundation in 1939—reached a membership of 1200 organizations and more than half a million unionized workers six years later. The National Federation of Sugar Workers grew from 78 organizations with 5393 members to 250 locals with more than 200,000 members. More than 20 new national, regional and local union federations were founded, dozens of parallel trade unions merged into single trade unions and the fragmenting heritage of organizing by specific trade was practically discarded. Dozens of trade union magazines and journals came on the scene with circulation exceeding 150,000 copies.

During these years, May Day Parades gained in prominence. Hundreds of thousands of workers marched every year and important economic and social gains for the working class were achieved. The CTC and trade unions achieved wage-hikes to the tune of 500 million pesos between 1940 and 1944, for a 108% increase versus an 84% increase in the cost of living. The minimum wage was substantially increased even for agricultural workers, the least paid. A great victory was the payment for all workers of 9.09% of earned salaries, or the equivalent of a month of paid vacation for every 11 months of work. In several sectors, the work week was set at 44 hours with the payment of 48 hours, rotating lists were established for maritime-dock sector and the payment of a subsidy for workers of this sector that were left without jobs due to the war.

Many displaced workers were accepted back at their jobs, including those who were laid off during the 1935 strike. Bosses and enterprises were deprived of the power they once had of firing workers without due cause, a measure harshly attacked by the oligarchy and foreign monopolies. Retirement laws for numerous sectors were passed. The Sugar Workers and Employees Pension and Social Assistance Fund—one of the Republic's most important social security institutions—was created.

This and many other achievements noticeably raised the influence and authority of the CTC and Cuban communists. The *Union Revolucionaria Comunista* Party (which in 1944 changed its name to *Partido Socialista Popular*) received 97,944 votes in the 1939 elections and garnered 200,000 votes in 1946. It secured 10 representatives in the House, three senators, 147 aldermen, two mayors and one minister without portfolio in the War Cabinet. The work of communists in the parliament and other responsibilities yielded very positive results for the country.

During this time, a strong youth and women's movement developed. The National Association of Small Farmers was also created, waging important struggles on behalf of workers in the countryside. Some of their demands were met, but the most serious problems remained. The so-called Cuban Federation of Small Farmers, a reformist trend, was also established. Cuban farmers and industrial workers were required to join these associations, which were generally run by the wealthiest members.

Government's discredit.- Despite advancements made, several vices, flaws and other evils inherent to the neocolonial republic were manifested: subordination to US imperialist interests (if muted by the common struggle against fascism), underdevelopment, corruption, the high cost of living, discrimination against Blacks and women, illiteracy, etc.

One of the most pressing problems of the period was the excessive price hikes of basic commodities. The war led to serious shortages of raw materials and of finished products with the logical increase in prices. With this pretext, a speculation race was launched by owners of large warehouses, tradesmen and middlemen in general, leading to sky-rocketing prices. A solution to this situation was sought through wage-hikes and price regulations, but corrupt officials and judges plotted with speculators and the black market was rampant. Popular discontent increased.

Political and administrative corruption, though it did not reach the levels of other times, was scandalous. The country was ruled without a budget law, the last one having been approved in 1938. Hence the abuse of credits and extraordinary budgets, contributing to the decline and squandering of state resources. Public health was a disaster. Credits for aqueducts, sewage systems, surgical and sanitary supplies, hospitals, etc. almost never reached their destination; cases of tuberculosis, syphilis, yellow fever, intestinal parasites and other diseases multiplied. Salaries of public employees were low and many of them were fired with changes of ministers or officials. Most amendments to the Constitution did not pass, and the text of the Magna Carta was practically dead.

During this period, students and the nation as a whole witnessed the worsening of a phenomenon first experienced in previous years: the university "*bonche*" (from the English "punch"). They were gangs of students officially enrolled in the university or in high schools that used mob-style threats to obtain grades without studying, receive salaries from jobs where they never worked, economic remuneration and other privileges.

"*Bonchismo*" had its origins in the widespread terrorism that resulted from the power vested in Machado's cronies after August 1933 to summarily execute without judicial processes. From that time, people settled accounts personally and took justice into their own hands. This phenomenon particularly developed after 1938 and led to a large number of assassinations and attempts against the lives of university students, professors and left-wing activists. Among the many victims was the incorruptible and energetic university professor Ramiro Valdés Daussa and the outstanding Communist worker Manuel Porto Peña. After 1944, "*bonchismo*" was still present in the sinister gangs that terrorized the country.

The government's image deteriorated rapidly, while the leaders of the PRC (A) took advantage of these negative aspects to unleash a relentless wave of criticism against the administration. They promised that if Dr. Grau were to be elected in the upcoming elections, all the country's problems would be solved.

Elections of 1944. Victory of Ramón Grau San Martín.- The new elections were held on June 1, 1944. The two largest electoral blocs ran in the elections: The governing *Coalición Socialista Democrática* (CSD)—Socialist Democratic Coalition— with Dr. Carlos Saladrias, leader of the Democratic Party, running as presidential candidate, and the opposition *Alianza Auténtico Republicana* party, with Dr. Ramón Grau San Martín as its candidate.

The CSD carried the government's discredit on its shoulders. The party's candidate, Dr. Carlos Saladrias, was opposed even by some sectors of the government itself. Besides being a conservative and unpopular figure, he lacked a coherent electoral platform to offer the electorate.

133

On the contrary, Dr. Grau San Martín, counted on the overwhelming support of the opposition alliance and other sectors that were unhappy with the government. Despite his anti-communism and demagoguery, the popularity he reached during his first presidential term (1933-1934) grew due to the shortcomings and vices of the current administration. He announced an ambitious and attractive program that brought hopes of improvement to the working class without frightening the ruling classes. There was another decisive element. Different from the 1940 elections, this time the president and the vice president would be elected by direct vote and voters were not compelled to check the boxes in only one of the ballot's columns. They could pick representatives from one party, senators from another and the presidential candidate of a third party.

This procedure allowed liberals and other members of the incumbent party to vote for congressional members of their government, while they gave their presidential vote to Grau. Thus, Grau San Martín garnered a landslide victory to the Presidency of the Republic while the incumbent coalition overwhelmingly won congressional seats and surpassed Grau's party in terms of aldermen and mayors elected in the country.

XIV
The "Auténtico" Governments. Failure of National-Reformism

On October 10th, 1944, with the coming to power of Dr. Ramon Grau San Martín, the administration of the Cuban Revolutionary Authentic Party began. This stage comprised two presidential periods: that of Grau San Martín (1944-1948) and Dr. Carlos Prío Socarrás (1948-1952). Except for the first two years—1944 to1946—the balance of which can be considered positive for the country, despite the serious evils that began to grow then, the rest of that stage was the greatest popular frustration in Cuban history since the Republic. These years saw the exhaustion of all possibilities for national-reformism and its definitive collapse, despite the very favorable economic conditions the postwar period had brought.

Initial steps for popular benefit.- During the first two years in power, the "*Auténtico*" administration adopted some measures that were favorable for the country's independent development and for improved living conditions, especially of workers. Even in the initial months, it handled public funds in such a way that despite having inherited a treasury with a 3.5 million peso deficit in October, it closed December with a 6 million capital surplus.

With industrialization as its objective, the government approved several decrees that were well received. Several pieces of legislation facilitated the entry into the country of means of production and raw material used by industries that emerged during the war. A considerable increase in the production of shoes, textiles, alcohol, beer, cork, medicines, toys, candies and canned fruit was recorded with the help of these measures. This growth, of course, was favored by the postwar period, which boosted internal demand and reduced the pressure traditionally exerted by the competition of US products.

An ambitious plan of public works—for which nearly 330 million pesos were earmarked—was drawn up, suggesting the need to expand the highway and road system and other works, as well as opening schools in the countryside to eradicate illiteracy. The implementation of this plan would fulfill some of the objectives proposed, although at the cost of extortion and misappropriation of resources.

Grau, fulfilling electoral promises, eliminated some taxes and cut others down; he forbid, by decree, the increase of rents and the eviction of tenants; he established sanctions for speculating merchants and set a minimum wage for public employees. He announced the carrying out of an agrarian reform. During Grau's four year term, the agrarian reform was limited to the temporary suspensions of farmer evictions, the apportionment of a 5400 hectare farm ("Casanova Sales", in Oriente), the beginning of a National Agriculture Census, the holding of cattle fairs and exhibitions, and the establishment of six cold storage plants, two fishing cooperatives, and two free markets in Havana.

The policies followed by Grau ware more beneficial for workers. Although at the beginning he made harsh statements about the leadership of the Confederation of

135

Cuban Workers (CTC), he soon changed his position and promoted workers unity. The 4th Congress of the Confederation took place in December, two months after his presidential inauguration. A united Board of Directors was elected at the Congress, headed by Communist leader Lázaro Peña. For the first time, the leaders of the National Labor Commission of the Cuban Revolutionary Party put aside their differences and anti-communism and formed a unified administration. Later on, it would be revealed that it was only a strategy they were forced to adopt due to the extraordinary strength, authority and prestige of the CTC and of Communists—a strategy to undermine unity from within and to take control of the leadership of the trade union movement. Moreover, Grau needed the support of Communist senators and representatives to obtain a majority in Congress. The only way to achieve that support—something they had achieved by early 1945—was by putting forward a program benefiting labor and popular causes.

At the same time that these positions were raised, Grau substantially increased salaries in a number of sectors; he eliminated the ease with which employers could arbitrarily dismiss workers; he regulated work to benefit the workers, he firmly confronted big plantation and sugar mill owners who rejected the legislation that favored workers and he even managed to arbitrate in some enterprises that had conflicts with their workers.

But perhaps the most significant step taken during the short 1944-1946 period was that of imposing what came to be known as the "sugar differential" on the US administration. In the 1945 harvest, the Cuban government retained 250,000 tons of sugar and sold them in Latin America at a price of almost 7 cents a pound, much higher that the price paid by the United States (3.67 cents). The difference between the two prices—the "differential"—which amounted some 40 million pesos, was used to subsidize food products that Cuba imported, to build rural schools, and to undertake other important projects.

Based on this experience, workers proposed—and Grau accepted—a formula that guaranteed a new "differential" every year, forcing the US to raise the price it paid for Cuban sugar in proportion to the increase in the cost of food products and other consumer items that Cuba purchased in that country.

To achieve this, and facing the tenacious opposition of sugar magnates, Grau included the prestigious labor leader Jesus Menéndez—a Black Communist—in the Cuban delegation that traveled to Washington to negotiate the sale of the 1945-1946 sugar harvest. A renowned economist and advisor to the National Federation of Sugar Workers, Jacinto Torras, was also included in the mission. Contrary to what he had promised, Grau maintained the same plantation owners heading the Cuban Institute for Sugar Stabilization in 1944, and named two US magnates for the commission that would negotiate the 1945 sugar harvest. But the appointment of Menéndez and Torras in 1946 was a step of irrefutable importance.

After obstinate refusals on the US side, and in the face of Cuba's determination, it was agreed to include a Clause of Guarantee in the contract of purchase and sale of sugar. According to the clause, price variations in the items Cuba imported from the US had to be calculated every three months. The price of Cuban sugar would be increased proportionally.

136

The product of the "sugar differential" (36 million pesos in 1946) was distributed among all those involved in sugar production, from workers and plantation owners. For the workers in particular, this "differential" represented an additional income of 29 million pesos that year.

Finally, in this initial stage, Grau nationalized the numerous military bases built by the United States on the island during World War II.

But as of 1946, Grau's government began a reactionary and anti-popular twist: giving up the "sugar differential", destroying trade union unity, wiping out most of the worker's achievements over decades of bloody struggles and during the first two years of the "*Auténtico*" government, an increase in political and administrative corruption, the promotion of a campaign in favor of presidential re-election—rejected by the people due to scandalous episodes in Cuban history—an increasing number of old bourgeois politicians in the government, the proliferation of gangsterism, the rise in the cost of living and increasing vices and evils of the neocolonial republic.

Administrative and political corruption.- In his first speech to Congress, President Grau proposed two conditions to prevail in the management of public funds: efficiency and honesty. But from the beginning of his term in office, inherited vices prevailed and spread in such a scandalous way that made "*Auténtico*" governments the most corrupt administrations in the history of the Republic.

The country continued to postpone budgets approved in advance, adding to them a long list of extra spending. A large number of government officials made exorbitant profits from plundering public funds and many of them become multimillionaires. Some sources for that enrichment included the National Lottery, Provision K of the 1943 Law #7, public works, Labor Retirement Benefits, mutual debts and the funds allocated to all the country's ministries and state agencies, as well as the obvious connivance with speculating business people, smugglers, bosses of illegal gambling and prostitution and with companies and owners who were violating the law. In order to separate himself from the mismanagement of state finances, Grau vetoed a bill setting up Bank Account Tribunals.

Most government officials, politicians and high-ranking authorities were involved in large-scale fraudulent businesses. To illustrate the situation, we will mention a few of them. Minister of Commerce Alberto Inocente Alvarez became notorious for his exchange of Cuban sugar for Ecuadorian rice, thus causing Cuba's positive commercial relations with Latin American countries to lose their prestige. Education Minister José Manuel Alemán spent over 200 million pesos of his Ministry in a brief span of time, amassing a personal fortune that was estimated in some 100 million pesos, or dollars. Meanwhile, Havana's honest and honorable Mayor Manuel Fernández Supervielle was denied his request for crucial resources to resolve the water supply problem affecting the capital city. As a result, the prestigious official committed suicide. We also saw the political schemes of José M. Alemán, who set up the so-called BAGA political group and financed his campaign with money from the Education Ministry's budget. The BAGA included, among other people, the nephew and sister-in-law of Grau San Martín. It was known that each representative's testimony in the House would cost the public treasury some $ 300,000. Amid an economically favorable situation for the country, Grau left a 68-million-peso deficit when his mandate ended. The scandal reached such a point that Case #82 was opened in 1950 against Dr. Grau San Martín and some of his administration's officials, charging them with the embezzlement of 174 million pesos; but all 6232 pages of the legal brief were stolen by six masked men one evening, making off with all evidence of the crime.

Another example of the prevailing disorder was an incident connected with the diamond that laid at the center of the Los Pasos Perdidos Hall, in the National Capitol building, marking kilometer zero of the national highway. On May 25, 1946, the precious stone was stolen without any further investigation on the robbery or its motives. Some 15 months later, June 2, 1947, the stone reappeared on Grau's presidential desk as mysteriously as it had vanished.

During the second term of the *Auténtico* Cuban Revolutionary Party, the PRC (A), corruption continued its rampant growth. In 1949 alone, President Prío Socarrás' family acquired 34 farms in three municipalities of eastern Pinar del Río province. Prío, who had been a modest lawyer before 1944, had become a multimillionaire by the time he stepped down from the presidency. A similar transformation was experienced by Eusebio Mujal, who had been officially designated as General Secretary of the Confederation of Cuban Workers, the CTC.

The abuse of State funds reached such a point, that despite large money collections, Prío Socarrás decided to negotiate a 200 million peso credit line with US banks. Strong rejection of the country's indebtedness plus the certainty that such funds would not be used for the country's benefit led to a massive and energetic popular protests; but congressional representatives saw the possibility for huge gains and the credit line was obtained.

The growth of gangsterism.- Dr. Grau took power in 1944 backed by several "action groups" which had previously opposed Batista and he decided to satisfy some of these groups' political and economic aspirations. He granted important posts in the country's police forces, military intelligence and other State agencies.

But this gesture did not satisfy the gangs' appetite and the distribution of political favors led to internal wars among the groups. Parallel to this, new political factions began to rise within the ruling cabinet and each of them tried to secure support from action groups. One method used by the factions was the physical elimination of their rivals. Finally, aside from using the police, the armed forces and other repressive bodies, the government used the gangs to attack labor unions, to impose its policies against the workers, to steal the organizations' money at gun point and to murder their leaders.

During the early years of the Grau administration and through the Prío government, numerous gangs emerged, whose names, because of their radical content or the figures they represented, made them attractive to the broad masses: Revolutionary Insurrection Union, Revolutionary Execution Tribunal, "Guiteras" Revolutionary Action, Revolutionary Socialist Movement, etc. In a report to the Court of Accounts published in March of 1952, Fidel Castro denounced that he knew of more than 2 100 jobs and "*botellas*" (false payroll registrations that allowed people to earn salaries without having to work) that had been distributed among gang members and hitmen. He provided names in each case and the number of privileges to which they were each entitled.

138

During the years of this "*Auténtico*" administration, there were hundreds of murders and attacks that were carried out by gangs, as well as shoot-outs among themselves. In an episode that shocked the nation, two of these gangs fought against each other at Orfila, in Havana's Marianao area, leaving six people dead and many others wounded, including women and children.

By early 1947, gangs had become so daring that they attacked with gunfire the Senate hall in an attempt to scare Senators into not signing a motion of no confidence against the Grau cabinet.

The outrageous character of these actions unleashed such a strong popular reaction that the Prío administration was later forced to pass what was known as "the Anti-Gangsterism Law". But the law proved useless against an evil that had its roots in the very heart of the *Auténtico* regime.

The anti-labor offensive.- The old desire to control the leadership of the labor movement and expel the Communists from it—something that opportunistic groups, particularly the National Workers Commission of the PRC, had been unable to achieve—was possible then thanks to the "Cold War" policy put in practice by the United States and the rest of the capitalist powers, and the advent of an Authentic administration in Cuba.

The defeat of Fascism in World War II resulted in profound transformations in the international scenario. First and foremost among them was the emergence of the Socialist camp. The colonial system also suffered a terrible blow, and independent, progressive, anti-imperialist governments came to power in many nations.

Headed by the United States, the forces of Imperialism and reaction in the world refused to accept those extraordinary achievements of mankind and pursued a warmongering, extremely aggressive policy against the USSR, and the newly-emerged Socialist states and liberated countries. Inside their nations, imperialists began a ruthless persecution against Communists and all progressive institutions and individuals—the witch-hunt, McCarthyism—and decided that the popular movements in the dependent countries, especially in Latin America, had to be crushed by all means.

To achieve this purpose, the United States promoted the ascent to power of authoritarian governments in the hemisphere, giving rise to the emergence of bloody military dictatorships in several countries beginning in 1947.

The existence of a strong trade union movement was an obstacle for the US's warmongering, hegemonic plans, so it had to be neutralized. This anti-labor drive was later plainly recognized by Serafino Romualdi, a high-ranking official with the American Federation of Labor, who wrote that "it is not enough that Latin American governments uniformly adopt the economic and military policy advised by the US government. If we do not manage to make the working movement of Latin American countries also follow that path, the Clayton and Truman Plans will be ineffective".

The oligarchy and trade unionists in the leadership of the PRC(A) fully agreed with these objectives. Although early during his term he was forced to respect the prestige, authority, and extraordinary popular support of the Communist and other leaders of the Cuban Workers Confederation of Cuban Workers, the CTC, and of most other unions, Grau was confident that he would be able to turn this situation around during his presidential mandate. That is why he began by introducing a policy in favor of workers and workers' unity as mentioned earlier, while placing ambitious individuals of known anti-Communist positions in the Ministry of Labor and other important posts.

Grau's virulent anti-Communism began to be felt in early 1947, when the Popular Socialist Party, which had collaborated with him since 1945, wrote him a public letter denouncing what they argued were four very negative aspects of his government: administrative corruption, the black market, his re-election efforts, and his close relationship with the fascist regime of Francisco Franco. Grau seemed to accept that criticism of his government, but he quickly resumed the attacks against Communists and insisted in their being expelled from the CTC and from the unions.

The masses though did not support that policy. In trade union elections carried out nation-wide in 1946, candidates who favored workers' unity recorded landslide victories in most unions. The situation repeated itself during the election of delegates to the V Congress of the CTC, scheduled to take place in April of 1947. These victories were scored in spite of the bribes, pressures, and manipulations by government officials. The Congress, which was finally held in May, was attended by some 900 trade unions, while nearly 200 unions under the control of the PRC(A)'s National Workers Commission refused to participate. Among the delegates there were some 300 Authentics who came out against the divisive tactics of their party leadership.

Unable to attain their goals either by democratic means or by pressures, threats, or legal manipulations, the government suppressed trade union democracy and embarked upon a path of imposition and terror. It arbitrarily dismantled union leaderships, and, assisted by its repressive apparatus and the gangs, raided locals, imposed leaders by decree, and murdered popular, experienced labor leaders of Communist and other political affiliations.

Immensely popular, traditional leaders like Jesús Menéndez, of the sugar workers; Aracelio Iglesias, of the harbor and maritime workers; Miguel Fernández Roig, of the tobacco workers, plus dozens of representatives from other sectors were assassinated during the Authentic government. The onslaught also reached campesino leaders, like Niceto Pérez and Sabino Pupo. The wave of murders even hit those who had initiated it, with Juan Arévalo, an old and discredited union leader and a trusted man of the US's AFL, killed in 1948, after he had gone over to the Latin American Association of Trade Union Workers, the ATLAS, an organization sponsored by followers of Argentinean President Juan Domingo Perón.

Two systems of parallel organizations were then established: on the one hand, the official trade union apparatus, headed by the notorious traitor of the Cuban working movement, Eusebio Mujal, and on the other, the non-official organizations, in favor of worker's unity, and fiercely persecuted, which continued to have Lázaro Peña as their chief figure.

Many of the gains of the working class were relinquished by the leadership of the official trade union movement in favor of companies and employers; others were preserved at the expense of the hard struggle and the blood shed by the working masses and their true representatives. The conflicting roles of the two organizations came to the limelight in the face of the great social problems that emerged then. With World War II over, the dumping of US products brought about the partial or total closing of factories, rampant unemployment and salary cuts. The modernization of sugar factories and other industries, Grau's renunciation of the sugar differential, and the reduction of the Cuban sugar quota in the US market affected both jobs and workers' incomes. The battles waged by the true working movement, and its frequent victories, became the sole guarantee workers had against the abdication of Authentic administrations and the betrayal of official trade union leaders.

The Truslow Plan.- Always attentive to the views of the United States, President Prío asked that a group of US experts be sent to Cuba to study the problems of the island's economy and suggest measures to solve them. Based on this request, a 17 member mission from the International Bank for Reconstruction and Development, headed by Francis Adam Truslow, traveled to Cuba.

From August to October of 1950, the so-called Truslow Mission analyzed the situation of the Cuban economy. Finally, in July of 1951, it presented a voluminous report with its findings. The document drew a more or less real picture of the technical and economic backwardness of Cuba without going into details as to its causes; it stated that there were serious management deficiencies like the improper use of public funds, negative budget and tax practices, etc., and proposed a number of economic, financial, and social measures to remedy the situation.

Some of those measures—less dependency on sugar, expansion of the sugar derivatives industries, boosting tourism, improving roads and communications, conducting a budget and tax reform—could have contributed to better management and greater economic efficiency. But nothing was said of measures of a fundamental nature, like an agrarian reform, the diversification of production and the development of a domestic industry, the creation of a national merchant marine, the search for new and more advantageous international markets, etc.

Instead of talking about these measures, the Truslow Plan opposed things like developing steel production or any other industry that did not offer incentives to US capital. At the same time, the possible benefits of the Plan would have been virtually null in the end since the profits obtained by US investors would not have remained in Cuba to be used for further economic development, but would have almost entirely migrated to the United States for the very benefit of the investor.

The huge advantages the Plan reserved for US companies and the closer dependency on the United States that it generated become evident when one looks at the kind of recommendations it made concerning measures to be taken by the Cuban government: tax cuts and tariff exemptions for the new investors; extending funds for private industry through the International Bank for Reconstruction and Development; revising the Mining Law to benefit foreign companies; reducing salaries in general but especially those of the sugar workers; making it easier for companies to fire workers. Special emphasis was placed on the need to create a strong employers' organization that, acting together with the labor leadership (i.e. the officially imposed leadership), could contribute to the implementation of the socio-economic policy recommended by the Plan.

At the same time that it dictated the labor policy to be followed by companies and the government, the Plan demanded that the latter allowed employers to fire a worker "without the need for explanations, through payment of an indemnification estimated on the basis of the worker's time of services;" to reduce salaries; to keep trade unions from participating in the organization of production; and to abolish previous workers' gains connected with seniority.

Despite the support of the official labor leaders, the struggle of workers' collectives made it impossible for Prío to implement the Truslow Plan during his term.

Other serious evils.- Coinciding with the anti-worker offensive unleashed by the Grau government, US investment in the Cuban economy began to grow, climbing from their all time low (some US$ 568 million) in 1946. The increase went mostly to the non-sugar sector of the economy (electricity, telephones, mining, rubber industry, pharmaceuticals, toiletries, textiles, etc.), in many cases in association with Cuban capital.

Despite their nationalist rhetoric and their statements against Latin American dictatorships, *Auténtico* governments basically followed Washington's designs. In 1950, when war is declared against the Democratic People's Republic of Korea, President Prío pledged to send a 25 000-strong Cuban contingent to fight side by side with US forces against the Korean people. But the popular outcry was such that the Authentic ruler was unable to keep his promise. Even Prio's mother, Doña Regla Socarrás, of *mambí* descent, came out against attempts to send Cubans to that war.

Under *Auténtico* administrations, the cost of living reached sky-high levels. The widespread popular unrest that resulted was brutally repressed, leaving fatal victims and numerous people wounded at the hands of the police. One of the victims was Carlos Rodríguez, a worker who died in September of 1951 as a consequence of the beating he received from the police during a demonstration against a bus fair increase.

Efforts to suppress the growing popular protests brought about abuses against civil liberties and rights: banning or violent dispersion of rallies and demonstrations; temporary and definitive closings of newspapers, radio stations and radio shows; raiding of offices of political parties and other opposition organizations; creation of new repression agencies, like the Subversive Activity Repression Group; continuous harassment of the People's Socialist Party and repeated attempts to declare it illegal; persecution and even murdering of not only opposition figures but also other personalities who clashed with the interests of certain political factions or gangs. Among those murdered, just to cite a few examples, were Carlos Martínez Junco, a high school student, killed in October of 1947 during a demonstration against corrupt officials in the Ministry of Education; ex-president of the University Students Federation and former Sports Director under the first Authentic administration, Manolo Castro, killed in 1948; Justo Fuentes Clavel, vice-president of the University Students Federation, murdered in 1949; and Alejo Cossío del Pino, an ex-State Minister under the Grau government, killed in 1952.

Complementary laws to the Constitution.- In his quest to give the impression that a favorable change had occurred in the country, Prío Socarrás announced a "**new paths**" policy that contemplated the approval of a series of complementary laws to the Constitution of 1940. Within this framework, Prío managed to pass a pompous Agrarian Reform Law that did not tackle any of the most important problems of the Cuban countryside; it merely limited itself to regulate the rents that land tenants were supposed to pay—a regulation that was never enforced—the creation of a Section for Rural

Consulting—that in practice never worked, to advise *campesinos* in their struggle against geophagy and to distribute several hundred hectares of land without affecting large landowners or offering resources of any kind to small farmers.

One of the most far-reaching measures was the creation of the *Banco Nacional de Cuba* (National Bank of Cuba) that began its operations in 1950. That same year, the Bank for Agricultural and Industrial Aid was also created, which mostly favored the wealthiest rural owners. Another one of the most popular demands was the creation of the Department of Treasury. Its creation was approved in 1950, but it did not begin to operate officially until 1952, so it never played any role during the Prío Socarrás Administration.

The *Partido del Pueblo Cubano* (Ortodoxo).- Since the beginning of the Authentic government several trends evolved within the leadership of the *Partido Revolucionario Cubano (Auténtico)*, two of which overpowered the others: one defended the democratic and nationalist theories advocated by the party's platform and the other sought to use power privileges for personal benefit, using whatever means—no matter how dishonest—to achieve this goal. Such diversity in trends reflected the ideological, political and social composition of the Authentic Party.

Contradictions increased in 1946 when, besides the worsening of vices, the Grau government took an obvious anti-popular and reactionary stance. On November 27 that year, the prestigious Authentic leader Manuel Bisbé accused Grau of governing only with those who flattered him, of giving old politicians the most important responsibilities and of allowing the corruption of some of his ministers. In December, five senators and nine representatives of the party created a fraction and agreed to jointly act within the PRC (A) under the leadership of Eduardo Chibás, a veteran fighter of the party against Machado since 1927 and an advocate of the principles that gave birth to the political organization. Chibás, as well as the other members of the fraction, criticized political and administrative corruption, the high cost of living, the rule of gunmen, the divisive policy within the trade union movement, the re-election campaigns and other evils. On March 12, 1947, they signed a document demanding "fundamental rectification" from Grau in the political, economic and social spheres.

But no changes came from the president and on May 15, 1947 they split from the party and founded a new political organization which took the name *Partido del Pueblo Cubano (Ortodoxos)*. When the reorganization of political parties took place a few months later, the PPC (O) came in fifth, with some 165.000 registered members.

The Orthodox Program called for economic independence, industrialization, agricultural diversification, nationalization of the main public services, the creation of a banking system, state control over production and exports, the end of racial discrimination, raising workers standards of living, elimination of gangs, administrative morality and balance among the various social classes.

Aware of the prestige of other bourgeois parties and of the impossibility for the communists and other left-wing organizations to gain power amid the prevailing "Cold War" and "McCarthyism" conditions, Chibás hoped to build an independent movement that would gain the support of the vast national majorities over a short period of time without the necessity of forging alliances with other parties. Hence his absolute rejection of electoral pacts as a fundamental principle of his political tactic.

143

However, the PPC (O) opened its doors to all who expressed their wish to join its ranks, as long as they accepted Chibás' leadership and the party platform, notwithstanding their ideological stand, political origin or class positions. With such an opening, the composition of the new party was very heterogeneous: former communist militants who had left the party but maintained progressive ideas, leaders of national-revolutionary or national-reformist tendencies, freethinkers and young people who understood the need for socialism; it also counted on the membership of large landowners and reactionary bourgeois, and representatives of the conservative wing of the Catholic Church.

In any event, despite the prevailing contradictions, Chibás guidance prevailed within the leadership of the PPC (O). With his charismatic personality he was the organization's soul. His fight against political and administrative corruption, his fight for the nationalization of the telephone and electrical companies and his support for other popular demands, earned the enthusiastic backing of hundreds of thousands of Cubans.

The Orthodox leader had fundamental contradictions with Marxism, and the formulas that he offered to face the evils that prevailed in the country did not provide thorough solutions. Debates between Communists and Chibás at times became very passionate; but generally they coincided on the denunciations of the same problems that affected the country and suffered similar attacks and reprisals, which is why they expressed solidarity with each other. Chibás always criticized the divisiveness of the Cuban labor movement, the assassination of its leaders, the violation trade union democracy and the attempts to ban the *Partido Socialista Popular*. In fact, among the island's political parties, the only serious and effective opposition against the disastrous Authentic Administration came from the Communists and the Orthodox.

The Youth Movement within the Orthodox Party became very important. Not only was it noticeable due to its massive affiliation and drive, but also due to its advanced ideas in the economic, social and political spheres—actually more advanced than those proclaimed in the Party's Platform. In 1948, they published a brochure with their "ideological and political thinking." They offered a profound analysis of the history of Cuba—with some misunderstandings, but generally accurate—which was quite different from the false approaches taken by bourgeois historians. They also accurately described the main problems affecting the country, drawing the conclusion that socialism was the only solution. However, they explained that prior to the establishment of socialism, a stage of national liberation was required. Many of the young members of this organization would play a fundamental role in subsequent struggles of the Cuban people.

Chibás brought the struggles against administrative corruption to the core of his political campaigns, considering that this was one of the main evils of the country's distressful situation. His symbol was a broom to sweep away the corruption. This is why in a short period of time the PPC (O) became a great mass party; it was not the party with the most members, but it did attract the most attention. In the 1950 elections, three years after the party's foundation, Chibás won a senatorial seat in Congress contested by Havana province; he received more than 200,000 votes, the most a candidate in a senatorial race had ever won.

But Chibás' political career and his own life would be shattered a short time later. Committed to denounce embezzlements, thefts and other immoralities by the Authentic government, he publicly accused one of the government's representatives, Aureliano Sánchez Arango and pledged he would produce concrete evidence during a widely-popular, live radio program that he hosted every Sunday on a national radio network. However, he could not keep his word to gather the evidence he announced he would have, and when Sunday came without the evidence, he gave a brief and emotional speech on his radio program—after which he committed suicide.

Chibás' death was a very severe blow for the PPC (O); its days as a great party were over with the demise of its founder.

The military coup of March 10th, 1952.- According to the laws of the nation, a new electoral process for general elections was due for June 1st, 1952. As months passed, the lack of prestige and the incapacity of the Carlos Prío Socarrás Government became more evident. The PRC (A) presented engineer Carlos Hevia as its presidential candidate, the *Partido Acción Unitaria* would take Fulgencio Batista as candidate and the PPC (O) offered Roberto Agramonte.

Hevia had the benefit of being the candidate of the ruling party and counted on the support of the political machines of six parties. But he had no following among the masses and, to top it off, he represented a regime hated by the people. For his part, Batista was rejected due to his background, for being a representative of militarism and of the pro-imperialist and oligarchic interests. He offered no hope for change. Agramonte, in spite of being a conservative professor, was the only hope for a transformation as he was the standard bearer of Chibás legacy.

He counted on the support of the PPC (O) which still was not discredited and although he rejected any kind of agreement with the *Partido Socialista Popular*, communists decided to vote for him. With their vote, they thought the defeat of the Authentic Administration would be certain. All opinion polls pointed to Roberto Agramonte as the favorite candidate to win the elections.

An extremely important factor within this electoral process—just as in previous moments of Cuban history—was the position of the United States. By this time, Washington had already lost its confidence in the Authentic governments and, in particular, its confidence in Prío Socarrás. Despite his submissiveness, he did not accomplish what he had been instructed to do by imperialism. Neither Grau nor Prío had succeeded in destroying the Cuban Communist Party which, despite attacks and attempts to disband it, still kept its prestige and authority and was already recovering from the latest aggressions. Communist leaders had been unexpectedly removed from the leadership of the labor movement and many of them were murdered. But the Party maintained a great deal of influence on the labor forces and, as a result, neither the monopolies nor the oligarchy managed to accomplish their plans.

Prío was not capable of sending a contingent of Cubans to join US troops in the Korean War, nor he did he sign a Cooperation Treaty on Navigation and Residence as the United States demanded, and he did not prevent Congress from supporting Puerto Rican independence fighter Pedro Albizu Campos. If, on the one hand, Prío tried to strictly carry out an anti-Communist, anti-labor and anti-popular policy as requested by the Americans, on the other hand he wanted to maintain a facade as a "nationalist", portraying himself as an enemy of Latin American dictatorships and supporter of Puerto Rican independence.

And in his eagerness to make himself rich, Prío had clashed with some powerful US interests. In 1950, when an influential US company tried to win a bid for some nickel mines in Oriente Province, Prio's government did not pay attention to the request. Instead, the bid was granted to a small Dutch firm, with the condition that in exchange, it would award participation in utilities to several individuals very close to the president.

These are some of the reasons why Prío and his cohorts no longer enjoyed US support.

The US government and the national oligarchy could least count on the Orthodox Party candidate, as they were fearful of the radical wing of that party and the possibility that the masses would give their popular, patriotic and anti-imperialist imprint to the Party if it ever won.

Consequently, only one of the candidates, General Batista, counted on US favor. Only he displayed the necessary conditions to frustrate a popular victory in the elections and to guarantee the continuity of the oligarchy and pro-imperialist order in the country. And Batista, desperate to return to power, assumed the role as a servant of Washington, the Cuban oligarchy and the military's most reactionary sectors.

Given that he did not have the slightest chance to be elected in the upcoming election, the "strong man" took power through a coup d'etat in the early morning hours of March 10th, 1952. The Authentic government crumbled in a matter of a few hours and Prío Socarrás fled the country without the slightest of resistance. A more openly terrorist and brutal period began for the Cuban people; but during this stage, the popular struggle would also reach it's highest moments, until the achievement of the final victory.

XV

The struggle against the Batista dictatorship. From the attack on the "Moncada" Barracks to the landing of the "Granma" yacht

Reactions to the coup d'etat.- The coup d'etat sent shock waves across the nation, as it amounted to the disruption of the island's constitutional order and due to the nefarious background of its perpetrator. The most alert sectors of society immediately understood that the coup was not staged, as Batista tried to make people believe, to frustrate a supposed self-coup that President Prío would inflict upon himself to perpetuate his mandate. The action, they contended, was aimed at thwarting the victory of the Orthodox Party and deterring the growing mass movement.

A few hours after the events, young lawyer Fidel Castro launched an impassioned Manifesto entitled "*Revolucíon NO, Zarpazo*" (Not a Revolution, but a Calamity) which bluntly denounced the spirit and purpose of the coup leaders, and foresaw the reign of terror that would ensue in Cuba. It called upon Cubans to fight against the dictatorship and warned: "once again there is a tyrant, but there will also be men like Mella, Trejo and Guiteras. There is oppression in the homeland, but there will be a day of liberty again". Aware of preparations for the coup d'etat, Fidel had already denounced it to the leadership of the Orthodox Party and had requested permission to make the denunciation through the party's radio station, but he was never authorized to do so.

Coup d'Etat, 10th of March of 1952

On the very same March 10, the *Partido Socialista Popular* strongly condemned the military operation, accused US imperialists of encouraging it, and urged members of all political parties to unite in battle for their democratic liberties and rights. The Party put forward several specific demands of immediate character. Other organizations like the unitarian trade unions, the campesino organizations, the Democratic Federation of Cuban Women and the Cuban Youth also came out in support of the orientations from the Communist Party. Days before the coup, the PSP had publicly denounced that a coup d'etat was in the making.

The University Students Federation appointed a commission that went to the Presidential Palace early in the morning of March 10. They offered the student's backing to President Prío, but did not receive the welcome they had expected and withdrew. On March 14, FEU approved a Declaration of Principles, in which they staunchly rejected the coup and called upon all truly democratic parties, organizations and groups to unite in support of several common goals. "The homeland is in danger", pointed out the FEU, "and we should honor it with our struggles".

In this way, since the first moments after the coup, three forces came out strongly against it. These were the forces that months and years to come, would play a major role in crucial battles: the group gathered by Fidel Castro, the members of the PSP and the organizations it led, and the students movement.

Bourgeois parties were affected by a severe crisis. Republicans, liberals and a substantial part of the democrats decided to join Batista, while weaker parties disbanded.

The *Partido Revolucionario Cubano (Auténtico)* saw Prio flee to the United States, where he began to conspire with some followers. They had access to abundant financial resources, but their actions, tinted with a sensationalist and putschist character, and lacking any popular backing, organization or orientation, ended up having no significance. In the meantime, Grau devoted himself to an innocuous verbal opposition, and played the game of the electoral mascarade orchestrated by the regime. Other *Auténticos*, like Miguel Suárez Fernández, joined the new governing body.

The *Partido del Pueblo Cubano* (Ortodoxo) condemned the military coup and requested the use of all "the active and passive forces of **legal resistance** provided by the Constitution". The party announced that it would appeal to the Supreme Court and the Constitutional and Social Guarantees Courts, and that it would take its position to the United Nations and the Organization of American States. But internal divisions within the party quickly developed. Emilio Ochoa, former candidate for vice president, who exerted great influence in provincial branches of the party, called for an alliance with the opposition, while Roberto Agramonte, former presidential candidate, continued an isolationist policy. Carlos Márquez Sterling, just like Grau San Martín, yielded and pledged himself to Batista. The main concerns of these politicians was the distribution, among themselves, of seats of representatives or senators, privileges, *botellas* as well as other posts in provincial and municipal governments.

University professors, professionals, and citizens in general decried the coup.

The reactionary dictatorship. Its first steps.- The first thing the **de facto** government did was to abolish the 1940 Constitution. Without any prior popular consultation, it imposed the so called Constitutional Statutes, that gave legal backing to all of Batista's despotic acts, including the new structures of power

148

and their functioning. Constitutional guarantees were suspended, and with them the right to strike and other democratic achievements.

The dictatorship dissolved the Congress of the Republic, and replaced it with the so called Consultative Council, a reactionary body, primarily made up of bankers, landowners, big business representatives, warehouse and shop owners, rich businessmen and traditional politicians, as well as labor union opportunists and mob elements. The dictatorship dissolved political parties, postponed general elections indefinitely and designed a code that ensured the electoral confirmation of the Coup d'etat. It dismissed and arbitrarily appointed mayors and aldermen, and concentrated in the hands of the Minister of Interior many of the tasks of these posts. It suppressed radio broadcasts with political content, prohibited meetings, assemblies, rallies and public demonstration of any character and disbanded at gun point peaceful rallies convened by workers and popular organizations. The dictatorship began a new wave of detentions, kidnappings and incarcerations of humble men and women, gave ministerial and police protection to gangsters imposed on the trade union leadership, prompted the breaking of diplomatic relations between Cuba and the Soviet Union, while it strengthened its ties with tyrant governments of Latin America. It also redoubled the maneuvers and efforts to send Cubans to fight under the command of the US military in Korea and increased the nation's war budget.

Regarding the labor movement, Batista was intent on continuing the policy of his predecessors. Although he ordered the suspension of all political parties, he took special measures with the *Partido Socialista Popular*. Right after the coup, the PSP headquarters and party locals in the provinces were sacked. In subsequent weeks, the offices of **Hoy,** the party's news paper, were raided, as well as the offices of numerous trade union and mass organizations led by the communists, like the Democratic Federation of Cuban Women. The offices of the magazines **Mella** and **La Ultima** suffered similar repressive onslaughts.

Arrests of communist militants, unitarian trade union leaders, and of progressive political leaders took place islandwide. On August 15th, the Consultative Council approved the creation of a special service to investigate all the immediate and long-term plans of communism, dubbed the "Investigative Committee on Communist Activities" (CIAC.).

Obviously, this repressive body not only targeted communists. It was also assigned the task of fighting all popular struggles and expressions of repudiation against the de facto government. The first acts of violence had already taken place, among them, the assassination of teenager Sergio Reina. Also, as a result of the coup, a savage aggression was ordered against the televised program "*La Universidad del Aire*", with the kidnapping and physical abuse of journalist Mario Kuchilán. The newspaper **La Palabra** suffered continued interruptions, as well as the televised program "Ante la Prensa". Neither journalist Mario Kuchilán, nor the above mentioned programs were linked to the *Partido Socialista Popular*.

Acts of violence increased after the creation of the new repressive body. On January 15, 1953, police attacked a powerful student rally that was protesting the desecration of a bust of youth leader Julio Antonio Mella, located near the grounds of the University of Havana. The police fired at the demonstrators, leaving 12 wounded, among them, Architecture Student Rubén Batista, who died several days later. That same day the police assaulted the workshop of sculptor José Manuel Fidalgo and destroyed many of his pieces of work, among them small statues of Martí with an inscription that read *"Para Cuba que sufre"* (For the suffering of Cuba). Students who distributed the **Alma Mater** periodical were arrested, and in May the government took actions to abolish university autonomy.

With the pretext of fighting communism, Batista perpetuated the absolute control of the CTC and trade unions through Mujal's followers. Charges against the killer of Labor Leader Jesus Menéndez, captain Casillas, were dropped and he was promoted to the rank of major. The assassins of labor leader Aracelio Iglesias were released from prison.

Another of the anti-labor measures adopted by the dictatorship was the prohibition of May Day parades for 1952. The suspension of constitutional guarantees was extended, and only the official Mujal-backed CTC was authorized to hold a meeting at the *Palacio de los Trabajadores.*

In terms of the economy, the government favored big business at the expense of an increasing cost of living for workers. In the months following the coup d'etat, the cost of living increased by more than 15%. Prices of beef, beans, suburban transportation and postal rates skyrocketed. Wages, salaries and pensions, except those of teachers and members of the Army, remained stagnated or were cut. Just between September 1952 and March of 1953, workers lost 53,026,400 pesos as a result of salary cuts.

Small farmers were also the target of the government's deceit and demagogy. Four months after Batista's take over, on July 17, he approved Decree Law 427 that forced land tenants to pay rents that amounted to the legalizing of land theft by US and Cuban landowners. The measure sparked the protest of small farmers from the locations of Realengo 18, Caujerí, Hato Estero, Rancho Mundito and other parts of the country. Grassroots labor organization supported the protests.

From its inception, the Batista government proved to be a docile servant of US interests. It followed the instructions of reducing sugar, tobacco, and other productions, and kept the national industry at the mercy of foreign competition. It signed numerous accords with the United States that translated into immense benefits for US companies and made scandalous concessions that included loans and credits to US companies at the expense of the national budget. An example was the case of the electricity and telephone monopoly. The government practically turned over Cuba's crude potential to US oil companies, while the production of nickel concentrates and cobalt, the country's third leading economic sector, was handed over to the Moa Bay Co. and Freeport Sulfur. US investments, considered at 713 million in 1951, rose to 1 billion by 1958.

Batista always rejected establishing commercial ties with the USSR and other socialist countries, reduced trade with Japan and European capitalist countries and reaffirmed Cuba's economic dependence on the US market.

Struggle tactics. The Popular Socialist Party.- Revolutionary forces coincided in their rejection of the **de facto** government, as well as in the strategic goal of toppling it, and establishing a broad-based democratic government. But sharp differences over the tactics to be employed soon developed.

The first political party that clearly outlined its tactical guidelines for the struggle was the Popular Socialist Party (PSP). As a strategic course, it proposed the struggle for a transitional government based on a broad coalition that would reinstate the Constitution of 1940 and all the democratic liberties and rights, and would call for immediate elections, so that the people could choose a government of national liberation, capable of developing a program with the transformations that the country demanded.

To achieve this goal, the Party called for the forging of unity in action among the working class, *campesinos* and all the other popular sectors (youth, students, women), and the creation of a common united front of political parties and organizations that would have the capacity to trigger mass mobilizations of such magnitude that the tyranny would be forced to desist from its repressive actions, re-establish constitutional rights and hold free elections.

The PSP, the Socialist Youth and organizations led by them (workers, women's and students) were committed to stage joint actions with the *Partido del Pueblo Cubano,* the Orthodox Youth, the FEU and other students organizations. This goal could not be achieved with the leadership of the PPC (O), but many of its members and cadres, and most of all the above mentioned youth organization, did join in the effort, forging a strong unity. Hence, the massive gatherings in favor of the Constitution, the Congress of Martí's Youth, the refusal to abide by Batista's statutes as well as many other actions conducted by youth against the Batista dictatorship, saw the active participation of communists and organizations led by the PSP. A permanent and effective solidarity was established among these revolutionary sectors.

But the same did not occur with the leadership of the bourgeois parties in the opposition, who under the table sought communist support, but in order to avoid clashes with the United States, refused any kind of formal alliance or pact with the PSP.

Despite the bonds established by the PSP with other revolutionary forces across the island its scope of relations was limited. The isolationist situation in which it was kept by the other parties, the persecutions that its members suffered, the prejudices against them, the intense national and international propaganda campaigns that tried to discredit them, and the disagreement of some sectors with some actions taken by the party, made it impossible to bring under its leadership the vast majority of the Cuban people. For these reasons, and without having the proper means and the indispensable forces, it was impossible for the PSP to lead the armed struggle against the tyranny. In the conditions of Cuba at that time, as Fidel Castro has expressed, that attempt would have resulted in a pointless holocaust.

Faced with that reality, the Party's only feasible move was the formation of a broad front, which helped to challenge the tyranny and force it to yield and also brought and end to the PSP's isolation.

In the meantime, the PSP expressed its opposition to preparations for a "counter coup" and putsch attempts organized by some politicians of the bourgeois opposition, arguing that these actions were being organized without the knowledge of the masses, by people who had no moral or prestige who were purely seeking political advantages.

The PSP later expressed its disagreement, albeit from different positions, with the insurrection tactics adopted by Fidel Castro and his movement. While it acknowledged the honesty, the courage and nobleness of this group of young people—and even expressed its solidarity with them—the PSP described Fidel's tactics as mistaken. The organization said that insurrection was a last recourse, to be used when all other possibilities of mass struggle were exhausted, that the armed struggle would be a result of the climax of mass struggle. The Party failed to perceive that, in Fidel's conception, actions were intertwined with mass struggle, and erroneously considered his actions as putschist. The PSP maintained this mistaken appraisal until late 1957.

Nevertheless, the Party did not question the armed struggle as a method. That's why it energetically rejected the position of ideologists and reactionary politicians linked to Batista and pro-imperialists, who tried to discredit that kind of struggle. It defended the people's right to rise up in arms. But again, it saw insurrection as **a last step** when all possibilities of mass struggle have become impossible. But for Fidel, it was appropriate to combine various forms of struggle, with armed insurrection as the decisive form to be waged **from the beginning** in order to overthrow the Batista tyranny and install a government that would materialize Cuba's national liberation and social emancipation.

The student movement.- The FEU and high school students organized continued activities aimed at denouncing the tyranny's anti-democratic acts and criminal repressive methods, attempting to draw to their mobilizations all people, all opposition parties, organizations and groups. They tried to create a socially unsustainable situation for the dictatorship. The FEU constantly issued appeals for the formation of a broad-based front against the dictatorship, without any exclusions. The front's immediate goal would be to replace the tyranny with a provisional government appointed by the students.

The decision to convene the people to pledge allegiance to the 1940 Constitution was enthusiastically welcomed. These activities began at the University of Havana, and then continued throughout the rest of the island. They took advantage of the baseball games, carnivals and other public activities to stage vibrant demonstrations against the tyranny. The public rallies, demonstrations and parades were convened to celebrate patriotic dates, to pay homage to martyrs of revolutionary struggles, to bury those who were being murdered, to protest against the crimes and abuses of the police force and to demand the release of detainees and political prisoners. A bust of Mella was installed on the plaza across from the University of Havana staircase on San Lázaro Street, and another bust of Antonio Guiteras was erected at the University's Pharmacology School. These rallies amounted to strong denunciations against Batista and his regime. They were generally repressed by the police, resulting in demonstrators killed, wounded and incarcerated.

An opportunity of exceptional importance for the student and popular struggles became available in January 1953, with the commemoration of the centennial of José Martí's birth. Martí's teachings against tyrannies and despotism, as well as all his patriotic ideals, were the highest banner the Cuban youth and people would wave. As the date approached, the FEU issued a document to be signed by the people", A Golden Book on Martí's Centennial", and disseminated a brochure containing some thoughts of the Apostle that were powerful political and ideological weapons in the fight against the dictatorship.

152

The celebration of the Congress of Martí's Youth, which wound up on January 27th, was a resounding success. It not only analyzed Martí's thought, but also made demands akin to the youth, energetically pronounced itself against the de facto government, and demanded the re-establishment of constitutional order. The importance of the event was expressed in its diversification. On hand were hundreds of delegates, representing different sectors of the Youth from the most diverse ideological trends and organizational membership.

Members of the University Students Federation and other students associations, from the opposition political parties, from workers, women, campesino organizations, etc., signed a "Martí's Youth Oath", through which they pledged themselves to the fight for the achievement of José Martí's most beautiful dreams which ended: "We swear to you, Great Teacher, to abide by the historic legacy that you bequeathed us, and give everything, even our own lives if necessary, to make of Cuba the independent, free, peaceful and happy homeland that you wanted it to be". Hundreds of thousands of youth from across the island signed this document.

On the night of January 27, leaving from the University's central staircase, the historic "Torchlight Parade" in honor of Martí swept the streets, with the attendance of thousands of young men and women and people from all walks of life. Among the demonstrators were many revolutionary youths working under the leadership of Fidel Castro to prepare the uprising. On the following day, in the afternoon, a huge popular parade, also organized by the students, closed the celebrations for the Centennial of the birth of the Apostle. In both the torchlight parade and the parade on the 28th, the crowd uninterruptedly chanted slogans of struggle: Down with Batista!, Down with the Dictatorship!, long live Martí!, Centennial with Liberty!, and Unity!

A year after the coup d'etat, the FEU declared March 10th as "Day of National Mourning" and began to air funeral music through powerful loudspeakers deployed at the University. The student movement expressed its solidarity with all victims of the tyranny, like that accorded to members of the National Revolutionary Movement —an insurrection organization led by professor Rafael García García. When these revolutionaries' plan of attacking the headquarters of the Batista Dictatorship Army in Columbia Fortress was discovered, and those involved in the actions were incarcerated, the students mobilized in their support, and many of them were sent to prison. The FEU called for a student strike and agreed to seize 13 University schools. Rocks were thrown at police cars, and high school students took over the building of Havana's Institute #1. The students movement also sided with the labor, campesino, small farmers and other popular sectors.

In June of 1953, the FEU strongly condemned the Montreal Pact, accord drawn up by traditional and discredited politicians opposing the Batista dictatorship. This manifesto was alien to the interests of the masses and did not respond to the needs of the country. The FEU stated its position: it called for unity among all members of the opposition, supported all Cubans who truly opposed Batista through any type of grassroots struggle, and fought all those who joined Batista's electoral mockery. The FEU fully adhered to the thesis of revolutionary insurrection.

This strict position would be maintained throughout the struggle against the Batista dictatorship.

The unitarian trade movement.- The Batista tyranny maintained a policy of imposing by force and supporting official trade union leaderships in CTC branches. It also forced workers to join these branches and pay fees to the controlled Mujalista organizations and threatened to fire them if they did not abide by this policy. This was a serious obstacle for the labor struggles.

Nevertheless, from the very first day of the putsch, workers demonstrations to condemn the coup continued.

The PSP leadership successfully managed to forge a unity of action among workers of all sectors and political creeds in defense of their class interests and against the government's economic and social programs.

One of Batista's principle objectives was to implement the principle recommendations of the Truslow Mission, centered around the creation of favorable conditions for foreign investors and the national oligarchy. So, new measures were taken to lower production costs and increase labor productivity, like the mechanization in the production of matches and cigars, in port operations and the shipment of sugar, as well as the upgrading of sugar mills and the development of maritime transportation through the use of ferries and seatrains. Moreover, procedures for the layoff of workers were expedited, money deriving from sugar differential agreement was withheld, salaries were lowered, sugar harvests were shortened and factories were closed. To facilitate the expansion of the US's "King Ranch" cattle monopoly, the eviction of hundreds of campesino families was ordered.

Numerous mobilizations ensued against this maneuvers of the dictatorship: parades, rallies, strikes, stoppages, massive occupations of work places and institutions, and slow downs on the job. To illustrate the situation, we will cite some of the actions. In September of 1952 more than 1000 textile workers from Cárdenas marched on Havana and took over the offices of the Labor Ministry to protest a 40% cut in subsidies for laid-off workers. The local population supported the action, and their demands were met. In October of the same year, over 15 000 tobacco workers in Las Villas went on strike to protest salary cuts, creating a united front. Placetas, Cabaiguán, Gaza del Media and Taguasco are declared "paralyzed towns". In December, 450 workers of "La Estrella" chocolate factory stage a work stoppage and occupy the factory, while the workers of the "Ambrosia Industrial" plant hold a sit-down strike. Workers from Havana's bus terminals initiate a slow-down strike. Employers of the "Lux" match factory seize the facility, which had been shut down and go on a hunger strike. Agro workers from Matanzas initiate the same action. On October 12, 1952, the Mujal-sponsored trade union calls for a parade in support of Batista to be held in front of the Presidential Palace, but labor forces turn the act into a demonstration of repudiation against Batista, crying **"Liberty!"**, **"Democracy!"**, **"Constitution!"**

Workers from sugar mills in Camaguey, Las Villas, Matanzas, and other regions of the country staged important demonstrations. They often had the support of dock, catering services and railroad workers, as well as the backing of *campesinos*. On May 20, 1952, during a rally at the former "Francisco" sugar mill (known today as "Amancio Rodríguez"), the army killed adolescent Sergio Reina, the first fatal victim of the Batista dictatorship. The struggles of *campesinos* from Realengo 18, Yaguajay, Alquízar, Virama, Rancho Mundito and other regions to protest evictions and to

The assault on the "Moncada" Barracks

express support for the Agrarian Reform were also held. In Oriente province a Committee in Defense of the Agrarian Reform was created. Tobacco and small fruit pickers, dock workers, sugar and construction workers made up the committee. The FEU expressed its solidarity with that committee. Similar organizations were founded in other provinces.

The unitarian labor movement, together with other sectors of the population, took part in rallies demanding the lowering of housing rent, against the sending of Cubans to the Korean War, to demand the payment of withheld salaries of employees from the Public Works Ministry, for the re-establishment of the 1940 Constitution and democratic rights. Despite the fact that May Day Parades were banned, the University Stadium was the site of one of such parades, as well as in other locations of the country, in which the popular demands of public workers were heard. Many workers were either imprisoned or beaten.

Similar actions continuously grew in number and importance during the dictatorship, placing in check the repressive forces and oftentimes frustrating their anti-labor offensive.

Fidel Castro's tactics.- When the coup d'etat took place Fidel Castro immediately realized that Batista and his henchmen would resort to any means, no matter how criminal, to keep themselves in power, that bourgeois politicians would not put up any significant opposition to the dictatorship, that all legal and peaceful means were closed for the people, and that therefore, the only hope to defeat the dictatorship and establish truly democratic rule in the country would be through the use of revolutionary violence.

During the first months, some bourgeois political groups and personalities began to conspire. They brought weapons shipments into the country, created organizations, recruited people and they even engaged in assassination attempts and other terrorist acts. Many honest citizens, desperate to fight against Batista, enrolled in these organizations. But their leaders, despite the fact that they had the money and the resources, were not eager to wage a real war against Batista, and time passed without the materialization of a serious insurrection struggle in the country.

Meanwhile Fidel, together with a group of comrades from previous struggles, and some youngsters that gradually joined him after the coup, remained for several months assessing the situation, and willing to assist any organization committed to the overthrow of Batista. In May of 1952, these young men assembled two radio transmitters to be used clandestinely in Havana city. But when they realized that the bourgeois insurrection groups were only playing at revolution, and that nothing was occurring with the focal point rebellion developed at the University of Havana under the leadership of Professor Rafael García Burkina, they devoted themselves to organize a movement of their own, a truly revolutionary movement. Fidel was convinced that there were objective conditions for a revolution. What remained to be created were the subjective conditions.

The experience of the 1933 Revolution demonstrated that the leadership of the movement could not be in the hands on bourgeois politicians, but in those of a group of fighters fully identified with the revolution's ideals, committed to face any danger and difficulties; that it was indispensable to include in this effort all those

156

forces interested in the toppling of the dictatorship, but under a single command; and that mass mobilizations—a decisive factor in a genuine revolution—could only lead to victory if at the same time there was an armed detachment capable of beating back the reactionary forces.

This is why Fidel's tactic consisted of using the most varied forms of struggle, but counting on the popular armed insurrection as the primary form. His steps were aimed at constituting an initial group, militarily trained, procure the indispensable armament and seize an important military fortress, with the purpose of sparking an uprising in the entire region, then call for a general strike and buy time for a mobilization that would raise the struggle to a national level. In the event that these actions did not succeed in bringing the dictatorship down, an irregular war would follow in the mountains and the countryside, similar to the struggle waged by Cuban *mambises* during the 19th century. Fidel summed up his goals with one phrase: "A small engine is needed to help start the big engine."

The assault on the "Moncada" Barracks.- Following these ideas, it was then decided to assault the "Moncada" barracks, headquarters to the "Antonio Maceo" Regiment in the City of Santiago de Cuba, capital of Oriente province. Due to its importance, the "Moncada" was the country's second largest military fortress in the country, with some 1000 troops. Its distance from Havana, would make difficult the sending of reinforcement troops to the Eastern Army. Moreover, Santiago is located on the Southern Coast, by the sea, and surrounded by mountains, conditions that would facilitate a rebel defense of the city once it was occupied, and would allow for a swift initiation of guerrilla warfare if the city had to be abandoned.

Historic considerations added to these strategic: the island's three independence wars had begun in Oriente, the popular uprisings in various moments of the Republic had also taken place there—even during the 1933 Revolution—its mountains were known by the armed resistance of *campesinos* against the landowners, and its people were always characterized by a spirit of rebelliousness.

Once the Moncada was occupied, the revolutionary forces would take police headquarters, the Maritime Police and Navy posts, as well as a radio station that they would use to proclaim to the people the purpose of the actions and to call them to join the struggle. In Fidel's conception, the armed uprising was inseparable from the mobilization of the popular masses.

In order to support the action on the "Moncada" it was decided to simultaneously seize the "Manuel de Céspedes" barracks in Bayamo, a city located in the center of the province which was a very important crossroads of land communications. This action would include blowing up the bridges over the Cauto River, to prevent the arrival of reinforcements from the Batista Dictatorship for the troops in Santiago.

The actions were planned in absolute secret. Besides Fidel, only two members of the movement's leadership, and their representative in Santiago de Cuba knew of the plans. The others knew that a decisive battle was to take place, but they ignored the details. The same concern was followed at the time of structuring the movement: it was carried out in a cell-like pattern, and security rules, in compliance with their clandestine character, were strictly observed. The organization had two

157

leadership committees: one military committee, under the leadership of Fidel, and a civilian committee, under the leadership of Abel Santamaría.·

Furthermore, the organization was selective. Following Fidel's instructions its members were to be recruited among the humble sectors of the population: workers, *campesinos*, employees, modest professionals. They were men and women, preferably young, with no political ambitions, not infected with the propaganda of anti-communism or the vices of traditional politics. In early 1953, the movement already had some 1200 members.

The weapons, uniforms and the necessary resources for the struggle were obtained without resorting to the aid of well-to-do people or corrupt politicians. The acquisition of those resources was mainly possible through the will and personal efforts of the movement's members. One young man sold his job and raised $300.00 "for the cause". Another sold all the equipment of his photo studio, his only means of income, while another pawned his salary for several months and he had to be stopped from doing the same with his furniture. One sold the equipment of his pharmaceutical laboratory. Another gave up his savings of 5 years, and there were many other cases of generosity and selflessness.

With the funds raised, 165 weapons were purchased, principally 22 caliber rifles and shotguns. Training and shooting practice soon began at the University of Havana, the *Club de Cazadores* from El Cerro and other places in the provinces of Havana and Pinar del Río. A small farm was rented (the "Siboney" farm), located in the outskirts of Santiago de Cuba, with the alleged purpose of turning it into a poultry farm. The weapons, uniforms and automobiles that would be used during the attack were sent to this farm, and combatants would gather there at the proper time.

The 26 of July was picked as the day for the action because it was a carnival Sunday, popular street parties in which people from various parts of he island traditionally came to the city, hence, the presence of young people from other provinces would not be seen as unusual.

The action.- On the dawn of that day, 135 combatants, dressed in military garb and led by Fidel examined the plan of action. They divided into three groups. The first was led by Fidel and would attack the fortress. The two others, led by Abel Santamaría , second in command, and Raúl Castro, would try to seize two important buildings adjacent to the fortress: the Civil Hospital, where the wounded would be taken care of, and the central offices of the local judiciary, or Palace of Justice, from whose roof-top the main action would be supported.

Once all participants were ready, the "Moncada Manifesto"—written by young poet Raúl Gómez García at the request of Fidel—was read. It described the attack on the Moncada as the continuation of the historic struggle for the island's full independence and liberty, proclaimed the revolutionary principles and the movement's objectives and made an appeal to the Cuban people's dignity and self-respect. Gómez García read his poem " *Ya estamos en combate*" ("We are already at war"), and Fidel addressed participants with this brief exhortation:

"Comrades: Within a few hours you shall win or be defeated, but at any rate, listen to me, comrades! at any rate this movement will triumph. If we win tomorrow, Martí's dream will come true much faster. If the contrary would occur, the gesture will serve an example for the Cuban people, to take on our banner and march onwards. The people will support us in Oriente and all over the island. Young men of the Centennial of the Apostle!, like in 1868 and in 1895, here in Oriente we are giving the first cry of LIBERTY OR DEATH!"

"You already know the objectives of the plan. Without any doubt it's dangerous and all those who leave this place with me tonight must do so voluntarily. You still have time to make a decision. Some of you will have to stay here due to a shortage of weapons. Those who are determined to go, take a step forward. Our motto is not to kill except as a last recourse".

Of the 135 revolutionary men and women, 131 took a step forward. The four that repented were given the order to return to their point of departure, and shortly after 4 o'clock in the morning, they all began to drive towards Santiago. The groups led by Abel and Raúl fulfilled their missions: the taking of the Civil Hospital and the Court House. The main group led by Fidel, arrived as planned to one of the checkpoints, checkpoint number 3. They disarmed the government troops there and went into the interior of the barracks. But a squad unexpectedly patrolling the area, and a sergeant who suddenly showed up on a side street, provoked a premature exchange of fire that warned the troops, who rapidly mobilized. Surprise, a decisive factor for success, was not achieved. The fight began on the outskirts of the premises of the fortress, and it became a battle of positions.

The revolutionaries were at a total disadvantage in the face of an enemy superior in weapons and troops and entrenched within the barracks. Another adverse element, an accidental one, was that the commando could not count on the support of several cars carrying some of the best weapons, because its crew got lost before they reached the "Moncada", in a city they did not know. Understanding that continuing the fight under such adverse circumstances would amount to a collective suicide, Fidel ordered a retreat.

The orgy of blood.- Right after these events, the dictatorship forces unleashed a brutal repression and wrote one of the bloodiest pages in Cuban history. Batista declared a state of siege in Santiago de Cuba and the suspension of all constitutional guarantees nationwide. He shut down the **"Noticias de Hoy"** newspaper, of the *Partido Socialista Popular*, and enforced print media censorship. Repressive forces were able to launch a savage repression against the rebellion without the risk of publicity. As to the assailants of "Moncada", Batista ordered the assassination of ten revolutionaries for each soldier killed in combat.

With the exception of a few revolutionaries who were able to escape thanks to the people's support, almost all the rest were capture, and a good part of them were murdered in the following days. Only six participants in the attacks of the barracks had actually died in combat, but the regime's repressive forces murdered 55 of those who had been captured as well as two people who hadn't even participated in the actions. Moreover, in contrast to the treatment given by the revolutionaries to the military personnel they captured, the rebels were savagely tortured before being killed, and later presented as if they had died in combat.

Sometime later, as he stood trial, Fidel denounced the extent of this crime's horror: "The killing did not take a minute, an hour or a full day. It took an entire week. The beating, the torture, the dropping of people off roof tops and the shooting did not cease for a single moment at the hands of those who were professionally trained to murder. The Moncada barracks was turned into a workshop of torture and death, and some undignified men transformed their military uniforms into butchers' aprons".

On the morning of July 26, after the retreat, Fidel returned with a group of combatants to the Siboney Farm, and followed by 18 men he left for the mountains to continue the struggle. During a week, they remained on the higher side of the mountain range, without water or food, while the Army was patrolling the base of the mountain. Scattered in small groups, some of them could cross the army lines; others turned themselves in the presence of the Archbishop of Santiago de Cuba. Fidel, with a few other of his comrades, totally exhausted, were surprised, as they slept, by a squad commanded by second lieutenant Pedro Manuel Sarría, on August 1st, 1953.

Although the massacre of prisoners had stopped due to the energetic reaction of the people, some of the soldiers wanted to kill Fidel and his two men on the spot. But lieutenant Sarría, an honest military officer, prevented them from doing so and told his troops: "Ideas cannot be killed". A while later, Sarría's convoy met with the Chief of Operations of the "Moncada" barracks, major Andrés Pérez Chaumont, the killer of many of the assailants. This officer urged Sarría to give him the prisoners, but Sarría flatly rejected that order, again saving the lives of Fidel and his comrades. He took them to the Santiago de Cuba prison, where they would be in less danger, and not to the "Moncada", as instructed by Colonel Alberto del Río Chaviano, Chief of Moncada's Regiment #1.

The trial.- Santiago de Cuba's local judiciary was transformed into an emergency court, the site of Trial 37 of 1953 against the imprisoned revolutionaries. It was September 21st. Some 60 people who did not participate in the actions were also accused, among them several leaders of the Orthodox and Authentic PSP parties. They were later released.

The assailants of the "Moncada" barracks maintained an exemplary attitude during the process. Despite the fact that they were handcuffed and heavily escorted during the trial, that troops kept their weapons pointing at them, and that they couldn't even consult with their defense attorneys, the young men reiterated during the lawsuit their revolutionary affiliation and their denunciations against the crimes perpetrated by the tyranny. Finally, 32 defendants were found guilty and 18 were acquitted. In the case of the acquitted, the jury failed to present evidence proving their participation in the 26 of July assaults in Santiago and Bayamo. The sentences ranged from 15 to 3 years in prison, and the two women combatants, Haydeé Santamaría and Melba Hernández, were given 7 month sentences.

Particularly harsh treatment was accorded to Fidel Castro. Since his incarceration in Santiago's municipal prison on August 1st, he was kept in solitary confinement, in total isolation, in violation of all juridical norms and of the Court's instructions. Thereafter, the military repeated and unsuccessfully tried to assassinate him using various means.

During the trial's first session, the young leader was forced to conduct his own defense since the attorney that was to act on his behalf was never authorized to interview him or to gather the indispensable information to adequately perform his role. But Fidel's accusations were so strong that once the second session was over, he was set apart from the rest of his comrades and tried separately.

The young defendant was denied even the most elementary rights to prepare his defense. He was not allowed to look at the trial's summary, or use literature needed for his defense, among them , works by José Martí. The trial began on October 16, behind close doors, in a small room of the "Saturnino Lora" Hospital's nursery school. Only 20 persons were allowed to witness the trial. His self-defense, that turned him from defendant into accuser, is one of the most moving and historically important documents in Cuban history.

For over two hours, wearing an old and faded toga that he was given for his defense, he rendered testimony that astonished some and made others tremble with irrefutable arguments not only concerning the illegal, immoral and reactionary character of the March 10th, 1952 coup d'etat, but also of the juridical and moral legitimacy of revolutionary violence to fight it. He made a most vigorous, accurate, courageous and irrefutable denunciation of the tyranny's horrendous crimes and arbitrary acts. He explained that the assault on the "Moncada", and the popular uprising that began with it, were a continuation of the nation's historical struggles for full independence and liberty, and were inspired in the noble yet radical ideas of José Martí, whom he called the intellectual author of the assault on the "Moncada". In his defense, Fidel expressed a revolutionary concept of the term "people", and assigned to it a decisive role as the subject of history. Fidel expressed his absolute trust in the Cuban people, above all in those people who made up the most humble classes and sectors. The optimist and fighting spirit displayed by the young leader, conveyed to the masses the firm conviction that the military setback in "Moncada" would not deter the triumph of the Revolution.

But perhaps the greatest importance of this self-defense was that, besides describing the worsening of the evils the Republic had suffered since its birth, it outlined a platform of profound national transformations in the economic, political, social and cultural spheres, around which the overwhelming majority of the Cuban people would unite. It was an advanced democratic-popular platform, written with a Marxist criteria, which reflected the highest aspirations that could be expressed within the objective conditions of that time. Its anti-imperialist slant was defined in the fact that the measures propounded were only to be accomplished if the wealth of the country was returned to the people and through the definitive breaking of the chains of neocolonial dependency. It was the program for the first stage of the Cuban Revolution.

After Fidel's self-defense and the judge's ruling condemning him to 15 years in prison, the trial was over. In the opinion of one of the magistrates who took part in it, that was the most important trial of the entire republican history. The immense popular upheaval that the attacks caused, the great sympathy and solidarity shown to the Moncada combatants, the honesty and the arguments of the defendants and Fidel's brilliant self-defense, turned the military setback at "Moncada" and "Céspedes" barracks into an important political victory.

As Raúl Castro, one of the main heroes of the attack on the "Moncada" barracks has noted, the fundamental meaning of the actions of the 26th of July resides in that they triggered off a period of armed struggle that did not end until the overthrow of the tyranny, they created a new leadership and a new revolutionary organization which repudiated the submission to US interests and the reformism advocated by the old bourgeois parties, they highlighted Fidel Castro as the leader and strategist of the popular war and the radical political action of the Cuban people, and they served as precursor to and experience for the organization of the "Granma" yatch expedition and the guerrilla warfare in the Sierra Maestra mountains.

The school of political prison.- The court ruled that the 30 male combatants of "Moncada" were to serve their prison terms at La Cabaña Fortress, located in Havana. But the Minister of the Interior instructed their transfer to the so called Model Prison, on the then-Isle of Pines (today, Isle of Youth), far away from the capital. The two women were interned at the National Women's Penitentiary in Guanajay, some 45 kilometers from Havana. A good amount of those who escaped the manslaughter or those who were acquitted for lack of evidence, continued involved in one way or the other in the fight against Batista.

The imprisoned young men were submitted to an isolation regime, without contact with the rest of the inmates. Particularly harsh was the treatment accorded to Fidel Castro, who on several occasions was held in solitary confinement, without the possibility of contact with his comrades, without access to correspondence, newspapers, radio or even sun light. This treatment led to a nationwide protest.

In spite of the adversity, the prison period was a great school for the "Moncada" combatants. They devoted their time to enrich their general culture and their political and ideological education, to reorganize the movement, to send instructions to the revolutionaries who were free, and to get ready for the continuation of the struggle once they were released from prison. The letters Fidel wrote in prison amount to a treasure of political and revolutionary education.

As an important tool for the improvement of their theoretical level, the combatants founded the "Abel Santamaría" Academy, where they received classes on History, Geography, Mathematics, Political Economy, Philosophy, English, Grammar, and other subjects. With much effort they began to build up a library which gathered some 600 books, representative of Cuban and universal culture, among them works by José Martí, and as well as titles by Marx, Engels and Lenin.

While in prison, Fidel secretly rewrote his self-defense **History will Absolve Me** and he figured out ways to send it to his comrades in Havana, who printed and distributed the text for the first time in 1954.

Repression and electoral maneuvers. Popular struggle.- While Fidel and his comrades served their sentences at the Model prison, the situation in the country became worse. The tyranny's repressive bodies stepped up their assaults against the people, violently dispersing strikes, demonstrations and public rallies. They assaulted and closed newspapers and radio programs. Detentions, torture and murders were rampant. The expulsion of Communists and their sympathizers from their jobs in public services and offices was ordered. Leaders and members of revolutionary or mass organizations, even many politicians from the bourgeois opposition, suffered daily abuse at the hands of the repressive forces. Not even the high Catholic hierarchy was respected: shortly after the attack on the Moncada, the police raided Havana's Archbishop See and delivering a blow to the head of Cardinal Arteaga.

The assassinations that attracted the most attention were those of Mario Aróstegui Recio, railroad worker from Camaguey province and member of the Orthodox Youth, and of Mario Fortuny, a former official of the Grau San Martín and the Prío Socarrás Administrations, and an outstanding leader of the Triple A. The Triple A was an insurrection organization founded by politician Aureliano Sánchez Arango of the PRC. This organization was forced to disband as a result of the detention or assassination of some of its members, the seizing of its weapons and the general persecution unleashed against its members. The organization's top leaders fled the country.

But Batista did not use repression just to remain in power, but also to impose on the people the policies demanded by the national oligarchy and the US upper classes. Through the use of force—he thought—he could attain, among other things, a decrease in the production of sugar, tobacco, rice and other staples, thereby facilitating the importation of US-made products at dumping prices and create favorable conditions for foreign investment: low salaries, companies authorized to fire workers, manageable trade union organizations, abusive intensification of labor, renunciation to the benefits of the sugar differential, tax exemptions for foreign capital and the granting of credits at the expense of the state budget, etc.

This planning included the construction of a canal that would link northern Cuba's sea waters with those of the South, splitting the island into two parts. This project, approved in August of 1954, was called the "Via-Cuba Canal", but the people dubbed it the "Break-Cuba Canal". The decision included the construction of commercial and tourism zones on both shores of the canal that would be ruled by special laws. The move would represent a great business deal for the concessionaire company *Compañía del Canal del Atlántico al Mar Caribe de Cuba, SA*. The company, made up of foreign capitalists and Batista's cohorts, was authorized to forcibly expropriate and evict owners or tenants living on zones adjacent to the canal. The concessionaire would be made for a period of 99 years and 500 million dollars would be invested in the project.

The overwhelming majority of Cubans rejected the project, not only for the consequences already mentioned, but also due to the threat it would entail regarding a direct US intervention, following the experience of the Panama Canal. Faced with widespread repudiation, after two years of immense efforts, the dictatorship was forced to abandon the project.

In the meantime, while the opposition was treated with an iron glove. Batista took steps to "legalize" his status without compromising his power. He called for mid-term elections for November 1953, but the electoral regulations he established were so outrageous that the only opposition party to registered was the PRC(A) of Grau San Martín. Rejection of the maneuver, even from bourgeois sectors, together with situation created by the attack on the "Moncada", forced the government to suspend the elections and make a new call for November 1st, 1954. To encourage massive participation of political parties the dictatorship announced the elections would be general, covering executive and legislative responsibilities, at national, provincial and municipal levels. Requirements for the inscription of political parties were relaxed.

Despite that, participation from the bourgeois opposition was limited only to the PRC (A) and a fraction of the *Partido del Pueblo Cubano (Orthodox)* led by the well-known landowner and politician Federico Fernández Casas. Four other parties that supported the government registered and made up the National Progressive Alliance: *Acción Progresista, Liberal,* and the *Union Radical* parties, and a fraction of the Democratic Party. Hence two presidential candidates would be in the race: Batista and Grau.

Revolutionary organizations and the people in general quickly understood that these elections would be a farce, and consequently, they denounced them with large mobilizations. At the very last minute, Grau withdrew from the race and the dictator remained as the sole candidate. The farce was consummated and Batista once again took the nation's presidency, now with the alleged backing of the elections. But no one was fooled.

Not long after the elections, in an obvious gesture of support to Batista's tyranny, US Vice-president Richard Nixon paid a friendly visit to Cuba. Besides the political backing, the northern neighbor was making important contributions to the strengthening of Batista's military might. One and a half years before the crimes committed against the assailants of the "Moncada" and "Carlos Manuel de Céspedes" barracks, US President, Dwight D. Eisenhower had described Cuba as among 8 Latin American countries that had received considerable military support and announced that in subsequent months, the island would receive 140 million pesos worth of military assistance.

Contrasting with this support, and as a response to the terror imposed by the tyranny, its anti-labor and anti-popular measures, the electoral farce, the complicity of various sectors of the bourgeois opposition and Washington's support to Batista, anti-government mobilizations multiplied. The most outstanding actions were those staged by the student movement, workers, women and progressive intellectuals. The student leadership radicalized, with the election of energetic José Antonio Echeverría in 1954 as the FEU's President. The women's movement was taken to the forefront by the fighting spirit of the Women's Civic Front of Martí Followers. In Santiago de Cuba, young revolutionary Frank País and Pepito Tey founded the *Acción Revolutionaria Oriental* ARO), that grouped hundreds of young men and women who continuously acted against the dictatorship . Soon, this organization's influence extended beyond the limits of Oriente province, taking on the name *Acción Nacional Revolucionaria.*

In Havana, another group of young people belonging to the National Revolutionary Movement, founded a year before by University professor Rafael García Barcena, devised a plan of sabotage actions, and some of its members were detained.

The revolutionary labor movement, the PSP, and the Socialist Youth played a main role in the continued popular mobilizations of the time. These organizations spearheaded the actions in many sectors. Protests grew in momentum and important strikes and work stoppages took place, mainly within the sectors of the sugar industry, the railroads, tobacco and transportation.

During this period (1953-1955) two regional events made important contributions to the impetus of popular demonstrations against the Batista tyranny. They also encouraged expressions of solidarity with Latin American peoples. The first event was the conspiracy and armed assault of the Guatemalan oligarchy and the US administration against the democratic government of Jacobo Arbenz. The second was the invasion of Costa Rica's northern territory by the troops of Nicaragua's dictator Anastasio Somoza. In both cases, Cubans marched to those countries to express their solidarity. Moreover, demands for the defense of Guatemala's democracy and Costa Rica's sovereignty sparked the organization of a powerful popular movement that Batista was unable to curb: the struggles against tyrannies and US interventions in sisters nations and in Cuba.

Amnesty: a resounding popular victory. Founding of the 26th of July Movement.- One of the issues that allowed for a great unity of views and actions in the struggle against the tyranny, was the demand of amnesty for all political prisoners, particularly for those who attacked the "Moncada" and "Carlos Manuel de Céspedes" barracks. From the very moment that the assailants were sentenced in 1953, the struggle for their release began. A wave of protests took place against the abuses they received in prison, particularly against the isolation that Fidel Castro was submitted to.

At the center of that activity was a Committee of Relatives of Political Prisoners, which assumed the leadership of the national campaign. For their part, the Federation of University Students (FEU), the *Partido Socialista Popular* (PSP) and the Socialist Youth and the Women's Civic Front of Martí's Followers, as well as many other political, social and mass organizations gave a decisive support to the demand. Print and radio media also made important contributions. The demand was expressed at all times and by all means possible; it ultimately became a national clamor. Tens of thousands of signatures were collected for a petition drive to demand their release. Even some conservative institutions joined the petition drive demanding amnesty.

In June of 1954, the Batista regime, in an effort to improve its image before the November elections, approved an amnesty law, but it did not benefit those who had committed violent acts that caused victims among members of the Public Forces, hence, it excluded Fidel Castro and his comrades. Once the elections were held and Batista felt secure, and in face of the overwhelming popular demand, he signed a parliament-proposed amnesty law. And although it was still limited, it did include Fidel and his followers. On May 15, 1955, Fidel Castro and the other imprisoned assailants of the barracks in Santiago and Bayamo were released. With this amnesty, the revolutionary forces, and the people had achieved their most important victory since the coup on March 10, 1952.

The popular reception given to the revolutionary group in Nueva Gerona, Isle of Pines, was impressive. Similar images would be repeated in Batabanó, in the railroad stations that their train would pass by on their way to Havana's railroad station. Messages of encouragement poured from the most committed opposition organizations and sectors (the FEU, the PSP, the Women's Civic Front, PPC leaders, Orthodox Youth, Mothers of Martyrs, etc.). All these gestures were a clear evidence of the mass support for Fidel Castro and his revolutionary ideals and actions. On that very March 15, a command from the *Acción Revolucionaria Oriental*, led by Frank País, expressed its welcome to the fighter's release by attacking Santiago de Cuba's *Club de Cazadores*, which ended with the seizing of numerous weapons.

In an interview with the press in the Isla de Pinos Hotel, as well as in his first statements to the Cuban people, Fidel expressed his commitment to stay on the island to fight the Batista government, rejected the electoral maneuvers sponsored by Batista with the connivance of some politicians from the opposition, and insisted on his and his comrade's decision to offer even their lives in the quest of the liberty of their homeland.

On board the steam boat that carried him from the Isle of Pines to the mainland, together with a group of supporters present during their release, Fidel outlined the ideas he had nurtured in prison to reorganize the movement and continue the struggle against the dictatorship. It was on board that boat where the movement's sympathizers agreed to name the organization "26 of July" (M-26-7), paying homage to the date of the heroic actions at the "Moncada" and "Carlos Manuel de Céspedes" fortresses.

Ever since, Fidel conducted a tireless activity aimed at unmasking he lies of Batista's spokespersons, denouncing the regime's crimes and abuses and convincing the people that Batista would not relinquish power peacefully. He visited some periodicals and radio stations to thank them for the campaign they waged demanding their release from prison, wrote some articles for **Bohemia** magazine and other newspapers, mainly **La Calle,** made statements to the press and tried to participate in public rallies and radio programs.

On the night of June 12, a group of revolutionaries led by Fidel met in a house in Havana, and integrated the first national leadership of the 26th of July Movement. It was made up of 11 members and had 5 working fronts: action, youth, finances, propaganda and labor.

While Fidel's intense activities continued and he became more popular among the people, the more notorious became the dictatorship's political bankruptcy. Its survival was mainly based on the terror it imposed and it was unable to resist any legal struggle. Hence, it then proceeded to close all channels of expression the young lawyer had access to. It did not grant permission for a public student rally on May 20, and prevented Fidel from going to the University. Politically oriented newscasts and radio programs were suspended. Journalists were assaulted and the **La Calle** newspaper offices were raided and shut down as terror was reinforced.

During the night of June 9, Jorge Agostini was murdered. He was a fighter from the Auténticos, a veteran from the Spanish Civil War, former Major of the Navy and former Presidential Palace Secret Services Chief during the Grau San Martín and Prío Socarrás administrations. This murder sparked heated protests from numerous national institutions, the FEU, the PSP and other political parties, and was vigorously denounced by Fidel Castro in an article entitled: "Faced with terror, faced with murder".

The repressive forces raided the homes of revolutionaries and detained, beat and tortured some of them , among them were attackers of the "Moncada". Some military officers charged with conspiring to rebel within the armed forces. The Bureau against Communist Activities (BRAC) was created. The arrest of Raúl Castro was ordered, falsely accused of having committed a terrorist attack, and plans for his assassination underway. The young revolutionary was forced to request asylum in Mexico's Embassy in Havana, and a short time later, he left for that country.

Under heavy surveillance, limited in his activities, deprived of the possibility of freely expressing his ideas, and under constant threat, Fidel left the country on July 7, 1955 for Mexico. Before leaving Cuba he said: "As all doors to civil struggles have been closed, there is no other solution but those of 1868 and 1895". He added: "As a follower of Martí, I believe it's time to take and not beg for our rights (…) I will be staying somewhere in the Caribbean. Of such trips, one does not return except with the tyranny beheaded at one's feet".

The organizing exile.- Fidel settled in the Mexican capital, and began to group the exiled revolutionary Cubans. He contacted Mexican friends and took part in various public rallies. In the meantime he kept correspondence with the comrades who stayed on the island, giving them instructions for the organization of the Movement all over the island, regularly communicating with them concerning the island's situation and the tactics to be followed in the struggle.

It's necessary to reach out to the people through all possible means, it is the main foundation of the revolutionary struggle, said Fidel. A month after his arrival in Mexico, Fidel wrote the "26th of July Movement" Manifesto #1, released on August 8th. It was the movement's first official document signed by its top leader, and it explained the its organizational a structure, its goals and the main means and methods of struggle. It analyzed the country's general situation in the economic, social and political spheres and explained the 15 main points of the Revolution's program that would be implemented once victory was attained.

The manifesto rejected the dubious agreement that the bourgeois opposition was orchestrating. And although it tactically admitted the holding of immediate general elections **without Batista,** it stated that a side from that, the only way out was armed insurrection. An issue of great importance was that Fidel conceived this struggle, not against the dictatorship, but against the regime that dominated the island over the last 50 years of neocolonial rule. The M-26-7 deposited all its trust in the Cuban people.

From Mexico, Fidel remained in contact with the Orthodox Party, and committed himself to encourage it to abandon peaceful methods, empty talk, hesitation and stagnation, and to assume a more resolute attitude in the face of the situation on the island. In this regard, he took advantage of the Congress of the Orthodox Party that on August 16th gathered the organization's representatives from all over the country, sending them a combative message that was acclaimed by the majority of participants. Numerous young people related with the 26th of July movement were present in the congress, and they managed the approval of Fidel's message as an official document of the Congress. Fidel also kept contacts with other activists on the island. Through them he would continuously receive information concerning the country's situation and he would direct the movement's activities.

In September, a historic encounter took place: Fidel Castro met with Ernest (Che) Guevara. The young Argentinean physician had settled in Mexico, after he had to leave Guatemala to escape the persecution unleashed by the US-imposed Carlos Castillo Armas regime. In Guatemala, Guevara had known Cuban revolutionary fighter Antonio (Ñico) López, assailant of the "Moncada" barracks. López made a good impression on Che when he told him about Fidel Castro and impressive episodes of the struggle against Batista. The encounter between Fidel and Che would be the beginning of a profound friendship and identified the brave internationalist fighter with the cause of the Cuban Revolution.

In late 1955, Fidel made a successful tour through various US cities (Philadelphia, New York, Union City, Bridgeport, Miami, Tampa, Key West). Accompanied by a valuable comrade, Juan Manuel Márquez, he committed himself to muster the numerous Cuban emigration in that country around the 26th of July Movement. Until that time, émigrés were scattered in their support of the Revolution , and Fidel's call would create a solid foundation for the channeling of support to the fight against the tyranny.

The tour was a complete success. Fidel spoke at emotion-packed pubic rallies, and instilled enthusiasm among the émigrés. At one rally held on October 30 at Palm Garden, New York, he made a historic promise: "I can responsibly inform you that in 1956 we shall be either free or martyrs".

When he returned to Mexico on December 10, he left behind a united and strong movement. From there, he issued the "26th of July Movement" Manifesto #2 for the Cuban people, dated Nassau, December 10th. It reiterated the goals and tactics of the movement, defined the protagonist role the masses would have in the Cuban revolutionary process, and called upon the émigrés to actively take part in the decisive battle.

Momentous rise in mass struggle.- While the movement led by Fidel Castro was reorganizing, and actions multiplied against the tyranny and the electoral masquerade, the divisions within the official trade union movement became more notorious, the entities guiding the workers' struggles strengthened and they became the protagonists of important actions.

Since the government offensive against the labor movement began in 1947, fighting committees or united front committees were created to channel workers' actions within trade union organizations that either had government-imposed management or were controlled by the Mujal-led labor organizations. Those committees, advised by Communists and led by activists from different political organizations, flourished islandwide following the Batista's military takeover, and headed numerous battles across the country. But they operated under different names and lacked a nation-wide an organizational structure.

As of 1953, and above all in 1954, a process of strengthening of these bodies began, and they became to be identified with a common name: *Comités de Defensa de las Demandas y por la Democratización de la CTC* (CDD)—Committees for the Defense of Demands and for the Democratization of the CTC. This process pointed to the creation of a national body that would gather all of the island's committees.

They did not amount to the creation of parallel trade unions, instead they were labor organizations whose aim was to force the yellow trade union leadership (pro-employer and pro-government) to act in defense of the interests of the working class.

One of the first conflicts in which the efficacy of such committees was put to test, was the February 1955 strike of shoemakers in Manzanillo against wage cuts and the government-ordered worker layoffs. In a meeting, all of the regions locals and the CDDs agreed to create a municipal labor committee, under whose direction the strike would be led. The movement began with the shoemakers, but soon became generalized. It brought to a halt all working activities in Manzanillo and drew the solidarity of shoemakers in other parts of the country, until it was finally victorious. In the heat of the strike, shoemakers in various municipalities of Cuba created local committees for the defense of the demands of their fellow workers, then they grouped around provincial committees and in a National Committee.

Labor actions grew in those places where the CDDs were created. They frequently were in the forefront of workers struggles, and occasionally gave their support to movements that were thriving under the leadership of other organizations. Three

168

important strikes staged in 1995 illustrated the rise of this fighting spirit: the strike of the "Estrella" sugar mill in Camaguey, the strike of Havana's bank workers and the national strike of sugar industry workers.

In February, the US company that owned the "Estrella" Mill, the Vertientes Camagüey Sugar Company, fired 57 workers. Faced with the passive complicity of the pro-Mujal trade union leadership, two workers organizations opposed the measure: the struggle committee led by the Communists and a group led by the PRC (A) affiliated workers. They convened a trade union assembly and agreed to paralyze the work of the mills until the company returned the fired workers to their jobs. Some 500 workers went into hiding in the countryside, hence the Rural Guard could find no labor force to put the mill back to work. After 14 days, the company acquiesced to negotiate with the committee, and the 57 workers were given their jobs back.

Between July and September of that same year, an important strike movement developed among the bank workers of Havana, who rejected attempts by private banks to deprive them of their right to organize unions. Besides, they demanded a 20% wage increase to meet the continued rise in the cost of living.

The leaders of the banking workers trade union(affiliated to the officially recognized trade union) adopted a fighting stance. The CDDs actively supported the strike, as well as the FEU, the electricity and telephone workers trade unions, the Partido Socialista Popular, many media outlets, Catholic organizations, etc. Solidarity stoppages occurred in many factories and workshops.

But the pro-government CTC leadership and the Banking Federation condemned the movement, dismissed the rebel trade union leadership and created a especial body to intervene the trade union organizations and replace all leaders that did not abide by the instructions of the Mujal-led leadership. To make things even worse, these yellow organizations supported the measures taken by the banking companies, that expelled numerous workers from their jobs, and backed the repressive bodies that persecuted strikers. So, betrayal, Threats and reprisals, combined with terror, led to the defeat of the strike.

Despite its failure, this strike was particularly important. Firstly, it showed a growth in unity and combativeness among workers within a sector that the ruling classes considered fundamental for the country's economic stability. The workers of this sector, considered as "trustworthy personnel", were carefully selected and enjoyed special benefits with respect to other sectors. Secondly, the breadth of class solidarity among the workers became more noticeable. Moreover, the strike forced the government and the Mujal-led trade union leadership to act against leaders and organizations officially recognized by the CTC with the same methods of imposition and terror that they used against the Unitarian labor movement, under the guise of the struggle against communism.

However, the most important action of the period was the strike of sugar workers staged in late December of 1955. The strikers were claiming the payment of the sugar differential, the reinstatement of 7.31% of their salaries—that had been discounted during the previous harvest—the return of fired workers to their jobs and other demands.

For several years, sugar workers had not been paid the money corresponding to the differential. But on this occasion, they demanded that payment with such force that the leaders of the pro-government CTC and of the National Federation of Sugar Workers (FNTA) were forced to decree a 48-hour strike. These leaders had previously reached an agreement with Batista, so that as soon as the strike broke out, a decree would be approved ordering payment of an additional 2.77% of the salaries to cover the differential, instead of the 7,5% that was supposed to be paid.

The CTC and FNTA declared the strike over and summoned the workers back to their jobs. But the CDDs and the provincial sugar federations of Las Villas and Camagüey provinces rejected the decree and decided to continue with the strike. They called on industrial and agricultural workers from nearby localities to join them, they seized churches, town halls and other buildings, and appealed to the solidarity of other working sectors (*campesinos* and small farmers, small traders and industrialists, etc.). The population backed the strikers by throwing logs, nails, pieces of glasses and other obstacles on streets, highways and rail roads in order to disrupt traffic, and by concentrating in plazas and parks. Economic life of these towns ground to a halt, and they became "ghost towns". More that 15 leaders of the Federation of University Students (FEU) moved to the different locations where the strike was on to take part personally and also to mobilize secondary level students in favor of the strikers.

The government tried to crack down on the movement through repression. There were hundreds of detentions, two people killed and many wounded. But the workers' actions grew in momentum, and political slogans like Down with Batista! and Down with Mujal were added to the original demands. On January 1st, 1956, the government issued another decree, ordering a differential payment of 4,2% of the salaries of sugar industry workers and 3,63% for agricultural workers, without making reference to any of the other demands.

The CDDs were not in agreement with the decree—which only amounted to a partial victory—and called for a continuation of the until complete victory. But the sugar workers' leaders from Las Villas and Camagüey, although they also rejected the solution, convinced workers to return to their jobs. When everything was back to normal, the CTC dismissed from their responsibilities the main trade union leaders in the two provinces due to the support they gave to the strike, just as they had done several months ago with he leaders of the banking trade union leaders.

This movement demonstrated the high level achieved by the workers' struggles and was a clear example of how actions in the pursuit of economic and social demands could be transformed into political battles against the government.

In February of 1956, weeks after the great sugar workers strike had ended, 100 delegates from some 500 trade unions from all over the country met clandestinely in Havana and created the National Committee for the Defense of Workers Demands and the Democratization of the CTC. This body, made up of 25 members from various political trends, from all industries and workers sectors and from the country's most important regions, had the responsibility of acting as a center of direction and coordination of the movement that was in the making nationally and would play a very important role in workers and all the people's struggles in subsequent years.

The electoral farce.- The bourgeois opposition, taking note of the momentum of the popular struggle, redoubled its efforts to find a negotiated settlement for the country's political crisis. The efforts done by the Press Block, the so called Committee for Democratic Independent Action (CADI), and other institutions, were centralized by the *Sociedad de Amigos de la República* (Society of Friends of the Republic) SAR. Born in 1948, this association had gained in strength after Batista's coup. Its members were representatives from the so called "civic institutions" (of social, professional, religious and masonry character, etc.) and by some personalities that self-proclaimed themselves impartial in political feuds.

The SAR was headed by veteran lawyer and diplomat Cosme de la Torriente, former Colonel of the Liberation Army, who was trusted by the US government and the main circles of the Cuban bourgeoisie. He had a vast experience in political mediation efforts, and in 1933 had gained recognition for his participation in the process of US mediation with the Batista dictatorship.

The SAR limited itself to defending the institutional path of the country by means of "representative democracy", and was opposed to the armed insurrection, terrorism or any other form of violence. Based on this reasoning, it rejected the coup of March 10, 1952. It tried to bring together opposition parties—always excluding communists and people linked to Fidel Castro—to negotiate an agreement with the dictator that would result in the formation of a provisional government, reestablish the 1940 Constitution, and that would call for general elections to return the nation to an institutional order. However, the organization did not keep faith with these demands. It was irresolute concerning the demands of guarantees for the respect of the people's will and some of its members often changed positions, even accepting some government proposals of partial elections and of constitutional elections presided over by Batista.

During the second semester of 1955, amid the growing force and radicalization of the mass movement and revolutionary violence, the SAR intensified its conciliatory efforts, in an attempt to thwart an explosion that would jeopardize the bourgeois-dominated system. These efforts had the support of the *auténticos* of Grau San Martín and Prío Socarrás, the two main factions of the Orthodox Party, the Nation's Movement, the Radical Liberation Movement, a faction of the Democratic Party and other political groups of lesser significance. *

The 26th of July Movement, the PSP, the FEU and other related organizations, sustained that the dictatorship would not renounce power through conversations and condemned any unprincipled agreement. But at the same time, they called on the masses to participate in the activities convened by the SAR and by the opposition parties, not to support the positions adopted there, but to energetically demand a resolute challenge to the dictatorship.

This is precisely what occurred in several rallies that took place in various parts of the country. A good example of that tactic was the meeting on November 19, 1955 in the Muelle Luz (a Havana dock). Convened by the SAR with the purpose of backing the "civic dialogue", one of the speakers was FEU president, José Antonio

---

* The Nation's Movement was a political party founded in 1955 by a group of personalities from various sectors, led by Jorge Mañachan, Orthodox leader, and José Pardo Llada, a journalist that enjoyed of great popularity at a time. The Radical Liberation Movement was also founded in 1955, by a group of Catholic intelectuals.

Echeverría, who declared himself in favor of a peaceful settlement of the Cuban crisis, but denounced the continued stubbornness of the government and warned that a rejection of immediate general elections with full democratic guarantees would lead to a popular insurrection as in 1868 and 1933. The huge crowd gathered there—mostly students and sympathizers of the 26th of July Movement and the communists—responded with sustained chants of Revolution!, and they turned the rally into a powerful demonstration against the dictatorship and the agreement.

At times, Batista encouraged the dialogue, but on other occasions he would show himself reluctant to hold talks with the SAR. He repeatedly denied to Cosme de la Torriente an interview the latter had been requesting and expressed his disgust over the mood injected by the masses into the opposition's public rallies. However, on December 29, alarmed by the powerful sugar workers strike and the rise of national rebelliousness, he accepted to meet with SAR's president and seemed to be willing to make some concessions. But on January 10th, 1956, when receiving him for the second time, he thought he had already gotten rid of the sugar workers storm and left the negotiations in the hands of lower-ranking officials. The dialogue had begun at the Continental House of Culture, but there wouldn't be any other interviews between Cosme and the dictator.

Two months later, on March 10th, during the celebration of the 4th anniversary of the coup, Batista completely dashed the hopes of the conciliators when he flatly rejected the realization of any kind of elections before 1958 and reiterated that he would not relinquish power until then. The "civic dialogue" had failed.

The founding of the Revolutionary Directorate.- The rise of popular effervescence and its organizational level by 1955 had an important expression in the birth of the *Directorio Revolucionario* (Revolutionary Directorate), the DR. The FEU had agreed to create an organization that, under its leadership, would gather the most radical elements of the students movement so that it would be in accordance with the needs stemming from the new period of struggle against the tyranny. Hence, during the year's last months, the Revolutionary Directorate was born, recreating the experience of the Students Movement that had developed in the 1930s, with adaptations to the new situation.

To a certain extent, the FEU was more broad-base than the Directorate. As a mass organization, it covered all students without making distinctions of political affiliations or views. However, the DR only would admit those students who had a staunch revolutionary commitment. But on the other hand, the DR was more encompassing than the FEU, because it would not only accept University students, but also young people from any study center, or from any sector or social class: handicraft workers, shop owners, industrialists, artisans, etc.

On February 24 1956, the FEU's President, José Antonio Echeverría, who was at the same time the DR's Secretary General, pronounced an important speech in the Master Lecture Hall of the University of Havana, in which he publicly proclaimed the foundation of the directorate. In his words, he warned about the uselessness of any attempt for a peaceful settlement of the country's crisis and pointed to the armed struggle as the only viable way to bail the country out of its situation. He stressed that the people were the protagonist of the struggle, that it was indispensable

172

to galvanize behind the struggle the efforts of all classes and cultural sectors, all revolutionary organizations, groups and elements, always respecting political motivations, tactics, possibilities and methods advocated by each and every one of the groups.

On that same day, the Directorate issued a "Manifesto to the Cuban people" explaining the reasons for its creation and disclosing its program, subdivided in 25 points. It denounced the ultra reactionary, illegitimate, criminal and despotic character of the government, analyzed the country's situation in all spheres of life, stated the historical need of a revolution that would radically transform Cuban society, that would free it of foreign capital and that would bring order based on political liberty, economic independence and social justice.

From then on, the Revolutionary Directorate's radical character would convert it into the most representative Cuban student organization in the battle against the tyranny. In fact, the FEU's political diversity subordinated it to the Directorate.

The "Conspiracy of the Pure".- The failure of the conciliatory efforts by the *Sociedad de Amigos de la República*, practically destroyed expectations for a peaceful solution based on free and democratic general elections, and reaffirmed for many sectors of the population the inevitability of revolutionary violence.

After Batista's speech on March 10th 1956, which dealt a final death blow to any peaceful illusions, a conspiracy began to brew within the ranks of Army officers. The conspirators set themselves the task of overthrowing Batista, re-establishing the 1940 Constitution, forming a provisional civil government headed by an apolitical personality and calling for general elections on October 10th of that year.

The conspiracy involved dozens of officers from various branches of the Armed Forces, and was headed by Colonel Ramón Barquín, military attaché of the Cuban Embassy in Washington, and major Enrique Borbonet. Among the plotters was then-first lieutenant José Ramón Fernández, who later became an outstanding revolutionary. The conspirators had had no involvement in the military coup of March 10th or any participation in the dictatorship's terrorist policies, which is why this plot was known as the "conspiracy of the pure ones."

The action was set to take place on April 4th, but there was a betrayal, and one day before the action, the main plotters were detained. They were submitted to a summary war trial, twelve of them were given sentences that ranged between 4 to 6 years in prison. The government took advantage of the opportunity to purge the army and some 100 officers were either separated from the ranks, retired, or transferred to other commands.

The particular relevance of this conspiracy was that it demonstrated the divisions within the upper echelons of the military, exposing as a myth the much-trumpeted "monolithic unity" of the armed forces around Batista.

The attack on the "Goicuría" Barracks. The situation in 1956.- A failed attack on the "Goicuría" Barracks, in the city of Matanzas, took place on April 29, 1956. Led by Reynold García, a worker with a long history of revolutionary struggle, and affiliated to the Authentic Party, he was a former member of the Triple-A. The group of assailants, in their majority military people, had been dismissed from the Army by Batista. Their purpose was to take the fortress over, seize its weapons and distribute them among the people to begin the insurrection.

However, all seemed to indicate that the military chiefs had been informed about the attack, because the assailants were ambushed and gunned down without any possibility of defending themselves. Ten plotters were killed, among them, the action leader. Others were captured and murdered later, while still others requested asylum in foreign embassies and left the country. The remainder were tried and sentenced.

Insurrection groups abounded during the first months of the year. The police discovered many houses being used to keep weapons and many people were either detained or murdered. In May, former president Prío was expelled from the country, under the accusation of taking part in subversive plans. The government suspended the paltry constitutional guarantees, raided schools in Havana, Santiago de Cuba and other cities, suspended radio programs and imposed press censorship. Public rallies were disbanded and repressive bodies reinforced their terror in order "to keep order".

The creation of the Revolutionary Directorate, which emphasized urban struggle, paved the way for the intensification of student actions (rallies, meetings, stoppages). They occurred daily and would generally end up in bloody clashes with police. In the view of the DR, these actions by the masses were useful to train the students for the armed struggle. Many leaders of the FEU and other youth organization, as well as leaders of the opposition, mainly Communists and orthodox, were often imprisoned, and assassinations increased. On May 15 Rubén Aldama, a black worker, and one of the organizers of the DR's secrete apparatus, was tortured to death. He was the DR's first martyr.

Despite the wave of crimes and abuses, the US ruling classes reiterated their support for the dictatorship. By late March, authorities from Southern Florida invited the dictator to visit that Southern state, taking into consideration "his loyal services in favor of democracy". He was even dedicated one special day, "The Batista Day", and was welcomed with high honors.

Faced with the turn of events, the PSP adopted the so called "line of August", which practically discarded the request for "immediate general elections with full guarantees for all opposition parties and groups". It then brought to the forefront the revolutionary general strike, to be followed by a popular uprising, tactic that had proved successful during the 1933 Machado dictatorship. The political forces had polarized.

Preparations in Mexico.- While the political climate on the island heated up, the group of revolutionary Cuban exiles, led by Fidel Castro, grew throughout 1956 and feverishly worked to fulfill their promise of being "free or martyrs" during 1956. They procured more than 10 houses that they used as lodging and to upgrade their general political and cultural knowledge.

The modest contributions that they received from Cuba collected among thousands of men and women, allowed them to speed up preparations as of February: they settled their first camp, bought their first weapons and started their military training. They rented the Santa Rosa Ranch, some 40 kilometers from Mexico City. It turned out to be a good training spot and an adequate place for the protection of weapons. Moreover, the ranch was located between a plain and mountains, a topography similar to the terrain they would be fighting on in Cuba. The chief of the camp was Ernesto Che Guevara.

174

The fund raisers made by patriotic clubs in exile, added to the money collected in Cuba. Mexican friends also contributed financially to preparations. Following the initiative of Carlos Maristany, a prominent personality of the auténticos, Fidel Castro and former President Carlos Prío Socarrás met. Socarrás contributed to preparations of the expedition with 20,000 dollars. The amount of weapons grew considerably, —they were purchased in several locations of Mexico and the United States. Military uniforms, boots and other supplies were also bought. Efforts were also made in Delaware, USA, to buy a Patrol Torpedo Boat, that would be used to carry the expedition to Cuba, but local authorities did not authorize the departure of the boat and the 8,000 dollars invested in its purchase were lost. Three months later, in a small town on the bank of the Tuxpan River, Fidel discovered an old leisure yacht on sale: the "Granma". He bought it and had it repaired. It would soon be sailing towards Cuba.

From the very beginning, the group of exiles had been organized militarily, following strict orders and discipline. They covered a rigorous training program that included long marches through nearby cities and mountains, shooting practice and personal defense. The military training, mostly included studies in guerrilla warfare tactics. In this subject, the group had the valuable support of colonel Alberto Bayo, former fighter with the Republicans in the war of the Spanish people against fascism.

But the mission was not easy: difficulties and setbacks, some very serious, had to be overcome. Besides the shortage of supplies and the failure of some plans, a police offensive against the revolutionaries was to be added beginning in the month of June, as well as one betrayal and two desertions. A campaign of hostility is launched against them sponsored by the Cuban Embassy in Mexico, while some bribed Mexican authorities acted in connivance with agents of the tyranny's Service of Military Intelligence and Cuban diplomats.

As a result, the police arrested many of the exiles between June and November, among them Fidel himself, as well as Ramiro Valdés, Juan Almeida, Che Guevara, Ciro Redondo, Julito Díaz, Universo Sánchez, Calixto García, María Antonia González, Alfonso Guillén Zelaya and other Mexicans, Colonel Bayo's son and many others. Some of them were tortured by Secret Service agents. The police raided several of the houses and the Santa Rosa ranch, and seized the weapons they found. The assassination of Fidel was even planned.

In Cuba a popular mobilization to demand the release of Fidel and his comrades erupted. Rallies in front of he Mexican Embassy in Havana took place, in other sectors of the capital and in other cities. Popular sectors in Mexico also mobilized in solidarity: Lázaro Cárdenas, former Mexican President, and a personality of great influence and prestige intervened, in favor of the revolutionaries, and the fighters were gradually released. Fidel was jailed 34 days.

These mishaps resulted in a waste of precious time, of valuable resources, and of great sacrifices. But once again, Fidel's commitment, unbreakable faith and endless capacity allowed him to pass the test. The group sought new houses and a new camp (in Veracruz, Boca del Río, Jalapa, Abasolo). They procured more weapons and took extreme precautions.

Throughout 1956, until November, while Fidel led all preparations in Mexico, he was also taking care of exile work in other countries, visiting Costa Rica and keeping abreast of the situation on the island. Besides the correspondence he maintained with leaders of the M-26-7 and the contacts with the emissaries that would go and come between Cuba and Mexico, the political and ideological work that Fidel maintained through interviews and articles he wrote mainly for the Cuban press was impressive. Most of them were published, not always in their entirety, by the popular **Bohemia** magazine.

In those articles, the Cuban leader would clearly explain the position of the 26th of July Movement against the agreement: he denounced the political scheming of the bourgeois parties that were seeking posts and favors, rebutted the slander campaign launched against him and his comrades by the dictatorship's officials and spokesperson, unveiled the origins of a plot that Rafael Leónidas Trujillo, the Dominican dictator, was planning against Cuba, and reiterated his uncompromising decision to initiate a popular armed uprising during that year.

His rebuttals to the accusations made by the Orthodox Party leadership against the 26th of July Movement were of great political and ideological importance. In his replies, Fidel exhaustively analyzed the class influence that affected the party, and condemned its silence in face of dictatorship abuses. That marked a fundamental split between the two organizations and Fidel's final split with the PPC(O).

However, while he used scathing language against those who supported the tyranny, and against those whose attitude had made them accomplices, Fidel encouraged unity among the Cubans who truly aspired to see the toppling of the Batista regime, even they didn't coincide with his tactics of struggle.

Within that framework of forging unity, the already mentioned talks between Fidel Castro and Prío Socarrás took place, as well as others between Fidel and leading figures of organizations linked with the 26th of July Movement: the Revolutionary Directorate and the Partido Socialista Popular.

Encounters with Frank País.- With the purpose of examining the development of revolutionary tasks and preparations that would guarantee a successful arrival of the expedition to the island, and the beginning of armed insurrection, Fidel met on two occasion with Frank País in Mexico City. País was the leader of the 26th of July Movement in Santiago de Cuba. For the first time the revolution's leader would meet the young teacher, who without reaching 22 years of age, had become one of the most intelligent, audacious, courageous and committed leaders of the M-26-7 in Cuba. The two meetings they held were enough for Fidel to put his absolute trust in País' ideological and moral qualities, as well as in the organizing and mobilizing capacities of this young revolutionary. The meetings also led to a very warm friendship between the two.

The Mexico Charter.- Fidel also met on two occasions in Mexico City, with the leader of the Revolutionary Directorate, José Antonio Echeverría, to coordinate actions against the dictatorship. The Directorate's main tactic was that of urban struggle, particularly in Havana. It systematically resorted to attempts against the lives of dictatorship officials and deemed necessary the physical elimination of Batista. Fidel, for his part, considered armed struggle in the mountains as the decisive element, supported by the masses from all over the country.

While meeting in Mexico, the two leaders did not concentrate on their differences, but on their cooperation, in bringing together efforts to hit the tyranny from all directions, according to the specific plans of each organization.

The agreements of those meetings were recorded in the so called "Mexico Charter", signed by the two leaders. In this document, the signatories rejected the call to partial elections in Cuba and expressed their understanding that the SAR and the political parties that supported it were not supposed to be begging for friendly settlements that only earned the Government's refusal, rejection and despise. They considered the social and political conditions as fitting, as well as logistic preparations well advanced to unleash the insurrection struggle in 1956, that would be aided in turn by a national general strike.

Important parts of the document focused on the conspiracy underway in Cuba by the petty Dominican tyrant Rafael Leónidas Trujillo, with the participation of a gang of Cuban gunmen and the complicity of a group of officers of the dictatorship's army, whose names were mentioned. The Charter denounced Batista's cowardice and his betrayal to the homeland, and it demanded that he give weapons to the FEU and the 26th of July Movement to fight Trujillo.

The top leaders of the M-26-7 and the Directorate pronounced themselves in favor of bringing together all of the country's moral, civic and revolutionary forces, and they guaranteed that the revolution would attain power without assuming compromises that would thwart the fulfillment of a program of social justice, liberty and democracy.

In the talks it was agreed that, in order to back up the landing of Fidel's contingent, the directorate would previously create a status of popular agitation island wide, and it would launch armed insurrection in cities, or at least in the capital, in coordination with the 26th of July Movement.

Contacts of the *Partido Socialista Popular* with Fidel.- The Partido Socialista Popular (PSP), a staunch supporter of unity among revolutionary forces, was moving towards strengthening its relations with the 26th of July Movement within and outside Cuba, seeking unity of action. Osvaldo Sánchez and various Party's cadres had spoken with *Moncadistas* in Mexico City. But the most important step in the development of these relations before the beginning of the insurrection, was the November meeting in Mexico City, between Fidel Castro and Flavio Bravo. Bravo went there as an envoy of the Party's National Executive Board.

The friendly meeting corroborated the identity of the strategic objectives of both organizations and also confirmed the party's lack of understanding with respect to the character of the insurrection that was in the making. It did not see the struggle's profound relation with the people, nor the role that the war would have on the mobilization of the masses. Hence the party's insistence in coordinating the landing with massive actions on the island.

The PSP considered, and it was so stated by Flavio Bravo, that Cuba's internal situation was unfavorable for a military action before December 31st. The economy had had a transitory respite, motivated by the results of the 1956 sugar harvest. But in the long run, economic prospects were dim. Considering this possibility, if the landing was to coincide with a powerful sugar workers strike, there would be full guarantees for the success of the operation. But the strike could only be effective after the beginning of the harvest, in January, and this is why the Party recommended—as Frank País had done before—to delay the departure of the expedition for 30 or 40 days.

Fidel replied that he understood the reasons cited by the Party, that they were solid, but that he had no other choice but to launch the struggle on the announced date, just as he had promised the people. He explained that at that moment he and his comrades were submitted in Mexico to intense persecution, that they were being arrested and that some of their houses had been raided and their weapons seized, and that in the event of delaying the operation, they were exposing themselves to losing everything: men and weapons. He expressed his hopes that once they reached Cuban shores, numerous uprisings would take place all over the country, and asked the Party for its cooperation, despite the fact that a short time remained before the departure.

Flavio reassured him that if the military actions responded to the interests of the masses, the PSP would not remain idle.

XVI
The struggle against the Batista dictatorship. The revolutionary insurrection

The "Granma" Yacht: a voyage to freedom.- October was about to begin and the departure day near, and taking into account the serious delay caused by detentions, the confiscation of weapons and the loss of training areas, it was necessary to accelerate the preparation of men. A new camp was found—the María de los Angeles ranch, near Abasolo, in Tamaulipas—and new groups arrived for training. Among the most recent recruits was a humble worker, joyful, audacious, and disciplined. It was someone not sent by the Movement, just another man among so many noble and generous ones, who would soon turn into a legendary guerilla fighter: Camilo Cienfuegos.

Training lasted until November 21st, the day when they received the order to quickly leave the area. Two of the men had disappeared, and if they told the authorities about the plans the revolutionaries had, the expedition might be lost. They moved to other locations and on the night of the 24th, all expedition members arrived at the port of Tuxpan, next to the river by the same name. Around 1:3O a.m., the yacht left silently, taking the hope of freedom for the Cuban people along with its cargo of 82 men. It was the early morning of November 25th,1956.

The "Granma" Yacht.

179

The November 30th insurrection.- Meanwhile in Cuba, the revolutionary forces tried to fulfill their commitment to facilitate the landing. The Directorate could not unleash an urban armed uprising, but it could perform several important actions. On the night from October 27th to the 28th, a commando from that organization carried out an attack at Havana's Montmartre cabaret, in which Colonel Antonio Blanco Rico, Head of the Military Intelligence Service (SIM), was executed.

In reprisal, police forces violently broke into the Haitian embassy a few hours later, assassinating ten young members of the Revolutionary Directorate that were taking refuge there. One of them, before dying, fired his revolver and killed Brigadier General Rafael Salas Canizares, the notorious head of Cuba's National Police. In these two actions, the tyranny's repressive apparatus lost, with these last actions, two of its most repulsive agents.

On November 27th, when the island was marking the 85th anniversary of the execution of the eight medical students, repressive forces tried to violently break up student demonstrations carried out in Havana, Santiago de Cuba and other cities. As a result, many people were injured, among them several policemen, wounded by stones thrown by the demonstrators. The universities in Havana and Santiago de Cuba closed their doors under the students' slogan of "No classes during Batista's dictatorship". The universities didn't open again until after the tyranny was defeated.

The Popular Socialist Party made arrangements to help the expedition members once they landed ashore. Oriente's Provincial Committee asked Manzanillo's Municipal Committee to provide every assistance possible, even to make sure they had the guides that the Party had prepared since it went underground. There were contacts between the 26th of July Movement in Santiago and in other places of the province; the Committees for the Defense of Demands called for a general strike, and Party and Socialist Youth militants participated in work stoppages, sabotage and other actions, along with the 26th of July members and the students.

Obviously, however, the center of all activities of support for the expedition members was the M-26-7 (26th of July Movement). The Movement began to prepare the necessary conditions in advance, throughout a vast area of the eastern province, in terms of weapons, men, supplies, communications, etc. Frank País gave that task to Celia Sánchez, a courageous, self-sacrificing and capable woman who was the person responsible for the Movement in that region. That assistance could not be provided at the moment of the boat's landing, because the Granma yacht arrived, as we'll see later on, at a spot that was not the planed point. But the apparatus that was created later fulfilled decisive roles.

Combatants in Santiago de Cuba and other cities also prepared to offer support for the expedition members with a popular uprising that coincided with the landing. Knowing that the Granma yacht was going to depart on November 25th, its arrival was calculated for the 30th and most of actions were planned for that date. The Movement prepared its forces throughout the country. On the 29th, transportation workers in Santiago went on strike. On the 30th, at dawn, the combatants took Santiago streets, wearing the olive green uniforms and the 26 of July armbands for the first time. They attacked the "Siboney" frigate and set the National Police headquarters on fire. They also occupied the Maritime Police station, junior high schools, hotels, the cathedral, and other buildings. The strike was general throughout the city. Over sixty prisoners escaped from the Boniato jail and many of them joined the struggle.

For several hours, the city was practically in the hands of the revolutionaries, who enjoyed the support and the sympathy of the population. Nevertheless, at noon, the revolutionaries were forced to fall back, since reinforcements arrived for the tyranny's forces, adding to its superiority in men and weapons. It was also discovered that the Granma landing didn't take place as expected. As they fell back, the revolutionaries were also protected by the people. However, snipers continued to harass the enemy forces in several areas of the city, resisting until December 2nd. During the November 30th actions, dozens of revolutionaries were wounded and ten of them died. Among those killed were José (Pepito) Tey, Tony Alomá, and Otto Parellada, dearly loved by the people of Santiago. The number of those arrested over the following days grew into the hundreds, both in Santiago and in other parts of the country.

Other important actions also took place on November 30th in Guantánamo, Contramaestre, Holguín, Puerto Padre, Palma Soriano and other eastern cities, where several actions were carried out. Among them: work stoppages, assaults on ammunition arsenals, the seizing of military posts and the burning of sugar cane plantations. One of the groups that joined the rebellion that day—the Sierra Canasta—kept its weapons until it later joined up with the Rebel Army. Other important actions were also carried out in several cities in the rest of the island's provinces.

The November 30th popular uprising, although it could not fulfill the proposed objective of supporting the "Granma" yacht landing due to the boat's delay, had tremendous significance: for the first time, Batista's bloody regime was attacked from several sides simultaneously. Those attacks marked the beginning of the revolutionary war—the immediate, glorious antecedent of which had been the assault of the Moncada garrison.

The promise fulfilled. The baptism of fire.- When the November 30th uprising took place, the "Granma" yacht was still far away from Cuba's eastern coasts. Several factors contributed to the delay: the bad weather they experienced since leaving Tuxpan for the Gulf, the excess cargo with respect to the ship's capacity, the malfunctioning of an engine for two days, etc., all of which led to the reduction of the boat's speed. Actually, the Granma yacht was not adequate, since it was designed to carry only a few people and there were 82 on this voyage, along with their weapons, knapsacks and other necessary items.

The delay caused scarcities of food, oil and drinking water which, along with other difficulties necessary to overcome, made the trip anguishing. First, they had to evade the surveillance of the Mexican navy and coast guards, and then the intense search for the expedition yacht by Batista's navy and the dictatorship's aircraft. One of the aviators, a communist who infiltrated in Batista's armed forces, told his party's leadership that he spotted the Granma yacht, a finding he of course did not report to his military superiors. Finally, they had to face the fury of a rough sea when approaching Cuba's shores, the sinking of an overloaded auxiliary boat and since they did not reach land where expected, they had to deal with dense mangrove swamps, bushes full of thorns and pointed leaves, persistent mosquitoes and gnats. It was almost daybreak, so there was the danger of being discovered by the enemy when the landing began. It was about six in the morning of December 2nd, 1956. The expedition members were at Las Coloradas, in Niquero municipality, on Oriente province's southwest coast.

By the time the rebel troops came out of the mangrove swamp and stepped on firm land, after two hours of arduous walking, the men were already in a devastating physical condition; they were exhausted and many were injured, uniforms and boots were seriously damaged; part of the weapons and ammunition were wet and many supplies were lost. But once again, revolutionary morale dominated adversity. Fidel's promise was fulfilled: the heroic fighters had returned to Cuba, ready to be free or to become martyrs.

Persecution of the revolutionaries was immediate. One hour after landing, the Batista army already knew where they were. The navy and the air force began bombing the Las Coloradas area, while the fictitious constitutional guarantees were suspended in four provinces (except Havana and Matanzas); an "operational situation" was declared in an extensive region of southwest Oriente and huge amounts of military supplies were sent to that zone. A wide circle was established around the area, aimed at eliminating the rebel contingent. The government ordered that Fidel Castro be killed as soon as he was captured, at the same time announcing that the guerilla leader was dead, with the purpose of confusing the people and discouraging the revolutionary fighters. It deceitfully promised clemency to those who gave up the struggle and surrendered to authorities.

The revolutionaries advanced towards the mountains with great effort, trying to reach them as soon as possible. On December 5th, they camped at a place known as Alegría de Pío, a sugarcane zone near the coast, where they were taken by surprise by the enemy's land and air forces. They suffered the first two casualties and were forced to deploy in several groups, hiding in nearby woods. Alegría de Pío was the guerilla's baptism of fire, as Comandante Ernesto "Che" Guevara called it later. The tragic and heroic situation there produced an historic phrase, pronounced by Comandante Juan Almeida Bosque. After hearing an intimidating demand to surrender shouted by one of Batista's officers, Almeida shouted back the response: "No one surrenders here, damn it!" (*Nadie se rinde aquí, carajo!*)

During the following days, the army captured a good part of the rebel contingent: it assassinated 20 expedition members in cold blood—Juan Manuel Márquez and Ñico López among them—others were sent to prison and those who managed to escape with the help of area *campesinos*, continued to march towards the Sierra Maestra mountains.

A few days later, on December 18th, at a place called Cinco Palmas, the disperse groups began to meet. The first one to arrive was led by Fidel and then the group of his brother, Raúl: eight combatants between the two. Upon receiving his companions and verifying they came with their uniforms, rifles and bullets, the leader of the Revolution exclaimed: "Now we have won the war!" (*Ahora sí ganamos la guerra!*).

Popular solidarity and terror by Batista followers. The Bloody Christmas.- Actions by revolutionary forces, in solidarity and support of the Granma combatants, took place in around the island a few days before and after the landing: train derailments, interruption of electric and telephone services, distribution of propaganda, attacks against newspapers that served the Batista dictatorship and against members of repressive forces, bomb explosions and other acts of terror and sabotage.

Arsenals of various types of weapons, Molotov cocktails, bombs, as well as uniforms, M-26-7 armbands and propaganda were discovered by the police in several cities (Pinar del Río, Havana, Matanzas, Santa Clara and Guantánamo among them).

The Popular Socialist Party directed the sabotage and student strikes which forced the government to divert its forces. At the same time, it initiated a campaign aimed at joining efforts to defend the expedition members, harassed by the army. On December 3rd, the day after the landing, the Party called on all opposition groups and parties, trade unions and farmer associations, the FEU (Federation of University Students), and other student organizations, to form a powerful single front against the tyranny, to protest against crimes it had committed and to defend the 26th of July combatants. It made new demands during that same week, and on December 12th it reiterated: "Today, regardless of our opinions on methods and tactics, there is a fact: July 26th followers have engaged in an action whose objective—to defeat the tyranny—is fair, and the government persecutes them and tries to wipe it out with the ferocity that characterizes despotic regimes. The tyranny's bloody hand must be stopped. We have to prevent the extermination of the insurrects. We have to leave behind the beast that has suppressed all signs of freedom and spreads terror throughout the national territory, that fills its jails with the opposition and constantly kills".

The urgency of this call responded to a real situation: the Batista army often killed those wounded in battle and also assassinated prisoners. Furthermore, repression against well-known militant opponents who could bring them support was added to the pursuit of the rebels. That's what happened, for example, in the northern zone of Oriente, where several large sugar mills and the Nicaro Nickel Company empire were located, and where there was a long tradition of workers' struggles.

In this area, an action group attacked a powder depot and blocked access to Santiago by road on November 30th, 1956.

And there, the tyranny's troops, headed by Colonel Fermín Cowley, decided to carry out a raid. Between the 23rd and the 26th of December, the army forcibly removed 23 men from their homes. They later appeared shot and hanged. Taking into account that these assassinations were committed during Christmas, this event has gone down in history as **Bloody Christmas**.

Several of the victims were prestigious leaders of the sugar workers; others were tobacco workers, miners, transportation workers, etc. The majority of them were 26th of July and Popular Socialist Party leaders, but there were also Orthodox, "Auténticos" and people without political affiliations. The fact that victims had different political memberships was a symbol of revolutionary unity that was forged during the struggle against the tyranny.

In Oriente province and throughout the country, a gigantic wave of condemnation was raised—without an answer—at the United Nations. The protest reached such an extent that it comprised all opposition parties, as well as the Rotary and Lions Clubs. Eleven months later, in November 1957, a 26th of July commando executed Colonel Cowley, directly responsible for this massacre as well as other crimes.

From then on, the bloody events multiplied in all provinces and cost the lives of thousands of revolutionary leaders and militants.

The guerilla consolidates. The year 1957.- The small guerilla group increased in size while advancing towards the Sierra Maestra mountains. It linked up with other groups of expedition members and several farmers and citizens from Manzanillo joined them. At the same time, a network of collaborators was created and the long walks served as training—tiring walks that were made difficult by hunger, fog, rain, uneven terrain, river crossings, and epidemics that affected the small group.

On January 17th, 1957, the guerilla soldiers fought their first victorious combat. The detachment, formed by only 32 men, with 22 weapons and very few bullets, attacked a small military barracks located at the mouth of La Plata river, which had a small but well-armed garrison. The attack lasted a little more than half an hour and the garrison suffered two casualties, five wounded and three prisoners. The guerilla forces, which did not suffer a scratch, captured eight rifles, a machine gun and some one thousand bullets, besides cartridge belts, boots, helmets, knives, clothes, and other supplies and some food.

The victory was modest, but it meant a lot for the future of the revolutionary guerrilla. After the disaster of Alegría de Pío, the taking of the La Plata barracks comforted the combatants, strengthening their morale, and demonstrated in practice that their idea of being able to defeat the army and arm themselves with the enemy's weapons was correct. For the first time, the guerilla group had more weapons than men. This action reached great national and even international importance; it proved that the armed movement existed and could win in combat, despite all the setbacks suffered. The action also proved that the government's story of the destruction of the guerilla forces was false.

That combat showed Batista soldiers a morale that was unknown to them: the humanitarian and fair treatment that the revolutionaries would always give enemy prisoners. The wounded received medical attention and were even given part of the scarce medicines the guerilla camp had; prisoners were set free. One of them joined the Rebel Army later. But the energy and firmness of the revolution before henchmen and informers guilty of crimes was also proved when one of them was executed at La Plata.

Thus, the first rebel victory set the guidelines that revolutionary combatants would follow throughout the entire war.

From then on, the guerilla forces gathered experience in the struggle and gained new victories, sometimes costly, before an army infinitely superior in men, weapons and other resources—an army that maneuvered to wipe out the rebel troops, followed its steps very closely, constantly bombed and machine-gunned it, infiltrated agents and tried to eliminate their supply base, forcing farmers to abandon their land, homes and livestock. More than once, air attacks or accidental factors provoked the deployment of the guerilla column.

A month after La Plata, deep inside the Sierra Maestra mountains, an important interview took place. Well-Known US journalist Herbert L. Matthews, of the **New York Times,** interviewed Fidel Castro. The interview, when later published, gave Cuba and the world the certainty that Fidel was not dead and that the revolution in Cuba was a reality.

The very same day of that interview—February 17th, 1957, and for the first time since landing—the M-26-7 national leadership met in the same camp. It was agreed, among other things, to prepare a group of combatants to strengthen the guerilla and to Prioritize the support for insurrection struggle in the mountains. In the first manifesto to the people of Cuba from the Sierra Maestra, Fidel offered information on the guerilla forces, its situation and activity, and oriented a series of important tasks: to intensify the burning of sugar cane fields and sabotage attacks against means of communications and other public services; to summarily execute torturers, murderers and other agents of the tyranny; to organize civic resistance in cities; to increase fund-raising for the Movement and to begin preparations for the revolutionary general strike, as the culminating point for insurrection.

Fulfilling the agreements, reinforcements began to arrive from the cities, combatants became familiar with the land and terrain and established increasingly closer links with those in the countryside. Farmers and agricultural workers, largely exploited, saw the rebel troops as their allies and defenders and an increasing number of them began to join the guerrilla. The latter, in turn, adopted an initially simple structure: the column divided itself into platoons and squadrons. It carried out a war of movement—"hit and run" tactics—without having a permanent territorial base. These tactics made it possible for the guerilla to evade the powerful enemy forces that fought against the rebel detachment following its first victorious combats.

The seizure of the garrison located at El Uvero, located by the sea on Oriente's southern coast, had great strategic, moral, and material importance. It had been reinforced in order to face any guerrilla attempt. It was a very hard combat that lasted almost three hours, in which six guerrillas died and nine were wounded, while army casualties were 14 dead, 19 wounded and 14 prisoners. A large amount of weapons, ammunition, medicines and equipment of various types were confiscated. The action, carried out on May 28th, 1957, ratified the convenience of the armed struggle as a fundamental means and strengthened the faith of the combatants, while it delivered a severe blow to the morale of the Batista army. Che Guevara characterized this event as "the victory that marked the coming of age of our guerilla", and added: "This action sealed the fate of the small garrisons located far from the enemy's largest groups, which were dismantled shortly after".

During the month of July, the inexperienced Rebel Army reached a considerable level of development: its positions began to be consolidated in the Sierra Maestra and the guerilla's nomadic stage began to be left behind. A new column separated from the original one, led by Fidel Castro: Column number 4. It began operations at El Hombrito, east of the Turquino Peak, under the command of Ernesto "Che" Guevara, who was already a Comandante. The two columns at times carried out actions separately and occasionally carried out combined combats.

On one occasion, on November 20th, the guerilla forces fought for seven hours, inflicting 100 casualties against the enemy.

In August, the guerilla front had managed to achieve certain territorial stability, which allowed Che to create a permanent base at El Hombrito, where workshops were organized and an armory, a bakery and a hospital were built. Poultry and pigs were raised, and a bomb shelter and a small dam were built. Eventually, a mimeograph was installed and **El Cubano Libre** began to be printed—the first newspaper of the guerilla, named after the one the Liberation Army had published last century.

The successful development of the guerilla struggle and Fidel Castro's growing prestige led some bourgeois opposition representatives to contact the rebel leader. In mid-July 1957, two well-known personalities climbed the Sierra Maestra to meet with him: Raúl Chibás, brother of the late founder of the Orthodox Party, and Felipe Pazos, renowned economist and president of Cuba's National Bank under of Prío Socarrás. They had the idea of creating a civic-revolutionary front of all forces opposing the dictatorship, on the basis of agreement to: Batista's resignation; the formation of a provisional government with a president appointed by the joint-civilian institutions; the celebration of general elections for all state, provincial and municipal posts under the norms of the 1940 Constitution. Moreover, the provisional government would develop a minimum program of indispensable economic, political, social and cultural measures, not as radical as those outlined by Fidel, but of great importance as an initial step towards transformations needed by the country. As a result of these talks, a document known as the "Sierra Maestra Manifesto" was issued, which gathered the agreements that had been reached. This meeting was an acknowledgment of the role the Rebel Army played as well as of Fidel Castro's concepts of strategies and tactics.

In the face of the failure of the general offensive launched against the guerilla, the tyranny's army intensified repression against the countryside, trying to destroy the support *campesinos* provided to the rebel forces. Dozens of farmers were assassinated in reprisal for the defeats of the Batista troops. But the crimes were useless: a "winter offensive" the troops began at the end of the year failed shortly after it had started.

Other manifestations of popular struggle.- During the entire year of 1957, along with the consolidation and development of the guerilla movement in the Sierra Maestra, the underground struggle increased notably in cities and in the countryside. This underground movement expressed itself in the most diverse ways: strikes, stoppages, demonstrations and mass mobilization; armed actions, sabotage, attacks; civil disobedience and resistance; propaganda; fundraising activities to bay food, medicines and clothes, as well as the recruitment of combatants for the guerilla and other activities. The M-26-7, the PSP, and the DR multiplied their actions, which many times were carried out in a coordinated way. Other fights against the tyranny were waged, and many opponents stated that were not happy with the passiveness and deceit of many political leaders.

Cuban women occupied a place of honor in the daily battle against the tyranny, both in the mountains and cities. Frequent demonstrations were held in which women carried banners and sang revolutionary songs—facing beatings, detention, torture and assassinations. On January 4th, 1957, in one of those daily demonstrations, over 200 women dressed in black, marching with signs that demanded: "Stop the murder of our children!"

The assault on the Presidential Palace and the "Corynthia" expedition.- On March 13th, following the tactics of "beating in the upper part", the Revolutionary Directorate (DR), followed by some PRC (A) militants and combatants from other affiliations, attacked the Presidential Palace, located in the capital of the Republic, with the purpose of executing Batista. If this objective was achieved, a call to the people to take to the streets would be made, so it occupied the main military positions in the capital and unleashed other actions, all of which should lead to the tyranny's defeat.

Although the revolutionaries managed to get to the Palace's third floor, they could not execute the tyrant, who had managed to escape, presumably using an interior staircase from his office.

While the Presidential Palace was under siege, a group led by José Antonio Echeverría, the Directorate's leader, stormed Radio Reloj. From the popular radio station's studios, Echeverría read part of a revolutionary proclamation announcing the execution of Batista. From there, he left for the offices of the Federation of University Students (FEU). But before arriving, his car was intercepted by police and after exchanging shots, the student leader was killed. Thus, the life of one of that generation's most outstanding young men and brave combatants was lost.

More than thirty attackers lost their lives in that action on March 13th and another four were taken by surprise and assassinated by the police weeks later, on April 20th. Fructuoso Rodríguez, FEU president after the death of José Antonio Echeverría, was among those later killed by the police.

Assault on the Presidential Palace

In honor of the Palace's assault, the students armed organization added the date of that historic event to its name. From then on, they called themselves the 13 de Marzo Revolutionary Directory (DR-13-M).

Realizing the possibilities for armed struggle in the mountains, the *Auténtica* Organization—an insurrection group loyal to former president Prío Socarrás— also sent an expedition to Cuba from Miami, which disembarked on May 24th in Cabonico Bay, north of Oriente. It was made up of some thirty men, under the command of Calixto Sánchez White, former leader of the official CTC (Confederation of Cuban Workers).

187

The expedition members tried to go into the Sierra Cristal, near to the landing spot, but they couldn't make it. Harassed by the tyranny's army, without guides, exhausted and hungry, 15 of them were captured and assassinated on May 28th, the same day the Rebel Army attacked the El Uvero garrison. This insurrection attempt is known as the "Corynthia" expedition, taking its name from the yacht that brought them.

Death of Frank País. General Strike.- On July 30th, 1957, the revolutionary movement suffered one of its most painful and costly losses: the death of Frank País, along with his companion Raúl, during an armed clash with the police on the streets of Santiago de Cuba. Besides being the M-26-7 national action leader, Frank had assumed the leadership of this organization in the cities when its leader, Faustino Pérez, was imprisoned. According to Fidel: "Frank was the most valuable, the most useful, the most extraordinary of our combatants".

On the 31st, the residents of Santiago took to the streets for the funeral of the young revolutionary. The rallying cry for strike soon spread throughout the city. Workers abandoned their factories and other work centers, commercial establishments closed their doors, and the streets were flooded by demonstrators. Despite the repression unleashed, strike actions expanded to the rest of the provinces, accompanied by sabotage to commercial establishments and public services, the seizure of radio stations, and even the declaration of "dead cities" in some places. Regardless of the unexpected and spontaneous character of the movement at the beginning, which prevented it from turning into a popular uprising capable of defeating the tyranny, actions extended in several places for a week. Although there were coordinated actions between the M-26-7, the Popular Socialist Party and the Revolutionary Directorate, and even contacts with the "*Auténtica*" Organization and the Young Catholic Workers, there was not enough time for this coordination to reach the indispensable level for an action of such importance.

The importance of this strike is that it showed the level reached by the people's political awareness, which in this case did not act moved by economic demands or material benefit, but with well defined revolutionary objectives. Moreover, it reaffirmed the decisive role of the general strike as a complement for armed insurrection in the struggle against the dictatorship.

The Cienfuegos Uprising.- The intensity of the struggle against the Batista regime and the growing integration of elements more valuable than the armed forces themselves, had one of its most complete expressions in the Cienfuegos Uprising on September 5th, 1957.

This action was the result of a conspiracy that developed mainly in Havana and Cienfuegos, and which involved officers, non-commissioned officers and soldiers from the Navy, the Air Force and the Army, with the participation of leaders and action groups from the 26th of July Movement, as well as other people involved, among them a representative from the Popular Socialist Party.

The plan consisted of the mutiny of naval and air force troops, the occupation of military installations and public offices and the call to a general strike, all of which was to lead to the defeat of the tyranny and the establishment of a government junta that would hand over power to the Rebel Army. The uprising of the Cayo Coco sailors, the seizure of the city and the possible retreat to the Escambray mountains to open a guerilla front there was also foreseen in Cienfuegos.

188

The date for the revolt had already been set—September 5th—but, at the last minute in Havana, it was postponed. But the delay was not known in Cienfuegos, so the uprising took place according to plan. Those who rose up took the Cayo Coco base, distributed weapons to the people and successfully initiated struggle in the city. They fought until the next day; but since the plan was not carried out in other places, the dictatorship could count on powerful reinforcements sent from Havana and other cities, and crushed the revolt.

The heroic action cost the lives of nearly 50 revolutionaries, most of them sailors, many of whom were murdered after they were arrested.

The Civil Resistance Movement. Terror increases.- Fulfilling the agreements of the 26th July national leadership at its February 1957 meeting, halfway through that year, the Civil Resistance Movement began to be organized throughout the country. Although there were M-26-7 militants as well as members of other organizations in its ranks, the stated purpose of the Civic Resistance was to bring together many opponents who did not want to take up arms or carry out sabotage, but who could economically contribute to the cause, boycott entertainment and other public activities, contribute with medicines and other resources, follow instructions of civil disobedience or express their rejection of the tyranny in other ways.

Thus, the Civic Resistance Movement, oriented by the 26th of July Movement, had an active participation in anti-Batista popular mobilizations and many of its members became outstanding leaders of the M-26-7.

Along with these activities, personal attacks and terrorist acts in general multiplied. During 1957, the number of explosives and bombs that went off in cities and towns increased continuously, numbering dozens in a single day. There was one day, June 30th, in which Havana was shaken by over a hundred explosions, so the date is remembered as "the night of one hundred bombs". In response, repressive forces also stepped-up terror, and the number of young people that were tortured and assassinated increased notably. Added to this number should be the many victims of premature bomb explosions, killed when they were being carried--due to lack of experience, anxiety or carelessness.

The execution of the tyranny's henchmen, guilty of torture and crimes, also became frequent. The case that had the biggest impact was that of Colonel Famín Cowley, Head of Regiment number 7, executed on November 23rd by an M-26-7 commando in Holguín. As explained before, Cowley was directly responsible for "Bloody Christmas", for the assassination of the "Corynthia" expedition members, and for other crimes.

As a reprisal for Cowley's death, the Army assassinated eleven Holguín citizens. The increasing revolutionary struggle and popular repudiation enraged the tyranny, rather than causing it to reflect. The number of crimes and abuses increased disproportionately. Reference has been made to many of them, but it is necessary to add some more cases due to the special connotation they had.

On October 21st, Bayamo went through a "Saint Bartholomew Night" of its own. The Batista army unleashed a wave of violence in that city, which resulted in 25 murders, numerous people wounded, home assaults, abuses and incarcerations. On December 18th, 7 men appeared hanged in Sancti Spiritus and 4 in Jovellanos.

A prestigious communist and leader of transportation workers, José María Pérez, was imprisoned and savagely tortured, as well as other communist workers and leaders Humberto Alvarez (sugar) and José M. Ramírez Casamayor (railroad). Well known politician and lawyer Pelayo Cuervo Navarro was found dead in the capital one morning.

Fifteen year old William Soler had the same fate, together with two companions—José R. Rodríguez López (18 years) and Rolando Poland Azoy (20 years). On the streets of Santiago de Cuba, Josué País (Frank País' brother), Floro Vistel and Salvador Pascual were shot to death. Teachers René Fraga Moreno and Ruben Bravo died at the hands of repressive forces in Matanzas and Holguín, respectively.

The Miami Pact.- In the face of the consolidation of the guerilla contingent in the Sierra Maestra and the rise insurrection struggle throughout the country, conciliating attempts on the side of the bourgeois opposition re-emerged (political parties and social institutions) with the purpose of stopping the revolutionary movement and putting an end to Fidel Castro's leadership. The Friends of the Republic Society was revived and new pacifist initiatives were launched by the Cuban Block of the Press, the Rotary and Lion Clubs, and many of the so-called "civic institutions". An Interparliamentary Commission was created to favor dialogue between the government and the opposition parties represented in the Congress. But Batista, after creating certain illusions in conciliators and entertaining them for a few months, finally rejected their main requests.

However, efforts to find a solution that would eliminate Batista from power without effecting the class interests of the oligarchy or those of US monopolies in Cuba were still being made. After a process of contacts and talks that ended in October 1957, representatives from numerous Cuban opposition parties and organizations met in the city of Miami: the Cuban Revolutionary Party (*Auténtico*), the Party of the Cuban People (Orthodox), the *Auténtico* Organization, the Federation of University Students, the Labor Revolutionary Directorate, The Democrat Party (a fraction of José R. Andreu and Lincoln Rodón), the 13 de Marzo Revolutionary Directorate and, supposedly, the 26th of July Movement.

The agreement these organizations reached, known as the Miami Pact, gave life to a so-called Cuban Liberation Council. On November 1st, its members signed a document in which they explained the basis of unity achieved and their objectives, as well as steps to be taken to obtain them. They opposed an electoral solution and proposed to form a provisional government, presided over by *Auténtico* economist Felipe Pazos, which would call for general elections within 18 months and implement a limited program, of reforms. For this purpose, they appealed for the help of the OAS and the UN.

The Pact altered the fundamental principles of the Sierra Maestra Manifesto—signed by Fidel Castro, Raúl Chibás and Felipe Pazos in February 1957— and since it was applied with an absolute lack of knowledge by Fidel, it tried to tie the hands of the July 26th Movement, by presenting it as something already accomplished.

The Miami Pact, which counted on the approval and encouragement of official US circles, brought about the most severe criticism and repudiation of the national direction of the 26th of July Movement and of the Popular Socialist Party. In a document dated December 14th, 1957, the rebel leader withdrew the

190

alleged representation of the M-26-7 before the Cuban Liberation Council, for assuming faculties that the organization had not given and for having talks and reaching agreements behind its back.

Fidel maintained that the important thing was not unity at all costs, but the basis of that unity, the way it was made viable and the patriotic intentions that encouraged it. He severely criticized the documents's indifference and cowardliness to omit the rejection of any kind of foreign intervention in Cuba's internal affairs; and not to energetically oppose the possibility of a military Junta to replace Batista. He denounced the underestimation with which signatories treated, in fact, the guerilla movement, and revealed the covert purpose of taking away from the Rebel Army its right to become the republic's armed forces, as swell as the intention of transferring the revolutionary movement's headquarters to exile. Instead of Felipe Pazos, Fidel supported Manuel Urrutia Lleo, a magistrate without political affiliation, to be the president of a provisional government. Lleo had maintained a dignified attitude in the trial against the "Granma" expedition members and, due to his radical positions, should pacify the US government and the Cuban bourgeoisie.

The Revolution's top leader did not close the door to unity talks, but reiterated that these talks must be based on respect for the principles raised by the rebel combatants, as legitimate representatives of the revolutionary people of Cuba. If these conditions are not accepted., warned Fidel, "we will continue the struggle by ourselves as we have done until today, without more weapons than those we can take away from the enemy in each combat, without more help than that of the suffered people, without more support than those our ideals provide us". And he concluded by affirming that "to fall with dignity, there's no need for company".

This rejection sealed the fate of the Miami Pact, which disintegrated without glory, showing that Fidel Castro and the Rebel Army were the real vanguard of the Cuban revolutionary movement, and that without this vanguard, no one could even dream of solving Cuba's problems.

New stage in the popular struggle and in the revolutionary war.- The underground struggle in cities and towns continued to grow when 1958 began. While the Rebel Army continued to expand its area of action, carrying out victorious combats, and came down from the mountains to attack enemy positions and to carry out important sabotage actions against properties of well known Batista followers. All this led to a higher stage of popular insurrection.

Throughout the country, especially from Matanzas to Oriente, the revolutionaries burnt sugar cane fields; they executed tyranny henchmen; planted explosive devises increased propaganda and popular mobilization against the regime, and prospects for a revolutionary general strike grew.

In February, a group from the M-26-7 in Havana kidnapped famous racing car champion Juan Manuel Fangio, who was going to participate in an international race sponsored by the government. The celebrated Argentinean racer was the tournament's main attraction, so they wanted his kidnapping to call the world's attention towards the situation in Cuba. The action totally fulfilled its purpose.

But the regime's repressive escalation also increased. The thousands of victims of torture and assassination caused great repercussion, among them the deaths of young

26th of July leader Orlando Nodarse in Pinar del Río, and Gerardo Abreu (Fontán) in Havana; prestigious workers leader Paquito Rosales from Manzanillo, who had been the first communist mayor elected in Cuba; Aleida Fernández Chardiet, and Catholic teacher Estherlina Milanés Dantin, who survived after being brutally tortured.

The fact that, under strong pressures, Batista decided to momentarily re-establish constitutional guarantees, made it possible for the people to be informed of the main crimes and abuses committed by the dictatorship, the rise of the mass struggle throughout the country and the successes of the Rebel Army. This gave new impulse to the struggle.

The battle carried out on February 17th at Pino del Agua was of great importance for the development of the revolutionary war. Pino del Agua was a small hamlet located south of Bayamo, surrounding a sawmill, on the Sierra Maestra's foothills. It was defended by a well armed and protected company. The objective was not to capture the town, but to force the army to send backup troops to help the surrounded barracks. The guerrillas would take advantage of this situation, intercepting all roads to trap and kill reinforcement troops.

Success was partial. Events did not take place exactly as planned, since through one of the main accesses to town, the enemy advanced protected by a wall of local women and children, forcibly used as shields. Once the action ended, the army murdered a group of 13 *campesinos*, most of them women and children. Batista army's counted some 25 dead, the same number of wounded, 5 prisoners and over 30 rifles, 5 machine guns and a cache of ammunition was captured. Rebel casualties were one dead and three wounded.

From that moment on, the Rebel Army combined movement war with position war, the latter tending to be more predominant.

A few days later, on February 24th, transmission of a rebel radio station—Radio Rebelde—began. It was located next to Column number 4's headquarters, headed by Che, in a place known as La Mesa. This radio station continued to broadcast during the entire war and played a transcendental role.

Also after Pino del Agua, conditions made it possible to substantially expand the operational area, creating new guerilla columns and opening other war fronts. Column number 7 was created in March 1958, headed by Major Crescencio Pérez which, together with the original nucleus, Column 1, headed by Fidel, and Column 4, commanded by Che, formed what has been called the First Front.

The "Frank País" Second Eastern Front.- During the first days of that same month of March, two new columns were created: number 6 and number 3, headed by Raúl Castro Ruz and Juan Almeida, respectively. These columns were assigned the mission of opening two new battle fronts east of Oriente.

After a long and hard march, Column number 6 entered a mountainous area located northeast of Oriente, an area of difficult access, which was called the "Frank País" II Eastern Front. It was a 12,0000 square kilometer territory, with a population of approximately 400,000 inhabitants. The area was considerably rich agriculturally (sugar cane, coffee, timber, etc.) and comprised numerous important industries, 15 sugar mills and two nickel processing plants, Nicaro and Moa, among them.

With the establishment of this Front, farmers in the region conveniently organized, groups of bandits that carried out attacks posing as insurgents were eliminated, guerrilla groups in the area re-organized, an air field and a bomb factory were built; and an intelligence service, a troop supply network, a public works section, a health department, some 40 hospitals and 400 schools were created.

The II Eastern Front played a decisive role in the revolutionary war. Over a nine-month period (from April to December, 1958), its troops waged nearly 250 combats, destroying over 30 of the tyranny's garrisons, inflicting some 200 casualties to the enemy, and capturing around 1200 weapons. The Front's forces multiplied during that time, and ended up with a total of 6 columns.

Other combat fronts.- At the some time, Comandante Juan Almeida, head of Column number 3, created the Third Front, which comprised an important portion of the Sierra Maestra, west of Santiago de Cuba. Other victorious combats were fought in this area. Its troops were a growing and constant threat for the capital of Oriente, and played an outstanding role in the final offensive in that province.

The incorporation of the DR-13-M and the PSP to the armed struggle in the mountains also consolidated during these first months of 1958. Since early November 1957, the Directorate had taken steps to open a guerilla front in the Escambray mountains, located on the center of the island, south of Santa Clara. Finally, a group of guerrillas established themselves there, in what was called the Second National Front of the Escambray. But its main leaders, far from obeying he Directorate's orders, made contact with Prío Socarrás, and abused farmers, stole and even committed murders, which led to their being expelled from the organization. They did not carry out any significant action against the Batista army.

On February 8th, 1958, the "Scapade" yacht expedition arrived in Cuba through Nuevitas bay, on the northern coast of Camaguey province. The expedition was headed by Faure Chomón, General Secretary of the Directorate. Well armed, the new combatants hoped to revitalize the Escambray front and reinforce the Directorate's activities in Havana with men and weapons, which they did. A few days later, the guerilla detachment came down from the Escambray and attacked the tyranny's troops in the towns of Cabaiguán and Placetas, and from then on carried out other notable actions. The guerilla force continued operations in the area until the end of the war.

On the other hand, the Popular Socialist Party, the PSP, had advanced in bringing its tactical concepts closer to those of the Rebel Army during the second half of 1957. Several of its leaders had been sent to the Sierra Maestra to exchange points of view with Fidel Castro, as well as with Ursinio Rojas, top leader of the Committees for the Defense of Demands in the sugar sector. In December of that year, the PSP decided to support the armed struggle and authorized its members to join the guerrillas. At the same time, the preparation of a guerilla detachment began in the Yaguajay area, north of Las Villas province.

The Yaguajay municipality had witnessed heroic *mambí* fighting during the 19th century independence wars and had seen strong *campesino* struggle during the Republic. Communists exerted a powerful influence in that territory, to the extent that it had been one of the only two municipalities in Cuba to elect communist mayors. The mayor of Yaguajay had been removed from his post after the 1952 coup d'etat. So the PSP decided tp place a Party figure, Félix Torres, a *campesino* leader as chief of the guerilla group, in that area Torres who would later become a comandante.

The detachment, which bore the name of "Máximo Gómez", had a unitary integration: its members belonged mainly to the PSP and the M-26-7. They had a supply network, a hospital, and published a newspaper. They carried out numerous actions, among them the seizing of Iguara and Zulueta and the attack on the city of Yaguajay. The group fought independently until the arrival of Camilo Cienfuegos and his column, to which they then subordinates.

The PSP also incorporated a number of its members into guerilla groups in other provinces, besides the important contribution it made in terms of leaders and militants to the Rebel Army in the Sierra Maestra. Those who created their own detachments and those who joined other guerilla groups or fronts were ordered to totally subordinate themselves militarily to the command of the Rebel Army's Staff and its top leader, Fidel Castro.

The electoral plans and dubious agreements. US maneuvers.- Coinciding with the revolutionary upsurge of early 1958, government electoral maneuvers and conciliating attempts of political parties and bourgeois institutions, encouraged by the US embassy in Cuba, re-appeared. Batista called for general elections, endorsing the presidential candidacy of one of his closest servants: Dr. Andres Rivero Agüero. Opposition politicians Ramon Grau San Martín and former Orthodox Carlos Márquez Sterling enrolled once again in to the farce, as well as other characters that later withdrew from the race, such as José Pardo Llada, Luís Conte Agüero and Emilio Ochoa. Sweetheart deals were made by the Friends of the Republic Society and group of Cuban institutions.

On March 1st, the hierarchy of the Catholic Church joined pacifist arrangements, with a document by the Episcopal Bishops that advocated for a government of national union, without excluding dictatorship representatives and presumably headed by Batista. A so-called Commission of National Concord, composed of well known representatives of the native oligarchy, was formed in order to put into practice the proposal of the Catholic bishops.

From the Sierra Maestra, Fidel Castro strongly rejected the dubious agreement. In letters addressed to journalist José Pardo Llada and to the news director of CMKC Radio in Santiago de Cuba, he rejected arrangements by the bishops and the Conciliation Commission, outlining the conditions that had to be fulfilled for him to accept a peaceful solution. Fidel wanted to express his criteria before a national press conference and called upon the tyrant to allow journalists into the Sierra Maestra so the truth of what was going on there could be known. Such permission was not granted. And, as on other occasions, it was Batista who put an end to the agreement, suspending constitutional guarantees again and imposing press censorship.

This attitude stirred up the discrepancies existing within the US government regarding support of Batista. For a few months, sectors that had understood the seriousness of the situation, and had made efforts to find an acceptable way out for bourgeois opposition and prevent the revolutionary triumph, remembering what had happened in August of 1933. But when the last conciliating arrangements failed, these sectors managed to have the United States suspend official weapon shipments to Cuba. With this measure, they hoped to give the impression that the US government was distancing itself from the Batista tyranny.

But in fact, Batista continued to receive military aid in a number of ways. The army continued to be advised by the US military. The US Naval Base at Guantánamo continued to be a source of supplies. Batista's military attaché in Washington met with generals from the Pentagon, in which they committed themselves to keep sending weapons to the dictatorship through the base, violating the established embargo. Moreover, covert transactions allowed for the delivery of rockets and other weapons from US territory. Batista's army also began to receive, with US help, weapons and other supplies from the Dominican Republic, Nicaragua, Britain, Israel and other countries.

In July 1958, a detachment of US marines arrived in Cuba, with the pretext of protecting an aqueduct that supplied the Guantánamo Naval Base with water, although popular protests and international pressures soon forced them to leave the country.

The April 9th Strike.- The idea that a revolutionary general strike, combined with armed insurrection, would put an end to Batista's dictatorship, gained extraordinary support during the first months of 1958. In March, many felt encouraged by the considerable expansion and effectiveness of the guerilla war in the mountains, and by strikes and mass mobilization in cities and towns, as well as by some popular victories in countries such as Venezuela.

Since the end of 1957, as a result of the creation of the 26th of July Movement's labor front in provinces and municipalities, the National Labor Front (FON) was created, formed exclusively by 26th of July trade union leaders under the leadership of David Salvador. This organization was given the task of organizing and carrying out a general strike on the labor sector; the Civic Resistance Movement would do it in professional, commercial and industrial sectors, and the National Students Front (also from the 26th of July Movement) would mobilize students. Armed actions in support of the strike were the responsibility of the Rebel Army in the countryside and of the 26th of July militias in the cities.

A manifesto was issued from the Sierra Maestra on March 12th, signed by Fidel Castro and by the head of the Movement in the plains, Faustino Pérez, in which instructions were given for the conduction of the strike. But on the 26th of that same month, knowing that the strike was being secretly organized without taking the CDD into account or other anti-Batista labor organizations, Fidel issued a new call which stated the need for the FON to coordinate its effort with all labor sections from organizations opposing the regime, so that all workers could join in the patriotic effort. However, these instructions were not followed.

At 11:00 am of April 9th, 1958, two national radio stations unexpectedly broadcast the call to the strike. There were numerous and heroic actions in Havana and in other places around the country, where work was partially paralyzed for a few hours, sabotage and popular demonstrations were carried out, as well as armed clashes between the army and the 26th of July militias. The city where the action was most successful was Sagua la Grande, which was taken over by revolutionary forces and completely paralyzed. The revolutionary forces fought against the regime's troops and forced them to fall back, firmly maintaining their positions for 24 hours.

The Rebel Army gave its full support to the general strike attempt, according to its possibilities at the time: part of its troops from the First Front went to the Cauto plain; the Second Front carried out attacks against important cities and towns, and the Third Front carried out daring actions near Santiago de Cuba.

Nevertheless, the strike did not work out well. The army, the police, and other repressive forces left a long trail of beatings, detentions and murders; more than 50 combatants were added to the list of martyrs of the Revolution, killed in combat or murdered. Marcelo Salado, an M-26-7 national leader, was among them.

When analyzing the causes of this bitter defeat, several things were pointed out: errors that led to the underestimation of enemy forces and the overestimation of the pro-strike ones; lack of real and effective coordination between revolutionary forces, mainly caused by prejudices against communists by many FON leaders; the underestimation of the role of the workers and lack of experience in the preparation of this kind of mass struggle.

Misjudgement and lack of experience led to the use of inadequate methods to organize and lead the strike: a great amount of general, abstract propaganda had been produced, but at the time of calling the strike, they appealed to secrecy and surprise, elements that are characteristic of armed actions but not of a mass movement. The concrete call to strike surprised the people, even many 26th of July leaders and militants, who were stunned. On the other hand, neither the Rebel Army nor the 26th of July militias were sufficiently prepared for the action.

This defeat was a serious blow to the revolutionary movement, but at the same time, it was a priceless experience. Fidel analyzed the causes of the failure in detail, warning that such errors would not be repeated and, with his usual confidence in the people, reaffirmed: "We have not given up the general strike as a decisive weapon in the struggle against the tyranny (...) A battle has been lost, but not the war".

Almost a month later, on May 3rd, the M-26-7 national leadership held an important meeting at Altos de Mompie, in the Sierra Maestra, where the results of the strike were critically analyzed and important agreements for the future of the revolution were made. The concept of the vanguard role of the Rebel Army and the supremacy of guerilla struggle prevailed, and Fidel Castro's prestige and authority were strengthened. Fidel was appointed General Secretary of the M-26-7 in the entire nation—including organizations in exile—and Commander in Chief of all forces, even the urban militias, which until that moment subordinated themselves to the movement's civilian leadership. Other changes included the appointment of a new head of the Labor Front at a national level, and the reorientation of the labor movement's unified activities, something on which Fidel had constantly insisted. As a result of the orientation, the National United Labor Front (FONU) was created several months later, in which all proletarian organizations confronting the dictatorship were represented.

The FF Plan: the tyranny's big offensive. Its defeat.- After the failure of the April 9th strike, the dictatorship estimated that the right moment to launch a massive offensive against the Sierra Maestra had arrived, which it had prepared for several months with the help of US advisors. The operation was called **FF Plan**

Revolutionary leaders at Sierra Maestra: Fidel, Raúl Castro, Che Guevara, Juan Almeida, Camilo Cienfuegos and Celia Sánchez (from the Spanish, *Fase Final* or *Fin de Fidel*, that is Final Stage or End of Fidel), and the tyranny hoped for it to definitely crush the insurrection. It consisted of an extensive military raid against all rebel forces, but mainly against the First Front, headed directly by Fidel, where the main blows were directed.

Batista's army moved some 10,000 men to the mountains, distributed in 14 infantry battalions and 6 companies, and supported by a tank company, aviation and the navy. At the beginning of the offensive, on May 24th, 1958, the Rebel Army had some 300 armed men, and its resources were very limited.

But Fidel had been expecting this offensive at any time, and he had taken key measures in advance. The territory was organized for the defense in every regard, the necessary resources for a long resistance were gathered. With full knowledge of the terrain and other factors at stake, a plan was designed to resist the enemy's advance, to eat away at it continuously until it weakened and to prepare conditions to move to the counteroffensive in due time. The rural population prepared itself to provide economic support for the rebel troops and to give them the necessary support in all aspects.

A decisive element should not be forgotten: the essential difference between the two sides. Certainly, the tyranny's army was powerful: at the moment of the offensive, it surpassed 40,000 men nationwide, without taking into account members of the Navy, the National Police and other bodies; it had been trained and had the advice of the best US specialists, and the United States government had provided it with all the necessary resources, including weapons and advanced technology for that time. However, the fact that it was a brutally repressive instrument of the oligarchy, with corrupt officers permeated by the worse vices—and faced with the purest, most conscientious part of the people— it was isolated and demoralized.

On the other hand, the Rebel Army was essentially formed by humble men and women, discriminated against and exploited, which had nothing to lose except their chains and a world to win. They knew that victory depended on their decision, strength and heroism, and that they were guided by a group of men like their Commander in Chief, who had demonstrated over and over again his exceptional capacity, confidence, firmness and unlimited loyalty to the people's cause. Fidel had taught them the reasons José Martí had to say that a just idea, from the bottom of a cave, is stronger than any army.

That is why, despite the overwhelming disadvantage in fighters, weapons and other material resources, the rebel troops were ready to suffer hunger and cold, to suffer all hardships in order to defeat the regime of shame and build a fairer society. Its morale was, then, unbreakable.

The enemy's offensive developed as Fidel had foreseen. The tyranny's army increasingly took positions of the First Front in three directions: but it did it at a high price, due to the rebel troop's strong resistance. Las Mercedes, Santo Domingo, Vegas de Jibacoa, San Lorenzo, Minas de Frío and other propositions fell into their hands. In turn, it clashed against rebel resistance in many points. The El Jigüe battle took place between July 11th and 20th, one of the most important actions of the entire war, in which a Batista army battalion was surrounded and defeated.

Major government forces also moved against the II Eastern Front, but they couldn't penetrate its defenses. In the face of their failure, the tyranny's aviation initiated a wave of savage bombings especially on the villages of that territory. The civilian population suffered the effects of fire bombs and demolition, of rockets and large caliber projectiles. These planes often refueled at the US Naval Base in Guantánamo.

In the face of these events, Commander Raúl Castro ordered the arrest of US citizens living in that territory, an order that was fulfilled and included a number of Marines from the Guantánamo Naval Base, who were captured as they passed by the area. A total of 49 were arrested. The objective of this decision was to force Batista to suspend bombings on the area and to call the attention of the world to these brutal attacks. Shortly thereafter, Fidel Castro ordered that the detainees be freed to avoid complications with the a US government; but the proposed objectives had already been obtained: bombings were suspended, the army gave up its offensive by land, the United States consul in Santiago de Cuba was forced to negotiate with the rebel leadership and the event had wide repercussions internationally.

During the month of July, the Rebel Army increasingly re-took lost positions, and on August 6th it captured Las Mercedes, a village where the enemy's last forces in the Sierra Maestra were located, and where it had began its great offensive in May. Batista's troops had suffered a major defeat.

Over 100 combats were carried out during the course of two months of operations--six battles of major importance, actions that cost some one thousand casualties to the tyranny's army, among them over 300 dead and 443 prisoners. The rebel forces counted 27 dead and 50 wounded, lamenting the loss of capable and heroic officers and soldiers such as René Ramos Latour, Ramón Paz, Angel Verdecia and Pedro Sotto Alba. The Rebel Army captured over 500 weapons: tanks, bazookas, machine-guns and rifles of various types and caliber, hundreds of mortars, radio equipment, over 100,000 bullets, etc. In the end, the rebel troops had almost tripled: now they were over 800 men.

After an irreparable setback, the dictatorship could only count, in Oriente, on the troops regrouped in urban areas. From then on and until the triumph of the Revolution, the rebel troops had the strategic initiative.

The Caracas Pact.- Very positive steps towards the unity of revolutionary forces were taken following the previously mentioned meeting at Altos de Mompie, and there were also unitary agreements with some parties, organizations and groups of reformist and even conservative tendencies. The most extensive and renowned effort in this regard was the so-called Caracas Pact, signed in Venezuela on July 20th, 1958, by representatives of the 26th of July Movement, the Revolutionary Directorate, the FEU, the Movement of Civic Resistance, the *Auténtica* Organization, the Montecristi group, the Labor Unity, Civic Institutions and the opposition fractions of the *Auténtico* and Democratic parties. The document was also signed by a former army officer and someone who called himself Secretary General Coordinator of the meeting, lawyer José Miró Cardona. The pact was also endorsed by the Popular Socialist Party, which was not present at the meeting, but that was the first to send a delegate to the Sierra Maestra—prestigious intellectual and communist leader Carlos Rafael Rodríguez.

The declaration, drafted in the Sierra Maestra with the decisive participation of Fidel, offered information on the country's situation and that of the struggle against the tyranny, and stated the need of joining efforts of all opponents in a revolutionary-civil front, the main pillars of which would be:

1) A common struggle strategy to defeat the tyranny through armed insurrection, achieving the formation of a powerful mass movement that would lead to a general strike and to an armed action throughout the nation.

2) The constitution of a provisional government that would lead the country to normality and guide it by a constitutional and democratic process.

3) A minimum program of government that would assure punishment to those guilty of Cuba's serious situation and that guarantees workers' rights, order, peace, liberty, the fulfillment of international commitments and the economic, social, intellectual progress of the Cuban people.

Signatory organizations asked the United States government to halt military aid and assistance of any type to Batista and reaffirmed their decision to defend national sovereignty and Cuba's anti-militarist and democratic tradition. They confirmed that war was not being waged against the republic's armed institutes, but against Batista, and called on all men of dignity within the armed forces to abstain from supporting the tyranny.

The document ended with this call: "We exhort all of the country's revolutionary, civil, and political forces to subscribe this declaration of unity, and later on, as soon as circumstances allow for it, we'll hold a meeting of delegates from all sectors, without exception, to discuss and approve the basis of unity".

The Caracas Pact had a purely political meaning, since true unity had been forged during daily struggle in the Sierra Maestra and the plains among revolutionary organizations and many militants from groups and parties who adopted combat and honest positions on their own. Some organizations only endorsed the declaration in a formal way, since the interests they represented did not allow them to put into practice the limited program they signed. That was the case, for example, of the Montecristi group, linked to the United States Central Intelligence Agency.

Conclusive expressions of the unity that had been forged in struggle were: the agreement of all truly revolutionary organizations in the strategy and tactics followed by Fidel Castro and their total incorporation to armed struggle; the rapid unification of the guerilla detachments from the Revolutionary Directorate and the PSP under the supreme command of Fidel and the Rebel Army; the carrying out of broad congresses of farmers and workers at the Second Eastern Front and of a national sugar plenary at General Carrillo, in Las Villas province; the constitution of the unitary leadership of the United National Labor Front, and other significant facts.

Farmers' Congress in Arms and Law Number 3 of the Rebel Army.- The Cuban revolutionary movement had always paid attention to farmers' problems, especially since the 1930's. Since 1953, **History Will Absolve Me** included the agrarian reform as one of the first laws the Revolution in power would approve. And when the Rebel Army and the "Frank País" Second Eastern Front consolidated, an Agrarian Bureau was created to take care of economic, social, political and cultural problems of the *campesinos*.

On September 21st, 1959, a *campesinos* congress headed by Commander Raúl Castro was carried out at Soledad de Mayarí Arriba, in Second Front territory, which was attended by 128 delegates—small growers of sugar cane, coffee, fruit, etc., and by numerous guests representing the Rebel Army, the labor movement and other sectors.

The event resulted in important agreements related to the struggle against latifundia and the problems affecting Cuban farmers, particularly the Second Front population; it approved the Regulations of the Regional Agrarian Committee, and elected a leadership headed by two campesino leaders of great prestige: Teodoro Pereira (President) and José Ramírez Cruz (General Secretary). The farmers' concrete support of armed struggle occupied an outstanding position.

The congress showed that farmers, along with workers -many of them agricultural- were the main force of the Rebel Army and of revolutionary power in the area.

A few days later, on October 10th, revolutionary agrarian reform was promulgated, Law Number 3 of the Rebel Army, signed by Commander in Chief Fidel Castro. This law recognized as owners, for the first time in Cuban history, farmers who cultivated State lands, as well as all tenants, subtenants, sharecroppers, colonists, subcolonists and *precaristas* (farmers who cultivated small portions of state land or land that had no owner), who occupied lots that were no bigger than 5 *caballerías* (67 hectares). The same law promised to eliminate latifundia when the Revolution triumphed.

Labor Congress in Arms.- On December 8th and 9th, 1958, a labor congress was held at Soledad de Mayarí Arriba, the same place where, three months before, the farmers' congress had taken place. Convened by the United National Labor Front (FONU), the event had a broad, unitary character. Attending the gathering were 100 delegates, who primarily came from the "Frank País" Second Eastern Front, but also from other areas nearby, which had not been freed yet, and who represented practically all production and service sectors. A considerable number of sugar worker leaders, who had convened a plenary of the sector, also participated.

The congress disallowed the CTC and the National Federation of Sugar Workers, both of them Mujal followers, and agreed on creating trade union commissions that would carry out free elections in all work centers of freed zones and debate work agreements with employers. The congress also decided not to continue paying the mandatory trade union fee that was officially established, as well as taxes, discounts and other payments that would contribute to the tyranny's financial support.

Other agreements were aimed at guaranteeing the production of sugar, coffee and other economic items of the area, the struggle for the payment of the sugar differential, and the donation of 20% of what was collected for this concept to the Rebel Army.

Agreements made began to be fulfilled immediately. At assemblies that were held, the workers expelled Mujal followers, they elected their new leaders freely and democratically, and agreed on their full support of the Rebel Army.

That regional congress constituted a very important step for the re-organization of social and economic life in freed zones, and to increase the workers' leading role.

New increase in underground struggle. Worsening of terror.- After a slight decline provoked by the failure of the April strike, the rhythm and significance of underground actions increased again, as of August. In September, a fire destroyed the Rancho Boyeros Airport almost completely; in November, the 14th Police Station was attacked, in Marianao, in which several policemen died and others were wounded.

Efforts were also made to frustrate general elections convened by Batista for November 3rd. An active propaganda campaign throughout the country and an extensive plan for sabotage joined the rebel troops' actions, which interrupted transportation on the highways, roads, and railways, stopped people who were running for office and prevented the normal functioning of many electoral precincts.

The overwhelming majority of the population stayed away from the polls—despite the regime's threats to fire or take other reprisals against those who did not vote; precincts were empty all day long, and the government had to fill the ballot boxes with false votes. Andres Rivero Agüero, Minister of Education and supporter of Batista, claimed victory in an electoral process almost no one acknowledged as legitimate.

The underground press occupied an important place in the intense propaganda work that brought the truth to the people regarding the situation in the mountains and plains, denouncing the government's crimes and abuses. Underground presses operated from the first moments the military dictatorship was established, but it grew with the development of the revolutionary process, enriched by the guerilla radio and newspapers. It efficiently counteracted press censorship and the closing down of many publications.

Carta Semanal, a Popular Socialist Party publication, began to be issued after the attack and closing down of **Hoy** newspaper, the day after the attack of the "Moncada" garrison. **Carta Semanal** came out regularly during the tyranny, despite the fact that its printing presses were discovered and that a number of its printers were arrested and tortured. Likewise, the PSP continued to publish the **Fundamentos** magazine, and other publications such as **El Campesino**, **Mensajes**, **Vida Económica**, **Arte y Literatura**, etc., while the Socialist Youth published the magazine **Mella**.

The 26th of July Movement published **Revolución** and the **Ultimas Noticias** bulletin, which later became **Sierra Maestra**. Another leaflet by the same name was published in New York, in addition to the publication of Cuban exile, and others in various provinces. **Vanguardia Obrera** played an important role in the proletariat's orientation. At the end of 1958, the 26th of July militias in Las Villas published **Milicianos**. Civic Resistance also had its publication: **Resistencia**;

202

the Directorate had **13 de Marzo**, and the FEU the **Alma Mater**. With **El Cubano Libre**, created by Che at the First Front, **Surco** from the Second Eastern Front, and **Patria** by the Rebel Army in Las Villas, an urgent need was satisfied in their respective battle fronts.

Moreover, hundreds of local publications circulated throughout the country which, along with fliers and manifestos, as well as the national underground press, were a decisive factor in the struggle against the tyranny. Some newspapers from opposition organizations could be added, as well as many other publications from the revolutionary organizations mentioned previously.

The extraordinary work of **Radio Rebelde** came to add to all these publications. Since February 24th, 1958, **Radio Rebelde** was a constant source of information, orientation and organization of the revolutionary movement both inside and outside Cuba, a daily message of encouragement and combat. Other underground stations also assisted, like **Trocha Libre**, which began broadcasting from Camaguey in December 1958.

A new wave of crimes by the tyranny matched corresponded with the increase of underground struggle. Not a single day passed without news of more murders; there wasn't a single municipality or neighborhood in Cuba, a single sector of the population, that was untouched by the bloody orgy. The number of women who were assassinated and tortured is incredible.

On August 1st, in answer to their protests of ill treatment, the Castillo del Principe prisoners in Havana, were machine gunned. During the second half of 1958, over 100 combatants from different political organizations were tortured and assassinated by the dictator's henchmen under the command of Jacinto Menocal, known as the San Cristobal Jackal. Dozens of young people—many of them unrelated to the struggle—appeared assassinated in cities and in the countryside, an indiscriminate reprisal for revolutionary actions.

To illustrate this, we will mention the names of some of the thousands of Cubans who were added to the long list of revolutionary martyrs during those months: Eduardo García Lavandero, brave combatant of the Revolutionary Directorate; sisters Cristina and Lourdes Giralt, members of the 26th of July Movement; Lidia Doce and Clodomira Ferrales, 26th of July messengers; PSP leaders Saturnino Aneiro and Carlos Rodríguez Careaga—the latter a leader of the United National Labor Front; Eliseo Camano, workers' leader of the 26th of July Movement; teacher Fulgencio Oróz, a Socialist Youth militant; 26th of July members Julio Rafael Ferro (Ferrito) and Ceferino Fernández Viñas, in Pinar del Río; and the main action leader of the M-26-7 in Havana, Angel Ameijeiras (Machaco).

Expansion of the war. The invasion to the West.- Before the beginning of the tyranny's summer offensive, Fidel had already foreseen its defeat and the unleashing of an unstoppable rebel counter-offensive. War zones had to be expanded as much as possible in order to develop the insurrection and as a determining factor for the success of that counter-offensive. With this, the dictatorship would be forced to spread out its forces, preventing their concentration in Oriente province and giving a new impulse to underground struggle in the cities.

Conditions to consolidate and broaden the war in Las Villas and Pinar del Río were prepared, the already existing fronts were strengthened and reorganized, and new ones were opened (the VI Front northeast of Oriente); a new one in the province of Camaguey). In the summer of 1958, besides detachments or groups operating in Las Villas, two guerilla detachments had already initiated their actions in Pinar del Río—one from the M-26-7 and another one from the DR-13-M. Guerilla groups also emerged in Havana and Matanzas.

Also noteworthy was the integration, in the First Front, of an all women's platoon that bore the name of "Mariana Grajales", the mother of the Maceos. The "Marianas", as they were called, had their heroic baptism of fire on September 27th, 1958, at the Battle of Cerro Pelado.

The Rebel Air Force and Navy were also born during these months, in Second Front territory, with the modesty that characterized the difficult conditions of struggle.

Following the strategy and the objectives outlined by the Commander in Chief, and with the decisive contribution of weapons, ammunition and equipment captured from Batista's army during their failed Summer Offensive, the Rebel Army achieved the minimum conditions necessary to send two invasion columns to the western and central regions of the island.

The two left the Sierra Maestra within days of each other. The "Antonio Maceo" Column Number 2, with some 80 men, left from El Salto on August 21st, 1958, under the command of Comandante Camilo Cienfuegos. Following a military order of the Commander in Chief, Camilo was given the authority to organize rebel combat units throughout the country, until comandantes from the provinces arrived with their columns to their respective jurisdictions; to apply the Penal Code and the Rebel Army agrarian laws on the invaded territories and to collect the contributions established by military resolutions; to combine operations with any other revolutionary force that was already operating in certain areas, and set up a permanent military front in Pinar del Río province that would serve as the invading column's operational base. Along with its main objective of extending the war to the island's western territory, Column #2 also had the mission of engaging enemy troops any time they appeared during the rebels' campaign throughout the island.

Commanded by Ernesto Che Guevara, the 150-men "Ciro Redondo" Column #8 left El Jíbaro on August 31st that same year. Guevara was appointed head of all rebel forces belonging to the 26th of July Movement operating in Las Villas province, both in rural and urban areas. Just like Comandante Camilo Cienfuegos, Guevara had the authority to collect contributions for his forces, to impose revolutionary laws, to coordinate operations with other guerrilla forces and to organize local combat units.

Comandante Che Guevara was also given the task of encouraging all rebel forces operating in Las Villas to make up a single army structure in order to unify the Revolution's military effort. Column #8 also had the strategic objective of engaging the enemy in the island's central territory and to intercept and paralyze the movements of enemy forces trying to reach eastern Cuba.

The march of the two invading columns became such a difficult task that it had a strong impact on the rebels' moral and physical strength. First, they had to make their way across steep terrain, then through swampy areas, enduring heavy downpours, and finally had to cross flooded rivers. They were even surprised by a strong hurricane just after initiating the invasion of the island. The rebel forces made most of their journey on foot and could only use horses or vehicles for very short distances. For that reason, many rebels saw their shoes worn and torn apart quickly, which slowed their march due to foot diseases and swelling. Hunger, thirst and insect bites hit the rebel troops and they spent entire days without food and were forced to drink muddy water from swamps and rivers.

At times, the rebels got lost due to the lack of guides. Added to that was enemy land and air persecution—sometimes intense—particularly in the plains of Camaguey; ambushes, chases and some combats which rebels tried to avoid in order to fulfill their mission. Although the guerrilla fighters found help from the rural population in many places, as well as support from revolutionary organizations, they had to face frequent delays and lack of back-up from city combatants.

Exhaustion and fatigue affected the morale of many men and it was necessary to appeal to their revolutionary principles. Despite occasional discouragement, there were very few cases of desertion. After 46 or 47 days of long walks, both columns reached Las Villas province, where they found much more favorable conditions created by local rebel groups. In combats along the march from the Sierra Maestra mountain range to Las Villas, both rebel columns lost three combatants each, four were wounded and one rebel was captured by the enemy. In those battles, Batista's army lost at least four men and rescued several others who had been wounded, while seven of its soldiers were taken prisoner by the rebel forces.

Campaign in Las Villas. The Santa Clara Battle.- Upon arriving in Villa Clara province, both columns had to unite all guerrilla fighters acting in the southern and northern territories of the province under the Rebel Army's single command. On October 8th, a day after arriving in Las Villas, Comandante Camilo Cienfuegos and his column reached Félix Torres' camp, in La Victoria Mountains near Yaguajay. That was the operational center of the Popular Socialist Party's Máximo Gómez detachment. That rebel force immediately came under Camilo's command and would take part in all coming combats.

Column #8, at Che's orders, arrived at the Escambray Mountains finding two different responses: The II National Escambray Front's hostile and arrogant reaction and the fraternal welcome given by the troops belonging to the 13th of March Revolutionary Directorate. This positive attitude materialized in the first contacts, during combats fought along Che Guevara's force and later formally in the so-called Pedrero Pact signed December 1st of 1958 by the 26th of July Movement and the Revolutionary Directorate.

Based on that pact, a civilian governmental commission for Escambray was set up just days after the signing. That commission was made up of representatives of both organizations.

The Pedrero document provided for provincial unity against the Batista dictatorship and called on remaining armed groups to come together for that commitment. The Popular Socialist Party immediately signed the agreement.

The troops belonging to Columns 2 and 8, along with those of the Revolutionary Directorate, jointly and sometimes separately fought important battles, attacked enemy military caravans, blew-up bridges, hit army reinforcements, sabotaged the November 3rd elections and practically divided the island into two parts, blocking the enemy's movements to the eastern part of the country. The military situation became so favorable in that province, that Column #2 was ordered to continue operations in Las Villas instead of heading for the western provinces.

On November 29th, powerful military reinforcements left Santa Clara for the localities of Cabaiguán and Fomento in order to destroy the rebel forces. Due to their superiority in the number of men and weapons, the enemy troops managed to recover some of its former positions. The rebel columns then applied a war of attrition and stopped the enemy's advance on December 2nd, forcing the army to withdraw with considerable human and material loses. The rebel counter-offensive would then take place.

The most important combats of that counter-offensive began to occur on December 15th. Amid intensive bombardment by Batista's air force, the rebel army would capture city after city: Fomento, Guayos, Cabaiguán, Placetas, Sancti Spiritus, Trinidad, Remedios, Manicaragua, Caibarién, Santo Domingo and Yaguajay, all the way up to Santa Clara, the dictatorship's last and most powerful stronghold in Las Villas province.

By that time, most sugar mills had been freed as well as most of the rural territory.

The government had good reason to have considered the defense of Santa Clara crucial, a city of 90,000 located in the heart of the island. The city was an important communications center with solid military fortresses defended by some 3000 troops—which increased by 1000 with reinforcements coming from nearby towns and from the capital—and permanently backed by the air force. Among reinforcements from Havana was a 22-car armored train considered unbeatable which was constructed especially to fight the rebel forces. The train was heavily equipped with machine guns, anti-aircraft weapons, a huge amount of war equipment and ammunition. It's crew included 408 soldiers and officers.

The forces belonging to Column #8 and to the Revolutionary Directorate, commanded by Ernesto Che Guevara, were made up of 300 well-armed, experienced troops of high political morale, later joined by 5000 recruits trained in the Escambray mountains.

The battle for Santa Clara began on December 29th under permanent attack by the dictator's air force. The rebels took the enemy's positions one by one: hills surrounding the city, the power plant, military facilities and public buildings used as shields by the dictator's troops (jail, court, provincial government palace, hotel, etc.). The rebels cut off communications between the city and the armored train, which they derailed and took over just as it began to move. In the action, all government troops were taken prisoner and the rebels seized a huge war arsenal on board the train.

The last enemy stronghold in the city surrendered on January 1st 1959 at noon: the barracks housing the "Leoncio Vidal" regiment. This was the most important military stronghold in Cuba's central region. With that victory, Las Villas became another newly freed territory.

Fidel Castro's victorious entry in Santiago de Cuba

The Rebel Army's final offensive. The triumph of the Revolution.-
The urgent need for an offensive against the dictatorship was encouraged by several factors: the broadening and consolidation of newly freed territories; the well defined administrative, political and military stability of the First, Second and Third Fronts the increase in the number of troops, weapons and war material belonging to the Rebel Army; the tremendous success obtained by the invading columns and the offensive carried out in the Second Front during early July; as well as the increasing danger of a military coup or US intervention in the war.

Following Fidel Castro's orders issued on November 13th for all rebel forces in Las Villas, Camaguey and Oriente, the offensive began by capturing the Bueycito mines five days later. On November 20th, the rebel forces unleashed their attack on Guisa, an important and well-defended town located a few kilometers away from Bayamo. The Battle of Guisa took the Rebel Army ten days of hard-fought combats, not only against locally deployed troops but also against nine different reinforcements which arrived one after another. Batista's army managed to mobilize more than 2 000 men, to fight only 300 rebel combatants. Just as the Commander-in-Chief described it in his war report: "the Battle of Guisa was a fight against planes, tanks and artillery".

Guisa was one of the most significant clashes of the war, resulting in more than 200 casualties on the enemy's side and a large amount of war material and weapons recovered by the rebel forces. Although it was a long and intense battle, the Rebel Army only lost eight men, including the brave Captain Braulio Coroneaux.

As the Battle of Guisa was taking place, forces from the Second Front attacked numerous enemy positions deployed in San Luis, Alto Songo, La Maya, Sagua de Tánamo, Guantánamo and other localities. The incipient Revolutionary Air Force played a significant role in the action and by December 9th, the rebel forces had their way clean to Santiago de Cuba.

Fidel assumed direct command of the rebel offensive against the capital of Oriente, which hit hard the western and northwestern bordering territories of Jiguaní, Puerto Padre, Chaparra, Manatí and other enemy positions. The Camaguey Front, aside from successfully engaging in numerous actions such as the occupation of army garrisons and government military headquarters, also successfully blocked all government reinforcement efforts in eastern Oriente. The rebel campaign in Las Villas successfully took place and armed actions in the island's western provinces continued to intensify.

On December 18th, amid victorious combats in the eastern territories, Fidel, Raúl Castro and Juan Almeida, gathered along the route to Santiago de Cuba where they were leading the invading forces from the three eastern fronts. During the next few days, the rebel forces began to take hold of enemy positions in that province and by December 30th, the enemy only had control of the cities of Santiago, Guantánamo, Manzanillo, Holguín and Victoria de las Tunas—which were all under heavy siege.

Under such conditions, the deterioration of Batista's army worsened—marked by an increase of desertions or of soldiers who jointed the rebel's side. Meanwhile, many Cuban bourgeois officials and US government representatives, as well as high-ranking officers close to dictator Batista intensified their efforts to reach a peaceful solution which excluded Batista. They had obviously foreseen the fall of the dictatorship and tried to save the bourgeois regime. Some conspiracy attempts were discovered, resulting in several officers arrested or forced into early retirement, while the US government continued to urge Batista to resign.

Many conspiratorial plans involved Army Colonel Ramón Barquín and Orthodox Conservative Raúl Chibás. In mid-December, the US State Department and the CIA expressed the need to quickly replace Batista by a military junta headed by people like Colonel Barquín. The US embassy in Havana favored General Martín Díaz Tamayo as Junta Chief. Tamayo was one of Batista's closest collaborators whose personal ambitions led to differences with the dictator. He began conspiring against Batista soon after.

On December 14th, US ambassador to Havana Earl T. Smith announced that his government had withdrawn its support of Batista, and two days later, Smith directly called on Batista to step down and hand over power to a military junta. Other military officers, including Brigadier Alberto del Río Chaviano, had also been supporting that decision for nearly a month. The 1958 events recall the historic pages of 1933 regarding the US intervention.

As part of conspiracies and political maneuvers carried out with the participation of the US embassy, General Eulogio Cantillo, Army Operations Chief in eastern Oriente province, expressed his willingness to negotiate an agreement with Fidel Castro to put an end to the national crisis. During their meeting on December 28th, General Cantillo committed himself to organize a military uprising in Oriente on December 31st and give up the positions that the government controlled.

Although the national situation was completely favorable to the rebel forces and the dictator's fall was imminent, Fidel accepted Cantillo's proposal in order to avoid more bloodshed. But Fidel demanded three conditions by Cantillo: the uprising should only take place in Santiago de Cuba and not in Havana, in order to avoid the setting up of a military junta; they must prevent Batista and his accomplices from leaving the country; and the US embassy must not be informed about the action.

Cantillo returned to Havana, he and Batista made their plan, and asked Fidel to postpone the action. The rebel leader realizes the treason by the enemy officer and orders the continuation of the rebel offensive against Santiago which he knew would only be a matter of hours. Gibara surrendered December 29th and many other coastal towns were also taken by the rebels on the 30th. The cities of Holguín and Victoria de las Tunas became free territories on January 1st and in the evening, the capital of Oriente, Santiago, also surrendered. With that victory Fidel's promise was accomplished: "The 1895 story will not be repeated! This time the *mambises* will enter Santiago de Cuba!"

With the victory of the Rebel Army in the three eastern provinces and the absolute demoralization of the army, Batista transferred the leadership of his armed forces to General Eulogio Cantillo, resigned the presidency and along with his aides, left Cuba on the eve of January 1st, 1959. In a misleading maneuver, Cantillo appointed the senior judge of the Supreme Court, Dr. Carlos M. Piedra, as Provisional President of the country—part of a plan jointly prepared with the US embassy to destroy the Revolution.

Upon learning of Batista's get-away and warning the people of attempts to take away their victory, Fidel Castro addressed the people from Palma Soriano, denouncing the treason and a military coup. He ordered all rebel commanders to continue armed actions on all battle fronts until the total surrender of the enemy, and he called for a general strike to break the plans of imperialism and oligarchy. Fidel ordered comandantes Camilo Cienfuegos and Ernesto Che Guevara to continue pushing toward Havana. Camilo had to take over Columbia camp—Cuba's top military headquarters from where the March 10th, 1952 coup was ordered—while Che had to assume control of the La Cabana headquarters—the second most important military fortress in Havana.

In a new and desperate attempt to control the situation, General Cantillo set hundreds of political prisoners free from the Isle of Youth penitentiary and, strictly following the instructions of US ambassador Earl T. Smith, Cantillo took Colonel Ramon Barquín—also in prison—to Havana and had him head the army. Barquín tried to have Fidel accept the post of Prime Minister of the provisional government but he refused to hand in the military command to the Rebel Army.

Imperialism and oligarchy could not frustrate the victory. Under the slogan *Revolución sí, golpe de estado no!* (Revolution yes, military coup no!), the Revolution's leader ordered rebel forces to attack Columbia camp. The general strike paralyzed the entire country, people armed themselves in cities and towns taking over garrisons, arresting Batista's henchmen in order to put them on trial and assuming control of cities and smaller towns.

The general strike successfully concluded on January 4th. The fabricated military coup failed and revolutionary power began to reign throughout the nation. Fidel's statement in Santiago had come true: "This time, luckily for Cuba, the Revolution will truly take power".

XVII
The victorious revolution.
Its consolidation and development

The Provisional Revolutionary Government. Initial measures.- The victory of the Revolution was greeted with overflowing popular enthusiasm. Rebel columns coming from Las Villas, headed by Commanders Ernesto Che Guevara and Camilo Cienfuegos were acclaimed as they went by cities and towns, and their arrival in Havana gathered hundreds of thousands, who cheered them and welcomed them. On January 8th, the Freedom Caravan, with Commander in Chief Fidel Castro at its head, entered the capital, as Havana residents jubilantly took to the streets. At Columbia Military Barracks, addressing the large crowd that had gathered there, Fidel Castro reaffirmed the goals of the Revolution, warned about the difficulties and obstacles ahead, and talked about the need for the Cuban people to stay closely united.

The population greeted the entrance in Havana of the Provisional Revolutionary Government, which had been officially proclaimed in Santiago de Cuba and had taken office on January 5th. As had been agreed, the provisional President was Dr. Manuel Urrutia Lleó, a magistrate. Urrutia had put together his Cabinet in Santiago de Cuba, appointing José, Miró Cardona, a wealthy lawyer, as Prime Minister.

But although both Urrutia and Miró had opposed the Batista dictatorship, they were conservatives, and with Dr. Roberto Agramonte, Minister of State, and Eng. Manuel Ray, Minister of Public Works, they put obstacles in the way of the profound transformations that needed to be taken.

Contradictions soon surfaced between the key figures of the provisional government and the true revolutionary power, represented by the rebel army. Even urgent measures taken during the first days of January, like the creation of revolutionary tribunals for the trying of war criminals, met the resistance of the President and the afore-mentioned ministers.

In numerous public addresses, Fidel Castro explained the basic aspects contained in the agrarian reform law that was being drafted, stressed Cuba's right to govern itself without foreign tutelage, and outlined steps to be taken. But by the end of January, people started showing concern over the government's slow pace.

In mid-February, the first ministerial crisis took place: the Cabinet resigned in full, and Fidel Castro, who up to then had remained as chief of the Rebel Army, assumes the post of Prime Minister. This change gives the Revolution a great boost, which is reinforced by the resignation in June of several ministers, and further accentuated with the popular solution in mid-July of a serious political crisis: in the face of opposition by President Urrutia to the enactment of the revolutionary laws, Fidel Castro puts into a practice a mass-centered political tactic and steps down as Prime Minister. Explaining his resignation in a TV appearance, he denounced the obstructionist, sell-out posture of the President. People then overwhelmingly demanded the resignation of Urrutia, who was replaced by Dr. Osvaldo Dorticós, a distinguished lawyer.

During this first stage of the Revolution—from January 1st, 1959 to approximately the end of 1960—a new Constitution is approved as well as a number of measures indispensable for the attainment of the old dream of economic independence, political sovereignty, real democracy, and social justice, all of which had been at the center of the struggle by the *mambises* during the 18th century and other patriotic fighters under the neo-colonial republic.

The Congress of the Republic was dismantled, together with the whole political and administrative apparatus of the dictatorship, whose members (Senators, Representatives, governors, mayors, councilors) had climbed to their posts by fraudulent means. The traditional political parties, totally in discredit due to their complicity with the dictatorship, automatically disintegrated. The politickers who had collaborated with dictator Fulgencio Batista were banned from any official public post for a period of up to 30 years. All these were measures that had been announced by the Revolution at the Sierra Maestra mountains, long before its victory, and which were now being implemented wit full and enthusiastic public support.

The Revolutionary Government decided to give exemplary punishment to those responsible for the murders and crimes committed under the dictatorship. In Cuban history, torturers and murderers of patriots and revolutionary fighters had always gone unpunished, and now people expected a change: the whole country was asking for death to the assassins. Revolutionary tribunals were established and public trials were held, with full guarantees for the culprits. And the appropriate sentences were passed, including capital punishment.

One other constant popular demand was that political and administrative corruption be eliminated, and that those who had become rich at the expense of workers' sweat and poverty be also punished. In early January, 1959, estimates indicated that more than 2 billion pesos (1 peso being the equivalent of US$ 1), had been dilapidated by the Batista regime, which left a public debt of 1 billion 350 million.

The Revolutionary Government began by confiscating all ill-acquired goods and properties, something that was also unprecedented. The Social Defense Code was changed to provide harsher sanctions for embezzlement, and the Ministry for Embezzled Property Recovery was established. The new ministry confiscated property belonging to the match manufacturing trust; the RECA oil consortium; the Cubana de Aviación Company; and the Rancho Boyero Airport. Fourteen sugar mills were impounded so that the dubious origin of their wealth could be investigated. Also the Associated and the Metropolitan bus companies, and the Cuban Telephone Company, the latter a US monopoly with dirty business connections with Batista. The Ministry for Embezzled Property Recovery took care as well of goods and possessions left behind by people fleeing the country. By April 1960, total wealth recovered amounted to 400 million pesos. The Revolution had put an end to the ominous "*botellas*" and to the embezzlement of public funds.

The old army, an instrument of oppression and terror, had been dissolved during the first days after the revolutionary victory, and the Rebel Army—"the people in uniform", like Camilo Cienfuegos had called it—had taken over the role of armed forces. In a further expression of national sovereignty, the US military mission, which had advised the Batista army, was sent off. The hated Urgency Tribunals and

212

the Criminal Hall II of the Supreme Court were dismantled. Also gone were the National Police, the Secret Police, and the rest of the repressive bodies of the oligarchy, which were then replaced by the National Revolutionary Police and other agencies capable of guaranteeing order and security or the country and the defense of the Revolution against its enemies.

The corrupt, sell-out leadership of the CTC and its unions, which had been imposed and sustained through anti-democracy violence, was wiped out by the working masses. Workers fired from their jobs under the dictatorship were reinstated. And the forcible eviction from private land of poor rural families ended for ever.

Aimed at eradicating traditional abuses against the population and improving their standard of living, the rates for telephones, electricity, and the prices of medicines, were drastically lowered. House rental was reduced by 50 percent, and a Urban Reform law was passed. All beaches were declared free for public use, thus putting an end to the centuries-old, odious existence of racially and socially discriminating exclusive resorts. A nation-wide effort was unleashed aimed at creating awareness among Cubans regarding their true equality, not only before the law but also in connection to jobs, education, and all other manifestations of social life. This was not a easy battle, as it had to contend with the deep-rooted racial prejudices that prevailed in the minds of a large segment of the Cuban population.

The Revolution created new sources of jobs, and numerous measures were introduced to eliminate the scorch of unemployment. By the end of 1959, social security was extended to the whole of the working population, and a monthly 40-peso minimum pension was established, an amount several times higher than most pensions, which in some cases were six pesos a month or even less. As the revolutionary process unfolded, social security was extended to all the population, and pensions raised to 60 pesos a month.

From the beginning, health and education were sectors to which the Revolution assigned Priority. Construction of hospitals, clinics, and dispensaries immediately began, especially in the most remote rural areas. The share earmarked for health in the national budget was considerably raised, and the training of doctors, dentists, nurses, and other health professionals was accelerated. Health care was provided free, including treatments and admissions in hospitals and other institutions. And while private medical practice was respected, the new doctors massively renounced it. Organ transplants, long treatments against diseases like cancer and leukemia, mental disorders, and others, and the most costly of surgical operations were made free for all who needed it. The foundations were laid for what would be Cuba's subsequent extraordinary development in the field of health.

Education was equally transformed. Faced with the horrifying scenario of one million illiterates, and 600 000 children without classrooms that contrasted with the 10 000 teachers without jobs, the Revolution decided to create 10 000 new classrooms, to cater especially to the need existing in the rural areas. At the same time, it began training voluntary teachers who, after going through short preparatory courses, went to work there where they were most necessary. Symbolic of the new Cuba, the Columbia military barracks—the country's largest—was handed over to the Ministry of Education and turned into a huge school complex under the new name of Ciudad Libertad. Likewise, the historic Moncada barracks, in Santiago de Cuba, also became a school complex, renamed Ciudad Escolar "26 de Julio". All in all, 69 military barracks were handed over to educational authorities and turned into schools. At the same time, an Education Reform Law was passed, aimed at improving the general standards of the educational system. The prices of textbooks were slashed down 35 percent, and conditions were created for the launching of the historic Cuban Literacy Campaign.

The Revolution took measures geared at weeding out many chronic evils of Cuban society. The gambling business (casinos, games of chance, pseudo-sports shows) was banned, thus depriving a group of unscrupulous entrepreneurs of a source of wealth that was largely based on the plundering of others. The National Lottery, one of the official institutions that best represented the prevailing corruption, was also banned. It was replaced by the National Savings and Housing Institute, which used the proceeds from the sale of tickets to build houses across the island. But this source of revenue based on a game of chance would later be eliminated, too.

Drug trafficking and organized contraband were also wiped out. Initial steps were taken to put an end to prostitution by striking at its roots: providing dignified jobs and the necessary re-education for the thousands of women who were victims of it. Mendicancy and the sad scene of neglected, barefooted children begging on the streets gradually disappeared. Only a few isolated—and even picturesque—traditional hoboes remained, like the well-known "*Caballero de París*" (Parisian Gentleman), with his long beard, his coat and his hat, who continued to wander the Havana streets, always refusing the assistance of social institutions.

The first Agrarian Reform Law.- Of all measures introduced by the Revolution in this stage, the most transcendental was certainly the Agrarian Reform Law, signed at La Plata, in the Sierra Maestra mountains, on May 17th, 1959. This law benefited more than 100 000 rural families, and dealt a mortal blow on imperialist domination in Cuba and the hated, old latifundia system. It wrote off the right of companies and foreign nationals to own land in Cuba, except in the case of small farmers. It also set the maximum land area that a company or an individual could own in 30 caballerías (402 hectares). This limit could be expanded to 100 caballerías, however, if they were used for growing sugar cane or rice, and even some other crops provided land was fully exploited.

Farms smaller than 30 caballerías could only be expropriated if they were not being exploited by their owners but were leased or given in usufruct to other farmers, planters, or landless peasants, whom the law turned into rightful owners of the land they had been cultivating.

If land being cultivated by a person did not exceed the 2 caballerías, it was turned over to him or her free of charge; if it extended from 2 to 5 caballerías, the person got the first 2 caballerías free, and was required to purchase the remaining, which could be done by installments.

Owners of expropriated land received indemnification through "Agrarian Reform bonds", which they could make good over a 20 year period. Widows and senior people whose only incomes came from land rents began receiving monthly cash payments amounting to those rents. Those monthly payments would later be paid to them for life. Owners who interfered with the law's implementation or who had left the country were not entitled to indemnification bonds.

214

Big landowners' farms that used hired labor were nationalized, but their operation was not dismantled. They continued to function as large agricultural production units, which would later become state farms and cooperative farms for sugar cane production (shortly after these cooperatives would also become state farms). State farms were indeed the embryo of the future socialist property in agriculture in Cuba.

The Law also provided for the establishment of the National Agrarian Reform Institute, which was empowered to guarantee the enforcement of the measure. Fidel Castro was appointed president of the Institute.

The Agrarian Reform law was not socialist in character. The 402 hectare limit represented a huge amount of land in private hands and allowed for the continued existence of a strong agricultural bourgeoisie. But the law was profoundly radical: it put an end to control over Cuban land of foreign companies and their allies on the island, the local latifundia class. Hence its national liberation-oriented, anti-imperialist, and revolutionary character, which explains, too, why after its passage imperialism and the internal reaction decided to openly oppose the Revolution.

This law, which was based on the principle that land should be owned by those who worked it, responded to the historic need of diversifying production; bringing economic development; and eradicating unemployment, poverty, and illiteracy. In the words of then Commander Raúl Castro, "without this agrarian reform there would not have been economic independence, industrial progress, or social well-being".

The Urban Reform Law: An original Cuban contribution.- One of the most pressing needs of Cuban society, as reflected in the program outlined by Fidel Castro after his attack on Moncada barracks in 1953, was solving the housing problem, a public demand that had never been met. An almost impossible dream for any tenant in Cuba was to finally become the owner of his or her house or apartment.

The Revolution immediately set out to try to make this popular aspiration come true. The rate for house rental had already been reduced, owners of idle plots were required, by law, to sell them to people seeking to build their own homes, and the National Savings and Housing Institute, with its ambitious housing construction program, had been established. But the most important measure taken in this connection was the Urban Reform law, passed on October 14th, 1960.

Unprecedented for other countries, this law was an original contribution of the Cuban Revolution. It turned the vast majority of Cuban into the owners of their houses. By paying rents that were reduced by 50 percent, Cubans covered the mortgage of their homes and became proprietors over a period of 5 to 20 years, depending on whether their houses were build before 1940 or after. Thanks to this law, more than one million Cuban families today own the houses where they live.

A characteristic worthnoting regarding this law but which is common to all Cuban revolutionary measures is that no landlord was abandoned to his or her own fate. Once they stopped receiving their rents, if they did not have other incomes, the state provided them with a life pension that ranged from 150 to 600 pesos a month, according to how much they used to make. If the former landlord had other incomes, then those were considered when determining his or her pension so that it would not be below or above the set limit.

So the Urban Reform law primarily benefited tenants by guaranteeing them ownership over their houses within a reasonable period of time but also small-scale landlords, who instead of relying on fluctuating, insecure rents now enjoyed a dignified life pension and were free the burden of taxes and expenses connected with maintenance and others. Those really affected by the law were the big real estate owners, who saw their rent incomes reduced to a maximum of 600 pesos a month.

Hence the enthusiasm with which the law was welcomed by workers, professionals, and modest landlords, who strengthened their support for the Revolution, and the disconformity with which it was met by the big real state owners, who reaffirmed in general their anti-Revolution positions.

The undeclared war against Cuba. The bloodbath that never was.- No matter how just, humane, and necessary the measures adopted by the Revolution, imperialism and the oligarchy were not ready to accept them, since they alter the foundations of the oppression and exploitation system that guaranteed their domination over the country.

From the very first days of January, 1959, the United States opened its doors, and gave shelter and protection to war criminals, embezzlers, and other notorious character who had served as their instruments in Cuba during the bloody tyranny of Fulgencio Batista. These elements immediately began to organize and arm themselves, with the complicity of the US's Federal Bureau of Investigations, the Central Intelligence Agency, and US authorities in general. On January 28th, a group of henchmen and spokespersons for the ousted dictatorship founded their first counter-revolutionary organization outside Cuba: *La Rosa Blanca* (the white rose).

Also in early January, the United States began a huge campaign against Cuba's decision to try and exemplarily punish torturers, murderers, and informers at the service of the Batista dictatorship. The US tried to portray actions connected with the rulings of the Revolutionary Tribunals as barbaric acts and assassinations, and accuse the Cuban government of conducting a bloodbath. Their chief aim of saving the lives of those who had unconditionally served their interests until a few days before; interfering with popular justice; and discrediting the Revolution. This campaign showed to what extent criminal, corrupt, pro-annexation elements of the Batista dictatorship were part of the imperial design against Cuba and an extension of the very US government. Those anti-Cuba campaigns would never stop thereafter.

By the end of January, in a fraternal, friendly visit to Venezuela, Fidel Castro announced the creation in Cuba in a short time of an news agency that would defend peoples of the world against the slander campaigns of their enemies. Shortly after, and with that aim, the Prensa Latina news agency was established.

During gigantic popular rallies in Havana, the nation protested with indignation the US complicity with local criminals and thieves, and the so-called Operación Verdad, or Operation Truth, began, aimed at countering the powerful imperialist campaign that was going on against Cuba.

The US government initially avoided a public involvement in plans against Cuba. One of its tactics then was using those running away from revolutionary justice, and the dictatorship of Rafael Trujillo, in the Dominican Republic, much like the US had used it before to send weapons to the Batista regime. So with the participation of US officials and Cuban counter-revolutionary elements, the Dominican dictator turned his country into a base for aggressions against Cuba.

By mid-January, 1959, news from the Dominican Republic spoke of mercenaries being recruited to launch an invasion on Cuba "as soon as discontent with the Revolution brewed". For seven months, numerous aggressions against Cuba are conducted from Dominican soil. Attacks were carried out against the Cuban embassies in Haiti and the Dominican Republic, and the Cuban ambassador in the latter, and raids conducted into Cuban waters and airspace, aimed at supplying weapons to alleged counter-revolutionary groups operating out of the Escambray mountains.

The Cuban government denounced the conspiracy to the world. In late June, Cuba had been forced to break diplomatic relations with the Dominican government. But by August, Trujillo's plans ended in total failure with the capture in Cuban territory of pirate planes, their crews, and their cargo of weapons.

Plots to assassinate Fidel Castro and other leaders of the Revolution began to feature high in aggressions against Cuba. As early as February 2nd, 1959, a US citizen was captured after he had illegally entered Cuba with the purpose of murdering Fidel. Hundreds of similar attempts would follow, with their organizers resorting to the most diverse of means, from long-range, high-precision rifles to poisons to bomb-pens to lethal germs and others.

One other early way of trying to destroy the Revolution was the training of cells of saboteurs, spies, and conspirators of different kinds, for their introduction in Cuba. The first of these groups was discovered and annihilated in the city of Regla, on the outskirts of Havana, in April of 1959. It was demonstrated that they had connections with US espionage agencies and were financed by supporters of the Batista dictatorship. That same month, two US nationals were caught while carrying out espionage and taking photos of the inside of the La Cabaña Military Fortress.

As the revolutionary process consolidated, the activity of the subversive groups increased. Sectors of Cuban society affected by the new measures, like the big landowners and real estate proprietors, members of the medical trust, and those involved in the casino and gambling business, in association with former military officers and Batista supporters, began to conspire. These were joined by people who turned their backs on the Revolution after they realized it was not going to help them in fulfill their selfish ambitions. The hierarchy of the Cuban Catholic church, with its close ties with the oligarchy, also played an active role against the Revolution during those early years.

US espionage agencies found in those circles excellent allies for their anti-Cuba efforts, and began training them, organizing them, and financing them. By mid-1959, they had set up numerous rings of conspirators and recruits for armed uprisings in Pinar del Río and other provinces.

Those early days of February, 1959, also saw the beginning of one of the most dangerous forms of aggressions against Cuba: the violation of its airspace and territorial waters by boats and planes coming from the United States—including US military boats and planes—manned by US citizens or by mercenaries of Cuban origin. Many could be the purposes of those raids: bombing and shelling towns, sugar mills, factories, power plants and other facilities; setting cane fields and oil refineries on fire; dropping weapons, explosives, and supplies to armed groups, espionage and sabotage rings; picking enemies of the Revolution and taking them to Miami; planting panic among the population; or simply triggering a violent reaction inside Cuba.

Great importance was attached to anti-Cuba propaganda and misinformation, an area in which the United States played a most active role. On May 12th, 1959, US ambassadors to South American nations met in Chile to coordinate a regional campaign against the Cuban Revolution. On the 17th, when the Agrarian Reform law was passed, the first US financed and sponsored radio station of the Cuban counter-revolution abroad, Radio Swan, began its broadcasts.

With the passage by Cuba of the Agrarian Reform law, the United States realized that diplomatic pressures, veiled threats, and political and propaganda campaigns were useless. Washington then decided to prepare a military operation against Cuba. In late May, a secret meeting took place in the US capital between Vice-president Richard Nixon and representatives of the Mafia and several US monopolies, in which Nixon pledges to overthrow the Cuban government.

Subversive groups, sabotages, raids, plots, and other counter-revolutionary activities multiplied thereafter. The discredit campaigns against the Revolution intensified, as did the exhortations on Cubans, especially professionals, to leave the country. In July, the US Senate authorized President Dwight Eisenhower to take measures of an economic character against countries that confiscated US property. The anti-Cuba escalate would continue in the months that followed.

In January, 1960, Allen Dulles, then Director of the Central Intelligence Agency, the CIA, proposed the US administration the creation of a Cuba project, and a task force in charge of executing project-connected actions was put together. In April, the CIA Chief of Station in Guatemala obtained from the Guatemalan President authorization to use Retalhuleu Ranch as air base and training camp for Cuban exiles.

After the signing of the Agrarian Reform law, defections began taking place, including well-known figures and even officers of the Rebel Army with ties to latifundia interests and reactionary circles. Most noticeable among them was the case of Commander Hubert Matos, chief of the Rebel Army in Camagüey province. Of rightist ideas, he came close to the high Catholic clergy and rich farmers of Camagüey, surrounded himself with people who shared his ideas, excluded people loyal to the Revolution from leading positions, and began a seditious movement in October of 1959. The sedition was suppressed quickly and without bloodshed by Commander Camilo Cienfuegos, who traveled to Camagüey specifically for that mission. Arrested, Hubert Matos was tried and given a 20 year sentence.

The most regrettable consequence of those events was the disappearance of Camilo Cienfuegos, whose plane got caught up in strong winds during his trip back to Havana, and plummeted down to the sea. More than two weeks of intense and painful search proved useless, and all over Cuba people wept the loss of one of their most beloved leaders. Since then, every 28th of October, people massively come to the sea-side in Havana and other cities and throw flowers to the water in remembrance of the revolutionary hero.

During the second half of 1959 and all through 1960, counter-revolutionary organizations, armed bands, and espionage rings—all of them financed, organized,

218

and supplied by the CIA—extended across the island, reaching all provinces. And as their banditry grew, so did the popular outcry, with ordinary people, workers, and students demanding weapons for the defense of the nation and punishment for the saboteurs and other enemies of the Revolution. The government decided then to reinstate the Revolutionary Tribunals, which had ceased to exist when the trials against war criminals had ended. It also decided to buy weapons abroad so it could distribute them to the people. The National Revolutionary Militia was established; it rallied workers, farmers, students, professionals, ordinary men and women who were ready to defend the revolutionary power side by side with the Rebel Army, the National Revolutionary Police, and other armed institutions.

On March 4th, 1960, the French boat "La Coubre", which had brought a shipment of weapons from Belgium, exploded in the Havana harbor. Booby traps placed by the CIA in the cargo went off as it was being unloaded, a criminal action that claimed the lives of 70 workers and wounded more than 200 others. The following day, during the burial of the victims, Fidel Castro launched for the first time the slogan that has become a permanent watchword for the Revolution in its struggle against its enemies: "¡Patria o Muerte!", Fatherland or Death!

US maneuvers at the OAS.- As early as June, 1959, the United States began pressing the Organization of American States, the OAS, to take a common action against Cuba. To this end, they promoted the holding of a Foreign Ministers' Consultative Meeting, which was scheduled for Santiago de Chile in August of that year. But the Cuban delegation ended up as the accuser, with the US unable to obtain a condemnation.

A year later, at the Seventh Consultative Meeting of OAS Foreign Ministers, held in San José, Costa Rica, in August 1960, the US managed to obtain a condemnation of Cuba on the ground of Cuba's admitted acceptance of Soviet assistance, which according to the OAS was an extra-continental power's intrusion in the Americas. During the course of the meeting, the US government announced the granting of a 600 million peso credit to be distributed among the governments of the countries there represented.

In response to this action, the people of Havana rallied at the city's Civic Square—today's José Martí Revolution Square—in a National General Assembly of the Cuban People, and approved the Havana Declaration. The Cuban document rejected the San José Declaration for attempting against the self-determination, sovereignty, and dignity of the peoples of the continent. It also denounced the endless interventions and aggressions of US imperialism against the Latin American peoples, and defended Cuba's right to receive assistance of any kind from the Soviet Union or any other nation, including military support in case the island was attacked.

This first Havana Declaration condemned the latifundia, the salaries of starvation, illiteracy, the discrimination against Blacks and native Americans, the repressive laws, colonial and neo-colonial exploitation, and the serious evils that affected the peoples of the Americas. It condemned, in sum, the exploitation of man by man and that of underdeveloped nations by the financial capital of imperialism.

This Declaration, which would later be ratified by the more than one million Cubans who signed it, took the island to the forefront of the defense of the interests, hopes, and aspirations of the Latin American peoples.

The economic aggressions.- Aside from organizing and controlling internal subversion on the island, waging a powerful diplomatic offensive against the Revolution, and training mercenaries to attack it, the US conducted a number of economic aggressions against Cuba with the aim of paralyzing the nation and destroying its revolution process. Cuba conducted more than 80 percent of its trade with the United States, which purchased almost all of the sugar the island produced. One of the first aggressions was to stop buying sugar from Cuba, with disregard for the fact that for almost a century the US had been a steady market for that Cuban product, that during the difficult years of the world wars Cuba had sold sugar to the US at extra-low prices, and that sugar production was the island's main economic activity and the sole means of subsistence for millions of people. The US distributed the sugar quota it had deprived Cuba of among other sugar producing countries, with which it also guaranteed the complicity of the oligarchies ruling those nations.

Not fully satisfied with this measure, Washington banned US companies and their subsidiaries in the world from exporting spare parts to Cuba. By so doing, the US dealt a severe blow to the island's economy since the overwhelming majority of Cuban factories, workshops, mines, rolling stock, etc. used US machinery. The US also cut off it supply of oil, vital for the Cuban economy. And when the USSR begins sending oil to Cuba, US oil monopolies, owners of the local refineries, refused to process it. The US topped all these measures, which by themselves would have been enough to paralyze any small, poor country, with a tight economic blockade that prohibited even the sales of foodstuffs and medicines to Cuba.

Together with this brutal economic offensive, the US began a campaign aimed at encouraging doctors, engineers, architects, teachers, professionals, technicians, and the skilled personnel employed in industries and services, to abandon Cuba. The US not only offered them jobs and high salaries, but it also tried to scare them into leaving Cuba by spreading the most incredible of rumors: that the Cuban government had decided to deprive parents of their rights over their children; that children were going to be sent to the Soviet Union with the most bizarre of purposes; that everything in Cuba was going to be in state control, including the most basic private properties; that a fierce religious persecution would be unleashes, etc. So the US opened its doors not only to the wealthy landowners, industrialists, politickers, pimps, henchmen, and elements of all sorts associated with the Batista dictatorship but it also started to lure thousands of qualified Cuban men and women, including more than 3000 doctors, all of whom the Revolution badly needed to stay in their positions.

The nationalizations.- The US government and its puppets now out of power in Cuba were confident that the Cuban people would not be able to stand such an all-out offensive, and would inevitably capitulate. Their arrogance prevented them from assessing the limitless force behind a true social revolution and the international solidarity. They were also unable to realize that their inhuman aggressions would only accelerate the revolutionary process.

So, the Cuban people responded to each aggression accordingly. A few days before the US deprived Cuba of its sugar import quota, Fidel Castro warned that "they may take away our sugar quota, but we will take away their sugar mills". On August 6th, 1960, 36 sugar mills, the oil refineries and the telephone and electric companies, all of them US property, were nationalized, an action that placed in national hands property worth 800 million pesos. On September 17th, US banks were nationalized. On October 13th, 383 lar-ge corporations and the rest of the banks, except the Canadian ones, were also nationalized. Then on October 24th, the remaining US companies in Cuba are nationalized.

On October 15th, Fidel Castro publicly announces that the program the Revolution had in mind when the attack on Moncada barracks, in 1953, had been implemented. The Revolution entered then a stage of socialist transformation, as evidenced by the nationalization of big companies owned by Cuban capital but which stood in the way of the further development of the revolutionary process.

In its clash with those responsible for Cuba's poverty and underdevelopment, the Revolution received a warm international solidarity. From the very first days after the victory, the peoples of Latin America and the world showed that they stood by their Cuban brothers and sisters. And the Socialist camp offered its resolute support. In February, 1960, a commercial agreement was signed with the Soviet Union, and on May 8th, diplomatic relations between the two countries were re-established. The USSR offered to buy all the sugar Cuba used to sell the United States, and to supply the island with the oil it could need. Commercial agreements were also signed with other Socialist nations.

Unable to buy spare parts from the United States, Cuba began the long and complex process of adapting or changing the technology of its industries, rolling stock, etc. The USSR spare no effort in trying to produce parts and equipment that could match the technology existing on the island.

Cuba, for its part, quickly began training the necessary personnel that would allow it to undertake its national development. The number of scientists, technicians, and skilled workers the island had in 1959, though insufficient, had been further depleted by the brain drain carried out by the United States during the very 1959 and 1960.

The Literacy Campaign.- Despite doubts cast by numerous personalities and organizations abroad, the Revolutionary Government embarked upon the task of eliminating illiteracy in one year: from January to December of 1961. One hundred thousand students, most of them from the cities, volunteered to go to all corners of the island and teach the illiterate how to read and write. These voluntary teachers were organized into detachments, which later became known as the "Conrado Benítez" Brigades, in honor of a young teacher assassinated by counter-revolutionary bandits.

These brigades were completed with another 120 000 ordinary Cubans and 12 700 young workers, who also volunteered to go and teach, an educational force that was trained and pedagogically supervised by close to 35000 certified teachers. This singular effort mobilized nearly 300 000 people.

The mission of the voluntary teachers demanded a great deal of understanding, sacrifice, will power, and resistance on the part of both the young educators and their parents. Many of the adolescents who took part in the campaign had never been away from their home. Now they found themselves living in remote rural areas, having to spend a whole year among people they did not know, who generally had life styles and customs different from theirs. They had to share the poverty in which many of their hosts lived, and in some cases help them after their classes with the daily work.

But the most serious problem lied in the fact that a large number of these young teachers had to carry out their honorable educational work in areas where counter-revolutionary bands operated. Their only means of protection were perhaps their books, and the awareness that they were conducting a peaceful and noble task. Yet, the peaceful and noble character of their work did not prevent that the armed bandits, in their criminal effort to destroy the early achievements of Revolution, would attack the young teachers and their militia protectors, brutally murdering several of them, like martyr teachers Conrado Benítez, Manuel Ascunce Domenech, and Delfín Sen. But all obstacles were finally overcome, and when the Literacy Campaign ended in December of 1961, more than 700 000 Cuban adults had been taught how to read and write, with the only exception of those with a learning disability. The latter accounted for only 3.9 percent of the population, a figure that represented the lowest illiteracy rate in Latin America, and one of the world's lowest. An incredible educational exploit had been realized, and Cuba could proclaim itself an illiteracy-free nation.

The Bay of Pigs Invasion.- In its effort to destroy the Cuban Revolution, the United States designed a strategy that included all possible fronts: political, economic, ideological, and military. The US organized and unleashed a counter-revolutionary war inside the very Cuban territory, via a combined bandit force of up to 3 000 armed mercenaries.

A vast propaganda campaign and a persistent psychological war were also being waged, based on anti-Communist prejudices and on the spreading of false rumors, which generated fear and uncertainty within the most backward segments of the Cuban population.

The wave of counter-revolutionary terror increased during the second half of 1960 and the first months of 1961, with the attempted destruction of industrial and agricultural facilities, means and ways of communications, schools, etc.; the setting on fire of department stores and shops in Havana, in which several workers lost their lives; assassination attempts against revolutionary leaders, especially against Fidel Castro; and the infiltration of armed terrorist groups.

On January 3rd, 1961, the US broke diplomatic relations with the Cuban government; several days later it announced the conduction of military maneuvers near the island, with the participation of more than 40 000 men and 150 naval units, including two atomic submarines. At the same time, the CIA was busy with the military training of thousands of mercenaries at camps in Florida, Guatemala, and Nicaragua.

The leadership of the Revolution had been denouncing, since January, 1959, each and every US aggression and interference. These denunciations acquired a stronger character in the face of the evident preparations for a military intervention. They were taken to the OAS, the UN, and other international fora, as well as expressed by Fidel Castro during his visits to Venezuela, Argentina, Uruguay, the US, and other countries. But more importantly, the Revolution had prepared the nation politically and militarily to face any contingency. Military schools had been established and were offering emergency courses; militia battalions are organized, with the immediate task of putting an end to banditry, especially at the Escambray mountains; and steps are taken to obtain the necessary weapons in the shortest possible time.

On December 31st, 1960, faced with the threat of a direct US military intervention, a general, nation-wide mobilization is ordered. On January 4th, 1961, the death sentence is established for counter-revolutionary crimes. Two days before, thousands of armed militia members had paraded through the Revolution Square, to mark the second anniversary of the victory and reaffirm the determination to defend at all cost the revolutionary power.

In early April, the US government is ready to invade the island by means of a mercenary force. In the morning of April 15th, eight US B-26 bombers that had taken off from a base in Puerto Cabezas, Nicaragua, conducted a surprise raid against the airfields of Ciudad Libertad, San Antonio de Los Baños, and Santiago de Cuba. Resorting as usual to treacherous procedures, the US disguised its planes with the markings used by those of the Cuban Revolutionary Air Force, to create the impression that an internal revolt was taking place.

The chief objective of the attack against the airports was to destroy on the ground the modest Cuban air force so it could not be used against the invasion. But the US failed in its purpose. The Cuban artillery, despite its lack of experience, was able to repel the attack, shooting down one of the enemy planes, with the death of the two members of its crew. The Cuban side recorded 53 people wounded, and 7 dead. One of the victims, a young soldier, expressed the Cuban people's determination to fight on when he wrote the word "Fidel" with his own blood on a wooden door next to where his dead body was later found.

The following day, April 16th, during the burial of the victims of the attack, addressing a huge crowd of armed militiamen and women, Fidel Castro proclaimed the socialist character of the Revolution, and declared a state of alert, aware that the bombing had been the prelude of the invasion. So, the Cubans who hours later fought the mercenary enemies would do so in the realization that they were fighting for Socialism.

The mercenary invasion, codenamed by its organizers as Operation Pluto, took place early in the morning of April 17th. The invading force—the so-called Brigade 2506—was made of 1 500 men, and had left Puerto Cabezas on board five US warships, escorted by other US naval units.

They landed at two separate points of Bay of Pigs (Playa Girón and Playa Larga), an area on the southern coast of the then Las Villas province. Their mission was to set up a beachhead and declare a provisional counter-revolutionary government, which would then request, and would immediately obtain, a direct US military intervention.

The place chosen was the right one: a narrow strip cut off from the mainland by a 10 kilometer long stretch of swamps. Only 3 dirt roads built after the Revolution connected the area with its vicinity, and the invaders thought it would be easy to block the entrance of Cuban forces via those 3 accesses. In addition, the Brigade was well organized, fully armed and equipped, and enjoyed all the necessary support.

But the US government and the mercenaries did not take into consideration two factors: the close unity that existed between the Cuban people and the Revolution.

and the strategic and tactical capability of Fidel Castro and the revolutionary leadership. People knew the invaders represented a sad past, and a return to the oligarchic domination and exploitation that the Revolution had brought to an end. They knew that the mercenaries had been escorted by the same forces that in late 19th century had frustrated the national independence efforts of the Cubans and had imposed a regime of oppression and plundering.

A glance at the composition of the invading mercenary Brigade was enough to realize that its purpose was to re-establish oligarchic control: 194 ex-military officers and henchmen of the Batista dictatorship; 100 big landowners; 24 big property owners; 67 real estate owners; 112 big merchants; 35 industrial magnates; 179 wealthy individuals; and 112 lumpen and anti-social elements. Many others were children or relatives of wealthy people who had lost their old privileges. Cubans, for their part, were assisted by their defense of a just cause, and the just obtained social and national emancipation.

At the same time, the accumulated experience and wisdom of the revolutionary leadership guaranteed the necessary popular unity and fighting readiness to face the aggression. Militia battalions from Cienfuegos, Matanzas, and Havana were quickly mobilized, as well as the Matanzas Militia Training School, a battalion of the National Revolutionary Police, and the artillery of the Rebel Army, all of them commanded by Fidel Castro.

Plans that had been previously designed for the defense of the whole of the national territory were simultaneously activated, and some 3 000 elements of known anti-Revolution positions, on whom the CIA was counting for internal support to the invasion, were immediately detained. A month before, the militia had dealt a demolishing blow on counter-revolutionary bands operating out of the Escambray mountains, and had also rendered useless US intelligence plans for that region.

Revolutionary forces heroically fought the mercenary Brigade, its naval units, tanks, and planes, with weapons that had timely arrived from the Soviet Union and Checoslovaquia. In less than 72 hours, they had defeated the enemy, with a toll of 89 mercenaries dead, 250 wounded, and 1 197 prisoners. It was April 19th, 1961. The Cuban side suffered hundreds of wounded, and 157 people dead, patriotic citizens who continue to be remembered as heroes today. Five days after, US President John F. Kennedy publicly admitted the US government's responsibility in the failed Cuban invasion.

From March to April of 1962, the Bay of Pigs mercenaries were tried; they were punished by depriving them of their Cuban citizenship and by having to pay a 62 million peso indemnification for material damages they had caused Cuba. Failure to provide that amount would result in the culprits having to serve a 30 year jail term, with compensating and compulsory work.

The Cuban government led it be known that it was ready to renounce that indemnification and turn the prisoners over to the United States if the US government agreed to acting so that a similar amount of US, Spanish, Nicaraguan, Guatemalan, and Puerto Rican patriots in jail for struggling against fascism, racism, colonialism, tyranny, and imperialism in their countries were also set free. But this proposal was unheeded, and finally the governments of Cuba and the United States agreed to exchange the prisoners for children's food and medicines amounting to the figure of the indemnification demanded by Cuba. For the first time in its history, the US was paying a war indemnification to another country.

Bay of Pigs Victory. Mercenary Prisoners

The Bay of Pigs victory consolidated the Cuban people's confidence in their own forces, confirmed the value of internationalist solidarity, and increased the prestige of the Cuban Revolution before the progressive world. It was not just a Cuban victory but a victory of all Latin American peoples in their struggle against imperialist and oligarchic domination. That was how progressive forces in the continent understood it, and they quickly raised their voices of support for the island under attack. Particularly moving was the position of Mexican patriot and revolutionary, General L Lázaro C Cárdenas, who volunteered to fight alongside Cubans against the invaders. He, too, understood Fidel Castro's assertion that "after the victory at Bay of Pigs, all peoples of Latin America were freer".

The unity of Cubans.- A decisive factor in the successful development of the Revolution was the unity of the Cuban people around their political and mass organizations, and the unity of those organizations around the revolutionary leadership. The unity of action that had been achieved during the struggle against the Fulgencio Batista dictatorship became organizational unity after 1959.

Although during the first months there were misunderstandings, different approaches to problems, and even errors, which could be expected in any great social movement like the one taking place in Cuba, agreement as to the objectives of the Revolution, and the need to defend it and make it advance prevailed. The new leadership knew that unity was indispensable and moved to educate the people in that realization. This is an area in which, as in many others, a key role was played by Fidel Castro, who has been at the heart of popular and revolutionary unity.

Following an initial period of internal clashes and struggles, the leadership of Confederation of Cuban Workers, the CTC, gradually got rid of opportunistic elements and methods it had inherited, while eliminating anti-Communist prejudices and re-establishing trade union democracy. The first CTC congresses were held in a climate of suspicion and contradictions within the national unions and the CTC itself. But the situation eventually normalized, thanks largely to the direct involvement of Fidel Castro. After a process of reorganization, the CTC came out with strengthened authority as the leader of the nation's working masses.

The peasant organizations integrated into the National Association of Small Farmers, the ANAP, which was founded on May 17th, 1961. The various farmers' structures that generally represented the interests of the wealthy landowners were dismantled, and their functions assumed by the ANAP.

As part of this unifying process, the Association of Rebel Youths, the AJR, was established in January of 1960. The AJR would later assimilate the other youth organizations, and also the Rebel Pioneers Union, founded in April of 1961. During the first congress of the AJR, on April 4th, 1962, the association changed its name to that of Young Communist League, and has remained at the heart of the struggles of Cuban youths through these years. Of the students' organizations, the most active one has been the University Student Federation, which has played a leading role in university transformation and actively participates in the revolutionary process. Meanwhile, the women's organizations that existed rallied under the Cuban Women Federation, which was established on August 23rd, 1960.

A valuable contribution of the Cuban experience to successful Socialist and national liberation revolutions has been the Committees for the Defense of the Revolution, the CDR's. Established in September of 1960 with the purpose of assisting with neighborhood surveillance against the growing terrorist actions, this peculiar social organizations have expanded their functions and become extremely useful for the Revolution in all fronts.

The CDR's are the largest mass organization in Cuba. They function at the level of city blocks and rural areas, and rally virtually all citizens older than 14, regardless of their occupations, ideology, sex, race, or other, provided they are not enemies of the Revolution.

Originally designed to watch against possible enemy actions in their areas, the CDR's soon began carrying out other tasks, like keeping the block tidy and clean; cooperating in health care-related activities (vaccination campaigns, blood donations, epidemics control, etc.); making sure children attended classes; collecting recyclable material; assisting in population and housing censuses and demographic research; assisting in electoral affairs; ensuring the free and democratic discussion by neighbors of proposed laws and government measures; cooperating with the police in the fight against crime; and others.

Virtually the whole of the Cuban population is grouped under the thousands of existing CDR's, with the membership of each usually not exceeding the 100 neighbors, who meet periodically, jointly discuss their problems, and democratically elect their representatives every year. These characteristics make it possible for the CDR's to successfully carry out such a wide range of functions as mentioned above, turning them into one of the most important organizations for the country, and one of the most bitterly hated by its enemies.

The Party.- After the 1959 revolutionary victory, the three organizations that had been more actively involved in the struggle against the Fulgencio Batista dictatorship retained their independence. They were the "26 of July" Revolutionary Movement, the most important one, led by Fidel Castro; the Popular Socialist Party; and the "March 13" Revolutionary Directorate. Of them, the only one that had a historically defined marxist-leninist stand was the People's Socialist Party, but there was agreement among all three as to the national liberation-oriented, socialist objectives of the process that was just starting. The sole exception was a wing of the anti-Batista movement, consisting of people who in general lines wanted a continuation of the capitalist system and the economic and political subordination to the United States.

These conservative positions, coupled with the existing anti-Communist prejudices and the low level of political and ideological awareness of a considerable segment of the Cuban population, plus the uncertainty and doubts that were there among many a revolutionary, made it impossible for an immediate merging of these organizations into a single party. Unity would not come without difficulties, and would largely be the result of the unifying steps that were being taken by mass organizations, as explained above.

But absence of a single party did not prevent the existence of close cooperation among the three organizations. Practically all fundamental decisions made by the Revolution came after consultations and common positions. At the same time, Fidel Castro and other top revolutionary leaders carried out an intense political and ideological drive through addresses, the press, direct contacts with the population, in which major national issues were discussed. Forces in action became ever more polarized, with the national masses consolidating their unity around the work of the Revolution and supporters of the bourgeoisie, pro- imperialist ideology going over to the enemy camp.

A major contribution to this unifying process, particularly the task of explaining and disseminating the fundamentals of marxist-leninist ideology, came by means of the Revolutionary Education Schools, proposed by Fidel Castro and Communist leader Blas Roca, on behalf of the new leadership. Initially under the "26 of July" Movement, these schools also became a project of the United Party of the Cuban Socialist Revolution and the Communist Party, organizations that will be discussed below.

This revolutionary instruction movement was founded on December 2nd, 1960, on the occasion of the 4th anniversary of the landing of the "Granma" boat; one of the most outstanding and prestigious Socialist Youth leaders, Lionel Soto, was appointed to head it. These schools constituted the first organ of a political nature that expressed the existing revolutionary organizations' unity of purposes and ideals.

A growing number of party members and active revolutionaries—mostly industrial and agricultural workers, teachers, military officers and soldiers, and representatives of the mass organizations (unions, farmers, women, youths, etc.)—went through the

227

different types of courses offered by this school system. The trainees—more than 155 000 up to 1966—were mostly people under 30 years of age. This movement would later be consolidated into the a party school network open for all party members island-wide. "Our Revolutionary Instruction Schools", once said Fidel Castro, "have filled an ideological vacuum, have trained tens, hundreds of thousands of Cubans".

Announcement of the First Central Committee of the Cuban Communist Party. Che's Letter. Founding of Granma Newspaper

The proclamation of the Socialist character of the Revolution in April of 1961 represented a major step forward in the merging of the revolutionary organizations. In June that year, the "26 of July" Movement, the Popular Socialist Party, and the "March 13" Directorate agreed to their dissolution in order to become one single party. Their unification gave rise first to the Integrated Revolutionary Organizations, which a year later became the United Party of the Cuban Socialist Revolution, and finally the Communist Party of Cuba. This last name was adopted during an important meeting in Havana from September 30th to October 1st, 1965, which also agreed to form the first Central Committee of the Communist Party of Cuba, appoint its leading apparatus and auxiliary commissions, and merge the dailies **Revolución**, founded by the "26 of July" Movement, and **Hoy**, of the Popular Socialist Party, into a single newspaper: **Granma**, the official organ of the new Party.

This was the culmination of the long process of unification of the island's revolutionary forces. Represented in the newly formed Central Committee of the

Communist Party of Cuba were all the heroic episodes of the last 40 years of the country's history, all major civil and military developments; manual and intellectual workers regardless of race, sex, or age; all revolutionary sectors. The new Party was entrusted with the colossal task of building the new society and leading the Cuban people in the defense of their homeland, their Revolution, and Socialism.

The Missile Crisis.- The defeat of the mercenary Brigade at Bay of Pigs made the US think that the only way of crushing the Cuban Revolution was through a direct military intervention. The US immediately embarked on its preparation.

But this did not go unnoticed for the Cuban government. On April 23rd, 1961, four days after the Bay of Pigs victory, Fidel Castro warned that a direct US aggression was all the more likely after the failure of their indirect attack; then on April 27th, President Osvaldo Dorticós met with the diplomatic corps to denounce that danger and ratify the island's determination to resist till the end.

The US stepped up its aggressive actions. On April 25th, Washington established an embargo on exports of any kind of products to Cuba, even those that had already been purchased and were waiting in US harbors.

Groups engaging in sabotage, espionage, and diversionist actions increased, as also did US support for the armed bands. New assassination attempts are plotted against Fidel Castro, other Cuban leaders, and supporters of the Revolution. An attempt to murder Carlos Rafael Rodríguez was aborted, but others claimed the lives of several members of the Rebel Army and the Militia in various parts of the country. The media campaign to make the US public opinion believe that by international law the US was allowed to send troops to Cuba intensified.

As part of their hostile plans, the US considered a self-inflicted aggression in connection with the Guantánamo Naval Base that would allow them to blame Cuba and provide a pretext for invading the island. With this aim, constant provocations took place from the US side of the base: marines shooting toward Cuban territory, some times for several hours; murder of a fisherman.

The number of violations of Cuba's airspace and territorial waters increased. In one single day—July 9th, 1962—US planes flew over Cuban territory 12 times. On another occasion, they launched rockets against eastern Cuba territory. US pirate boats attacked units of the Cuban Revolutionary Navy: three Cubans die during one of those attacks; 17 others were lost in another one.

Meanwhile, Washington stepped up its pressures on Latin American governments so they unconditionally support US plans against Cuba. It accompanies its pressures with bribes: an assistance program for Latin America, the so-called Alliance for Progress, portrayed as a solution for the region's problems. In late 1961, Venezuela and Colombia broke diplomatic relations with Cuba; in January, 1962, the 8th Consultative Meeting of OAS Foreign Ministers, in Punta del Este, Uruguay, suspended Cuba's membership in the organization for its "incompatibility with the inter-American system".

From late 1961 to early 1962, the US designed the so-called Operation Mongoose, approving 33 tasks to be carry out against Cuba in a graded way. The plan was expected to end with an internal rebellion in October of 1962, the pretext for the US military intervention. Hundreds of CIA officials were involved in the plan. In late September, the US Congress passed a "joint resolution" authorizing the President to use force against Cuba—an invasion if necessary—to put an end to "the aggressive and subversive work" of the Cuban Revolution in the western hemisphere.

In late September and up to beginning of October, military forces were concentrated near Cuba; US President John F. Kennedy called 150 000 reservists into active duty; an additional 150 000-strong force comprising several divisions was regrouped in Florida and Texas; and a hemispheric meeting convened by the Secretary of the US State Department was held in Washington, to impose the anti-Cuba plan on Latin American countries.

The Cuban government denounced the offensive to the world since it began, and responded to each aggressive US action. As Cuba was being expelled from the OAS, a Peoples Conference was being held in Havana, with the participation of relevant political and intellectual personalities of the hemisphere. The meeting denounced the US government as the disrupter of peace on the continent, and proclaimed that Cuba's fate was the fate of 200 million oppressed people in Latin America.

Also in response to the OAS agreement, more than one million persons met in Havana in a new National General Assembly of the Cuban People, and approved the Second Havana Declaration, a document of an extraordinary political and ideological value that analyzes the serious situation in Latin America, its main causes, and the way to solve it. The Declaration asserted that where all peaceful ways were closed for the peoples, the armed insurrection was indispensable, and that "the duty of every revolutionary is to do the revolution".

In 1961, the Cuban Revolutionary Armed Forces began streamlining and improving their structures and composition, and the government appealed to the Soviet Union to speed up its shipments of weapons and combat equipment necessary to guarantee the island's defense. On May 29th, 1962, the USSR proposed to deploy in Cuba medium and intermediate range missiles, an offer that was accepted considering its significance for the general strategic strengthening of the Socialist block, and what it meant for Cuba's own defense. It was decided that the signing of this military agreement be announced in November, during a visit to Cuba of Soviet Prime Minister, Nikita S. Jruschov. In August, the deployment of 42 medium range nuclear missiles began, together with the sending to Cuba of IL-28 medium range bombers and a 43 000-strong Soviet military contingent. The Soviet troops would be directly subordinated to the government of the USSR, their mission being to support the Cuban Revolutionary Armed Forces in case of a foreign aggression, in full respect of the island's sovereignty and legal order, and without the right to occupy Cuban territory or carry out any other actions not connected with their cooperation role.

But before the Soviet-Cuban military agreement was announced, when US forces were ready to launch their aggression against the island, evidences were presented to President Kennedy of the missiles' presence in Cuba. The situation changed altogether, since it was no longer an issue of a military operation against Cuba but an international conflict in which the Soviet Union, a nuclear power, was involved.

The US immediately mobilized its army, navy, and air forces, not only in the western hemisphere but also in Europe and the Far East. It increased its reconnaissance flights over Cuba; activated its nuclear bomb carrying B-27 bombers; considerably reinforced Guantánamo Naval Base; and, on October 22nd, ordered a naval blockade of Cuba. US planes began flying low over Cuban territory.

Fidel Castro, Commander in Chief of the Cuban Forces, ordered a nation-wide military state of alert. Cuba requested an immediate meeting of the UN Security Council; denounced before the world the new and dangerous US adventure; and stressed the island's sovereign right to repel any enemy aggression and ask any friendly nation for assistance. The Soviet government placed its armed forces in full combat readiness; issued a declaration condemning the naval blockade and the rest of the US's aggressive measures; and warned Kennedy about the possible consequences of those aggressions.

Cuba declared that it would not allow its ships to be inspected by US forces, and that it would shoot against enemy planes entering its territory. On October 27th, the batteries of an anti-aircraft rocket group at Banes, in eastern Cuba, shot down a U-2 plane that was violating the island's airspace.

A wave of solidarity with Cuba was generated world-wide, while UN Secretary General, U Thant, intervened, in an effort to find a solution to the conflict. Exchanges took place between the Cuban and the Soviet governments, and Jruschov maintained an active correspondence with President Kennedy. As a result of that Soviet-US correspondence, the USSR accepted to withdraw its missiles from Cuba in return for the expressed US commitment not to attack Cuba and stop its allies from doing it. And so, the Missile Crisis came to its end.

The Missile Crisis. October, 1962

The very same day that the agreement was known in Cuba, on October 28th, Fidel Castro made a public statement expressing the position of the Cuban

231

government, which had not been consulted with regards to the compromise. Cuba set forth five conditions as a true guarantee against a US aggression. These conditions, which came to be known as "the five points", were the following:
—End to the economic blockade and all measures of commercial pressure against Cuba by the US in the world.
—End to all subversive activity, the dropping and infiltration of weapons and explosives, the organization of mercenary invasions, the infiltration of spies and saboteurs, all of them actions originating in the United States or in other countries that acted in complicity with the United States.
—End to pirate raids from bases in the United States and Puerto Rico.
—End to all violations of our naval and airspace by US warships and planes.
—US withdrawal from Guantánamo naval base, and return of that occupied territory to Cuba.

The Missile Crisis once more showed the world the US arrogance, and its disregard for the sovereignty of other nations. It also demonstrated the Cuban and Soviet interest in the peaceful solution of conflicts, preserving Cuban sovereignty, and preventing a world nuclear catastrophe. It also proved that Fidel Castro was right when he said that the defense of the Cuban Revolution could not be trusted to external forces but had to rely on readiness and patriotism of Cubans. Lastly, the conflict evidenced the high morale, serenity, unity, and courage of the Cuban people, who did not yield before the dangers, and were ready to fight and die for the defense of their dignity and freedom. Cuba showed, again in the words of Fidel Castro, that it may not have had nuclear missiles, but it had "long range moral missiles that cannot be dismantled, that will never be dismantled".

The harassment against Cuba continues.- President Kennedy's commitment not to carry out a direct or indirect military attack against Cuba did not mean the end of the harassment. On the contrary, the economic blockade stayed in place, as did the subversion and the other forms of aggression, some of which adopted new, more barbaric and reckless methods.

Intensifying the economic blockade, in December of 1962 President Kennedy decided to impose sanctions on ships from capitalist countries that touched Cuban harbors; shortly after, he would announce that ships used for trading with Cuba would not be allowed to carry merchandise purchased by the US government. The US then compiled a "black list" of countries trading with Cuba, and threatened to cut off economic and military assistance to them.

The US Treasury Department decided to freeze all Cuban assets in the United States, including bank deposits, and prohibits any transfer of dollars from or to Cuba. It also embargoed all assets belonging to Cubana de Aviación Airlines, including several planes. Numerous other measures are taken, with the aim of starving the Cuban people into submission.

Internal subversion also increased. The banditry of counter-revolutionary groups continued up to 1965, especially at Escambray, in central Cuba. A mountainous, hard to reach area, Escambray had not benefited from the early revolutionary transformations as much as the rest of the country had, and there was even little awareness in general regarding the changes that were going on. At the same time, numerous elements of the so-called Escambray Second National Front stayed in the area after 1959, entrusted with the implementation of the Agrarian Reform law. Some of them committed abuses and arbitrary actions that local residents associated with the Revolution. And since the political work in the area had been extremely poor then, enemy bands were able to plant fear, confusion and mistrust among the rural population. At Escambray the bandits committed abominable crimes, for which, though, they would be made to pay later. All these factors combined, making it possible for the counter-revolutionary bands to operate in this area longer than they did in other regions.

The struggle against these bands was waged by an army made up mostly of workers and farmers, many of them local residents, supported by the Revolutionary Armed Forces, the Ministry of Interior, and the Militia. Organized under battalions, this force successfully fought the armed bandits, while the Party and the mass organizations teamed up to raise the political awareness of the rural population. In January 1965, Cuba announced that the bandits had been totally eliminated.

Aside from controlling the bands and providing them with supplies, Washington continued organizing and infiltrating into Cuba spy and sabotage rings, with the aim of undermining the island's economy and murdering revolutionary leaders and followers. Cuban security forces repeatedly penetrated and dismantled these rings, capturing their members and sentencing them to long prison terms. In November of 1962, the chief of CIA operations in Cuba was apprehended. The man, a former military officer under the Batista dictatorship, revealed all CIA plans against the Revolution.

Mercenary boats, and even US military planes and ships, continued carrying out attacks against Cuban industries, cities, and ships. Soviet and Spanish ships would also be victims of those aggressions while in Cuban and international waters. Some enemy planes were downed, and ships captured. The Cuban fishing fleet was frequent prey of attacks, its boats sunk or hijacked, and its crews murdered and kidnapped. Sometimes, Cuban fishermen were detained, taken to Key West, and arbitrarily condemned by US judges.

These attacks and kidnaps gave rise to huge demonstrations, many of them before the US Interest Section in Havana. Hundreds of thousands of people would parade day and night in front of the US office, until the fishermen were finally handed over to Cuba.

The Cuban government responded with measures of its own to those crimes and abuses. Once, in February of 1964, water supply to the US naval base at Guantánamo was cut off, only to be re-established after the fishermen were released. At times, Cuba would reciprocate by imposing large fines on US citizens caught violating the island's naval or air space. And there were occasions when the Cuban navy recovered the hijacked vessels, and even apprehended the perpetrators.

It is during these years that the United States began the practice of hijacking Cuban planes in mid-air, actions that frequently put in jeopardy the lives of innocent national and foreign citizens. Up to 1975, some 100 Cuban airplanes had been hijacked, never to be returned. Several hijack attempts were aborted thanks to the courage shown by the crew on board, who at times had to pay with their lives. Hijackers would usually be received as heroes in the US, thus encouraging this hated international practice. Later, the US government would suffer the consequences of such actions—US planes, too, being frequently forced to land in Cuba—and an anti-hijack agreement would be signed between the two countries.

US-sponsored and encouraged counter-revolutionary terrorism has also adopted the form of kidnappings and assassination attempts against Cuban diplomats, officials, and internationalist workers. In August, 1976, two members of the Cuban diplomatic staff in Buenos Aires, the Argentinean capital, were kidnapped, and disappeared. Previous similar actions had occurred, like the attempted kidnapping of a group of Cuban volley-ball players in Puerto Rico, during the 10th Pan-American Games.

At the same time, attacks involving bombs, machine guns, and rifles have been perpetrated against Cuban ambassadors and consuls, and Cuban offices abroad, among them the UN Permanent Mission in New York, the Interest Section in Washington, and Cubana de Aviación Airlines representations in the world. Aside from the United States, these criminal actions have also taken place in countries like Canada, Mexico, Chile, Jamaica, Argentina, Venezuelan, Barbados, Panama, Puerto Rico, Portugal, England, Portugal, and others, leaving numerous deaths, wounded, and considerable material damages.

One other form of harassment against Cuba—provocations from within Guantánamo Naval Base—also increased during those years. The US marines offended verbally and with gestures Cuban frontier guards, and frequently shot at them, wounding them at times, and even causing the death of two of them: Ramón López Peña, killed in July of 1964, and Luís Ramírez López, in May of 1966. Meanwhile, other violations of the Cuban territory occurred. In December of 1964, Che Guevara denounced that that year alone there had been 1 323 provocations from within the base.

Those first revolutionary years were also marked by the intensification of US pressures on Latin American governments with the aim of isolating Cuba and conducting a collective action against it. In March, 1963, President Kennedy affirmed: "We will build a wall around Cuba". Some governments of the continent resisted t he US pressures, especially Mexico, which never yielded to them. Yet, although not as a unanimous decision, the OAS again pronounced itself against Cuba, which it had expelled from the organization in 1962.

During the 9th Consultative Meeting of OAS Foreign Ministers, held in Washington in July, 1964, a resolution was passed urging the governments of the region to break diplomatic relations with Cuba, and calling on people on the island to rise against the Revolution. The OAS document also carried the threat of a military action on Cuba. It violated the Río de Janeiro Treaty, the UN Chart, and the very OAS Chart, and was based on accusations that the organization was never able to prove, regarding an allegedly aggressive Cuban policy that it considered to be dangerous for peace on the continent.

234

The Cuban people strongly rejected the accusation, and at a mammoth rally in the capital of the then Oriente province, they approved the "Santiago de Cuba Declaration", a dignified reply to the OAS action. The document defined the OAS as "totally lacking the moral and the right to judge and punish Cuba". It denounced the United States and tyrannical, oligarchic governments of the region as the ones responsible for subversion and for the danger of a war on the continent. Cuba presented a long list of concrete facts to back its accusation, and described as "an unprecedented, cynical act that the victimizers should proclaim themselves judges and try to further punish the victim".

The Santiago de Cuba Declaration warned that if there was not an end to the aggressions, the training of mercenaries, and the infiltration of spy and sabotage rings, weapons and explosives into the island, the Cuban people would "consider themselves equally entitled to assist with resources available revolutionary movements in those countries that interfered in the internal affairs of our nation".

In rejecting the threats of a military aggression carried in the OAS resolution, the Cuban declaration stressed the Cuban people's determination to defend their independence at all costs. It concluded with the well-known phrase by General Antonio Maceo: "Whoever tries to get hold of Cuba will end up biting the dust of its soil drenched in blood, if he has not died in the fight!"

In fulfillment of the US-imposed OAS agreement, several Latin American governments broke relations with Cuba.

From the very beginning after the revolutionary victory, the United States constantly called on Cubans to flee their country, encouraging them to clandestinely leave for the US, while preventing regular travel between the two countries. Washington went as far as taking away the passports, and legally prosecuting, students and other US citizens who visited Cuba. The ban on travel led people opposed to the Revolution, and those making up the traditional Cuban migratory flow to the US, to resort to unlawful means of reaching US territory. The relatively short distance that separates Cuba from the coast of Florida made sea trips the most frequent type of illegal travel. But these trips usually involved small, unseaworthy vessels, a number of which capsized during the journey, with their passengers at times getting killed.

Faced with this situation, in October of 1965, the Cuban government, whose policy had always been one of not standing in the way of those wishing to leave the country, created conditions at a coastal place called Camarioca, near Matanzas city, so that Cubans seeking to go to the US could picked up there by boats coming from Florida, provided that the vessels were in seaworthy conditions. Unable to stop the flow that ensued, the US government agreed to signing an accord whereby a Varadero-Miami charter airlift was established for those traveling to the US. This was the first migratory agreement to be concluded between the two countries.

Biological warfare.- Among the most criminal aggression that the US has carried out against Cuba is the spreading of toxic substances and germs over the island, causing the outbreaks of diseases that have affected people, plants, and animals. Only a deliberate enemy action could caused these epidemics in a country whose high level of public health care and flora and fauna protection is recognized by the most competent, specialized regional and international organizations.

As early as January, 1965, Cuban authorities discovered near Santiago de Las Vegas, in Havana province, a balloon that in breaking spread an unknown white substance. Then in September, 1968, a foreign expert hired by the CIA introduced a virus that destroyed coffee plantations. In 1971, an African Swine Fever epidemic wreaked havoc on the porcine cattle of the western Cuban provinces.

But the biological warfare intensified after 1979. That same year, a third of all Cuban sugar cane plantations was affected by an epidemic of **sugar cane rust**, while **blue mold** infested 90 percent of the tobacco fields. These were both diseases Cuba had eradicated many years before.

In 1981, an epidemic of **hemorrhagic dengue** spread across the island, affecting more than 35 000 people in a few months, and causing the death of 150 of them, mostly children. Other infectious diseases, like **hemorrhagic conjunctivitis**, have also strangely proliferated.

Aside from the victims that this criminal activity has caused among the population, and its great damages on the country's basic crops, Cuba has had to make overhuman efforts, dedicate huge resources, and take extreme measures to stop and eliminate those epidemics, and recover from the considerable losses they have brought for the national economy.

All these forms of aggression have been systematically taking place along the 37 years of revolutionary power.

Economic development from 1963 to 1975.- From 1963 to 1975, means of production gradually became social property. In October of 1963, in the face of the rural bourgeoisie's counter-revolutionary attitude, a new agrarian reform law was passed, reducing maximum land ownership by a private individual to 5 *caballerías*, or 67 hectares. Farms exceeding that extension were nationalized, which dealt a decisive blow on the counter-revolutionary landowners. With this, 70 percent of all land went to national hands. Farmers received the official promise that this would be the last agrarian reform law; any further move towards higher forms of land ownership would only occur on the basis of farmers's willingness.

At the end of the nationalization process, private property in agriculture lied only with small farmers, who owned 30 percent of the nation's land, and some means of transportation, which continued to be the personal property of those directly operating them.

During the first decade of revolutionary power, economic development was not at the center of the government's attention. The ruthless US economic blockade and the continued aggressions of different types forced authorities to devote a large number of resources to defense, if only to guarantee the survival of the Revolution. For several years, the revolutionary government had to maintain more than 300 000 men over the arms, with the subsequent military use of resources that could have otherwise gone into general production.

Nonetheless, efforts were made to begin the country's industrialization and the modernization of agriculture. The stock of tractors grew considerably, and sugar cane lifting machines and combined harvesters were introduced, with a view to making sugar cane harvesting a more humane, less labor-intensive activity. Cuban workers had agreed to contribute 4 percent of their salaries to industrialization, which together with state financing and Soviet assistance, allowed for the creation of hundreds of industrial plants, like the Alquitex Textile Factory, in Alquízar, west of Havana; the Mechanical Plant and the INPUD Home Appliance Factory, in Santa Clara, in the center of the island; the "Cuban-Soviet Friendship" Construction Material Plant and the "30th of September" Industrial Conglomerate, in Santiago de Cuba, on the eastern part, and others.

At the same time, Cuba began training scientists, technicians, and skilled workers, and major research centers and training institutions were established, among them the "José Antonio Echeverría" Technical University, the Soils and Oceanology Institutes, etc.

From 1965 to 1970, Cuba concentrated most efforts in attaining a 10 million ton sugar harvest. The accelerate growth of the population and consumption, the need to obtain resources for industrialization, and the urgency of considerably increasing exports demanded that special emphasis be put in greater production of the country's number one industry.

But the targeted 10 million ton sugar production was not attained. Original estimates had failed to consider that industrial investments remained lower than required, that labor was not enough, and that voluntary work, albeit in heroic proportions, would have been unable to cover the manpower deficit. In addition, there were organizational problems, and wrong administrative and economic management methods. However, sugar production reached a record 8 537 600 tons, the highest in the nation's history.

Aside from the aforementioned miscalculations and deficiencies, other mistakes were also made during those years. Moved by the desire to rapidly improve the living and working conditions of the population, numerous measures were taken that were not consistent with the country's real capabilities. A policy centered around gratuities was set forth, with daycare centers, sports events, lunch, house rent for low income families, working clothes, uniforms, boots, and others, being free from payment. Taxes were gradually phased out, and subsidies increased.

At the same time, production costs and economic control were neglected; the career of Public Accountancy was written off university programs; salaries were paid with disregard for actual work done; payments among enterprises were discontinued; and the national budget practically ceased to exist.

In addition, boundaries blended between the political work of the Cuban Communist Party and the executive functions of government, and the role of trade unions and mass organizations was dangerously weakened.

Aware of these shortcomings, in early 1970, the Cuban leadership began addressing them with a view to correcting them. The consolidation of the Revolution, and the perception that a direct US military aggression then (1970-75) was not in sight, allowed for more than 150 000 defense personnel to be employed in other spheres, and for greater emphasis to be placed on economic development.

Sugar cane agriculture, especially harvesting, experienced growing mechanization, with a subsequent reduction of manpower requirements. In 1975, some industrial and agricultural branches had grown considerably, like oil refining, fishing, construction, power generation, and the production of nickel, steel, lubricants, cement, fertilizers, eggs, and other foodstuffs. The area of cultivated land also increased considerably, as did the volume of water in dams, and roads and other communications infrastructures. The Cuban merchant marine grew ninefold.

Social and cultural advancement.- Noticeable was also the development attained in other important fields of social and cultural life. The 1959-1960 initial educational measures were reinforced by a law that nationalized education in general and made it free; a mass high school scholarship program that kicked off after the literacy campaign with 40 000 children of workers and farmers; free technical and professional on-the-job courses; the establishment of high school nighttime courses for workers; a large-scale adult education program that extended to all workplaces on the island; a university reform whose academic and organizational changes included the establishment of teacher training institutes, a university scholarship program, an expanded number of careers, and the combining of study and work.

Build upon a principle outlined by Cuba's National Hero, José Martí, in the 19th century, the blending of study and work was applied at all levels of education, from primary school on. In 1966, the first student work experiment was conducted, with schools going to work in the field for 35 days. Then, during the 1968-69 school year, the first "secondary schools in the countryside", popularly known by its Spanish acronym of ESBEC's, opened up.

Over this period, primary school enrollment extended to all children between 6 and 12 years of age, with school enrollment in general, and the number of graduates from all specialties, also recording a sharp increase when compared to the situation in 1958.

The big educational transformations opened up new horizons for cultural development. Numerous new, specialized cultural institutions were established, like the National Council for Culture, the National Arts School, the Ballet School, and the National Monument Commission, and the cultural entities that existed when the revolutionary victory also experienced a boost. The National Association of Cuban Writers and Artists was founded, and immediately began a intense culture promotion work, together with other agencies like the Cuban Film Institute and the Cuban Journalists Association.

Emerged during those early years, the strong amateur artist movement comprised some 20 000 groups nation-wide by 1975. Hundreds of thousands of students also participated in activities connected with this movement.

Books, too, attained an amazing relevance, as did the network of libraries. Casa de las Americas, one of the continent's most prestigious literary centers, has also played a major role in bringing Cuban culture close to the most progressive sectors of the Latin American intellectual world.

In line with the high priority given to health care, the network of hospitals, polyclinics, dental clinics, blood banks, maternal homes, hygiene and epidemiology laboratories, and biomedical research institutions had extraordinarily grown by 1975. The number of graduates from health-related careers and medical professionals multiplied several times. Diseases like poliomyelitis, malaria, and diphtheria were eradicated, while gastroenteritis, tuberculosis, tetanus, and other infectious diseases were greatly reduced. Infant mortality had dropped more than 50 percent compared to 1958, and life expectancy was 15 years higher.

The Revolution showed great concern for children from a very beginning. A great number of daycare centers were build, to benefit working mothers and provide children under 6 years with pre-school education, in close association with both the family and society. In 1975, there were more than 650 daycare centers, catering to the young children of 50 000 working mothers, figures that would considerably increase as the revolutionary process continued.

Cuba has also experienced an amazing sports development after 1959. All aristocratic sport clubs were made available to the general population, as were also all sports facilities, whose number was gradually increased. An end was put to professionalism, and tens of thousands school teachers were trained so that they could provide physical education classes. The National Institute for Sports, Physical Education, and Recreation was established, aimed at promoting, organizing, and directing sport activities in the country. Among the main sport institutions created were the "Comandante Manuel Fajardo" Higher Institute for Physical Education; the sports initiation primary and secondary schools; the provincial teacher training physical education schools; and the Sport Medicine Institute. And the up to then non-existing sports implement industry was founded.

As a result of this huge effort, Cuba began ranking high in sports events world-wide, as opposed to its poor previous performance in international competitions.

One other sphere of Cuban life that underwent an unimagined transformation was social security. The Revolution immediately adopted measures aimed at eradicating unemployment, an effort that was greatly assisted by the boom in agriculture, industry, construction, education, health, and other social services. Unemployment came indeed to be replaced by a shortage of labor.

Job discrimination against Blacks and women also disappeared. Social security was extended not only to all workers but laws were passed guaranteeing social assistance to all citizens deprived of a source of income for reasons not imputable to themselves.

But the desire to reward workers who did outstandingly well led to an error: a resolution was approved allowing those workers to retire with a pension equivalent to 100 percent of their salaries. This measure, which later turned into a law, ended up being negative, since the it exceeded the country's very ability to honor it, extended beyond predicted limits, and led to the retirement of many workers who, in terms of their physical and general capabilities, could have continued to make a valuable contribution. But if anything, this measure, like the whole social policy of the Cuban Revolution, demonstrated the deep concern that existed since the very beginning for the well-being of those men and women who selflessly assisted in the nation's progress.

Latin Americanism and Internationalism.- A characteristic that has marked the work of the Cuban Revolution has been its internationalism and its Latin Americanism. Born of the desire to the genuine longings and aspirations of Cuban society, the Revolution would not have been able to stand by its set goals if it had not come into close connection with nations that had already carried out their socialist transformation, or with countries sharing similar problems and difficulties as Cuba.

The ties Cuba built with the Socialist camp represented a new type of relations between nations and peoples, based as they were on fraternal treatment and cooperation, respect to sovereignty, and self-determination. It would have been extremely difficult for Cuba—and for any small, underdeveloped nation, for that matter—to successfully stand up to the relentless harassment coming from the world's strongest, most aggressive of powers.

At the same time, the cause of the Cuban Revolution was that of dependent, colonial countries, especially those in Latin America, which struggled for national emancipation and social progress. This is why internationalism was always a fundamental principle of the Revolution's foreign policy and its permanent position before the world.

From the very first years of the Revolution, Cuba offered shelter and assistance to persecuted progressive fighters, and extended its moral, political, and many times material solidarity to other fighting people: Viet Nam Democratic Republic, the South Viet Nam National Liberation Front and Government-in-Arms; Laos; Cambodia; Palestine; Congo; Angola; Mozambique; Ethiopia; Guinea-Bissau; Cape Verde; and others.

In October, 1960, the Cuban Institute of Friendship with the Peoples was established, aimed precisely at guiding those relations. Cuba also upheld the work of the Movement of Non-Aligned Countries, of which it was a founding member in 1961, and one of its most active players ever after. It sponsored as well the holding in Havana, in January, 1966, of the Tricontinental Conference, during which the Organization of Solidarity with the Peoples of Asia, Africa, and Latin America, the OSPAAL, and the Latin American Solidarity Organization, the OLAS, were established. Those organizations have played an active role in the struggle of the Third World countries against imperialism, colonialism, and other forms of oppression and exploitation.

Of particular importance was Cuba's solidarity with the heroic struggle of the Viet Namese people. Diplomatic relations with the Asian nation began in 1960; in 1969 Cuba established an Embassy in the jungle of South Viet Nam, an official expression of the ties that already existed between the two peoples. At the UN and all international organizations and fora Cuba denounced the US genocide. It held solidarity with Viet Nam rallies and functions to show moral and political support, and also made material contributions to the Viet Namese people. The "Ho Chi Minh" Construction Contingent, medical brigades, and other Cuban workers lent a helping hand, and even offered their blood, to the beleaguered nation. An active role was played as well by the Cuban friendship association with Viet Nam.

The Cuban Revolution also showed active solidarity with the discriminated and oppressed people in the United States, and with progressive sectors in that country. The civil rights movements, and those against the discrimination of Blacks, Indians, Latinos, and other national minorities, against the sending of US soldiers to Viet Nam and other wars, and against the incarceration of democratic activists like Angela Davis, have had ample and strong Cuban support. This explains, to a large extent, the warm and fraternal welcome that Fidel Castro has received when he has visited New York on the part of the black masses in Harlem and other popular sectors, as well as the growing and moving solidarity with Cuba of those US sectors, in contrast with the ever more hostile attitude of US administrations.

But if the international solidarity of the Cuban Revolution has been intense in general, it has been ever more so towards Latin America, for geographic, historic, cultural, and other reasons. This was a tradition that began last century with Simón Bolívar and José Martí, two of the most illustrious precursors of Latin America unity, found its continuation in the patriotic, anti-imperialist and revolutionary struggles waged during the Republican period in Cuba, and was also included in the Moncada revolutionary program set forth by Fidel Castro as early as 1953.

In April, 1959, at Central Park in New York, Fidel Castro reiterated: "Cuba has turned into the hope of the Americas; that hope should be saved. We speak in defense of the peoples of Latin America..." The voice of Cuba has always been that of the oppressed and exploited Latin America, and Cuba has always called for the unity of Latin American and Caribbean nations as an indispensable step in the way of the solution to the continent's problems. In its first and second Havana Declarations; in the Santiago de Cuba Declaration; in its criticism of the US's Alliance for Progress; in its defense of the sovereignty and self-determination of nations; in its denunciation of the US invasions of the Dominican Republic, Grenada, Panama, etc.; in its support for the Argentinean people's sovereignty over the Malvinas, or Falkland islands; in its repudiation of the foreign debt and the unequal terms of trade; in each and every one of the big battles waged by its Revolution, Cuba has always fought for the present and the future of the peoples of the Americas.

No government has done more for the independence of Puerto Rico that the Cuban government. The Puerto Rican issue has been taken by Cuba before all international organizations; two illustrious Puerto Ricans, Juan Juarbe Juarbe and Doña Laura Meneses de Albizu Campos, were recognized as Cuban citizens and appointed members of the Cuban Mission to the UN; and Puerto Rican *independentista* fighters have always found solidarity and a second homeland in Cuba.

The popular and democratic government of Salvador Allende in Chile received the multifarious assistance of the Cuban people, and when it was ousted in complicity with the United States and a fascist dictatorship was installed, Chilean refugees also found in Cuba a second homeland.

At the same time, Cuba has assisted with doctors, nurses, field hospitals, equipment, medicines, food, and hundreds of thousands of blood donations victims of earthquakes in Peru, Nicaragua, Chile, Armenia, Iran, etc.

One characteristic of this internationalist humanitarian solidarity is that it has been offered regardless of the ideology of the government whose people have received it, and without stopping to consider whether those governments had diplomatic relations with Cuba.

The island has also fraternally welcomed youths, women, teachers, writers, artists, doctors, scientists, students, and other people from the continent who have freely and exhaustively debated in events Cuba their problems and possible solutions to them. Some of these events have resulted in the emergence of important regional entities, like the Latin American Student Organization.

Ernesto Che Guevara: "For ever onward till victory!".- One of the most outstanding expressions of the internationalism of the Cuban Revolution dates back from its first decade: the national liberation project undertaken by Commander Ernesto Che Guevara.

Internationalist fighter against the Batista dictatorship, one of the Revolution's top military chiefs, President of the National Bank, Minister of Industries, promoter of the "new man" spirit among the youth, initiator of voluntary work, theorist, militant activist, legally recognized as Cuban citizen by birth, Che Guevara's greatest aspiration was, however, to liberate Latin American peoples from imperialist oppression.

From the very beginning, Che had told Fidel Castro of this desire. On May 25th, 1962, addressing a function on the occasion of the Argentinean National Day, he described himself as part of an army fighting on every corner of the world, and predicted that there will be other May 25ths when celebrations like that day's would be held not in Cuba but in some other place "under new symbols, under the symbol of victory, the symbol of socialist construction, the symbol of the future". Then in 1965, when he considered that the Cuban Revolution could do without his presence, he left the island, asserting that other places in the world needed his modest efforts. His last official Cuban mission was in December of 1964, when he chaired the island's delegation to the UN General Assembly, which he addressed on behalf of Cuba.

Che Guevara's absence from public life on the island gave US-controlled enemy media a pretext to launch a campaign against the Revolution and its leadership. They reported, among other things, that Che had been executed in Cuba due to discrepancies with Fidel Castro, and accused the top revolutionary leadership for his murder. Posters appeared in several countries portraying Ernesto Guevara Lynch, Che's father, demanding that Fidel Castro handed over the body of his son. An indignant Guevara Lynch denounced the slander, but news agencies failed to carry his denial.

Che clandestinely arrived in Congo (later Zaire, and today the Democratic Republic of Congo) with a group of Cuban fighters, heeding a request by the liberation movement of that African nation; their mission was to provide military instruction to the guerrilla fighters there. Che and his men placed themselves under the command of the Congolese chiefs and expressed their desire to fight alongside the guerrilla in those operations that it so decided. They refuse any privileges, and demand that their living conditions be the same as those of the local fighters.

Che set up military training and general education schools, and worked as advisor, and Spanish, Mathematics, and French teacher. He provide as well medical care for both guerrillas and local residents. He and his men took part in more than 50 military actions against South African, Belgian, and other European mercenaries, to whom they inflicted major defeats, although at the cost of losing some valuable comrades. In Congo, Che suffered from Yellow Fever, which he managed to overcome.

In November, 1965, the Congolese decided that Cubans should return, and Havana ordered their withdrawal. In seven months, they had carried out their mission, in which Che Guevara was able to apply his military and political experience, as well as his medical knowledge, which together with his solidarity he made available in a truly humanistic and internationalist spirit. Upon leaving Congo, the Cubans left a feeling of gratitude and sympathy among the guerrilla and the local population alike. In addition, they had acquired a new type of fighting experience, which somewhat departed from the Cuban one.

On October 3rd, 1965, during an important meeting in which the Cuban Communist Party adopted that name and formed its first Central Committee, Fidel Castro read a moving farewell letter by Che, which the brave guerrilla fighter had addressed him. Che had written it in Havana, for it to be read in due time. It was deemed appropriate to read Che's letter during that transcendental, solemn meeting, to put an end to enemy intrigues, and considering that it did not reveal information that could lead to Che's whereabouts.

In his letter, Che points to important moments lived next to Fidel, and he frees Cuba from any responsibility in connection with the new mission he had embarked upon: "I formally resign from my positions in the leadership of the Party, my post of Minister, my rank of Commander, and my Cuban condition. Nothing legal binds me to Cuba; only bonds of a different nature, which cannot be broken as can appointments to posts(...)Other nations of the world call for my modest efforts. I can do that which is denied you because of your responsibility at the head of Cuba, and the time has come for us to part".

Che also referred to the pride he felt next to Fidel and the Cuban people during sad and luminous days like those of the Missile Crisis. He reaffirmed his identification with Fidel Castro's principles and assessments, and with the foreign policy of the Revolution. He expressed confidence in the future of his children, who remained in Cuba, and asserted that "if my final hour finds me under other skies, my last thought will be of these people, and especially of you".

His mission in Congo over, Che returned to Cuba. But he could not wait to begin his liberating work in South America. He asked Fidel to allow him to take with him a group of highly experienced comrades who had fought with him in Cuba and Zaire; he picked them, and was authorized to undertake his new mission. After the training and general preparations in Cuba, Che clandestinely left the island on October 23, 1966, following a puzzling itinerary that landed him in Bolivia eleven days after, on November 3rd. He was being expected by several comrades, who had been preparing conditions for the revolutionary project.

Shortly after, the guerrilla group was organized, an urban network established, the field explored, and foundations laid for the armed struggle in the mountains. On March 23rd, 1967, the group waged their first combat, which was disastrous for the Bolivian troops. Che named the movement Bolivian National Liberation Army, and began compiling a field diary. On March 31st, the group comprised 29 Bolivians, 16 Cubans, and 3 Peruvians.

As soon as the Bolivian government learned of the presence of the guerrilla, it asked the US, and the intelligence services of Argentina, Chile, Brazil, Peru and Paraguay, for assistance. The Bolivian Army immediately began receiving US military advise, weapons, equipment, and other supplies, many of which came from the Panama-based US Southern Command. The CIA also took an active participation in the anti-guerrilla actions; some of the CIA agents were of Cuban origin. Indeed, the US Army and the CIA were the ones directing the whole operation.

The Bolivian people, especially students and miners, carried out huge solidarity demonstrations. Miners even agreed to donate one day of their salaries for the guerrilla. But the Alfredo Ovando government declared a state of siege; suspended constitutional guarantees; and unleashed a savage repression. On June 24th, taking advantage of the San Juan festivities, the Army went into the mines, conducting one of the worst workers's onslaughts in the country's history. Mining leaders who survived were arrested, and the movement dismantled.

A long, tormenting ordeal began for the guerrilla, which initially waged several victorious actions. Serious complications emerged: CIA and Bolivian intelligence agents managed to penetrate the group; desertions took place, some of them implying first hand information for the Army; contact is lost with the rearguard group, La Paz, and Havana; actions of indiscipline, some of them serious ones, occurred; and although peasants had lost their fear of authorities, they hesitated to join the guerrilla.

On the other hand, despite its shortcomings, the Bolivian Army was overwhelmingly superior in number; thousands of men followed the guerrilla fighters' every step, and managed to surround them, while planes constantly bombed their camps. Heroic actions were commonplace, but irreparable deaths also occurred: Eliseo Reyes, Antonio Sánchez, Carlos Coello, Martínez Tamayo, Tamara Bunke, Vilo Acuña, Inti Peredo...

On October 8th, at a place called Quebrada del Yuro, the guerrilla group bravely fought the Army. Wounded on a leg, his rifle rendered useless, Che found himself also without bullets for his pistol. The Army closed in on them, and Che was taken prisoner. Next day, October 9th, 1967, he was murdered in cold blood, following orders by US and Bolivian authorities.

Solidarity with Angola, Ethiopia, Nicaragua, and other countries.- Faced with a racist South African aggression supported by Zaire and by mercenaries from other countries, the recently independent People's Republic of Angola requested Cuban military assistance. Cuba sent an internationalist contingent to that African nation, which eventually built up into a 53 000—strong force. Over a 15 year period, more than 337 000 Cubans serviced in Angola, waging alongside their Angolan comrades numerous and important battles, like the one at Cuito Cuanavale. The invaders' total defeat would come, though, at the cost of more than 2 000 Cuban lives.

The Cuito Cuanavale victory not only saved Angola's independence but also decisively contributed to that of Namibia, and was a major factor in the elimination of **apartheid** and the transformation of South Africa into a democratic, non-racist Republic.

No less important has been the assistance offered by more than 50 000 Cubans in reconstructing Angola, among them builders, doctors, teachers, and other workers, who had to do their jobs amid the terror unleashed by the UNITA counter-revolutionary bands. Many were the Cuban civilian victims at the hands of UNITA terrorists.

One other form of Cuban cooperation with Angola has been through the granting of scholarships. More than 8 000 Angolan students have graduated on the island thanks to this scholarship program.

Non-racist South Africa has also enjoyed the solidarity offered by Cuba. Over 200 Cuban doctors currently work in several provinces of that big African nation.

In 1978, when Somali troops invaded Ethiopia, a country with a young revolutionary government, Cuba also heeded the request for assistance made, and sent 40 000 internationalist fighters, who alongside the Ethiopian soldiers, defeated the aggressor, forcing it to withdraw.

Cuba also gave permanent moral and material solidarity to Nicaraguan patriots after they ousted the Anastasio Somoza tyranny, one of the continent's oldest and bloodiest. Construction workers, doctors, educators, and others served in the Central American nation, fighting backwardness, ignorance, and poverty. Among those internationalist workers were more than 6 700 teachers who, organized under the "General Augusto César Sandino" Contingent, went to the most isolated rural areas and there where they were more badly needed. And when several of these teachers were murdered by armed "contra" gangs, 100 000 of their colleagues on the island volunteered to take the place of those fallen. When the Violeta Barrios government came to power, upon its request, a medical brigade stayed in Nicaragua, cooperation that is still going on.

The Chernobyl nuclear disaster in Ukraine, which affected a large number of people there, moved Cuba to offer hospital and medical assistance to the victims, especially children. A special camp was set up at one of the island's finest beaches, where more than 15 000 Chernobyl children have received specialized treatment. In Ukraine itself, Cuban doctors have also assisted victims of the regrettable accident.

In sum, tens of thousands of Cubans have served in cooperation the island has extended to some 60 countries of the world; they have worked as teachers and educational advisors, doctors and health professionals in general, builders, sports trainers, and experts in different branches of the economy, science, and culture. And at one point, 25 000 foreign students rom Asia, Africa, and Latin America were studying in Cuban schools.

Civil Internationalist Cooperation of the Cuban Revolution.

The amazing fact that a small, poor nation like Cuba, besieged by the world's most powerful and aggressive country, has been able to contribute with so much assistance to so many other countries is explained chiefly by two things: the fair and friendly treatment Cuba received in its relations with the Socialist camp, particularly with the USSR, which allowed the island to overcome great obstacles; and the Cuban people's internationalist consciousness, which emerged and consolidated during their struggle of centuries against national and foreign oppressors, and attained its highest expression in the work and ideals of the Cuban Revolution and its leader, Fidel Castro, both permanent examples of revolutionary humanism and internationalist solidarity.

XVIII

Towards Socialism. Crisis of the world's Socialist system and US escalation against Cuba. Resistance and struggle.

Improvement of socialist democracy. The First Congress of the Cuban Communist Party.- 1975 was a special year for the Cuban Revolution. The year1970 had marked the beginning of a process of analysis of the work done by the revolutionary government in its first decade as well as the experiences of other socialist countries. This process reached its highest point in 1975 when the Cuban Communist Party held its first congress.

That congress had a strong impact on the party's internal life, since it was the result of the fruitful political work carried out on the grassroots level. At this political event the Central Committee and other party leadership entities were elected for the first time, statutes and a Political Platform—practically its first program—were drawn up and other ideological and organizational issues were defined. But as the Communist Party was the society's and the state's leading force, its congress had tremendous significance for the country due to the important and decisive national problems dealt with in the congress and the accords and resolutions approved: the draft of the Republic's Constitution, the improvement of the different branches of People's Power, the island's new political and administrative division, the economic management and planning system as well as the political, ideological, economic, social and cultural policies of the party and government.

The congress ratified Fidel Castro as the Central Committee's First Secretary and Raúl Castro as its Second Secretary, also electing a 13 member Political Bureau, a 9 member Secretariat and a Central Committee made up of 112 permanent members and 12 alternate members.

The Constitution of the Republic.- The Constitution bill was drawn up by a commission chaired by Blas Roca Calderío and later subjected to a process of political debate that included practically all citizens above 14 years of age. The bill was analyzed in party meetings at the grass roots level, trade unions, the Committees for the Defense of the Revolution, the CDR's, the Cuban Women's Federation, the National Association of Small Farmers, the Young Communist League, the Cuban University Students Federation, the High School Students, Army and Interior Ministry units, and Cuban missions abroad.

At the meetings some 10 thousand proposals were presented to modify the constitution bill or to add to it and 5 500 000 people voted in favor of the bill as it was written. The commission introduced the most relevant proposals and the document was discussed and approved by the Cuban Communist Party Congress. Two months later, on February 15th, 1976 the constitution bill was taken to a popular referendum in which 98 percent of the island's eligible voters participated, that is to say, citizens above 16 years of age. The document was approved by 97.6 percent of the island's voters. The Magna Carta went into effect on February 24th, 1976.

Juridically the Constitution consecrates the profound transformations that took place in Cuba during the first 15 years of the Revolution. Its main principles are the following:

—The Republic of Cuba is a socialist state of workers and *campesinos* and other manual and intellectual workers. All power belongs to the working people and that power is based on the firm alliance between the working class and the *campesinos* and other categories of working people in the city and countryside. The Communist Party is the leading force in society and the state. The latter must render all its support for the social and grass roots organizations that represent the specific interests of the population.

—Cuba is a sovereign state; it considers null, void and illegal the treaties, concessions or pacts agreed upon on unequal terms or that ignore or undermine its sovereignty over any part of the national territory. The Republic of Cuba is part of the world's socialist community, shares the principles of workers internationalism and of combative solidarity among the peoples, and grants political asylum to those persecuted for their struggle in favor of national freedom, democracy, social justice, equality of all men and women, social progress and socialism.

—Cuba is guided by a socialist economic system, based on the social property of all the people over the means of production and on the elimination of man's exploitation of man. Personal property is guaranteed over the goods that come from individual work and over the means that are not used to exploit other people's work.

—The state protects the family, maternity and marriage; it guarantees education, culture and the fundamental rights of all citizens, banning any discrimination by race, sex, color or national descent. At the same time all citizens have equal duties.

The Constitution established the composition, function and aims of the People's Power institutions, which are based on socialist democracy, the unity of power and democratic centralism. At the same time it determined the composition, organization and function of the island's judicial system. It established the principles of the Cuban electoral system, and established universal, equal and secret vote for all Cubans above 16 years of age, though voting was not made compulsory.

This first constitutional text of 1976 established a direct vote for delegates to the municipal assemblies of People's Power and an indirect vote for the delegates to the provincial assemblies and deputies to the National Assembly. But this and other principles were changed in 1992.

The Second and Third Congresses of the Cuban Communist Party (1980 and 1986 respectively) gathered the experiences of the policies applied by the party and the state in all spheres of the island's life. Upon discussing the Call to the 4th Congress in 1991, which included critical and serious analysis by the Cuban people, the masses expressed, among other issues, the need to make some changes to the text of the existing constitution.

The congress took on those proposals and a year later, in July, 1992, the National Assembly—the only institution authorized to modify the constitution—discussed and approved the changes through the vote of two thirds of its members.

The reforms were the result of various factors, including 15 years of experience in the implementation of the constitution approved in 1976; changes had occurred in the world after the collapse of the socialist community and the disintegration of the USSR, to which we'll refer later, as well as the situation created in Cuba as a result of those developments and of stepped up attacks by US imperialism.

Many of the articles of the island's constitution merged, were shortened, increased or redefined and some were eliminated. New chapters and articles were also added. We'll later refer concretely to those changes that we consider most important.

The reforms included new chapters and articles related to the declaration of a **state of emergency**, to the property of joint ventures and other legally established economic associations, to the treatment of foreign residents in Cuba, to the Defense and Popular Councils, issues that were not included in the 1976 text. The reforms granted *campesinos* more possibilities to associate with each other. Articles that referred to Cuba's relations with the socialist community were eliminated since that community had disappeared.

A new article emphasized the freedom of religious beliefs, the separation between the church and the state, and the relations between both. The old text included an article that dealt with this issue in the same spirit of respect to all creeds, but now there are two articles. The new article grants more independence to the church.

The constitution now not only reaffirmed the Communist Party's Marxist nature but also its devotion to the thought of Cuban National Hero José Martí, an element that appeared in the prologue of the 1976 Constitution and in all programs of the Cuban Revolution, but not as an article in the Magna Carta.

Most reforms had to do with the People's Power institutions and the island's electoral system. They offered clear and precise definitions of **province** and **municipality** and the role each must play. The municipal assemblies were given more responsibilities, since they are the institutions more directly linked to the population's problems. The reforms regulated everything related to the **Popular Councils** and granted the direct vote to elect delegates to the **provincial assemblies** and to elect **deputies**. Before, the vote was indirect for the two levels.

The People's Power institutions.- In line with what was established in the constitution of the Republic, Cuba implemented the country's new political-administrative division in 1976 and an improved organization of People's Power.

The Revolution had previously adopted some non-essential changes in the country's political-administrative division, but a careful study of that structure, that took into consideration the economic, political, geographic, demographic characteristics of each area, showed the need for a profound change. Then, instead of six provinces, 58 regions and 407 municipalities, the nation decided to eliminate regions and divided the national territory into 14 provinces and 169 municipalities. One of them—the Isle of Pines—(called the Isle of Youth today) was granted the category of **special municipality**, directly supervised by the central power.

The new system of People's Power was established on the basis of that division. During the first years of the victorious Revolution different government forms had been rehearsed in the provinces, regions and municipalities. In 1974 an experiment was done in the province of Matanzas which gave way to the system established in the 1976 Constitution.

According to this system, the National Assembly is the supreme organ of state power, the only entity with constituent and legislative authority. It is elected every five years and at the same time the National Assembly elects a Council of State from among its members, with a President—who also chairs the Council of Ministers—a first Vice-President, five other Vice-Presidents, a Secretary and another 23 members. The National Assembly designates the Council of Ministers proposed by the President of the Council of State.

In addition to the provincial and municipal assemblies—supreme organs of state power at local levels—Popular Councils have been created to represent certain demarcations. The Popular councils are made up of the delegates of the electoral districts included in each demarcation. They are granted a great deal of authority to work for the efficiency of production and services in each territory and to meet the population's health, economic, educational, cultural and social needs. The delegates of each Popular Council elect the council's President from among its members.

For the election of delegates to the assemblies of People's Power, each municipality is divided into **electoral districts** which are not part of the island's political and administrative division. They are created to elect the delegates and to facilitate their relations with their voters or constituents. An electoral district can neither have less than 250 voters nor more than 3000.

The first step to elect delegates consists of holding an **assembly of nomination of candidates.** For that, each district is divided into smaller areas so that each nomination assembly won't have hundreds of participants, but rather, a reduced number. The assembly must be attended by half of the area's voters, who can freely propose the number of candidates they wish.

The Communist Party doesn't nominate or elect; any person who lives in the area, with no mental or judicial impairments, has the right to nominate or to be nominated whether or not he or she is a party member, regardless of his or her political, religious or philosophical beliefs, sex, race or social origin. The assembly can approve or reject the proposed candidates by a majority of votes. Not more than 8 candidates and not less than 2 can be nominated in an electoral district. In Cuba there can't be a sole candidate. One delegate is elected by each district.

The nominated candidates make up the district's slate. Explicit biographies of the candidates are written and placed in public places along their pictures. During election day all candidates appear on the electoral ballot, then voters voluntarily and freely elect their delegates by direct and secret vote. The count is made immediately after the polling station is closed, before the eyes of voters and under the custody of two pioneer children who stay in the polling station during the entire day. If no candidate gets more than 50 percent of the votes, a second round is held with the participation of the two candidates who obtained the most votes. No one can be a delegate or deputy if he or she doesn't obtain more than fifty percent of the votes.

It is worthwhile noting that in spite of the fact that voting is not compulsory, the voter turnout has been very high in all elections. The lowest was registered during the first balloting in 1976 when 95.2 percent of voters participated. The highest was obtained in February of 1993 with 99.57 percent.

All representative organs of state power are elected and renewable at certain periods of time. Those elected have to periodically report back to their constituencies concerning their performance, and voters are entitled to revoke them through referendums at any time. If more than 50 percent of voters agree to revoked the delegate, he is dismissed and a substitute is elected.

Another characteristic of the delegates and deputies is that their condition doesn't give them personal privileges or economic benefits. As a rule, they must develop their activities in the people's power institutions without affecting their jobs as workers, professionals, *campesinos*, students, economic or service officials and without receiving any additional salary.

The style of socialist democracy followed in Cuba doesn't end with the electoral system we've just explained here. In addition to the election of leaders by the people, the report tack assemblies in which the performance of leaders is analyzed, and other forms of participation, one of Cuban democracy's most peculiar and significant characteristics is the direct discussion, by the masses, of the island's most important bills and projects.

This discussion is conducted through political and grass-roots organizations. The draft law is studied by members of the party and the Young Communist League, the UJC, who together have one million members; by the Confederation of Cuban Workers and its affiliated unions, with three million workers; the National Association of Small Farmers, with more than 200 000 *campesinos*; the Cuban Women's Federation, with three and a half million members; the University Students Federation, and the High School Students Federation, with nearly half a million youth, as well as by social institutions like the National Union of Cuban Writers and Artists, the Union of Cuban Journalists, the UPEC, the Economists Association, etc. But the largest of all are the Committees for the Defense of the Revolution, the CDR's, whose membership is made up of 84 percent of the island's population above 14 years of age and which allows for debate among 7 and a half million people. It's difficult to find a citizen who is not involved in such debates in one way or another, since most of the island's citizens belong to more than one grassroots organization.

In this way, the island's socialist democracy guarantees that no corner of the country or sector of the Cuban society is left out in the discussion of each basic document scheduled to be implemented, or without stating their opinions or suggestions, which are later collected and analyzed by the corresponding institutions.

That process of discussion has taken place concerning laws like the Constitution bill, the Family Code, the Labor Code, the Social Security Law, the Housing Law, the Law against Indolence and others. Other Communist Party documents have also gone through this process, including the Party Program and the Call to the Cuban Communist Party's 4th Congress.

Gains, failures and rectification (1975-1989).- The years that followed the important institutional changes that took place between 1975 and 1976 were characterized by remarkable progress in the more efficient use of the country's productive resources, as well as significant gains in the country's economic and social development, and in efforts to increasingly meet the population's needs. But they were also years of growing objective internal and external difficulties, of serious mistakes and deficiencies, above all in the implementation of the economic management and planning system.

The Gross Social Product registered an important increase up to 1986 and, though it suffered a slight decrease, in 1988 it was 167 percent higher than that of 1975. The value of exports and imports, investments, personal consumption, per capita income and other indicators also increased, though some difficulties were reported in 1986 and 1987.

Sugar harvests produced over 7 million tons of sugar, far above those before the triumph of the Revolution, and the 1989 harvest reached 8 124 thousand tons. Cuba reported a remarkable increase in electricity generation, and in the production of steel, nickel, fertilizers, citrus, paper and cardboard, vegetables and root vegetables, construction materials, as well as fishing, construction, agricultural machinery, industries—including six new sugar mills— hydraulic works, forestry and other areas. New thermoelectric plants were built to provide electricity to 90 percent of the island's population and considerable progress was made in the construction of the Juraguá nuclear power station in Cienfuegos. The movement of innovators and inventors also reached gigantic dimensions.

Sugar cane agriculture had a fleet of 90 thousand tractors and most of the sugar cane was harvested with combines. The **microbrigade** system was created to build houses: it consisted of groups of workers who temporarily left their work centers to construct buildings that would later be distributed among workers in their centers. If between 1949 and 1958 eight hundred houses were built annually, in the 1980-1985 period 66 thousand homes were constructed every year. In addition, 85 percent of Cubans became owners of their homes. The microbrigade system was neglected in 1985 and housing decreased, but it was later revitalized.

During the same period social security and welfare remarkably increased and the island's health care system registered a significant development. The network of health institutions multiplied dozens of times compared to 1958 and covered all of the country's population. Among the many health centers created we'll cite as examples the "Hermanos Ameijeiras" clinical-surgical hospital—one of the island's most modern—and the "Juan Manuel Márquez" pediatrics hospital in Marianao.

The **family doctor** system was implemented to meet the health needs of residents in limited urban and rural areas and to care for the health of each one of the area's families. The system complemented the country's network of hospitals and polyclinics. In 1990, **family doctors** covered 90 percent of Cuba's population.

Traditional endemic diseases were eradicated, including TB, polio, diphtheria, tetanus, measles, typhus and chicken pox. Infant mortality went down from more than 60 per one thousand live births in 1958 to 10.7 in 1990; life expectancy went up from 65.8 to 75.2 and the number of doctors reached one for every 284 inhabitants.

The number of professors, researchers, teachers, doctors and other university professors grew every year, obtaining the highest graduations in Cuban history up to that date. Several institutions related to social sciences were set up, including the Center for Studies on Martí and the Institute of History of the Cuban Socialist Revolution and Communist Movement. The latter merged in 1987 with the Academy of Sciences' History Institute and the Center for Studies on Military History to form

252

the current Cuban History Institute. A significant growth was reported in the number of day-care centers, schools, enrolled students, graduates, students on scholarships, cultural institutions and other educational and cultural indexes.

Sports developed every quickly. Cuba increased several times the titles obtained in international competitions and ranked among the world's top ten nations in the area.

In 1980, Cuba had the privilege of sending to outer space one of its citizens, Lieutenant Colonel Arnaldo Tamayo Méndez, who became the first Latin American cosmonaut during the first Cuba-USSR joint flight with Soviet cosmonaut Yuri Romanenko.

The area of science and technology was particularly boosted, examples of which we'll cite to illustrate this assertion. The National Scientific Research Center the CENIC was wet up, as well as the Genetic Engineering and Biotechnology Center, the "William Soler" Children's Surgery Cardio-Center—the largest in the world—the Immuno-Essay Center and the Nervous System Regeneration and Transplant Center.

Modern techniques were introduced, including equipment capable of destroying kidney stones, making Cuba the first Third World country to install this technique; a nuclear magnetic resonance equipment, the first in Latin America; the EVALIMAGE system created by the CENIC to visualize and analyze CAT scan images; the CID-7060 alpha-numerical and graphic videoterminal created on the island, and the Cuban carbon dioxide laser scalpel.

Brain transplants began in Cuba in that period as well as liver, heart and heart-liver transplants. Kidney transplants continued successfully on the island. For the first time in the world, Cuba introduced the vaccine against meningitis in 1985. Other important Cuban contributions to world medicine were introduced, like the human leukocyte alpha interferon, the policonasol (PPG), the discovery of a substance made of human placenta capable of curing vitiligo, the first high-temperature ceramics semi-conductor; the successful treatment of retinosis pigmentosa, and the skin growth factor. The island's pharmaceutical and biotechnological industry reached important development levels.

These and other not less important gains in several of the island's spheres were obtained in an unequal struggle against enormous difficulties. During those years the price of products and raw materials that Cuba imported increased, and the prices of the items the island sold decreased on the world market. Sugar had a price far below its production cost. Interest rates and foreign debt payments increased, as well as shipping tariffs. Between 1975 and 1979 alone the currency exchange rates were reduced by 53 percent.

Those were years in which great economic losses were reported due to several hurricanes and other natural disasters, and to the great damage caused by crop diseases like the **sugar cane rust** and the **tobacco blue mold**. In the first five years of the 1980's serious deficiencies and mistakes in economic management were added to the previous calamities.

The most urgent economic areas were not prioritized; there were excessive expenditures and little revenues in production as well as an immobility of resources. Economic efficiency was measured by the cost of investment and not by results. Payrolls were excessively large in production and service centers. Difficulties were reported in construction. The role of microbrigades was underestimated. There were serious problems in planning the island's economic and social development and volunteer work was underestimated.

Beginning in 1985, the country's leadership began a policy of "rectification of errors and negative tendencies" to overcome the situation.

All the difficulties of that stage, somewhat alleviated by the economically just relations with the USSR and other socialist countries, and by the country's beneficial integration into the Council for Mutual Economic Assistance, the CMEA, were seriously worsened, however, by the tightened economic blockade against the island and stepped up US aggression.

The US increased its attacks against the island to thwart the Cuban Revolution's gigantic efforts to raise the levels of the island's economic, political, social and cultural development.

The Barbados terrorist bombing and other US terrorist acts.- In the 1975 -1989 period, the US government continued its efforts to starve out and terrorize the Cuban people into surrender, employing all methods, including acts of repugnance and loathing.

After realizing that hijacking Cuban vessels and aircraft didn't bring about the results it expected, the US's Central Intelligence Agency, the CIA, planned the terrorist bombing of a Cuban civilian aircraft in midair. In July, 1976, CIA agents planted a bomb in a Cuban commercial airplane in Kingston, Jamaica that didn't destroy the yet in midair but at the airport because its departure had been delayed. But the passengers of a Cubana de Aviación airliner that left from Barbados on October 6th the same year were not that lucky.

Two bombs were planted in the aircraft's luggage hold, turning the jet into flames moments after it took off, killing 73 people traveling on board. 57 Cubans, 11 Guyanese and five Koreans died. All of them were workers, students or athletes. The murdered Cubans included the island's junior fencing team, which was returning home following an overwhelming victory in a sports tournament in Venezuela. Six of the murdered Guyanese had been chosen to study medicine on scholarships in Cuba.

The perpetrators and the masterminds of the crime were found, and some of them tried in Venezuelan courts in a process that had many irregularities. The CIA managed to save its main agents: one was released and the other one broke out of jail by walking out of the prison's front gate. The latter, who went underground, continued carrying out terrorist missions in other countries of the area. The agent who directed the attack served two years in US prisons for other crimes and is now peacefully living under the protection of US authorities.

The crime sparked massive popular demonstrations against the US government and its terrorist agents, and led Cuba to put an end to a recently signed bilateral agreement with Washington on the hijacking of airplanes.

During those years attacks on Cuban embassies and diplomats abroad increased and members of the Cuban community abroad advocating dialogue with Cuba were murdered.

Another example of the morale of the CIA-sponsored counterrevolutionaries was the arson at the "Le Van Tam" day care center in Havana on May 8th, 1980. 570 children under 6 were trapped in Cuba's largest daycare center as a result of the fire, since the terrorists had set fire near the elevators in the ground floor, closing

254

all exits. Only the heroism of workers, fire fighters and neighbors, including adolescents between 12 and 14 years old, avoided a tragedy.

Another method implemented during those years to destabilize and isolate the country from the international and Iberoamerican community was that of creating problems ion the embassies based in Havana. In some cases, with the complicity of foreign diplomats and officials, counterrevolutionary and antisocial elements began taking over embassies and the residences of ambassadors based in Havana. Their aim was to request the political asylum that the US and other countries had denied them through normal procedures.

The attacked embassies, among others, included the Vatican's Nunciature, the embassies of Peru, Venezuela and Ecuador, and later the embassies of France, Spain, the Federal Republic of Germany, Czechoslovakia, etc. The most spectacular and serious case of the period was that of Peru's embassy.

As a rule, the Peruvian government did not grant entry visas to people who requested them through normal procedures, but did grant them to those who illegally entered the embassy without being persecuted, thus encouraging their illegal behavior.

In response to that irresponsible conduct, and following the murder of a Cuban military officer, the Cuban revolutionary government withdrew the guards that protected the embassy and, in an official statement, warned that no Cuban who forcibly entered a foreign embassy would receive a safe-conduct to leave the country. At the same time, Cuba warned that if diplomatic immunity was used as a pretext to legalize crime, protect common criminals, violate Cuban law and create a climate of insecurity for foreign representatives in the country, it would take all necessary steps.

Following the Cuban government's decision to stop protecting diplomatic installations, many seeking to leave the country began entering the Peruvian embassy, at one point reaching over 10 thousand people. They were mostly lumpen elements and petty criminals. They also included, however, people who didn't agree with the Revolution. The Cuban government didn't adopt any measure against those who entered peacefully; on the contrary, they were allowed in and out freely, and even to return home to wait for their exit visa—something which thousands of them did—and if any country granted them visas they were allowed to leave Cuba. In addition, they were given food, health care and medicines.

When the people learned about the murder of the Cuban guard, large popular demonstrations were held to support the Cuban revolutionary government and to reject the assailants and the Peruvian government's attitude.

On April 19th of that year, on the occasion of another anniversary of the victory of Playa Girón, a gigantic demonstration was held in the capital, called a "March of the Combatant People". For more than 13 hours, over one million people marched from Havana's Seaside Drive to Peru's embassy on the beautiful 5th Avenue, proclaiming their support for the Revolution and their condemnation of the anti-social elements and counterrevolutionaries who had entered the embassy. That demonstration acquired such dimensions that international news agencies, including those from the United States, had to admit—amidst anti-Cuba attacks—that the overwhelming majority of Cubans supported Fidel and the Revolution. Similar marches took place the following weeks and months, particularly on mayday, to mark International Workers Day, and on may 17th, to mark Campesino Day. Those great mobilizations received the solidarity of the progressive and revolutionary forces in the Americas and the world.

The attack on the Peruvian embassy, however, was not an isolated development, but rather, part of a gigantic provocation organized by the United States and its servants. During those days, some 700 counterrevolutionaries gathered in the front of the US Interest Section in Havana, an individual launched a car against a popular demonstration; the fire at the "Le Van Tam" daycare center, serious incidents took place at the Ecuadorian embassy; the South American governments subservient to Washington accused Cuba of violating established norms on the right to asylum and the United States announced threatening war games around the island. Cuba answered with popular demonstrations across the island and with military maneuvers nationwide that would only end when the US stopped theirs.

Boats coming from Florida began arriving in Mariel port on April 21st with the aim of picking up relatives who wished to go to the United States. The Cuban government gave them all the opportunities they needed, giving way to a maritime bridge between Mariel and Florida used by nearly 125 thousand people. Despite its protests and threats, the US could not prevent the arrival of what it called the "wild tide"; Washington, however, rejected the newcomers and jailed many of them. The "*marielitos*" had lived in a socialist Cuba all their lives. And despite their vices, they perceived the injustices of US society. They were rejected by the Miami-based counterrevolutionary groups and began an unfortunate Odyssey.

The Revolutionary Government firmly upheld the principle of authorizing the departure of those who legally requested it and not granting safe-conduct to leave the country to those who broke into embassies.

The Santa Fe Committee's Report.- From 1980 on, US harassment against Cuba was officially included in the Republican Party's platform. The Interamerican Security Council put a group of experts called the Santa Fe Committee in charge of drawing up a document on Cuba and the policy to follow toward that country, a policy which would be implemented by the Republicans once they took power.

In May of that year, the committee wrote a report whose main points are the following: the United States cannot accept the existence of a socialist Cuba; the island must pay a high price of its anti-imperialist and revolutionary policy; the first step against Cuba must be frankly punitive, breaking all diplomatic relations, including the expulsion of Cuban diplomats at the Cuban Interest Section in Washington. According to the Committee, the US was to "resume" exploration of the Caribbean area, stop the dollar flow to Cuba from US tourists, establish a counterrevolutionary radio station openly sponsored by the US government and encourage a domestic rebellion on the island. The document states: "if propaganda fails, a liberation war against Castro must be launched".

In line with those recommendations, the US government took direct charge of radio broadcasts beamed to Cuba, and opened the so called "Radio Martí" (1986), sparking the interruption by the Revolutionary Government of the migration agreement with the United States reached in 1984. In 1989 Washington assumed the high cost and even greater responsibility for opening a TV channel bearing the same name and aims—a failed attempt since Cuba managed to totally interfere the TV signal.

In the mid 1980's, the US took its anti-Cuba campaign to the UN Human Rights Commission and named a counterrevolutionary terrorist, who had been a police officer during the Batista dictatorship, as the head of the US delegation to that UN body. In addition, the US stepped up air espionage over Cuba by using SR-71 "Black Bird" planes and rehearsing a mass air strike against the island's western region. US President Ronald Reagan met with Cuban American counterrevolutionaries in Miami, nratified his support for them and launched new threats against Cuba.

War of All the People, collapse of the Socialist block and Special Period in Peace Time.- In view of the US's aggressive escalation, the revolutionary leadership took the necessary measures to face all of the enemy's possible variants, including a total blockade of the island and an air, sea and land invasion by US troops.

The Cuban military strategy is based on the **War of All the People**. The strategy is not to wage an exclusive war with a professional army. Every Cuban citizen—man, woman or child—has a specific role to play in the different fronts: military, economic, political and ideological, sanitary, cultural, etc. The decision is to fight the enemy with all the country's forces to repel the aggression, or if the country is taken over by the enemy, to make life impossible for the occupation forces.

The Cuban Revolution has trained all the people for that situation, which has been conceived as a **Special Period in War Time**, and whose worst stage would be a so-called **Zero Option.**

Certain events that took place in the world, however, created a serious situation for Cuba, even though a direct military conflict with the United States didn't occur. It was the swift process that in only three years led to the collapse of the socialist block and the former USSR. Its impact was so harmful for Cuba, above all in the economic sphere, that the government thought it necessary to declare a **Special Period in Peace Time.**

The US's fierce economic blockade against the island, and its pressures on its allies since the early days of the Revolution, had forced Cuba to concentrate most of its economic and trade relations with the USSR and other socialist countries. In 1990, more than 80 percent of the island's foreign trade was carried out with the socialist block, but when it disappeared—leading to tremendous instability in those countries, accompanied by radical changes in their policies and concepts—the former socialist block's relations with Cuba deteriorated immensely.

In February, 1990, Fidel Castro foresaw the possibility of an economic crisis of unpredictable dimensions, and called on the people to prepare to face the worst contingency that might be created as a consequence of severe restrictions in supplies, primarily raw materials, food and fuel, in a way that we can be able to resist the most adverse conditions and continue, as much as possible, our development programs. The crisis predicted by Fidel didn't take long to occur. The island lost 75 percent of its imports and more than 95 percent of its foreign markets for its products. Fertilizers, animal feed and herbicides disappeared as well as parts of the island's industry, essential raw materials, medicines, textiles, and other resources.

A second blockade was now added to Washington's, which had already cost the equivalent of 43 billion dollars. In addition, trade was ever more unequal, interest rates and foreign debt services grew and the world's economic crisis worsened.

As a result of those factors, the Cuban economy suffered an astounding decline: in 1993 it had plunged by more than 34 percent compared to 1989. Sugar production in 1995 decreased to 3.3 million tons—the lowest in the history of the Revolution. the lack of electricity paralyzed part of the country's life and seriously affected the island's inhabitants with frequent "*apagones*", or blackouts, and with cuts in TV programs, movie and theater functions and other cultural and recreation activities. Many enterprises, factories and other production and service centers reduced their activity or shut down, leaving more than 100 thousand people jobless, though not defenseless. There was a serious shortage of medicine, medical instruments, school supplies and others. The issue of newspapers, magazines, books and other publications was equally shortened.

Despite that grim picture, Cuba managed to maintain the principal gains of the Revolution. No "shock" market economic policies were applied in Cuba. Most unemployed workers were relocated in other work centers, and the rest, some 11 thousand, began receiving 60 percent of their salaries and had the chance to carry out other activities as self-employed workers. Social security and welfare programs increased; pensions were not affected; no salaries were held back for any active workers. Not a single school, hospital, polyclinic or day care center was closed. The number of university professionals grew. Infant mortality continued decreasing, except for 1994, in which it went up slightly. But in 1995 it went down again to 9,4 per one thousand life births.

Strategy to face the Special Period.- Following the collapse of the socialist block, Cuba was forced to join a system of international economic relations based on unequal exchange and other norms that rule the capitalist world, totally unfavorable for underdeveloped countries. Cuba had to reorganize its economy without giving up the essential principles that guided and have guided the Revolution, nor its main achievements and efforts to continue developing the socialist project as much as the difficult and complex conditions of today's world would allow.

Firstly, Cuba reorganized its economy and domestic finances. The Cuban government planned to make the most efficient use of its own resources, though this sometimes meant going backwards concerning the gains achieved in the fields of science and technology. Cuba again began to use the oxen and the plough and other manual techniques that had previously been left behind. The policy adopted years before of replacing imports and increasing exports was imperative.

The government adopted measures to reorganize its internal finances: the abolition of some free services, creation of taxes —non-existent for many years—, a price policy that maintained a minimum quota accessible to low income families, and other measures aimed at reducing the amount of money in circulation and the budget deficit.

In the agricultural arena, authorities set up the so-called Basic Units of Cooperative Production, with all possible aid for their members; idle land was handed over to families who wanted to form, and agricultural markets were opened so that individual farmers, "plot owners", cooperative members and some state farms could sell their products on a free market basis. By mid 1996, 33 percent of the country's arable land belonged to the state, 42 percent to the UBPC's, 10 percent of the agricultural production cooperatives and 15 percent to private *campesinos*.

A very important decision was the authorization and encouragement of self-employment, which in 1996 was an additional source of jobs for 208 000 people (retirees, housewives, workers who needed an extra income and jobless people).

But a country like Cuba, which depends a great deal on foreign trade to obtain foreign currency, it is essential to buy fuel, food, machinery, raw material and other products that meet the needs of 11 million inhabitants. That's why foreign currency was allowed to enter the country and Cubans were authorized to have it. Above all, tourism, foreign investment and exports are playing a decisive role in the fight to overcome the **Special Period**.

Despite all difficulties, tourism has been growing steadily and mixed associations and other types of foreign capital investment have developed satisfactorily. In mid 1996, there were 212 joint ventures with business executives from 50 countries and an investment capital of 2.1 billion dollars. 668 foreign firms are represented in Havana. And Cuba's National Bank maintains relations with some 500 banks from the world over.

The principles upon which those relations are based have been set by the new Foreign Investment Law of 1995, which established favorable conditions for foreign investment in Cuba. The island's social and political stability, its skilled labor force and other factors guarantee the success of their enterprises. On the other hand, Cuba obtains benefits from these relations since foreign investors contribute capital, know-how and markets, which the Cuban side cannot obtain by itself. In addition, joint ventures provide jobs—53 thousand at present—and the Cuban government doesn't lose the property occupied by those enterprises.

Investment in Cuba is totally different from that of neocolonial Cuba, when foreing monopolies were the absolute owners of all the means of production and of the earnings, generally evading taxes and exerting a negative control over the island's economic and political life.

Recovery begins.- The strategy followed to face the challenges of the **Special Period**, had its first positive signs—though still very weak ones—in1994, more evident in 1995, and consolidated and extended in the first six months of 1996. First, the dangerous economic decline came to a halt, and following a more than 34 percent decrease in 1993 compared to 1989, the economy began to slightly recover by 0.2 percent in 1994, 2.5 percent in 1995, and grew by 9.6 percent in the first semester of 1996. The sugar harvest played an important role in that book since the island produced more than one million tons of sugar compared with the previous year. Another important factor has been the foreign financing obtained for the production of sugar, tobacco and other crops. An approximately five percent economic growth is expected for 1996, since economic activity is less intense in the last six months of the year.

Important results have been obtained in the production of nickel, tobacco, fertilizers, oil extraction and refining, steel, fish, cement, vegetables, as well as in construction and tourism. Many factories that had stopped working are again producing, and some at full capacity. In the first six months of 1996 global employment grew; more than 51 thousand people got jobs. Blackouts have been reduced as a result of an increase in electricity production.

Imports and exports steadily increased and foreign trade has remarkably diversified: Cuba has trade with 97 countries.

259

The reorganization of internal finances has made progress: financial liquidity and the budget deficit were reduced despite the fact that the average wage and social security and welfare benefits are on the rise, and that prices in the agricultural markets went down by 10 percent. The value of the Cuban peso went up by 58 percent compared to 1995.

Infant mortality has been the lowest of all times: 8.2 per one thousand live births (in late June, 1996). Life expectancy is 75 years and there is a doctor for every 193 inhabitants. Since 1959, Cuba has also graduated more than half a million university professionals, and there's a professor or teacher per every 13 students.

The Torricelli Law, the Helms-Burton Law and other recent aggressions.- The collapse of the European socialist regimes, one after the other, sparked a great euphoria in US government circles and in the Miami-based counterrevolutionary groups.

They not only enjoyed the terrible blow socialism and national liberation received, but also expected that something similar would occur in Cuba. As they didn't believe in the autoctonous and independent nature of the Cuban Revolution, and believed Cuba was a Soviet satellite, they were convinced that the Caribbean island would suffer the same destiny as the popular European democracies.

The Cuban American ultra right wing elements predicted that the collapse was a matter of days or weeks. Political hustling began over the organization and establishment of a new government that would replace Fidel Castro's, and even agencies were set up to deal with claims over properties confiscated or nationalized by the Revolution and with other arrangements related to the return of those groups to Cuba. The most aggressive elements even planned a generalized massacre of revolutionaries on the island.

Months went by, however, and no signs of disintegration were felt. The economic crisis increased but steps were taken to face it, and the political situation was stable: the people repeatedly expressed their support for the Revolution.

Concerned and upset, the US government decided to lend a hand to the collapse of socialism in Cuba by taking measures against the island, further tightening its economic blockade and increasing the forms of aggression that it had already been practicing.

In mid 1992, ultra right wing representative Robert Torricelli introduced in the House a bill bearing his name—which was later passed—and which reiterated the US's decision to use all means necessary to crush Cuba, including starving the Cuban people to death.

Among other things, the Torricelli Law gives the US President authority to apply economic sanctions to countries that have trade relations with Cuba; bans subsidiaries of US companies based in third countries from trading with the island; rules that no ships that touch Cuban ports to carry merchandise or passengers to Cuba are allowed to enter US ports for a six month period and severely restricts money remittances to Cuba. The law's aim is to consolidate years of US pressures on third countries to isolate Cuba, all of which had failed.

But the Torricelli Law had the same fate as other US instruments of pressure against other countries. Despite the law, Cuba continued expanding its foreign trade and obtaining financing for certain economic areas; companies from several nationalities began to invest in Cuba and to establish other economic ties; the crisis stopped an signs of recovery were seen at the end of the tunnel. Elections held in Cuba in February, 1993, in the midst of the special period, brought about an overwhelming support for the Revolution: 99.7 percent of voters went to the polls and only 7.03 percent of them cast blank or null ballots.

The US government's most aggressive circles and the Miami-based counterrevolutionary groups lost patience with this new failed anti-Cuba policy. They prioritized domestic subversion on the island, social unrest, terrorist acts and provocations, for which they counted on the personal participation of officials from the US Interest Section in Havana and with an avalanche of CIA agents who infiltrated the island and repeated calls to subversion by counterrevolutionary radio stations based in Florida. More than one thousand hours of radio transmissions are beamed against Cuba weekly on 17 frequencies. In April, 1994, a well known spokesperson for the Miami anti-Cuba elements demanded "three days to kill" when the Revolution fell.

On July 15, the "13 de Marzo" tugboat, moored in Havana's port, in unseaworthy conditions, was robbed by people who wanted to leave the country and to whom the US had not authorize legal entry into its territory. Warned of the boat's bad sailing conditions, they didn't stop and other vessels tried to intercept it. The kidnapped tugboat clashed with another boat and sank immediately after. Despite efforts by the crews of other vessels and the coast guards, only 31 people were rescued. Another 32 died.

From that date on, and encouraged by the US government and the Miami based counterrevolutionaries, there was a wave of boat hijackings, occasionally accompanied by murders, and many people built makeshift rafts to cross the Florida Straits, causing the loss of many human lives in the journey. On August 5th, Fidel Castro warned that if the US insisted on encouraging the illegal departure of Cubans, the island would not stop them—a decision that was implemented a week later.

US President Bill Clinton refused to adopt measures to discourage the illegal exits, but on August 19th, in view of the flow of rafters that arrived at US shores, he announced he wouldn't give refuge to any person arriving illegally at US coasts. For the first time in 36 years, the US government stopped encouraging Cubans to follow that dangerous route. In addition, Clinton ruled that the rafters captured in US or international waters would be sent to the US's illegally occupied Naval Based in Guantánamo or to other US military installations in other countries to decided on their destiny later.

Weeks later, on September 9th, Cuba and the United States signed a migration agreement that reflects the US's commitment not to admit illegal immigration and regulates the flow of legal immigrants. That agreement, welcomed by large sectors of the Cuban community in the US, was angrily rejected by the most aggressive counterrevolutionary sectors.

But despite the US government's positive change of attitude on the migratory issue, Clinton enacted a series of new anti-Cuban measures: no remittances of packages to Cuba would be allowed, except for medicines; air traffic between the US and Cuba would be limited to flights aimed at carrying legal immigrants into the US and counterrevolutionary radio transmissions would be increased.

On August 5th, counterrevolutionary disorders occurred in two Havana neighborhoods—Habana Vieja and Centro Habana—whose main perpetrators were anti-social elements. But the working people themselves, who mobilized immediately, put an end to the incidents without using weapons. President Fidel Castro personally appeared on the scene to lead the mobilized workers. The gigantic popular demonstrations that followed flatly thwarted any destabilizing attempt.

Another important failure for them was the result of the elections held in July, 1995. The enemies of the Cuban Revolution had carried out a desperate campaign to prevent the people from taking part in the balloting, which they thought was easy since voting is not compulsory in Cuba and ballots are secret. Hence, the electoral race in fact became a true plebiscite. Despite the enemy's efforts, 97.1 percent of eligible voters went to the polls; only 4.3 percent cast blank ballots and the ballots of 7 percent were annulled. That is to say, more than 85 percent of the island's electorate clearly expressed its support for the Revolution, which in the conditions of the most serious economic crisis over the past 36 years, translated into an extraordinary victory for revolutionary power.

In response to the new failure, the US government's ultra right wing sectors linked to the Cuban American counterrevolutionaries, took new and more dangerous steps in their anti-Cuba escalation. Nine bills against Cuba were discussed in the US congress during 1995, which later concentrated on the Helms-Burton Law, aimed at stopping foreign investment and paralyzing foreign financing and supplies to Cuba, as well as legalizing US support for the counterrevolutionary groups inside the island and the government that would be established in Cuba once the Revolution were overthrown.

That law is taking the same direction as its predecessor—the Torricelli Law. It constitutes, however, a more flagrant violation of the Cuban people's human rights and of the sovereignty of other countries in the world, including the US's allies. It also violates the norms and principles that rule international law and economic relations among nations.

In the first place, the Helms-Burton Law legalizes all measures adopted against Cuba by all US administrations. It forces the US government internationalize the US blockade against the island through the UN Security Council, making it compulsory for all countries. It demands from the US government an annual detailed report before the US congress on Cuba's economic relations with other countries.

The law demands the most strict application of sanctions against US citizens who violate the orders, licenses, regulations or resolutions on the US blockade (travel ban, prohibition of money remittances or donations of any kind). These sanctions include 50 thousand dollar fines and the confiscation of any property used to violate the laws of the embargo.

In order to boost subversion, Helms-Burton authorizes all types of support for the counterrevolutionary groups inside Cuba and grants the US the right to determine what type of government, society and relations Cuba should have after the Revolution is overthrown. That practically means Cuba's annexation to the US.

A condition for the US to accept that type of Cuban government would be the total return of all properties nationalized by the Revolution that belonged to US citizens or companies. That aspect of the legislation would not only benefit US citizens who had that nationality when the confiscation occurred, but also those who later adopted that citizenship. If the properties are not physically returned, a "full and total" compensation (three times as much as its real value) is demanded.

Adopting extraterritorial authority, that law grants US courts the right to admit any claim made by US citizens supposedly affected by the loss of their property in Cuba and to rule on the issue. If a citizen from a third country has invested in that property or "traffics" with it, he or she can face a suit or sanctions, like the suspension of entry visas into the United States. Those sanctions will also be extended to the closest relatives of the person sanctioned, his or her spouse and children.

The Helms-Burton Law's arbitrary and inhumane nature, which is aimed at starving the Cuban people to death, ignores the sovereign equality of states and violates the principles of international law. The law was opposed not only by the world's progressive and democratic forces and by the advocates of the sovereign rights of all nations, but also by the US Democratic Party itself, and particularly President Clinton, who feared a negative reaction from US allies.

However, a provocation designed by terrorist groups in Florida linked to the Republican Party's most reactionary wing, served as a pretext for Clinton to radically change his mind and assume the position of his political enemies. It's been said that the turn was decisively the result of Clinton's weak ethical principles and his electoral calculations just months before the elections in which he was again running for president.

The provocation of February 24th, 1996.- Since the triumph of the Cuban Revolution thousands of US pirate planes have violated the country's air space. Those violations have been used to bomb towns, factories, stores and other economic facilities; to burn sugar cane plantations, refineries, and oil deposits; to provide terrorist groups and rebels with explosives and other military equipment; to introduce spies and saboteurs; to carry out biological warfare or throw propaganda calling for unrest and subversion. More than 25 such violations occurred just in the months before February, 1996.

Cuban authorities reported the incidents to US civil aviation agencies, pointing out that the pirate flights also violated US laws. Besides committing those violations, through Miami based radio and TV, terrorist leaders boasted of their flights over Cuban territory and over the Cuban capital, vowing to continue doing so. US authorities, however, did nothing concrete to prevent the flights though sometimes they said they were concerned. The Cuban government harshly reiterated that it wouldn't continue tolerating such flights, since "patience has limits".

In the morning of February 24th, 1996, three pirate planes from the terrorist organization "Brothers to the Rescue", coming from Opalocka airbase in Florida entered Cuban air space, but returned north when they saw Cuban military aircraft. Hours later, the pirate planes came back to Cuba and were warned that air zones north of Havana were on the alert and that, if they entered those activated areas, they could be shot down. A terrorist leader on one of the planes answered that they knew, and that they would enter anyway. It was an obvious challenge to the sovereignty of the island's air space.

Two of the aircraft that penetrate Cuban airspace were shot down. The head of the terrorists—on a third place—kept himself protected in international airspace, avoiding the fate of his subordinates.

This incident sparked a new campaign against Cuba by the US government. Immediately after the aircraft were shot down, as if everything had been planned, President Clinton announced new measures against Cuba including: approving the Helms-Burton Law, giving up to the mostly Republican congress; urging the UN Security Council to condemn and sanction Cuba; indefinitely calling off visits by Cuban Americans to the island and raising more funds for increase the broadcasts of the so called "Radio Martí".

At the Security Council's request, the International Civil Aviation Organization, the ICAO, named a commission to investigate everything related to the incident occurred on February 24th. The United States manipulated that commission, refused

to give it access to valuable evidence, falsified others, and obtained a confusing, contradictory and biased report that the ICAO plenary didn't approve. Instead of adopting it, that agency passed a balanced resolution that was sent to the Security Council with the report. This time despite pressures, neither could the United States get the Security Council to sanction Cuba.

This battle waged by the US superpower to isolate Cuba has brought about completely opposite results: the island's prestige and authority have increased, while discontent over and opposition to US arrogance has reached unimaginable dimensions. Not a single government in the world has come out in favor of the Helms-Burton Law. Particularly firm positions against the law have been adopted by the governments of Latin America and the Caribbean, Canada, Russia, Vietnam and other countries; international organizations like the Non-Aligned Movement, and regional organizations like the Organization of American States, the OAS, the European Union and the Group of Río, as well as figures of very different political tendencies. Particularly significant is the firm opposition adopted by Mexico and Canada, two countries associated with the United States in the free trade agreement. For the first time ever, the OAS reached an agreement opposing the United States, which was left alone in that regional body: the rest of the other member countries rejected Helms-Burton.

By late August, during Clinton's unsuccessful visit to Mexico to garner support for the law, the Mexican Foreign Minister rejected all unilateral and extraterritorial initiatives aimed at isolating Cuba. A document handed over to a US envoy by a Mexican senator read: "With profound indignation Mexicans have received the abominable Helms-Burton Law. Its shameful nature will never be accepted in a nation full of dignified legacies such as those of Benito Juarez, Our Nation's Hero, of which we boast and learned that **respect for the right of others is equivalent to peace.** Condemnation remarkably increased in August, when another extraterritorial measure that violates the principles of sovereignty and international law was approved in the United States: the D'Amato Law, which provides for sanctions against any country that invests in Iranian or Libyan oil industries. The fact that a government that has practiced the most condemnable forms of terrorism in the world proclaims itself the judge of other governments accusing them of terrorists is considered gross sarcasm.

On the other hand, if it's true that US hostility against Cuba has reached unimaginable levels, solidarity with the Caribbean island has acquired impressive dimensions worldwide, including among the US people. Friendship societies, political movements, religious sectors, figures of the most different political or ideological tendencies and affiliations, carry out a permanent labor to support the island politically and morally and engage in important material aid drives that have helped ease the population's most pressing needs. Work brigades from several countries visit the island and make their contribution to the country's development and the people's resistance. Support for Cuba has increased over the past few years in international organizations and forums: for four years in a row, the UN General Assembly has overwhelmingly rejected the blockade of Cuba.

Particularly noteworthy is the US solidarity movement. Not only communists and left wing organizations play an important role in that movement, but also artists, scientists, professionals, students and religious institutions. Even sectors from the US capital and prominent politicians are coming out for an end to the blockade and aggressions, for a negotiated solution to the problems between Cuba and the US. Solidarity brigades (the "Venceremos" sand the "Antonio Maceo", etc) increased, as well as groups of students who visited the island in a friendly gesture.

One of the most impressive demonstrations of that US solidarity are the caravans that frequently tour different US states under the sponsorship of the religious organization Pastors For Peace and with the cooperation of other Canadian religious groups, their brave challenge to the US blockade against Cuba, their odyssey on the US-Mexican border, and their heroic attitude when they held a successful "fast for life" for 94 days demanding the return of 395 computers to be sent to Cuba that US authorities had impounded. Those beautiful solidarity acts are, at the same time, battles waged by the US's progressive people to defend their own rights, included in their country's constitution, and permanently violated by their government.

Another demonstration of recognition and growing respect for Cuba are the island's relations with the Cuban community abroad. Despite the distance that have separated them from Cuban soil, the hostile environment and the anti-Cuban work done by the counterrevolutionary pressure groups, a large section of that community has known how to preserve their language, idiosyncrasies, habits and traditions, their love for their homeland and national feelings. In that hostile environment, they have come out for an end to the US war against Cuba and for developing normal and stable relations between Cubans on the island and those who reside abroad. And both those Cubans and the Revolutionary Government have taken serious steps in that direction.

In November, 1978 the Cuban government held its first contacts in Havana with a group of representatives from that community. In April, 1994 the conference "The Nation and its emigration" took place also in Havana with the attendance of 221 guests from 30 countries. Important common ground was found in that conference, which was later strengthened at the second such meeting held in October, 1995, with the participation of 332 guests from 34 countries. Today there is a stable communication with that patriotic sector of Cubans, who, despite not necessarily agreeing with socialist ideology, agree with the Cuban Revolution's objectives of national unity, full independence, sovereignty and peaceful and mutually beneficial relations among all nations, including the United States.

History does not stop.- Today, in August, 1996 Cuba successfully steps up efforts to continue forward. 38 years after the triumph of their Revolution, the Cuban people keep writing glorious pages of their admirable history. With the conquest of their true independence in 1959, their long battle is not over: before, they struggled to earn a dignified position in the community of really free countries, today, they are fighting to uphold the dreams come true.

This is a battle of all the people, who know they own their destiny; a battle for the future of all the oppressed and underdeveloped peoples of the Americas, of all the exploited and forgotten peoples; a battle for the honor, validity and victory of socialism.

The small Caribbean island's children are fighting this battle standing on the ashes of the oppressive power and raising the star of independence and liberty on their three-colored flag.

266

XIX

The Cuban Nation at the Threshold of the 21st Century

The last five years of the 20th century witnessed a number of key events that came to reaffirm the historic transcendence of the Cuban Revolution and the rightness of the Socialist choice made by the Cuban people. The pages that follow focus on this period of time.

A sustained recovery. The economic recovery began in 1994 continued in 1996, at such a pace that between 1995 and 1998 the rated growth of the Gross National Product (GNP) was 3.5%, despite the protracted economic war on the part of the United States and the heavy toll of hurricanes and other adverse weather conditions. In 1999 the economy grew 6.2%, and then 5.6% in the year 2000. These figures represent a significant advance considering that in 1998 the US blockade resulted in losses of some 70 billion dollars for Cuba.

But the country moved ahead regardless of this damage, caused mostly by the so-called Helms-Burton Law, which seeks to stop foreign investment from flowing to Cuba. By mid-2000, there were 390 foreign investment deals of different kinds, 59% of which had been concluded after passage of the afore-mentioned law. And of the approximately 4.3 billion dollars worth of contracted foreign capital, 40% also came after the law's enactment.

Thanks to the economic recovery, the excessive amount of money in circulation, which in 1994 had reached the 12 billion pesos, had been reduced to a more proportionate 9.7 billion by 1999, with the budget deficit also falling from almost a third of the GNP in 1993 to 2.4% in 1999. In addition, the Cuban peso greatly revalued: if during the first years of the Special Period it traded at a rate of 125 to 150 pesos per one US dollar, in the year 2000 the dollar trades for only 20 to 21 pesos.

Several are the branches of the Cuban economy that have played a role in the recovery. The most dynamic sector has been tourism, which has been growing at a rate of 21% annually, regardless of the fact that the US government keeps a ban on US citizens travelling to Cuba and tries by all means, including the use of terrorist agents, to thwart the island's tourism development. In 1997 there were several bomb attacks against tourist facilities in Havana, one of which, at the Copacabana Hotel, claimed the life of young Italian Fabio di Celmo. Cuban authorities captured the perpetrators and discovered the accomplices of these terrorist actions, which stopped thereafter.

Significant increases have also been recorded in nickel production, power generation, oil and gas extraction, textiles, fertilizers, fruits and vegetables. By mid-2000, virtually all sectors of the economy have experienced a reanimation, including the areas of consumer goods and services. Sugar production, which had declined to a record-low 3.2 million tons, started a slow recovery in 1999, surpassing the 4 million tons in the year 2000.

But these production increases are not yet enough to go around, so while they have not had a direct impact on the subsidized monthly supply of staples and goods that each and every Cuban gets the production increases can for the time be found, however, at the agricultural and industrial markets at unsubsidized prices, and at shops that sell products in hard currency.

Slowly but surely, foreign trade has also recovered. The end of 1999 recorded a commercial activity to the tune of 5.5 billion dollars. Cuba was by then trading with 146 countries, with Spain and Canada as its chief partners followed by Venezuela, the People's Republic of China, and the Russian Federation.

At the same time, care has been taken to preserve the basic gains of the Cuban Revolution, in areas like public health, social security, sports, and others. The infant mortality rate has remained under 8 since 1996, and in the year 2000 it was 7.2, the lowest in the whole of Latin America. A similarly positive trend can be observed in the areas of maternal death; life expectancy, that stands at more than 75 years; the number of doctors—one per 168 inhabitants—which makes Cuba the country with the highest per capita number of doctors in the world; among several other important social indicators.

Numerous epidemic and endemic diseases have been eradicated, like poliomyelitis, diphtheria, child and newly-born tetanus, ordinary and congenital measles, posparoiditis meningoencephalitis, whooping cough, and others. A key factor in this achievement has been the systematic mass vaccination campaigns, the nation-wide health-care network, and the general improvement of health conditions. Also playing a role in the health panorama are the approximately 400 rural aqueducts that have been built over the last decades. Success is equally being scored in the effort aimed at obtaining a vaccine against AIDS and other vaccine proto-types to fight certain cancerous tumors, all of which are evidence of Cuba's scientific potential and of how much Socialism cares for scientific development.

Significant, too, are the achievements in education. Pre-school education reaches 98% of the children population from 0 to 5 years of age; all children from 5 to 11 years attend primary school while 95% of the students expected to study in the seventh and eighth grades do so. From 1990 to 1998, despite the economic hardships, more than 300 thousand students graduated as university professionals for a total of over 700 thousand such professionals trained during these four decades of Revolution.

But the magnitude of the achievement goes beyond the mere figures. An idea of the kind of education that Cuba offers can be given by the results of a survey conducted in 11 Latin American nations by the UNESCO-sponsored *Laboratorio Lationamericano de Evaluación de la Calidad de la Enseñanza* (Latin American Laboratory for the Assessment of the Quality of Education). The study, which included mathematics and language tests to third and fourth grade pupils, easily set Cuba in the place of honor.

At the same time, a growing number of Cubans have finished their master's degrees in sciences or are researchers, technicians, and scientific personnel in general. And major breakthroughs and contributions are recognized world-wide in fields ranging from medicine to genetics to pharmacology. The teaching of arts and letters, and the works of Cuban artists and writers, for their part, continue to receive international acclaim.

In sports Cuba also continues to score high. At the 17th Olympic Games held in the US city of Atlanta Cuban athletes won 25 medals—9 gold, 8 silver, and 11 bronze—and Cuba ranked eighth among participating countries. And at the Sydney Olympics, in September of 2000, Cuba won an even higher number of medals: 29, which breaks into 11 gold, 11 silver, and 7 bronze titles. Despite having obtained more medals Cuba came in ninth, as developed nations had prepared better for the games, more and more athletes, in search of profits, changed flag and competed for the rich nations, and the trend to link sports to profits accentuated. At Central American and Caribbean games Cuba continues to be number one, and at Pan-American level it ranks second. In baseball, boxing, weight lifting, judo, volleyball, and others Cuba has shown to have the greatest of potentials.

The political and ideological battle. In addition to the hard struggle that Cuba is forced to be permanently waging in the face of the US government's on-going economic, biological and terrorist war, the Island is immersed in an equally intense ideological battle as it has to be constantly dismantling discredit campaigns organized abroad while wrestling domestically with the evils associated with the growing and indispensable relations with the capitalist world.

A new boost has been given to the work of political schools under the Communist Party, the mass organizations, and other institutions. Emphasis is also placed in the teaching of history at all levels of education; the study of the ideas and the work of José Martí; and instilling in the younger generation an ethics based on the precepts of both Martí and Marx.

Since late 1999, round tables and open tribunes are regularly been held to discuss issues of national and international interest. These enlightening programs are carried nation-wide and also internationally via the Cuban TV and radio networks, with the additional contribution of the print press. They have become events that one way or another draw the attention of the whole population, especially children and young people, and have demonstrated an immense capacity for both mass mobilization and education. Then there is University for All, a education modality that brings the knowledge of higher education to every Cuban home via television.

Renewed emphasis has been given to the work of centers and institutions devoted to the study of the José Martí legacy. They include the *Casa Natal* and the *Fragua Martiana*, established before the advent of the Revolution but which had been systematically neglected, as well as others created after the victory of the Revolution, like the *Centro de Estudios Martianos*, and more recently the *Memorial José Martí* and the *Oficina del Programa Martiano*, the *Sociedad Cultural José Martí* and the *Movimiento Juvenil Martiano*. The number of departments devoted to the study of José Martí at Cuban universities has increased as have the wide-spread José Martí Youth Seminars. And the bibliography on José Martí has been greatly enriched, as well as the number of periodicals dealing with the life and work of the beloved Cuban National Hero.

The patriotic, anti-imperialist, and internationalist tradition of the Cuban people, and Cuba's history and national culture in general, well explain Cubans' solid defense of their political and ideological positions. In December of 1996, the Cuban National Assembly (Parliament) passed the Cuban Dignity and Sovereignty Reaffirmation Act in response to the Helms-Burton Law. In March of 1997 Cubans endorsed the *Mambises** of the 20th Century Declaration, which expresses their determination to resist and overcome the imperialist circle. Then in 1999 the Baraguá** Oath was proclaimed. These two documents were debated nation-wide and received broad public support.

To these shows of high political awareness on the part of the Cuban people and of the solidness of the revolutionary power one could add other outstanding political events, like the 5th Congress of the Cuban Communist Party and the funeral ceremony in honor of Commander Ernesto Che Guevara, both in 1997, as well as the 1997, 1998, and 2000 People's Power elections.

Held in October of 1997, the Cuban Communist Party congress reviewed the country's overall situation, setting the general lines for the continued economic recovery and for ideological work. Among the congress' chief decisions were the issuing of an Economic Resolution, which has guided economic activity since, and the passage of the document "The Party of the Unity, the Democracy, and the Human Rights That We Defend," which had been widely and freely debated by the population at more than 230 thousand grass-roots assemblies.

The congress renewed the Cuban Communists' confidence in the future of both Cuba and humanity, as expressed by Fidel Castro in his report central to the meeting when he noted that "revolutionary ideas will live as long as there are revolutionaries, patriots, persons of noble heart; as long as there are people who carry within themselves the best of human virtues."

Delegates to the Municipal Assemblies of the People's Power were also elected in October. More than 96% of the electorate voted in those elections, and 14 533 delegates were voted into office nation-wide. Blank and spoiled ballots accounted for a little over 7% of the votes cast, which meant that nearly 93% of the votes were valid ones.

Later, in January of 1998, elections were held for 601 deputies to the National Assembly (Parliament) and for 1 192 delegates to the Provincial Assemblies. Voter turnout reached the 98.35%, and blank and spoiled ballots amounted to only 5%.

At these elections, the overwhelming support for the Revolution also became evident in the so-called united vote (voting for all candidates on the ballot). The united vote ended up accounting for 94.39% of all valid votes, which meant that all candidates were elected with the backing of more than 94% of the votes cast. Fidel and Raul Castro, the two top leaders of the Revolution, were elected by 99% of the possible votes.

The last elections of 20th century Cuba were those for Municipal Assembly delegates, held in April of the year 2000. Although voting is not compulsory in Cuba, voter turnout was 98.06%. Valid votes accounted for 94.13% of those cast as blank and spoiled ballots were only 5.87%. The total number of delegates elected was 14 686.

....

* *Mambises* is the term Cubans used to denominate the 19th century independence fighters.

** *Baraguá* is the name of a place of great historic significance in eastern Cuba. It was here that General Antonio Maceo turned down a Spanish peace offer that implied peace without true independence.

Posthumous homage to the Heroic Guerrilla and his Comrades-In-Arms fallen in Bolivia. The official ceremonies and activities organized following the discovery, transfer to Cuba, and final laying to rest of the remains of Ernesto Che Guevara and six of his comrades killed in action in Bolivia became a vigorous expression of Cubans' internationalist and revolutionary sentiments, and their respect for patriots and heroes. Buried in Cuba, next to the Guerrilla Commander were Cubans Carlos Coello Coello, Orlando Pantoja Tamayo, Alberto Fernández Montes de Oca and René Martínez Tamayo; Bolivian Simeón Cuba Sanabria; and Peruvian Juan Pablo Chang-Navarro Lébano.

In June, 1997, following a long search by a team of Cuban scientists and experts assisted by Bolivian and Argentinean personnel, the remains of Che and his afore-mentioned comrades were found in Bolivia. Flown to Havana, the remains stayed in provisional custody at the Granma Hall of the Cuban Armed Forces' headquarters, until the monument being built in their honor at Santa Clara city, in central Cuba, was completed. The funeral ceremony finally took place from October 11th to the 17th, days that were declared as official mourning.

Before their transfer to Villa Clara, the remains were laid at the José Martí Memorial, in Havana, so that the people of the Cuban capital could pay tribute to the heroes. Fidel and Raul Castro joined other Cuban government leaders as they conducted the first guard of honor before the remains; several hours after more than a million Havana residents had paraded before the carcasses, in a show of heart-felt respect, love and admiration.

Along the road to Villa Clara, more than 300 kilometers away, hundreds of thousands also gathered in tribute, and at the José Martí Library, in Santa Clara city, residents filed for hours to equally show their respect.

The remains were finally put to rest on October 17th, at the memorial built for them at the Ernesto Che Guevara Revolution Square, in Santa Clara, where Commander in Chief Fidel Castro delivered the main speech. Fidel Castro highlighted the moral, humane, and revolutionary stature of Che Guevara, and pointed to the symbolism of the remains being in Cuba.

"I see Che and his comrades," said Fidel "as reinforcements, as a troop of invincible fighters, a troop comprising not only Cubans but also Latin Americans, who come to fight next to us so that jointly we can write new glorious pages in history (…) Not all epochs and circumstances call for the same methods and tactics. But nothing can stop the course of history; its objective laws have perennial validity. Che focused on these laws, and he had an absolute faith in man."

Other of Che's comrades-in-arms whose remains have also been found have been equally honored here, among them the Argentinean-German-Cuban Haydée Tamara Bunker Bíder, known as *Tania la Guerrillera* (Tania the Guerrilla Fighter). By the end of the year 2000 the remains of thirty guerrillas, including Cubans, Argentineans, Bolivians, and Peruvians, were being kept at the Santa Clara memorial.

The Cuban People Suits the United States Government. The more than 40 year old war against Cuba on the part of the United States has resulted in huge material and human losses and damages for the island. This state of war has been turned the official US policy towards Cuba, and Washington's responsibility for the

271

damages of all kinds caused has been fully documented in the United States over the years, including numerous declassified US official documents.

Based on those facts, and in strict compliance with legal procedures, two legal suits were brought before the Havana City Civil and Administrative Provincial Court. The suits were established on behalf of eight social and mass organizations in Cuba, which combinedly rally almost the entire Cuban population: the Cuban Trade Union Central (CTC), the National Association of Small-Scale Farmers (ANAP), the Cuban Women Federation (FMC), the José Martí Young Pioneers Organization (OPJM), the Committees for the Defense of the Revolution (CDR), and Veterans of the Cuban Revolution Association (ACRC).

The first of these suits, titled "The Cuban People Suits the Government of the United States for Human Damages," was introduced on May 31st, 1999, and it demanded that Washington pay a total of US$ 181.1 billion as reparation for the loss of 3 478 Cuban lives and for damages against 2 099 other persons, who have been seriously injured, maimed, or rendered disabled as a result of US actions.

The second law suit, titled "The Cuban People Suits the Government of the United States for Economic Damages Caused Cuba," was established on May 3rd, 2000, and called for an indemnification of US$ 121 billion to compensate for damages and prejudices, particularly direct and indirect economic losses caused Cuba as a result of actions promoted, organized or conducted by the US government.

The suits state that both the human and the economic damages were caused by actions ranging from political to military, economic (the blockade and other anti-Cuba laws and measures), biological, diplomatic, psychological, propaganda, terror and sabotage, espionage, physical aggression to logistic support for armed counter-revolutionary gangs and mercenary groups, raids against Cuban territory, encouraging defection and emigration (especially illegal emigration), attempts to kill Cuban leaders, the threat of nuclear extermination and even direct aggression by a mercenary army.

For several months, hearings were held in connection with the law suits. Witnesses and victims of these actions, relatives of victims, Cuban security and military officers, and every Cuban with a legitimate argument to make appeared in court. Their accounts made Cuba go through a dramatic re-creation of the horrendous crimes the island and its people have had to suffer at the hands of successive US administrations. The process included the exhibit of declassified US documents, and reports compiled by Cuban security forces.

The hearings ended with a ruling by the courts that sentenced the US government to paying the afore-mentioned indemnification: US$ 181.1 billion for human damages, and US$ 121 billion for economic damages caused Cuba.

Achievements in foreign policy. The end of the 20th century saw an increase of US hostility in the diplomatic arena. But this did not deter Cuba in its efforts to expand its ties with the world. By mid-2000, Cuba had diplomatic relations with 171 countries, and belonged to 20 of the most important, elective UN agencies in addition to numerous other regional and international organizations.

A growing number of countries, organizations, and personalities condemn the US economic war against Cuba. Among those that have expressed opposition to the blockade, the Helms-Burton Law, and other anti-Cuba measures set forth by the

United States are the FAO and other UN agencies, the Movement of Non-Aligned Countries, the Association of Caribbean States, the Rio Group, the Latin American Integration Association, the Interparliamentary Union, the Union of African Parliaments, the Union of Arab Parliaments, as well as the European, the Latin American, the Central American, the Indigenous, and the Andean parliaments.

Similar positions have been held by the UN Conference on Human Settlements (Istanbul, 1996), the Food Summit (Rome, 1996), the CARIFORUM (Santo Domingo, 1998), the Summit of the Group of 77 (Havana, 2000), and other international fora. Heads of states from dozens of countries have issued declarations deploring the US circle against Cuba, among them the Pope, during his 1998 visit to Cuba.

Of significant importance are the votings of the UN General Assembly against the US blockade, which reflect growing support for Cuba.

VOTINGS AT THE UN GENERAL ASSEMBLY ON RESOLUTIONS IN FAVOR OF AN END TO THE US BLOCKADE SUBMITTED BY CUBA

Year	In Favor	Against	Abstentions
1996	137	3	25
1997	143	3	17
1998	157	2	12
1999	158	2	8
2000	167	3	4

In 1998, Washington was for the first time defeated at the UN Human Rights Commission, in Geneva, where since 1992 the US government had been, through pressures and threats, imposing successive anti-Cuba resolutions. Sixteen countries supported the US document while nineteen opposed it, and eighteen abstained. In 1999, the US delegation managed to impose its anti-Cuba resolution by the difference of just one vote.

Cuba continued to have an active participation in the Ibero-American summits, from the VI to the X, held respectively at Santiago de Chile and Valparaiso (1996); Margarita Island (1997); Oporto, Portugal (1998); Havana, Cuba (1999); and Panama City (2000). The Havana summit was particularly significant as the US government and its closest associates in the region tried hard to disrupt it. Yet, the meeting stood out for its level of representativeness, detailed organization, successful development and results, as well as for the respectful, serious, and profound way in which the most diverging of opinions were expressed, in an atmosphere of absolute freedom and frankness.

The Havana summit addressed issues of great importance for the people of Ibero-American and Caribbean nations. It also condemned the Helms-Burton Law and the US blockade. In frustrating US efforts to thwart the meeting, Ibero-American countries demonstrated that nations can and should stand for sovereignty.

Cuba has also been active within the Movement of Non-Aligned Countries, at summits of this organization, at the Latin America-European Union summit held in Brazil in 1999, and in all other agencies of which Cuba is a member.

The visit by Pope John Paul II. Among the dozens of visits by foreign dignitaries in the last five years of the century, that of the Pontiff of the Catholic Church and Head of State of the Vatican, Pope John Paul II (Karol Josef Wojtila), had a special significance. The Pope visited Cuba from January 21st to 25th, 1998.

Cuba was the only Latin American country that the Pontiff had not visited, which lent itself to readings of different kinds, as it was known that the hierarchy of the Cuban Catholic Church had taken a stand of opposition to the Revolution during the early years after its victory, in January of 1959. In addition, reactionary circles in the US and the Cuban counter-revolution abroad had been trying hard to keep the visit from taking place.

Responding to the call made by the Communist Party, the Church, the government, and local organizations, hundreds of thousands (believers and non-believers, Catholics and followers of other faiths, Party members and non-Party members) welcomed the Pope and cheered him along the more than 20 kilometers from the José Martí airport to the Apostolic Nunciature. At the very airport, President Fidel Castro read a welcoming statement expressing respect, friendliness, and satisfaction over the visit. The Pope then conveyed his greetings to the Cuban people and authorities and said thanks for the heart-felt welcome.

During his stay in Cuba, John Paul II and the papal entourage met with Fidel Castro and other government leaders, spoke to 300 Cuban intellectuals at Havana University, gave open air masses in four different provincial capitals (Santa Clara, Camagüey, Santiago de Cuba, and Havana, the national capital), and held a liturgical celebration with Church and lay representatives at the Havana Cathedral, among other activities.

The religious ceremonies were marked by their organization, by the discipline and enthusiasm of the hundreds of thousands (from all walks and creeds) who participated, by the presence of local government and political authorities alongside religious dignitaries, by the absence of political propaganda or proselytizing, by the general public respect shown towards the papal message and the words of almost all bishops, and by the broad coverage that all mass and religious functions received.

During the cordial encounter between John Paul II and Fidel Castro the Cuban leader presented the Pope with a copy of the first edition of the biography of the renowned Cuban teacher and priest Félix Varela, originally published in New York in 1878. The Pope in turn gave the Cuban President a mosaic from the Holy See with the image of Christ on it that is a replica of an ancient Byzantine piece kept at the crypt of the Saint Peter's Basilica in Rome.

During his visit to the University of Havana, the Pope prayed in silence before the urn with the remains of Presbyterian Félix Varela, kept there since 1912. Responding to the welcoming words of University Rector, Dr. Juan Vela Valdéz, the Pontiff paid tribute to Varela and Martí, whose virtues, he said, have been inherited by the Cuban people.

The visit by the head of state of the Vatican ended with a solemn farewell ceremony. In his words, on behalf of the Cuban people, President Fidel Castro thanked the Pope for honoring Cuba with his visit, for his expressions of love for the Cubans, and for his words all, even those with which he might have disagreed. In reply, the Pope noted that "the Cuban people cannot be deprived of ties with other peoples." He called for an end to "unjust inequalities" and "the limits to the fundamental liberties" and deplored "the restrictive economic measures imposed from outside, which are unfair and ethically unacceptable." John Paul II expressed confidence in the future of Cuba and wished material and spiritual prosperity for the Cuban people, whom he described as "protagonists of their history."

On January 28th, three days after his return to Rome, the Pope devoted his entire general audience that week, before 8 000 pilgrims from Italy and the world, to brief them on his just-ended visit to Cuba, which he termed unforgettable. He said that during his stay on the Island he had been surrounded by a sea of people, who had given him "a moving welcome." The Pope then dedicated a thought of special recognition to the President of the Republic of Cuba, Dr. Fidel Castro, and other authorities."

The Pope's visit to Cuba was especially significant. The negative atmosphere that had been created as a result of the campaigns abroad completely disappeared, and the Cuban people gave a demonstration of education, culture and political maturity. The Pope received a spontaneous, natural, respectful and warm treatment in Cuba; in return, he left a image of countless merits as a dignitary, among them his firm determination to overcome all his physical handicaps, his hard work, and above all his courage and independent stand in deciding to come to Cuba despite the enormous pressures and forces that had stood in the way of the visit.

At the same time, the visit demonstrated the solid revolutionary convictions of the Cuban people, their unity, and their firmness. Cuba opened its doors wide to thousands of foreign journalists, who enjoyed full freedom of movement and work. In the words of President Fidel Castro, the visit was a historic event and a new exploit of the Cuban people.

Relentless solidarity. Seeing that the Cuban people are successfully resisting, the US government has intensified its economic war and has stepped it up with new aggressions. In late 1996 and early 1997 planes coming from the US spread a Thrips Palmi Karay insect plague over Cuban territory, an insect that attacks practically all plants. The plague caused heavy damage on crops, especially that of potatoes.

In July, 1997, the US House and the Senate passed the Graham Amendment (under the Defense Allocation Law), which defined Cuba as "a national security threat for the US," although numerous US civil and military personalities, including the head of the South Command, have asserted otherwise, i.e. that Cuba poses no military threat to the US.

In October of the year 2000 the US Congress placed new obstacles to the sales of food and medicine to Cuba while drastically reducing the opportunities for US citizens to visit Cuba. At the same time, it allowed for Cuban funds that had been arbitrarily frozen in the US to be given to reactionary elements based in Miami. Adding insult to injury, these restrictive measures, which were even criticized by the then US President Bill Clinton have all been presented as a flexibilization of the blockade.

In the face of this growing aggression, actions in solidarity and support of Cuba have intensified world-wide. New solidarity organizations have been established, which have come to complement the work of countless other government and non-government organizations that set up solidarity brigades to come and work in Cuba and collect donations for people on the island. Among the 19 working brigades from all continents that travel to Cuba every year are the **Venceremos**, the **Antonio Maceo**, the **Maceitos**, the **Cruz del Sur**, the **Latin American**, and the **Nordic** brigades as well as two **José Martí** brigades, the **US Freedom to Travel Caravan**, and others.

Events of solidarity with Cuba have been nationally organized in over one hundred countries during the last few years, as have numerous regional an international conferences. These solidarity with Cuba meetings are regularly attended by thousands of delegates. The II World Solidarity Meeting, held in Havana from November 10th to the 14th, 2000, drew 4 347 delegates from 118 nations, and was marked by the enthusiasm and militancy with which participants defended Cuba's right to be the master of its own destiny.

Among the many agreements that derived from this meeting was that of declaring 2001 "International Year of Solidarity Against the Blockade, the Cuban Adjustment Act and All Imperialist Maneuvers Against Cuba." It was also agreed that the 10th of October—the date that marks the beginning of Cuba's struggle for independence—would be marked as World Day of Solidarity with Cuba.

Particularly important have been the numerous meetings held in Cuba among Cuban and US youths, scientists, teachers, students, athletes, and others, as well as the decisive solidarity shown by the US people during the seven month struggle for the return of Cuban child Elián González.

Solidarity with Cuba has also been expressed in many other ways, as in the establishment of sister city relationships between Cuban and foreign cities, and in the aid provided by states, international agencies, and popular organizations when Cuba has been faced with natural disasters.

Support for Cuba in the defense of its sovereignty and against the blockade and other anti-Cuba laws has equally been expressed in agreements and declarations promoted by numerous organizations during international meetings and events. Participation of Fidel Castro and other top Cuban officials in conferences and other conclaves world-wide, at Ibero-American summits, and others, have systematically resulted in mass rallies and demonstrations in favor of Cuba.

The US has been unable to globalize the blockade while, in contrast, there has been a growing international effort towards globalizing solidarity with Cuba.

Cuba, an example of international solidarity. The collapse of Socialism in Europe and the intensification of the economic war against Cuba that followed combined to produce a profound economic, a crisis that to a lesser or greater extent affected each and every aspect of life on the island. The suffocating shortages forced the population to make great sacrifices, which still continue for many in spite of the recovery that has been taking place.

276

Yet, economic constraints have not kept the Cuban people from extending their fraternal solidarity to many nations in a wide range of fields. That solidarity has been mainly expressed in two directions: the struggle internationally to bring solutions to the most pressing economic, social and cultural problems of the underdeveloped world, and the voluntary, free, and selfless contributions that Cuba has been making to Latin American, Caribbean, African, and Asian nations in areas ranging from health care to education to construction, sports and others.

At countless international events Cuba has proposed, and demanded, solutions to issues like poverty, lack of health and education, hunger, the foreign debt, the unfair terms of trade, the destruction of the environment, and other evils affecting the third world, which are mostly the result of the exploitation and the plundering being conducted by the rich imperialist powers.

On the other hand, Cuba has continued to share its achievements and progresses with nations of the hemisphere. The island has been well-known since the early years after the revolutionary victory for its contribution to the peoples' liberation from oppression and the defense of their independence. Some 400 thousand Cuban troops have fought in the defense of just causes world-wide, and Cuban blood has been shed in the defense of the sovereignty of many sister nations. And more than 80 thousand Cuban civilian workers, among them thousands of medical doctors, have offered their services in more than 100 countries. Since 1959, 11 medical brigades with more than 400 members have traveled to countries of all continents, including Europe, to help alleviate the effects of earthquakes, hurricanes, volcanic eruptions, floods, and other natural disasters.

In the last few years, Cuban health workers have been at the center of one of the most heroic, selfless episodes of solidarity. In February of 1998, when Peru suffered the effects of "El Niño" a team of Cuban professional and technicians immediately traveled to the area carrying medicines, blood serum, medical instruments and material to assist the affected population.

In September of 1998, President Fidel Castro called on the international community to help Haiti, which had been devastated by hurricane Georges. Considering Haiti's serious health care situation, including its high infant mortality rate, the Cuban leader proposed that developed nations (like Canada, Japan, France and other members of the European Union) contributed with medications for a program that, under World Health Organization supervision, could have saved 25 thousand Haitian lives annually. Cuba volunteered to provide the necessary medical personnel for the ambitious project.

A similar call was made by Fidel Castro several days later, this time in favor of the Dominican Republic, which had been equally hit by the hurricane. Aside from its call, Cuba renounced its share of internationally assistance (Cuba had also been affected by the storm) so that it could be channeled to the Haitian and Dominican peoples; in addition, Cuba decided to send medical brigades to Haiti and the Dominican Republic, where Cuban health experts remained for 42 days, working in local hospitals and providing general assistance to the population.

In November of that year, the Cuban government issued a declaration of support for Central American nations faced with yet a bigger natural disaster: that caused by hurricane Mitch, which had then left more than 11 thousand people dead. Cuba strongly supported the plea made by affected nations, which demanded that tariffs be eliminated for some of the region's export products; that the European Union removed tariffs barriers; that a reconstruction program be set in motion for Central American with the support of the World Bank, the IMF, Inter-American Development Bank, and the Central American Integration Bank; that the international community put together a regional emergency group for the provision of fresh aid for the isthmus; and that the foreign debt of Nicaragua and Honduras be written off and that of Guatemala and El Salvador be alleviated. Cuba also expressed its readiness to provide affected nations with all the necessary medical personnel for as long as their presence might be needed.

Before the floods had receded, Cuban medical brigades had arrived in Honduras and Guatemala, an assistance that quickly extended to Nicaragua, Belize, and El Salvador. In its solidarity gesture Cuba had disregarded the fact that the governments of some of those nations had maintained an extremely hostile attitude towards the island. Cuba went as far as canceling the debt that one of those countries—Nicaragua—had contracted with Havana, which amounted to over 50 million pesos.

The Cuban government also made other concrete proposals to the international community. It said that if one of several countries with greater resources than Cuba provided the medications, it would send all the necessary medical personnel so that in the short and medium terms a comprehensive medical care program could be implemented in the affected nations. Cuba also volunteered to provide, immediately, free, and for as long as necessary, two thousand medical doctors for Honduras, Guatemala, and any other country of the region that might need them.

And seeking to help solve the longer-term health care problem of the area, Cuba offered to provide 500 medical scholarships a year for Central American students. It proposed that an "Ibero-American Program for the Comprehensive Health Care Development of Affected Central American Nations" be designed and implemented. By the time Cuba launched its proposal there were already six Cuban medical brigades doing relief work in Honduras and Guatemala, made up by more than 100 doctors and other medical personnel.

This assistance was gradually expanded to other Latin American, Caribbean, and African nations, where thousands of Cuban doctors and technicians have been working. One of the latest examples is Venezuela, a country that in 1999 suffered the heaviest rains and worst floods of the century, leaving tens of thousands of people dead, more than 200 thousand people homeless, and losses exceeding the US$ 2 billion. The rains had not stopped when the first 447 Cuban medical experts, with all necessary equipment and medications, had already arrived and were assisting the local population. By November of the year 2000 this assistance was still being provided to Venezuela.

At the turn of the century, more than two thousand Cuban medical experts were paying services in countries of the world.

Meeting with a group of Cuban doctors, nurses, and health technicians working in Gambia, Africa, in August, 2000, Fidel Castro described the international medical assistance program being implemented by Cuba as "a true revolution in the field of medical care." A month later, participating in the so-called Summit of the Millenium, the Cuban leader addressed the situation of AIDS in Africa. Fidel Castro offered the United Nations, the World Health Organization, and African nations the necessary medical personnel to not only fight the AIDS epidemic but also to combat other health problems in the continent while training a local medical staff. In addition, Cuba has an agreement with Venezuela whereby a number of patients and sick persons travel to Cuba to receive medical care.

At the same time, Cuba is training as doctors hundreds of youths from other countries. In the face of the natural disasters befallen Central America and the Caribbean in recent years, and given the region's acute shortage of doctors and medical experts, the Cuban government decided to step in and help train doctors. During the holding in Havana of the 9th Ibero-American Summit, in November, 1999, Cuba inaugurated the Latin American Medical Sciences Faculty, which every year will be receiving 500 new students from the region. The school, which started with just one thousand students is presently training 3 300 youths from over 20 countries. It is expected to eventually accommodate between 8 and 10 thousand students from all over the world, including Africa.

Cuba has also offered to train youths from US minorities and marginalized sectors of the US society. In September, 2000, the president of the Cuban National Assembly (Parliament), Ricardo Alarcón, announced that for the benefit of the Black caucus of the US Congress, the island was ready to receive, beginning that year, 250 Afro-American youths (together with another 250 Latino and other minority youths) to be trained as medical doctors in Cuba, for a total of 500 scholarships for US students in the year 2000.

Announcing the Cuban offer, Alarcón noted that "there is also a Third World within the US, where millions of native Americans and Afro-Americans live in poverty and are deprived of adequate medical care," and that Cuba was extending its medical training program to also include them.

Aside from the students at Havana's Latin American Medical School, 240 Haitian youths are also being trained as doctors at Santiago de Cuba; these figures are irrespective of the about one thousand other foreign students who are presently studying medicine in other Cuban faculties, for a total of more than 4 500 world youth being presently trained as doctors on the island. In general, 8 220 foreign scholarship students are currently studying different careers in Cuba.

Cuba also started an International Sports Trainers College for the benefit of youths from the Third World, particularly Latin America.

The Cuban government is assisting as well in the establishment of medical faculties in African countries, like Gambia, where its has already sent medical professors.

True to its solidarity vocation, socialist Cuba continues to share its scientific, technical, and cultural achievements with other peoples of the world that might need it.

The fight for the return of Elián. One of the most impressive battles waged by the Cuban people against US Imperialism and its Miami acolytes was that in demand of the return to Cuba of six-year old child Elián González Brotón.

On November 25th, 1999, Elián was found floating, off the coast of Florida, tied to an inner tube. The boat that was illegally carrying him and a group of other people to the United States had capsized, causing the death of most people on board, including Elián's mother. Elián, who had been found in a delicate health condition, spent two days in a Miami hospital. And although the six-year old was able to give his father's telephone number in Cuba, the US Immigration and Naturalization Service (INS), in violation of US laws and of existing migration agreements with Cuba, gave the child's custody to distant relatives in Miami, despite these individuals' dubious records and their connections with Cuban-American ultra-right, extremist groups.

Acting on a request by Elián's father, Juan Miguel González Quintana, the Cuban Foreign Affairs Ministry approached the US Interest Section in Havana with an official petition for the return of Elián to his family in Cuba, in compliance with international law. But Elián's relatives in Miami, in connivance with anti-Cuba elements of the Cuban-American National Foundation (CANF) and resorting to all possible legal subterfuges, refused to release the child. Thus started a public opinion battle that went on for seven long months.

Financially supported by the CANF, the Miami relatives hired lawyers and managed to keep Elián in virtual isolation, making it even difficult for his father and grandparents in Cuba to communicate with him. They tried by all means, including psychological ones, to make Elián renounce his Cuban identity in favor of well-known US capitalist symbols. Even psychiatrists were hired—it was later learnt—in an effort to confound the child's mind. So what was eminently a family issue was turned into a political campaign against the Cuban Revolution.

Five weeks after Elián had been found, the INS finally recognized that Elián's father was the only person who could represent the child and speak for him. Yet, in open violation of US laws, the INS not only did not immediately return Elián to his father but gave the Miami relatives the opportunity to start a legal procedure in which it was not the father who was speaking for the child but those who were practically holding him hostage. And when the INS finally instructed that Elián be reunited with his father, the Miami relatives and their CANF financial and political sponsors refused to do so.

The CANF had bribed, blackmailed, and cajoled judges, journalists, legislators, mayors, priests, and local authorities, and was branding as spies of the Cuban government anyone who in the US favored the return of Elián to his Cuban family. They had gone as far as seeking that the US Congress grant Elián the US citizenship, even against the stated will of his father.

The kidnappers and their lawyers dangerously prolonged the legal procedure while launching an offensive in which not only local authorities but even the two presidential candidates got involved, with the expressed aim of getting Elián's father, Juan Miguel González, to defect and stay in the US.

But the Cuban nation did not sit idle by. One week after Elián's return had been requested and seeing that the Miami claque had no intention of releasing him, the Cuban people started a series of huge demonstrations in support of his father's position. In Havana and other Cuban cities "open tribunes" were set up so that people could express their views on the issue. Round tables on Cuban radio and television kept the population informed of the latest developments regarding the case. These round tables addressed issues like the kidnappers' violation of Cuban, US, and international laws, their efforts to manipulate the child's mind, the low moral and social standards of the Miami group, the CANF's notorious history, the dirty political maneuvers and corruption involved in the case, and the contradictory positions within the US government. The Cuban people also took careful note of the growing sentiment within the US public opinion in favor of the child's return, and of how much public attention the case had generated.

Huge popular marches and parades were held in Cuba, rallying mothers, grandmothers, youths, children, students, professionals, workers and farmers, all of whom demanded that Elián be returned to his father. On one single day, December 10th, 1999, nearly 2 million people participated in demonstrations in 17 cities across the island.

In demanding the return of the beleaguered child, poetry also played a role, as can be seen in this poem, dated January 1st, 2000:

NEW YEAR FOR ELIÁN

The homeland grows. Despite the fierce North
its steady course it firmly keeps,
and every January brings forth
renewed hope and belief.

But in the marsh of their rage
the enemies of Cuba do not rest,
and the bluer the sky for Cuba turns
the restless that they get.

Blinded by fury, in their claws
it is a Cuban child they now hold,
their tentacles around him,
they cling to him, they won't let go.

They snatch him from the person that he loves,
from the warmth of his island, from his home,
and wrap him in a cluster of strange stars
so that his lonely star he won't recall.

But wounded in its heart, the homeland rises
and in a single voice,
a single shout comes from its throat:
"let the child be returned to his beloved soil.

And so the cry for justice lingers on,
grows as time passes, with time grows,
only to stop the day, the bright new daybreak
when Elián finally finds his way home.

As a place for popular reunion and debate regarding the Elián ordeal, but also so that it could be used in the future as a forum of discussion of important Cuban or world issue, on April 3rd, 2000, the José Martí Anti-Imperialist Open Tribune was inaugurated in Havana, by the city's well-known sea-side drive, and across from the US Interest Section. Dominating the square is an imposing statue of the Cuban National Hero holding a child with one arm as he points with the other, in accusation, towards the US office.

In the middle of the battle for the return of Elián, the child's grandmothers traveled to the United States, in an action that had great impact on the US public opinion. But US public support for Elián's return reached its peak when on April 6th, 2000, Elián's father arrived in the US and asked the US people for support so that he could be reunited with his six-year old son.

In the face of the unanimous demand of the Cuban people, the world outcry, and the very US public opinion that favored the return of Elián to his family in Cuba, and given the kidnappers' rejection of any arrangement, US Secretary of Justice, Janet Reno, ordered the use of force to rescue Elián, in a swift and successful operation that took only minutes. The child was reunited with his father, and following a US Supreme Court ruling he returned to Cuba, on June 28th, 2000.

Juan Miguel González gave a true example of fatherly love, courage, tenacity, firmness of principle, and confidence in the Cuban people and their Revolution. It was thanks to his brave conduct, to the heroic, relentless struggle of the Cuban people, and to the active international solidarity that the tragedy generated, including the support of the vast majority of the US society, that the maneuvers of the anti-Cuba Mafia and the US ultra-right were defeated.

The outcome provided the occasion for the Cuba-American mobs in Florida to show their true nature; while Elián was flying back home, a female demonstrator in Miami begged before the cameras: "Oh, Lord, please, knock that plane down, knock it down!" Attitudes like this could not be more revealing.

The battle for Elián left valuable teachings and experiences, among them:
—It showed once more, in an indisputable way, the existence of two incompatible life outlooks: on one hand the humane, noble conduct of the Cuban people and Revolution, ready to run whatever risks in the defense of the legitimate rights of one of its children, and on the other hand the de-humanized, unscrupulous behavior of the Cuban-American Mafia and the US ultra-right, who were ready to ruin the happiness and the life of a six-year old child in order to hurt the Cuban people and their Revolution.
—It helped further unite the Cuban nation while reaffirming the wisdom and humanism of the Cuban leadership, especially Fidel Castro. It also showed the great moral, ideological, political, and cultural values of the Cuban people, particularly the level of political and social awareness attained by Cuban children and youths. The whole Elián issue greatly strengthened the militancy of the masses in Cuba, and their convictions in the rightness of justice and dignity.
—It highlighted the importance of different mass struggle modalities—open tribunes, round tables, popular marches—which revealed themselves not only as powerful

weapons but also as true expressions of the national culture, and of the political, ideological, and revolutionary awareness of the Cuban people.

—it showed that there are great moral reserves in the US society, which may prove fundamental once the US people understand the rightness of a cause and the need to defend it.

—it demonstrated that the terrorist Cuban-American Mafia in Miami, the brainchild of the US government, which has supported it for decades, has become a true Frankenstein capable of defying the very US government, openly violating US laws, and undermining in so doing the prestige of that nation and its institutions.

But the return of Elián did not mean the end of Cuba's struggle against the US aggression. The different mass mobilization modalities that emerged during the struggle for the child's return continue to be used today to oppose the US blockade and to fight other anti-Cuba maneuvers by the reactionary US ultra-right and its Cuban-American counter-revolution. Outstanding in this struggle is the demand for an end to the so-called Cuban Adjustment Act, in effect since 1966, which allows for Cubans reaching US territory—irrespective of the means used to travel there—to be granted permanent residency in that country.

Existing only for Cuban nationals, this law has become the main incentive for Cuban illegal migration to the US, involving even the traffic of human beings, which systematically claims the lives of men, women and children. So notorious are the effects of the Cuban Adjustment Act that it has come to be known on the island as "the killer law." Cubans also continue their fight against the US's Helms-Burton Law, passed in 1996.

Attempts to kill Fidel Castro during the 10th Ibero-American Summit. The new modalities of mass mobilization and struggle that proved so successful in the Elián episode have been effectively used more recently to denounce and expose a plan to assassinate Cuban President Fidel Castro during the 10th Ibero-American Summit held in Panama in November, 2000.

The same day of his arrival in Panama City, the Cuban President denounced by means of an official declaration that terrorists elements—organized, directed, and financed from the United States by the Cuban-American National Foundation, the notorious CANF—were already in Panama with the mission of murdering him. The head of the assassins was no other than well-known terrorist Luís Posada Carriles, the direct perpetrator of countless criminal and murderous actions, among them the blowing in mid-air of a Cuban passenger plane with 73 people on board, near Barbados on October 6th, 1976.

These terrorists were based in the US and Central America; Posada Carriles is known to have lived in El Salvador, where he moved about freely in spite of the fact that the Salvadoran government was well aware of his criminal records and his contacts. Posada and his accomplices had introduced explosives and weapons in Panama and planned to assassinate Fidel Castro during the Cuban leader's visit to the University of Panama, where he was scheduled to address a student rally. Given the high power of the explosives that the terrorists were going to use, the action could have claimed the lives of hundreds of students, teachers, and other people.

Thanks to the detailed denunciation made by Cuba, Panamanian authorities were able to capture and imprison Posada Carriles and three of his henchmen; their weapons and explosives were also seized. The Cuban government has requested the terrorists' extradition. As the new century began Panamanian authorities had not made a final decision as to how to proceed.

In summary, with the advent of a new century, 42 years after the victory of their Revolution, the Cuban people continue to add pages of glory to their admirable history. Their attainment of true independence in 1959 did not mean that their struggle had ended: before, they were struggling to hold a dignified place within the concert of free nations, and today they struggle so that that dignified position is maintained and upheld.

Theirs is the battle of a whole nation, a people that knows that they are the masters of their own destiny. But theirs is also a battle for the future of Latin America, oppressed and underdeveloped, a battle for all marginalized, poor peoples of the earth. A battle for honor, dignity, and Socialism.

The children of this small Caribbean island are waging that battle, standing tall upon the bits and pieces of the yoke they tore apart, as they hold high the colors of their flag, with its lonely, free star.

Minimum bibliography

Aguirre, Sergio: *Eco de Caminos*. Ciencias Sociales Publishing House, Havana, 1974.

Alarcón Ricardo: *Una ley que viola todo el derecho internacional*. Analysis of the scope and content of the so called Helms-Burton Law. Editora Política Publishing House, Havana, 1996.

Almeida Bosque, Juan: *La Sierra Maestra y más allá*. Editora Política Publishing House, Havana, 1995.

Alonso, Guillermo and Enrique Vignier: *La corrupción política y administrativa en Cuba. 1944-1952*. Ciencias Sociales Publishing House, Havana, 1973.

Alvarez Batista, Gerónimo: *III Frente a las puertas de Santiago*. Letras Cubanas Publishing House. Havana, 1983.

Alvarez, Justina: *Héroes eternos de la patria*. Venceremos Publishing House. Havana, 1964.

Alvarez Mola, Verónica, et al: *De Tuxpan a la Plata*. Orbe Publishing House. Havana, 1979.

Armas, Ramón de: Eduardo Torres-Cuevas and Ana Cairo Ballester: *Historia de la Universidad de la Habana. 1728-1978*. (2 volumes). Ciencias Sociales Publishing House. Havana, 1964.

Báez, Luis: *Memoria inédita*. Conversations with Juan Marinello. SÍ-MAR S.A. Publishing House, Havana, 1995.

Benítez, José A: *David Goliat Siglo XX*. Granma Publishing House, Havana, 1967.

Cantón, José: Vladimir Barbeito and José Acosta: *Los regímenes precapitalistas. Cuba*. Revolutionary Instruction Schools, Havana, 1966.

Cantón Navarro, José: *Algunas ideas de José Martí en relación con la clase obrera y el socialismo*. Second unabridged edition. Editora Política Publishing House, Havana, 1961.

Castro, Fidel: *Entrevista concedida a la agencia EFE*. On Latin America's foreign debt Editora Política Publishing House. Havana, 1985.

Castro, Fidel: *Fidel y la Religión*. Conversation with Friar Betto. SÍ-MAR S.A. Publishing House, Havana, 1994.

Castro, Fidel: *Ideología, conciencia y trabajo político*. Editora Política Publishing House, Havana, 1986.

Castro, Fidel: *La historia me absolverá*. Edition, Preface, Introduction and Notes by Pedro Alvarez Tabío and Guillermo Alonso. Council of State's Publishing Office, Havana, 1995.

Castro, Fidel: *Nada podrá detener la marcha de la historia*. Interview with Jeffrey Elliot and Mervin Dymally on several issues. Editora Política Publishing House, Havana, 1985.

Castro, Fidel: *Un encuentro con Fidel*. Interview with Gianni Mina. Council of State's Publishing Office, Havana, 1987.

Castro, Fidel: *Un grano de maíz*. Conversation with Tomas Borge. Council of State's Publishing Office, Havana, 1992.

Castro, Fidel: other speeches, presentations, interviews and writings published by *OR Publishing House,* publications, booklets and books. It includes Main Reports from different Communist Party congress and speeches at international fora.

Castro Ruz, Raúl: *La Operación Carlota ha concluido! Victoria del internacionalismo cubano.* Editora Política Publishing House. Havana, 1991.

Castro Ruz, Raúl: *Selección de discursos y artículos. 1959-1986.* (2 volumes). Editora Política Publishing House, Havana, 1988.

Information Center of the Revolutionary Orientation Division of the Cuban Communist Party's Central Committee: *Cronología, 25 años de Revolución. 1959-1983.* Editora Política Publishing House, Havana, 1987.

Information Center of the Revolutionary Orientation Division of the Cuban Communist Party's Central Committee": *Cronología de la Revolución. 1984-1989.* Editora Política Publishing House, Havana, 1991.

Center for Studies on Military History: *Moncada: la acción.* Editora Política Publishing House. Havana. 1981.

Center for Studies on Military History: *Moncada: motor de la Revolución.* Editora Política Publishing House. Havana, 1983.

Center for Studies on Youth: *La Asociación de Jóvenes Rebeldes.* Abril Publishing House, Havana, 1986.

Cinco Palmas. Bulletin of the Council of State's Publishing and Historic Affairs Office, Havana, year I, number 1, may 1994. Primarily an article by Pedro Alvarez Tabío: "Nature and stages of revolutionary war in Cuba".

Collazo, Enrique: *Los americanos en Cuba.* Ciencias Sociales Publishing House, Havana. 1972.

Young Communist League's National History Commission: *La invasión: estrategia fundamental en nuestras guerras revolucionarias.* Cuban Book Institute, Havana, 1972.

State Committee on Statistics: **Anuario estadístico. Cuba.** All annual editions from 1975 to 1988 and previous and later reports. Havana.

Constitución de la República de Cuba. Havana, 1992.

Constituciones de Cuba. 1869-1940. Editora Política Publishing House, Havana, 1978.

Cronología de la Revolución. 1959-1965. Revolutionary Instruction Schools. Havana, 1966.

Cupull, Adys, and Froilán González: *UN hombre bravo.* Capitán San Luis Publishing House, Havana, 1994.

Chomón, Faure: *El asalto al Palacio Presidencial.* Ciencias Sociales Publishing House, Havana, 1969.

Declaraciones de la Habana y Santiago. Editora Política Publishing House, Havana, 1965.

D'Estéfano, Miguel A.; José M. Galego and María del C. Solana: *Fidel y el tercer mundo.* Chinh Tri Quoc Gia Publishing House, Hanoi, 1994.

Diario de la guerra. Edition and Introduction by Pedro Alvarez Tabío. Council of State's Publishing Office, Havana, 1986.

Días de combate. Prologue by Luis Pavón, Book Institute, Havana, 1970.

Diez, Tomás, et at: *Selección de artículos y documentos para la historia del movimiento obrero y la revolución socialista de Cuba*. (7 volumes). Revolutionary Armed Forces Central Political Division, Havana, 1984.

Revolutionary Armed Forces Central Political Division: *Moncada: antecedentes y preparativos*. Editora Política Publishing House, Havana, 1980.

Revolutionary Armed Forces Central Political Division: *Historia de Cuba*. Book Institute. Havana, 1971.

Documentos históricos . Introduction and notes by Gonzalo de Quesada y Miranda. University of Havana Publishing House, 1965.

Documentos políticos . International Policy of the Cuban Revolution. (2 volumes). Editora Política Publishing House, Havana, 1966.

Domínguez, Ofelia: *50 años de una vida* . Book Institute, Havana, 1971.

Duarte Hurtado, Martín: *La máquina torcedora de tabaco* . Ciencias Sociales Publishing House. Havana, 1973.

Escalante Font, Fabián: *La guerra secreta de la CIA*. Capitán San Luis Publishing House, Havana, 1993.

Fernández Retamar, Roberto: *"Nuestra América": cien años y otros acercamientos a Martí*. SÍ-MAR S.A. Publishing House, Havana, 1995.

Fernando Rios, Olga: *Formación y desarrollo del Estado socialista*. Ciencias Sociales Publishing House, Havana, 1988.

Ferrera Herrera, Alberto: *El Granma: la aventura del siglo*. Capitán San Luis Publishing House. Havana, 1990.

Gálvez, William: *Camilo. Señor de la Vanguardia*. Ciencias Sociales Publishing House, Havana, 1979.

García Galló, Gaspar Jorge: *Esbozo biográfico de Jesús Menéndez*. Editora Política Publishing House, Havana, 1978.

García Oliveras, Julio: *José Antonio Echevarría: la lucha estudiantil contra Batista*. Editora Política Publishing House, Havana, 1979.

Gómez, Juan Gualberto, et al: *La lucha antimperialista en Cuba*.(compilation). Edición Revolucionaria, Havana, 1976.

Grinevich, E. and B. Gvosdariov: *Washington contra la Habana*. Progreso Publishing House, Moscow, 1982.

Grobart, Fabio: *Trabajos escogidos*. Ciencias Sociales Publishing House. Havana, 1985.

Guerra, Sánchez, Ramiro: *Azúcar y población en las Antillas*. Ciencias Sociales Publishing House. La Habana, 1970.

Guerra Sánchez, Ramiro: *Manual de historia de Cuba. Nacional de Cuba* Publishing House. Havana, 1964.

Guevara, Ernesto (Che): *El Diario del Che en Bolivia*. Notes by Adys Cupull and Froilán González. Editora Política Publishing House. Havana, 1987.

Guevara, Ernesto (Che): *Obras. 1957-1967*. Casa de las Américas. Havana,1970. (2 volumes).

Guevara Lynch, Ernesto: *Mi hijo el Che*. Arte y Literatura Publishing House. Havana, 1988.

Hart Dávalos, Armando: *Cambiar las reglas del juego.* Interview with Luis Báez. Letras Cubanas Publishing House. Havana, 1983.

Historia de la Revolución Cubana Selection of speeches on historic issues. Editora Política Publishing House, Havana, 1980.

Historia de una agresión. The trial against the Bay of Pigs mercenaries. Venceremos Publishing House, Havana, 1962.

Ibarra Cuesta, Jorge: *Cuba: 1898-1958. Estructura y procesos sociales.* Ciencias Sociales Publishing House, Havana, 1995.

Ibarra Guitart, Jorge R.: *La S.A.R.: dictadura, medicación y revolución.* Ciencias Sociales Publishing House, Havana, 1994.

Cuban History Institute: *Historia de Cuba.* Volume I. Editora Política Publishing House, Havana, 1994.

Institute of History of the Communist Movement and the Cuban Socialist Revolution: *Historia del movimiento obrero cubano. 1865-1958.* (2 volumes). Editora Política Publishing House, Havana, 1985.

Institute of History of the Communist Movement and the Cuban Socialist Revolution: *J.A. Mella. Documentos y artículos.* Introduction, notes and chronological synthesis by Erasmo Dumpierre. Ciencias Sociales Publishing House, Havana, 1975.

Izquierdo Canosa, Raúl: *Días de la guerra.* Editora Political Publishing House, Havana, 1994.

Lechuga, Carlos: *En el ojo de la tormenta*: F. Castro, N. Jruschov, J. F. Kennedy and the missile crisis. SÍ-MAR S.A. Publishing House, Havana, 1995.

Lefrán, Manuel de J.:*!!...y llegó el Comandante y mandó a parar!.* Felipe Torres Trujillo Workshops, Camaguey, 1994.

León Cotayo, Nicanor: *Sin ramo de olivo.* Cuban US relations under the Ronald Reagan government. (2 volumes). Editora Política Publishing House, Havana, 1988.

Le Riverend, Julio: *La República. Dependencia y revolución.* Book Institute, Havana, 1973.

Le Riverend, Julio: *Historia económica de Cuba.* Book Institute, Havana, 1967.

López Segrera, Francisco: *Cuba: cultura y sociedad.* Letras Cubanas Publishing House, Havana, 1989.

Mencía, Mario: *La prisión fecunda.* Editora Política Publishing House, Havana, 1980.

Foreign Ministry: *Historia de una usurpación.* The US naval base in Guantánamo Bay, Havana, 1979.

Miranda, Caridad: *Trazos para el perfil de un combatiente.* (On Frank País). Oriente Publishing House, Santiago de Cuba, 1983.

Miranda Fernández, Lucinda: *Lázaro Peña, capitán de la clase obrera cubana*. Ciencias Sociales Publishing House, Havana, 1984.

Moreno Fraginals, Manuel: *El ingenio.* (3 volumes). Ciencias Sociales Publishing House, Havana, 1973.

Núñez Jiménez, Antonio: *Geografía de Cuba.* Editora Pedagógica Publishing House, Havana, 1965.

Núñez Machín, Ana: *Rubén Martínez Villena*. Ciencias Sociales Publishing House, Havana, 1974.

Pacheco González, María Caridad; Orlando Cruz Capote and Humberto Fabián Suárez: *Apuntes para la historia del movimiento juvenil cubano.* Abril Publishing House, Havana, 1987.

Padrón, Pedro Luis: *Qué república era aquella!* Ciencias Sociales Publishing House, Havana, 1986.

Pérez Concepción, Hernán: *Selección de lecturas de historia de Cuba.* History School, University of Havana, 1975.

Periodo Especial . Press Information Center, Havana, 1996.

Pichardo Viñals, Hortensia: *Documentos para la historia de Cuba*. Ciencias Sociales Publishing House. Volume I, Havana, 1971.

Pichardo Viñals, Hortensia: *Documentos para la historia de Cuba.* Ciencias Sociales Publishing House, Volume III, Havana, 1973.

Pichardo Viñals, Hortensia: *Documentos para la historia de Cuba.* Ciencias Sociales Publishing House, Volume IV (First Part), Havana,1980.

Pino-Santos, Oscar: *Aspectos fundamentales de la historia de Cuba,* Beijing, 1963.

Pino-Santos, Oscar: *Cuba. Historia y economía.* Ciencias Sociales Publishing House, Havana, 1983.

Plataforma Programática del Partido Comunista de Cuba Revolutionary Orientation Division of the Cuban Communist Party's Central Committee, Havana, 1975.

Playa Girón, la gran conjura . Capitán San Luis Publishing House, Havana, 1991.

Portuondo del Prado, Fernando: *Historia de Cuba*. Nacional de Cuba Publishing House, Havana, 1965.

Portuondo, José A.: *Bosquejo histórico de las letras cubanas.* Foreign Ministry, Havana, 1960.

Portuondo López, Yolanda: *30 de noviembre*. Oriente Publishing House. Santiago de Cuba, 1986.

Programa del Partido Comunista de Cuba. Editora Política Publishing House, Havana, 1986.

Regalado, Antero: *Las luchas campesinas en Cuba.* Revolutionary Orientation Commission of the Cuban Communist Party's Central Committee, Havana, 1973.

Riera, Mario: *Cuba política, 1899-1955*. Modelo S.A. Publishing House, Havana, 1955.

Rivero Muñíz, José: *Tabaco. Su historia en Cuba.* History Institute, Academy of Sciences, Havana, 1965.

Roa García, Raúl: *La Revolución del 30 se fue a bolina.* Book Institute, Havana, 1969.

Roca, Blas: *Los fundamentos del socialismo en Cuba.* Páginas Publishing House, Havana, 1943.

Rodríguez, Carlos Rafael: *Letra con filo.* (3 volumes). Ciencias Sociales Publishing House, Havana, 1973 and 1987.

Rodríguez García, José Luis: *Crítica a nuestros críticos.* Ciencias Sociales Publishing House, Havana, 1988.

Rodríguez García, José Luis, et al: *Cuba: Revolución y economía. 1959-1960.* Ciencias Sociales Publishing House, Havana, 1985.

Rodríguez Herrera, Mariano: *Con la adarga al brazo.* Young Communist League's National History Commission. Book Institute, Havana, 1978.

Rodríguez, Juan C: *Hombres del Escambray,* Capitán San Luis Publishing House, Havana, 1990.

Rodríguez, Juan Carlos: *La batalla inevitable.* Capitán San Luis Publishing House, 1996.

Roig de Leuschsenring, Emilio: *Cuba no debe su independencia a los Estados Unidos.* La Tertulia Publishing House, Havana, 1960.

Roig de Leuschsenring, Emilio: *Los Estados Unidos contra Cuba libre.* (4 volumes). Office of the City Historian, Havana, 1959.

Rojas, Marta: *El juicio del Moncada,* Ciencias Sociales Publishing House, Havana, 1988.

Rubiera, Daysi, and Miguel Sierra: *Testimonios sobre Frank.* Oriente Publishing House, Santiago de Cuba, 1978.

Ruiz, Raúl: *Los órganos del Poder Popular.* National Assembly of People's Power, Havana, 1979.

Seis leyes de la Revolución. Ciencias Sociales Publishing House, Havana, 1973.

Sergueiv, F.: *La guerra secreta contra Cuba.* Progreso Publishing House, Moscow, 1983.

Serviat, Pedro: *El problema negro en Cuba y su solución definitiva.* Editora Política Publishing House, Havana, 1986.

7 documentos de nuestra historia. Book Institute, Havana, 1968.

Cuban Society of International Law: *Agresiones de Estados Unidos a Cuba revolucionaria.* Ciencias Sociales Publishing House, Havana, 1989.

Soto, Lionel: *La Revolución del 33.* (3 volumes). Ciencias Sociales Publishing House, Havana, 1977.

Soto, Lionel: *La Revolución precursora de 1933.* SÍ-MAR S.A. Publishing House, 1995.

Tabares del Real, *José A.:Guiteras.* Ciencias Sociales Publishing House, Havana, 1973.

Taladrid Herrero, Reinaldo and Barrero Medina, Lázaro: *El chairman soy yo.* Trebol Publishing House, 1994.

Tauler López, Arnoldo: *Las ideas no se matan.* Ciencias Sociales Publishing House, Havana, 1988.

Theses, resolutions and other documents of the four congresses held by the Cuban Communist Party (1975, 1980, 1986 and 1991)

Toro González, Carlos del: *Algunos aspectos económicos, sociales y políticos del movimiento obrero cubano (1933-1958).* Arte y Literatura Publishing House, Havana, 1974.

Torres, Félix: *Memorias*. (Unpublished)

Un pueblo invencible. Prologue by general Sergio del Valle Jimenez. On the 1962 Missile Crisis. José Martí Publishing House, 1991.

Valdés Vivó, Raúl: *El gran secreto: cubanos en el camino Ho Chi Minh*. Editora Política Publishing House, Havana, 1990.

Various authors: *Apuntes de la prensa clandestina y guerrillera del periodo 1952-1958*. Cuban Journalists Union, Havana, 1973.

Various authors: *Historia de la Revolución Cubana*. Introduction by Nicolás Garófalo Fernández, Pueblo y Educación Publishing House, Havana, 1994.

Various authors: *Los balseros cubanos*. Ciencias Sociales Publishing House, Havana, 1996.

Various authors: *Reportajes de la nueva vida. Veinte años de educación revolucionaria*. Letras Cubanas Publishing House, Havana, 1980.

Vergara, Joaquín J., et al: *Del Pinero al Granma*. Editora Política Publishing House, Havana, 1989.

Iglesia Martínez, Teresita: *Cuba: primera república, segunda ocupación*. Ciencias Sociales Publishing House, Havana, 1980.

Zanetti, Oscar, and Alejandro García: *Caminos para el azúcar*. Ciencias Sociales Publishing House, Havana, 1987.

NOTE: This bibliography is not a compilation of works studied or consulted by the author, but a small part of them. Its objective is only to provide readers with some sources in which, if they so wish, they can expand their knowledge of given historic aspects. As a rule, too specific issues or books with many volumes are excluded from this bibliography. Neither do we mention periodical publications, documents, articles or booklets, reports or writings by many Cuban government and Communist Party leaders, whose list would have been endless. Nevertheless, we thought it necessary to include concrete works on sugar and tobacco—basic Cuban economic branches—biographies of certain figures, and books of documents which, despite their several volumes, could be of invaluable help.

Index

Big Offensive. Its Defeat.- The Caracas Pact.-Farmers' Congress in Arms and Law Number 3 of The Rebel Army.- Labor Congress in Arms.- New Increase in Underground Struggle. Worsening of Terror.- Expansion of the War. The Invasion to the West.- Campaign in Las Villas. The Santa Clara Battle.- The Rebel Army's final offensive. The triumph of the Revolution.

The Provisional Revolutionary Government. Initial Measures.- The First Agrarian Reform Law.-The Urban Reform Law: An Original Cuban Contribution.- The Undeclared War Against Cuba. The Bloodbath That Never Was.- US Maneuvers at the OAS.- The Economic Aggressions.- TheNationalizations.- The Literacy Campaign.- The Bay of Pigs Invasion.- The Unity of Cubans.- The Party.- The Missile Crisis.- The Harassment Against Cuba Continues.- Biological Warfare.- Economic Development from 1963 to 1975.- Social andCultural Advancement.- Latin Americanism and Internationalism.- Ernesto Che Guevara: "For EverOnward Till Victory!".- Solidarity with Angola,Ethiopia, Nicaragua, and Other Countries.

Improvement of Socialist Democracy. The First Congress of the Cuban Communist Party.- The Constitution of the Republic.- The People's Power Institutions.- Gains, Failures and Rectification (1975-1989).- The Barbados Terrorist Bombing and Other US Terrorist Acts.- The Santa Fe Committee's Report.- War of All the People, Collapse of the Socialist Block and Special Period in Peace Time.- Strategy to Face the Special Period.- Recovery Begins.- The Torricelli Law, the Helms-Burton Law and Other Recent Aggressions.- The Provocation of February 24th, 1996.- History Does Not Stop.

A sustained recovery. The political and ideological battle. Posthumous homage to the Heroic Guerrilla and his Comrades-In-Arms fallen in Bolivia. The Cuban People Suits the United States Government. Achievements in foreign policy. The visit by Pope John Paul II. Relentless solidarity. Cuba, an example of international solidarity. The fight for the return of Elián. Attempts to kill Fidel Castro during the 10th Ibero-American Summit.

Se terminó la impresión de esta obra,
en los talleres gráficos de
Editorial Linotipia Bolívar
y Cía. S. en C.,
de la Calle 10 No. 26-47, tel.: 360 04 55,
en el mes de Febrero de 2003.
Bogotá, D. C., Colombia